MUSIC LIBRARY AND RESEARCH SKILLS

JANE GOTTLIEB

The Juilliard School

Property of
Nyack College
Manhattan Center

PEARSON

Prentice
Hall

Upper Saddle River, New Jersey, 07458.

Library of Congress Cataloging-in-Publication Data

Gottlieb, Jane
  Music library and research skills/Jane Gottlieb.
    p. cm.
  Includes bibliographical references and indexes.
  ISBN-13: 978-0-13-158434-1
  ISBN-10: 0-13-158434-0
  1. Musicology—Information resources.   2. Music—Information resources.
  3. Musicology—Study and teaching.   4. Music libraries—Handbooks, manuals, etc.
  5. Musicology—Handbooks, manuals, etc.   6. Music—Bibliography—Methodology.
  I. Title.
  ML3797.G68 2009
  780.72—dc22   2008026109

Editor-in-Chief: Sarah Touborg
Marketing Director: Tim Stookesberry
Executive Editor: Richard Carlin
Editorial Assistant: Emma Gibbons
Marketing Manager: Wendy Gordon
Marketing Assistant: Jacqueline Genovese
Senior Managing Editor: Mary Rottino
Production Liaison: Fran Russello
Senior Operations Supervisor:
  Brian Mackey

Cover Design: Margaret Kenselaar
Cover Illustration/Photo: Wolfgang
  Amadeus Mozart. *Le Nozze di Figaro:* autograph
  manuscript of finale. The Juilliard Mauscript
  Collection.
Manager, Cover Visual Research & Permissions:
  Karen Sanatar
Composition/Full-Service Project Management:
  Bruce Hobart, Pine Tree Composition, Inc.
Printer/Binder: Bind-Rite Graphics

Credits and acknowledgments borrowed from other sources and reproduced, with permission, in this textbook appear on appropriate page within text.

Pearson Education LTD., London
Pearson Education Singapore, Pte. Ltd
Pearson Education Canada, Ltd.
Pearson Education–Japan
Pearson Education Australia PTY, Limited

Pearson Education North Asia, Ltd.
Pearson Educación de Mexico, S.A. de C.V.
Pearson Education Malaysia, Pte. Ltd.
Pearson Education Upper Saddle River,
  New Jersey

10 9 8 7 6 5 4 3 2 1
ISBN-(10): 0-13-158434-0
ISBN-(13): 978-0-13158434-1

For My Students

and in memory of my teacher
Suki T. Sommer
(1935–2008)

CONTENTS

Acknowledgments

Many individuals have contributed to my work on this book, both profession-ally and personally. I am indebted to my students—all those I have had the privilege of working with in my years teaching bibliography to the doctoral students in Juilliard's C.V. Starr Doctor of Musical Arts program and, prior to that, in the three years I taught master's students at Mannes College of Music. They have helped me refine the course over the years, reminding me of what was truly impor-tant to them as performers and aspiring scholars.

This book would not have come to fruition without the inspiration and edi-torial acumen of Richard Carlin, Prentice Hall's executive editor of music. I wish to thank Suki Sommer, who taught me (and many others) how to be a music librar-ian; Joseph W. Polisi, president of The Juilliard School, whose support of Juilliard's library and scholarly initiatives have been key to my work; Bruce Kovner, who, by donating one of the world's most extraordinary collections of music manuscripts to Juilliard in 2006, allowed me to work closely with treasures by the greatest com-posers of the classical repertoire; dear L. Michael Griffel, who first taught me how to teach bibliography, and whose work as a teacher, writer, and editor exemplifies the highest standards of scholarly excellence; the late Richard F. French, director of Juilliard's doctoral program from 1987 to 1993, who tried (unsuccessfully at first) to teach me that "less is more" and who ultimately believed in me; my read-ers and colleagues James P. Cassaro, Amy Gottlieb (who also happens to be my sis-ter), Richard Griscom, Alan Klein, Barbara Mackenzie, Russell Merritt, Jane Penner, Patricia Thomson, Brien Weiner, and James Zychowicz. I could not have completed this book without the assistance of my team of very gifted editors, Noah Opitz, Alan Richtmyer, and Lisa Robinson, and Linda Solow Blotner, who expertly prepared the index. Laura Macy of Oxford Music Online graciously answered numerous questions and allowed use of the examples from *Grove Music Online*. Dr. Norbert Gertsch and Wolf-Dieter Seiffert of G. Henle Verlag shared their wis-dom on composer thematic catalogs, as did Philip Gossett and Christoph Wolff.

Many people deserve recognition for their suggestions. I am especially grate-ful to Ken Keaton, Florida Atlantic University; Richard Griscom, University of Pennsylvania; Janice Dickensheets, University of Northern Colorado; John Wagstaff, University of Illinois at Urbana-Champaign; Jane Edmister Penner, Uni-versity of Virginia; and Karen Jung, Southeastern Louisiana University.

My family has been immensely supportive of a project that has occupied me for many years, and each has made some contribution to the book: my beloved mother (and honorary music librarian) Edythe Rosenberg, my sister Amy Got-tlieb, brother Michael Gottlieb, and partner Peggy Collen. My dear friend Richard Greenberg, brilliant playwright and master chef, offered countless forms of encouragement.

My most profound expression of gratitude is reserved for my brilliant, beautiful, and kind neurological team, Dr. Carolyn D. Brockington and Dr. David J. Langer, who fixed the problem that threatened my life and inspired me to finish this book: they will forever be my royalty.

Finally, this book is dedicated to my students, whose expert performances and superb musicianship remind me of why I went into this business in the first place.

Jane Gottlieb

Preface

The legendary Library of Alexandria, thought to be the repository of all knowledge in the ancient world, has been adopted as the model for the *Alexandria Digital Library* (http://www.alexandria.ucsb.edu/); Johannes Gutenberg, the man who established the age of printing with his famed Gutenberg Bible, has had his name and achievements memorialized through *Project Gutenberg* (http://www .gutenberg.org/wiki/Main_Page), one of the first projects to disseminate free online versions of works no longer protected by copyright; recordings of music are downloaded from the Internet for personal iPods; students expect librarians to answer reference questions via instant messenger services and may rarely visit the library in person; the search engine Google and online bookseller Amazon have morphed into information providers through large-scale book-scanning projects done in cooperation with libraries; and, the megalibrary database OCLC has made its resources available to all through www.worldcat.org.

How can the music bibliography course adapt to such changes? The traditional course, whether taught by librarians or by musicologists, was usually based on creating index-card descriptions of sources (primarily book sources) that were deemed to represent the foundation of music research. The standard text for such classes was *Music Reference and Research Materials: An Annotated Bibliography* by Vincent Duckles, first published in 1964 with 1,155 entries; its most recent fifth edition, prepared by Ida Reed and published in 1997, boasts 3,500 entries. Duckles, which includes clear annotations and references to reviews for each source, was the ideal compendium for a music bibliography class. It is now woefully out of date, and, to my knowledge, no one has yet come forward to take on a comprehensive update.

I have been teaching music bibliography classes to graduate-level music performers for more than 20 years: first at Mannes College of Music and, since 1987, to doctor of musical arts candidates at The Juilliard School. In the first years of my teaching, I based the course on the way I had been taught—that is, using the Duckles approach. (I still have my index box of note cards from my music and performing arts bibliography classes at Columbia University taught by Professor Suki Sommer.) Each week students were given an extensive list of reference tools in various genres (bibliographies of music literature, dictionaries, thematic catalogs, discographies) and asked to become familiar with them by preparing index-card descriptions of each source and responding to those treasure hunt–type questions that some of us find to be so much fun ("Which libraries own copies of the original edition of Dussek's "Sufferings for the Queen of France"?*) My assumption was that even if the students weren't preparing index cards (and few were doing

---

* The answer can be found in RISM A/I.

so), they would at least become familiar with the sources needed to answer such a question. Although this worked to some extent, like many of my colleagues, I was frequently challenged by my students to explain why any of this work was relevant to their lives as musicians. (The response of "it is because I say it is" goes only so far). It eventually became difficult to create questions that would introduce students to even a small portion of the ever-growing number of sources and to bring them away from focus on each tree to a view of the forest.

The approach I have since adopted (and the one embodied in this book) is based on broadly conveying concepts of music research through an understanding of the tools that provide information about music: what exists, how it is arranged, and how to best use available music reference sources to undertake research. I now ask students to create their own research projects, in which they will discover how the topic is covered by available reference tools, and identify and evaluate relevant sources as well as lacunae. (The question of "why is this relevant" is largely mute when the project is self-generated.) Students are expected to understand different formats of literature about music (books, dissertations, periodical articles, etc.), and to use them appropriately.[1]

In my view, it is unlikely that we will someday have a comprehensive sixth edition of Duckles. As Donald Krummel wrote in his review of the fourth edition (1988) "Duckles is no longer the conceptual model, either for teaching graduate students or for developing library reference collections."[2] Since the time of Krummel's writing, librarians, publishers, scholars, and students have embraced guides to research as the preferred model for reference tools, from published books to pathfinders on library Web sites.

ORGANIZATION OF THIS BOOK

Chapters 1 through 6 of this book examine sources of information *about* music (music literature sources). The arrangement of these chapters mirrors what I advocate to be an ideal research process—one that begins with library catalogs as our universe of information on music and proceeds through bibliographies of music literature, dictionaries and encyclopedias, composer bibliographies, and periodical indexes. (The rationale for this approach is explained in more detail on pp. 44–50.)

Chapters 8 through 10 discuss sources of information on the music itself, encompassing manuscript source studies, repertoire guides, and thematic catalogs. The latter chapter, the lengthiest in this book, includes extensive information on the arrangement of catalogs, as well as details on composer complete works editions.

(It should be noted that Chapter 4: Composers, Performers, and Composer-Performers contains primarily sources of literature *about* the individual, while Chapter 10: Thematic Catalogs, contains primarily catalogs of the music itself.)

Although there is an overall concept to this organizational scheme, each chapter is designed to be self-contained, so an instructor may utilize its resources as best fits into his/her own approach.

The book is broadly inclusive in its subject matter, with coverage of popular music, jazz, and world music sources as well as sources on western art music; publications are included as of fall 2007, with selected additions of major resources that appeared as of March 2008. All Web site addresses were verified in April 2008. A companion Web site maintained by the author will include quarterly updates.

I am a bibliographer at heart and was tempted to include additional listings of tools such as composer biographies, historical series, and manuscript facsimile editions. Recognizing that these listings would have been unwieldy and out-of-date almost immediately, I opted instead to direct users to other places where such information may be found.

The narrative discussions in the book are designed as brief introductions to respective subjects and are followed by citations to relevant literature for more comprehensive information. I have generally tried to follow the principle of "lead and get out of the way" by presentation of some basic issues followed by references to the work of expert scholars who will elaborate on these issues.

The book is filled with examples, or "real-life scenarios" that demonstrate use and relevance of selected tools. My colleagues can doubtless create additional examples from their own experiences as librarians and scholars.

Although the ever-quickening pace of change in our profession creates its own challenges, I find it an exciting time to be a music librarian and instructor. I have always been inspired by Vincent Duckles's quote from the preface to his first edition of *Music Reference and Research*,

> "This guide has been designed to illuminate the bibliographical resources for music scholarship. Implicit in its organization is the concept that bibliography is an approach to knowledge, a way in which the student can progress towards mastery in his [sic] chosen field of specialization within the larger dimensions of the field of music."[3]

With utmost respect to Duckles and all those who have formed our foundation of music scholarship, I hope that this *Music Library and Research Skills* book will illuminate paths to knowledge.

NOTES

1. This approach is largely consistent with recently published standards for Information Literacy for music students developed by the Music Library Association. See Paul Cary and Laurie Sampsel, "Information Literacy Objectives for Undergraduate Music Students: A Project of the Music Library Association, Bibliographic Instruction Subcommittee," *Notes* 62, no. 3 (March 2006): 663–679.

2. Donald Krummel, review of *"Music Reference and Research Materials: An Annotated Bibliography,* 4th ed. by Vincent H. Duckles and Michael Keller, *Notes* 46 no. 1 (Sept. 1989): 64–66.

3. Vincent Duckles and Ida Reed, *Music Reference and Research Materials: An Annotated Bibliography,* 5th ed. (New York: Schirmer Books, 1997), xiii.

CHAPTER

1

Libraries and the Universe of Information on Music

OVERVIEW

Music Libraries and Collections

This book takes as its premise the centrality of libraries for music research. Libraries house a wealth of materials documenting music from all historic periods and regions of the world: music scores, books about music and related subjects, sound and video recordings in all formats, manuscripts, and archival collections. Whether one visits a library physically in person or virtually via the Internet, libraries and the collections they house enable students, researchers, and performers at all levels to pursue searches for information about music as well as searches for music itself.

If libraries are so central to research, why do students and researchers sometimes avoid them? Admittedly, libraries can be intimidating. It may not be immediately obvious how to find materials, or even how to find someone to ask. Libraries are not bookstores or cafes. Although some public and academic libraries now allow users to bring coffee cups (usually with stipulations that the cups have lids), many others do not, for the simple reason that spills can be damaging to the materials or to the library furniture.

Library catalogs do not always operate in the same way as Google searches. Even though an ever-increasing number of library catalogs are Web based, and many use Google-type search boxes, music libraries around the world still house vast amounts of materials that are accessible only via old-fashioned card catalogs. Moreover, only a small portion of the materials housed in libraries have been digitized. It is unfortunately all too easy for individuals who have grown up in the age of the Internet to believe that all information is available in digital form, and, therefore, all things worth knowing are found through a Google search. Even Google's initiatives to partner with libraries to create Web-searchable digital content (described later) cannot eliminate the need for libraries as repositories of the world's recorded knowledge, or the need for librarians to aid users in accessing and evaluating information.

This chapter provides some basic information on the nature of library collections and different types of libraries, along with tips on searching library catalogs and the Internet for music research. Gaining some familiarity and level of comfort with one's local library often makes it easier and less intimidating to approach other libraries with research inquiries. And, of course, success with one research project encourages pursuit of other projects.

RULES FOR SUCCESSFUL MUSIC LIBRARY USERS

Rule No. 1: Pester the Librarian (Either in Person, Via Phone, E-mail, or Blog, Depending on the Service Offered by the Library)

The first item in the American Library Association's "Code of Ethics" for library professionals is the following: "We provide the highest level of service to all library users through appropriate and usefully organized resources; equitable service policies; equitable access; and accurate, unbiased, and courteous responses to all requests."[1] Users should expect no less from the librarian or information specialist they encounter in any library, whether the encounter is in-person or via phone or e-mail. If you find yourself ignored or treated rudely, or if your question is not answered to your satisfaction, persist until you gain some information that can assist with your query. (Or, as a colleague recommends, wait until the shift changes and another librarian comes on duty.)

Rule No. 2: Participate in a Reference Interview

One of the primary roles of a reference librarian is to engage the user in a "reference interview" to find out what he or she is specifically seeking. Whether as a result of shyness or feelings of intimidation in libraries, users often ask very general or broad-based questions. For example, a student may come to the library and ask for information about late Beethoven works. When probed further by the librarian, it turns out that the student would like to find information about Beethoven's String Quartet, op. 131. In the case of music, it is especially important for the librarian to clarify whether the user wants a score or recording of the work or *information about* the work.

STUDENT: "I'm supposed to do an assignment on late Beethoven works."

LIBRARIAN: "Is there a specific work you were asked to study?"

STUDENT: "String Quartet, op. 131."

LIBRARIAN: "Would you like a score, recording, or information about Beethoven and his late quartets?"

STUDENT: "All of the above."

With this information, the librarian is then able to help the user locate appropriate materials.

Rule No. 3: Understand the Difference between Answering Factual Questions and Exploring Those Questions Requiring More In-Depth Original Research

It is fairly easy to find out that Beethoven composed his late quartets in the years 1824–26. This is primarily a factual question: a question that typically begins with "who, what, where, when." It is much more difficult (and, in fact, probably more interesting and rewarding) for musicians to explore analytical elements of these complex late works and the extramusical factors that led Beethoven to compose them.

Similarly, while it is a fact that Natalie Maine of the Dixie Chicks publicly criticized President George Bush in 2003 prior to the U.S. invasion of Iraq, it is more complicated (and, again, probably more interesting) to explore how popular music performers have engaged in political controversies in the past century.

Rule No. 4: Knowledge of the Literature about Music and How It Is Organized Helps Users Pose Better Questions

Educated users tend to ask better questions. By gaining more familiarity with the literature about music, students and researchers at all levels can work to refine their own questions, knowing where to find the answers to factual questions and gaining a sense of how more complex questions have been explored by scholars. This is an especially important exercise for students who need to identify original research projects for their graduate-level theses and dissertations.

Often very broad topics must be broken down into manageable units. For example, a student wishing to compare the phenomenon of global hip hop to the globalization of early jazz will need to begin by researching each topic separately.

Finally, there are many times when careful research will reveal that a subject has been so thoroughly studied that there is little to add. However, the only way to find out is to take the journey, which many find to be quite rewarding in itself.

The Whole Is Greater Than the Sum of Its Parts: Bibliographic Databases and the Library without Walls

The technological innovations of the last half century have made it possible for researchers to gain access to information about holdings of library collections far from their own locales.

Computerization of library catalogs began in the late 1960s, when the Library of Congress and other library organizations developed standards of MARC cataloging, or machine-readable cataloging. The use of computerized catalog records in turn led to the development of large bibliographic databases, notably OCLC (Online Computer Library Center) and RLIN (Research Libraries Information Network) which could be used by libraries for shared cataloging, interlibrary loans, and other types of resource sharing. These databases contain millions of *bibliographic records* representing the holdings of thousands of libraries worldwide—our "library without walls" and our universe of music information. Without the development of computerized cataloging and shared databases, users would need to travel physically to library sites to search their paper-based card catalogs. Few of us can now imagine this world.

OCLC's WorldCat

OCLC and RLIN, the two largest bibliographic databases, merged in 2006, with OCLC taking the lead as the primary database provider for libraries. OCLC's WorldCat (www.worldcat.org) presently boasts of including "more than 1.2 billion items in more than 10,000 libraries worldwide."[2]

WorldCat is freely available to individuals via the Internet; in many libraries, it is hosted via a broader collection of databases titled FirstSearch. The latter incorporates a selection of subscription databases (some of which will be described in Chapter 6).

WorldCat and Interlibrary Loan

WorldCat is a central tool used by librarians and library users for identifying items that may be borrowed via interlibrary loan, the process through which libraries lend materials to other libraries on behalf of their users. Libraries have varying policies regarding interlibrary loan requests: some will allow users to generate their own interlibrary loan requests, while others require that they be generated by the user's home library. Often the lending library charges a modest fee for the transaction. Some libraries pay these fees directly, while others require the individual to cover the payment. Interlibrary loan requests are usually done through library networks. Note that most libraries do not lend audio or video recordings via interlibrary loan.

REAL LIFE SCENARIO

You have come across several mentions of the book *It's Not About a Salary: Rap, Race, and Resistance in Los Angeles* by author Brian Cross. Your library does not own a copy of this book, which was published in 1993. WorldCat locates copies in dozens of libraries in your area, which you may request via interlibrary loan, either directly or via your library's interlibrary loan office.

Perhaps as a result of the predominance of Amazon.com searches on the Web, WorldCat is intentionally user-friendly, with its author field search of "first name last name," instead of the more traditional library search protocol of "last name, first name." In addition to books, scores, and recordings, WorldCat includes articles and a range of electronic resources. The search for Brian Cross's book, for example, will also bring up a review of the book by Reebee Garafolo published in the journal *Popular Music,* vol. 15, no. 1.

Google (and Others) Work with Libraries

As noted earlier, Google has developed several important initiatives that involve partnerships with libraries.

Google Books

In late 2004, Google announced a partnership with five large research libraries—Harvard University, Stanford University, the University of Michigan at Ann Arbor, the University of Oxford (England), and the New York Public Library—to digitize millions of volumes in their collections. This group has since expanded to include other large collections, such as those at Cornell University and the University of California, as well as European partners, among them the Bavarian State Library and Ghent University Library. The project allows complete viewing of titles that are no longer protected by copyright (i.e., books published prior to 1923) and selected viewing for those titles still under copyright protection.[3] Google Books also links to WorldCat entries, encouraging users to find a title in a library collection when it is not available in digital form.

Google is not alone it its book-scanning projects; Microsoft, Yahoo, Amazon, and the nonprofit library organization Open Content Alliance have also joined the race to create a universal library on the Web. (Comparisons are frequently made to the third-century B.C. Library of Alexandria, which, prior to its destruction by fire, was considered the world's largest library.)

Google Scholar (http://scholar.google.com).
This tool allows searches of selected scholarly literature, including "peer-reviewed papers, theses, books, abstracts, and articles."[4] Researchers should be aware, however, that Google Scholar indexes only a portion of the literature; it should, therefore, be used in conjunction with other databases (see Chapter 6).

What's NOT Online

In a few words, much of significance is not found online. Given the gigantic size of OCLC's WorldCat and the ease of searching computers, it is easy to assume that bibliographic records for all library materials can be found online. This is not the case, however, and in many libraries it is still necessary to search the card catalog or the card catalog in book form.[5] When visiting a library in person or via the Internet, check to see how much material is listed in the online catalog, and how users may access information on the materials that have not yet been converted to computer-based bibliographic records. (Libraries use the term *retrospective conversion* to refer to the process of converting card catalog bibliographic records to formats that can be read via online catalogs.) In particular, original music manuscripts and rare printed editions are not well represented in online databases, as many libraries have not converted their holdings of these rarities to computer format.

Researchers should also note that music holdings of European libraries are not universally found in WorldCat. One should check some of the major sources on libraries noted later, and consult individual catalogs directly, as needs arise. A valuable resource is the Web portal www.theeuropeanlibrary.org, which offers unified Web searching to holdings of selected European national libraries.[6] Also of note is the Library of Congress's *Z39.50 Gateway to Library Catalogs* http://www.loc.gov/z3950/, which provides access to library catalogs from around the world.

Digital Collections

Libraries and archives worldwide have taken advantage of digital technologies to develop Web sites with rich collections of text, images, and sound and video files.

Digital music collections range from the Staatsbibliothek zu Berlin's "Beethoven Digital" (see p. 13), with the full text facsimile of Beethoven's Symphony no. 9, to the Library of Congress's "American Memory Project" Web site, with digital reproductions of sheet music collections and sound files (see p. 15).

Beyond Books: Archives and Archival Collections

The term *archives* refers to collections that document the history of an organization or an individual through materials created in the course of their daily activities. For an organization, archival records may encompass memoranda and correspondence created by the organization's administration throughout its history. For an individual, archival records may encompass correspondence and other unpublished documents, such as birth and marriage records. Because of the nature of archival collections, they are typically cataloged as *groups* of materials, rather than as individual items, as would be found in a library catalog. Searching archival collections involves searching finding aids or folder lists that describe the holdings of the collection. See Figure 1–1 for example, the finding aid for the Agnes De Mille collection on the New York Public Library Dance Division Web site: http://www.nypl .org/research/manuscripts/dance/dandemilleawards.xml or Figure 1–2, Woody Guthrie Manuscript Collection, Library of Congress American Folklife Center: http://memory.loc.gov/ammem/wwghtml/wwghome.html.

The archivist determines the organization of the folders and then lists the contents of each folder. Fortunately for researchers, technology for posting printed finding aids on Web sites was developed in the late 1990s, allowing many institutions to make their finding aids available electronically.[7] Examples may be found on the Web sites of many of the national libraries listed in the following section.

Archival materials usually fall into the broader category of *primary sources,* indicating the source closest to the creator. (For further discussion of primary sources, see Chapter 8: From Manuscript to Published Edition). *Secondary sources* refer to sources further removed from the creator. Thus, published books based on study of primary sources are secondary sources.

Rule No. 5: Do Your Homework with a Thorough Review of Secondary Sources before Consulting Archival Collections

Most major reference sources give Leonard Bernstein's birth date as March 25, 1918. Locating this information in his papers at the Library of Congress (http://lcweb2 .loc.gov/faid/faidfrquery.html) would require much digging to find his birth certificate and is probably unnecessary unless there is a controversy. It is generally more difficult to use archival collections; usually, appointments must be made in advance, and users are required to wear special gloves or follow other procedures that ensure the preservation of the materials.[8]

Rule No. 6: Trust but Verify

That said, there are sometimes discrepancies between major reference sources, or times when it is certainly necessary to verify information in the primary source materials. This issue will be explored further in Chapter 8.

FIGURE 1–1   Finding Aid for Agnes de Mille Collection, Dance Division, New York Public Library for the Performing Arts

The New York Public Library

Guide to the de Mille, Agnes, 1905-Collection, ca. 1914-1984.

(S) *MGZMD 37

Jerome Robbins Dance Division

The New York Public Library for the Performing Arts
40 Lincoln Center Plaza
New York, NY 10023-7498

Jerome Robbins Dance Division, New York Public Library.
40 Lincoln Center Plaza
New York, NY 10023-7498
(212) 870-1657
dance@nypl.org
http://nypl.org/research/lpa/dan/dan.html

Processed by:Diane Coburn Brüning
Date Completed:February 1985
Encoded by:Apex Data Services; revised by Dan Santamaria
Date Completed:September 26, 2003; revised 2004

Encoding funded by the generous support of the Gladys Krieble Delmas Foundation.

Table of Contents
Descriptive Summary
Administrative Information
Biographical History
Container List
  I. Correspondence, 1902-1943
  II. Writings of Agnes de Mille
  III. Choreographic and Production Notes
  IV. Financial Papers
  V. Agnes de Mille Dance Theatre (Heritage Dance Theatre)
  VI. Honorary Degrees and Awards
  VII. Legal Documents, Certificates, and Personal Memorabilia
  VIII. Miscellaneous Writings
  IX. Miscellaneous

Descriptive Summary ▣

Title: de Mille, Agnes, 1905-Collection, ca. 1914-1984.

Collection ID: (S) *MGZMD 37

Creator: de Mille, Agnes

Size: 1696 folders in 49 boxes

Repository: The New York Public Library for the Performing Arts
                      Jerome Robbins Dance DivisionNew York, New York

Abstract:

Languages Represented: English

Administrative Information ▣

Source: Purchase, 1984. Agnes de Mille. Received: 1984.

Access: Walter Prude and Agnes de Mille correspondence, boxes 4 - 7, until the earlier to occur of the death of both de Mille and Prude or the year 2004.

Preferred Citation: de Mille, Agnes, 1905-Collection, (S) *MGZMD 37, Jerome Robbins Dance Division, The New York Public Library for the Performing Arts.

Biographical History ▣

Agnes George de Mille, dancer, choreographer, writer and spokesperson for the arts, was born September 18, 1905 in New York. She was the daughter of playwright William Churchill de Mille (1879?-1955) and Anna George de Mille (1878-1947), who was in turn the daughter of writer and single-tax advocate, Henry George (1839-1897). Agnes' uncle was the film producer/director, Cecil B. de Mille (1881-1959). She had a younger sister, Margaret (1908-1978).

In 1914, the de Milles moved to Hollywood where William was joining forces with Cecil in the motion picture industry. Agnes attended the Hollywood School for Girls, graduating in 1922, and went on to graduate from University of California in 1926 with a degree in English. William and Anna separated that year, being divorced in 1927, and Agnes spent that summer after graduating traveling in western Europe with her mother and sister. William married Clara Beranger, a colleague in the movie industry, in 1928 and lived with her in California for the remainder of his life.

Agnes' formal dance training did not begin until early adolescence in California with Theodore Kosloff. She did some performing in college shows although she did not train continuously during her college years. Soon after graduating, she began to give solo recitals and later with Warren Leonard in her own works. Her mother helped her produce these and accompanied her to concerts in various cities in the United States and in Europe. During this period, she settled once again in New York, at first living with her mother and sister, and then on her own.

Agnes moved to England in 1932 where she continued her dance training in ballet with Marie Rambert. She performed in her own work and those of her peers such as Antony Tudor under the auspices of Rambert.

http://www.nypl.org/research/manuscripts/dance/dandemilleawards.xml

FIGURE 1–2 Finding Aid for Woodie Guthrie Collection, Library of Congress American Folklife Center

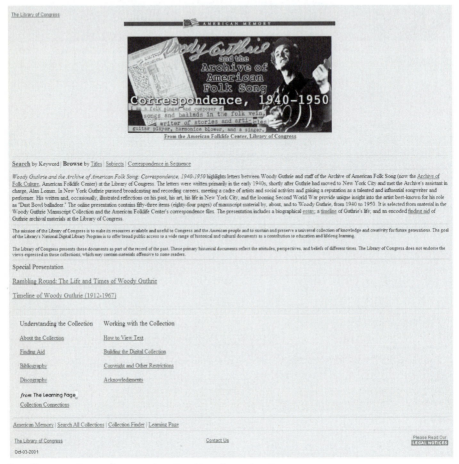

http://memory.loc.gov/ammem/wwghtml/wwghome.html

Where to Find Information about Music Libraries

The *Grove Music Online* article on "Libraries" includes a detailed history of the development of music libraries worldwide, along with an extensive listing of libraries arranged by continent and city. The listing also includes references to printed collection catalogs.

RISM Series C, "Directory of Music Research Libraries" (see p. 180), includes information on music research libraries around the world. In general, the RISM Series C entries for each library are more detailed than those found in *Grove Music Online*.

The chapter on "Catalogs of Music Libraries and Collections" in Vincent Duckles's *Music Reference and Research Materials*, 5th ed. (New York: Schirmer

Books, 1997), pp. 391–496, lists published catalogs of libraries and selected special collections alphabetically by city.

The Music Library Association (MLA) is the professional organization for music libraries and music librarians in the United States. Founded in 1931, MLA currently has 1,731 members and subscribers. Its journal, *Notes*, includes articles on music librarianship and collections, as well as book, music, and media reviews. For further information, see the organization's Web site: www.musiclibraryassoc.org.

The International Association of Music Libraries, Archives and Documentation Centres (IAML) currently has about 2,000 individual and institutional members in some 45 countries.[9] Founded in 1951, the organization fosters cooperative international projects to further access to music in libraries, archives, and documentation centers around the world. Among its cooperative projects are the "4 Rs," which have arguably transformed scholarly access to music: *RISM (Répertoire International des Sources Musicale), RILM (Répertoire International de Littérature musicale), RIdIM (Répertoire International d'Iconographie musicale)*, and *RIPM (Retrospective Index to Music Periodicals)*; all of these projects will be discussed in more detail elsewhere in this book.

IAML publishes a quarterly journal, *Fontes Artis Musicae*, which includes articles on music librarianship in member counties, as well as regular reports on many of its cooperative projects. For further information, see the organization's Web site: http://www.iaml.info.

Classification Schemes

Libraries use standardized classification schemes to organize materials in their collections by subject areas; the classification schedules most commonly found in music libraries in the United States today include the Library of Congress (LC) Classification scheme: http://www.loc.gov/catdir/cpso/lcco/ and the Dewey Decimal Classification (DDC): http://www.oclc.org/dewey/versions/ddc22print/.

Familiarity with the classification scheme used in a particular library is certainly valuable, as it may allow the user to locate materials with relative ease, especially when browsing in an open-shelf collection. Library classification schemes cannot be used alone, however; it is always preferable to rely on the catalog to locate materials, rather than solely on browsing, as one might do in a bookstore.

BROWSING: PROS AND CONS

Even though browsing in open-stack collections in libraries or bookstores is a wonderful way to discover materials serendipitously, it is important to remember that in circulating collections, browsing provides a picture of the collection only at a given time. Materials may be checked out or shelved in the reference area or in another location in the library. Again, the catalog will provide a much more accurate picture of the collection.

TYPES OF LIBRARIES AND SELECTED LISTINGS

Public vs. Private, Research vs. Circulating

This section presents a summary of the different types of libraries in which music collections may be found, with brief information on a few selected libraries in each category. This information is generally limited to the library's Web site address, significant digital collections created by the library, and selected publications of a bibliographical nature. Additional information about the library may be found through its Web site, as well as in the sources noted earlier (RISM Series C, *Grove Music Online* article, and Duckles's list of published collection catalogs). Unless otherwise indicated all lists are arranged alphabetically by name of library within each category.

Libraries define their user communities and access policies based on the population they serve. In general, public libraries serve the public in a particular community and are typically supported by citizens' tax dollars. Nonresidents of that particular community may need to pay special access fees to take materials out or access subscription databases.

University, college, and conservatory libraries support the needs of the school's students, faculty, and staff. Funding is provided by the university, and if a public university (such as a state college), by tax dollars. Some university, college, and conservatory libraries are open to nonstudents; others are not.

Library Etiquette

The most important principle of library etiquette is to inquire in advance as to access policies. Most libraries post this information on their Web sites. As a researcher or student, you are guaranteed a better reception if you follow the library's access policy, rather than show up unannounced. Users should also check library hours and vacation schedules in advance of a visit: many European libraries are closed for part of the summer. It is also important to check about credential documents required for access: some libraries require letters of introduction for students or scholars to view rare materials. See, for example, the access card requirements for researchers at the Bibliothèque Nationale de France: http://www.bnf.fr/pages/zNavigat/frame/version_anglaise.htm?ancre=english.htm.

It is also important to know the distinction between *research collections* and *circulating collections*. The former term usually refers to large collections that house unique and rare materials, such as manuscripts, rare editions, and archival collections; such materials rarely, if ever, circulate, either to their user communities or via interlibrary loan networks. The materials are housed in closed-stack areas, and users can browse only by consulting the catalog. Circulating collections are those that lend materials, usually to members of a defined user community. Materials are often arranged on open stacks to allow for browsing. Some large public libraries, such as the New York Public Library for the Performing Arts, house research and circulating collections in the same building.

National Libraries

National libraries are government agencies supported by government funds. Composers, authors, and publishers are sometimes required to deposit copies of their works through systems of "copyright deposit," a policy that helps create vast collections of materials. National libraries house research collections; materials usually do not circulate. Selected national libraries with large music collections include the following:

Bavarian State Library (Bayerische Staatsbibliothek)
http://www.bsb-muenchen.de/index.php?L=3
Music Department: http://www.bsb-muenchen.de/Music.94.0.html?L=3

The Music Department of the Bavarian State Library (the state library of Bavaria, one of Germany's 16 states, with Munich as its capital city) serves as the copyright deposit library for Bavaria. It currently holds more than 36,000 music manuscripts, 347,000 scores, 78,000 sound recordings, and approximately 132,000 books and periodicals.[10] The Bayerische Staatsbibliothek also serves as the center for the German offices of RISM and RIdIM.

Selected Publications
Bayerische Staatsbibliothek. *Katalog der Musikdrucke (Catalog of Printed Music): BSBMusik.* 17 vols. München: K. G. Saur, 1988–90.
_____. *Katalog der Musikhandschriften: Bayerische Staatsbibliothek.* 3 vols. München: G. Henle, 1979–89.
_____. *Katalog der Musikzeitschriften: BSB-MuZ (Catalog of Music Periodicals): Bavarian State Library.* München: K. G. Saur, 1990.
_____. *Katalog der Notendrucke, Musikbücher, und Musikzeitshcriften (Bavarian State Library. Catalog of Printed Music, Books, and Periodicals on Music).* 2nd ed. München: K. G. Saur, 2001. (CD-ROM)

Berlin Staatsbibliothek
Preussischer Kulturbesitz, Musikabteilung mit Mendelssohn-Archiv http://staatsbibliothek-berlin.de/deutsch/abteilungen/musikabteilung/index_en.html

The Berlin Staatsbibliothek houses some of the world's most significant music manuscripts, among them the autographs of J. S. Bach's Mass in B minor and St. Matthew and St. John Passions; Beethoven's Fourth, Fifth, and Ninth symphonies; as well as an almost complete collection of Mozart's operas.[11] As its entry in RISM Series C indicates, "The Staatsbibliothek is the greatest music library in Germany with source materials from Bach to Schumann, as well as unparalleled collections of German printed music from 1800–1945."[12] During World War II, many of the Berlin Staatsbibliothek's holdings were dispersed to libraries in Eastern Europe for safekeeping and have only recently been identified. (A selected listing of sources related to this subject is provided next.) The postwar division of Berlin led to separate libraries in East and West Berlin; the two were finally united in 1992 and moved to their present location in 1997.

Selected Sources on Discovery of Materials from the Berlin State Library following World War II

Hill, Richard S. "The Former Prussian State Library." *Notes* 3, no. 4 (Sept. 1946): 327–50; 404–10.

Lewis, Nigel. *Paperchase: Mozart, Beethoven, Bach—: The Search for Their Lost Music.* London: Hamish Hamilton, 1981.

Mann, Brian. "From Berlin to Cracow: Sixteenth- and Seventeenth-Century Prints of Italian Secular Vocal Music in the Jagiellonian Library." *Notes* 49, no. 1 (Sept. 1992): 11–27.

Plamenac, Dragan. "Music Libraries in Eastern Europe: A Visit in 1961." *Notes* 19, no. 2 (March 1962): 217–34.

Sackman, Dominik, and Susan Gillespie. "Classical Music: A State Secret." *Musical Quarterly* 82, no. 1 (Spring 1998): 160–89.

Whitehead, P. J. P. "The Lost Berlin Manuscripts." *Notes* 33, no. 1 (Sept. 1976): 7–15.

Selected Berlin State Library Publications

Becker, Heinz. *Giacomo Meyerbeer: Weltbürger der Musik: eine Ausstellung der Musikabteilung der Staatsbibliothek Preussicher Kulturbesitz Berlin zum 200 Geburstag des Komponisten, vom 31 Oktober 1991 bis zum 5 Januar 1992.* Ausstellungskataloge Staatsbibliothek Preussicher Kulturbesitz 38. Weisbaden: L. Reichert, 1991.

Elvers, Rudolf, und Hans-Günter Klein. *Ludwig van Beethoven 1770–1970. Autographe aus d. Musikabt. d. Staatsbibliothek Preussicher Kulturbesitz, Ausstellg. 1–30 Dez 1970 im Mendelssohn-Archiv der Staatsbibliothek.* Ausstellungskataloge Staatsbibliothek Preussicher Kulturbesitz 1. Berlin: Staatsbibliothek Preussicher Kulturbesitz, 1970.

George, Dieter. *Handschriften aus Südostasien: Ausstellung der Orientabteilung der Staatsbibliothek Kulturbesitz im Haus am Lutzowplatz vom 8. Januar bis 13 Februar 1977.* Ausstellungskataloge Staatsbibliothek Preussicher Kulturbesitz 7. Berlin: Staatsbibliothek Preussicher Kulturbesitz, 1976.

Jaenecke, Joachim. *Georg Philipp Telemann: Autographe und Abschriften: Katalog.* Staatsbibliothek Preussicher Kulturbesitz. Musikabteilung. Kataloge der Musikabteilung. Erste Reihe. Handschriften 7. München: G. Henle, 1993.

_____. *Joseph und Michael Haydn: Autographe und Abschriften: Katalog.* Staatsbibliothek Preussicher Kulturbesitz. Musikabteilung. Kataloge der Musikabteilung. Erste Reihe, Handschriften 4. München: G. Henle, 1990.

Klein, Hans-Günter. *Ludwig van Beethoven: Autographe u. Abschriften: Katalog.* Staatsbibliothek Preussicher Kulturbesitz. Musikabteilung. Kataloge. Reihe 1: Handschriften 2. Berlin: Merseburger, 1975.

_____. *Wolfgang Amadeus Mozart Autographe und Abschriften: Katalog.* Staatsbibliothek Preussicher Kulturbesitz. Musikabteilung. Kataloge. Reihe 1: Handschriften 6. Kassel: Merseburger, 1982.

Staatsbibliothek zu Berlin und Biblioteka Jagiellonska, eds. *Music Manuscripts of the Staatsbibliothek zu Berlin—Preussischer Kulturbesitz and of the Biblioteka Jageillońka in Kraków.* München: K. G. Saur, 1998—2009. (microfiche) (Microfilm copies of autographs from the Staatsbibliothek in Berlin that were moved to the Jagellonion Library in Cracow, Poland, as well as microfilms of the collection of the Sing-Akademie zu Berlin.) For complete listing see http://www.saur.de/index.cfm?lang =DE&ID=0000006658.

Digital Collections

Beethoven Digital (the complete score of Beethoven's Symphony no. 9) http://beethoven
.staatsbibliothek-berlin.de/.

The Berlin State Library also hosts Malvine, an online database of postmedieval
manuscripts and letters housed in European libraries: http://www.malvine.org/
malvine/eng/about.html.

Bibliothèque Nationale

http://www.bnf.fr/
Music Department: http://www.bnf.fr/pages/collections/musique.htm

Established in 1942, the Department de la Musique of France's Bibliothèque
Nationale presently encompasses the libraries of the Paris Conservatoire and the
Opéra. Its holdings include more than 2 million items, among them significant
manuscripts (such as the manuscripts of Mozart's *Don Giovanni* and Beethoven's
Appasionata Sonata), autograph letters, and archival collections (called *fonds*). It
also serves as the copyright deposit library for France, thus adding significant holdings of printed and recorded music each year. Holdings since 1991 are listed in the
library's online catalog: Bn-Opale: http://catalogue.bnf.fr/.

Selected Publications

Bloch-Michel, Antoine. *Lettres autographes conservées au département de la Musique.*
Paris: Bibliothèque nationale, 1984.

Brossard, Yolande, ed. *La collection Sebastian de Brossard, 1655–1730: catalogue (Department de la Musique, Res. Vm. 8 20).* Paris: Bibliothèque nationale de France, 1994.

Écorcheville, Jules. *Catalogue du fonds de musique ancienne de la Bibliothèque nationale.*
8 vols. Paris: Société internationale de musique, 1910–14. Reprint, New York: Da Capo
Press, 1972.

Lesure, François. *Catalogue de la musique imprimée avant 1800 conservée dans les biblio-
thèques publiques de Paris.* Paris: Bibliothèque nationale, 1981.

Massip, Catherine, and Cécile Grand, eds. *Catalogue des manuscrits musicaux antérieurs à
1800 conserves au Département de la musique A et B.* Paris: Bibliothèque nationale de
France, 1999.

Digital Collections

Gallica Anthologie
http://gallica.bnf.fr/anthologie/page.asp?T2-2-9-MUS.htm.

British Library

http://www.bl.uk/

The British Library in London houses one of the world's most extensive collections of printed music and manuscripts. A description of the British Library's
music collections is found at http://www.bl.uk/collections/music/music.html.

Among the many highlights of the British Library's music collections are the
Stefan Zweig Collection, the Paul Hirsch Collection, the Royal Music Library
Collection, and more than a million published scores in its "Printed Music" collection.

A detailed and informative list of catalogs and collections are available at http://www.bl.uk/collections/music/musiccatspecial.html.

Most of the music manuscript holdings are available online at http://www.bl.uk/catalogues/manuscripts/.

The library's extensive holdings of printed music are listed in Baille, Laureen. *The Catalogue of Printed Music in the British Library to 1980*. 62 vols. (New York: K. G. Saur, 1981–87). Holdings listed in this catalog along with post-1981 holdings are found in the library's "Integrated Catalog": http://catalogue.bl.uk/F/?func=file&file_name=login-bl-list.

Selected Publications

http://www.bl.uk/catalogues/listings.html

Banks, C. A., Arthur Searle, and Malcolm Turner, eds. *Sundry Sorts of Music Books: Essays on the British Library Collections: Presented to O. W. Neighbor on His 70th Birthday*. London: British Library, 1993.

Searle, Arthur. *The British Library Stefan Zweig Collection: Catalogue of the Music Manuscripts*. London: British Library, 1999.

Selected Digital Collections

http://www.bl.uk/onlinegallery/homepage.html

The British Library's "Turning the Pages" software allows viewers to experience major sources in digital form by turning the pages of the text. Among the items featured in this program is Mozart's own Thematic Catalog, *Verzeichnüss aller meiner Werke,* with links to audio excerpts. http://www.bl.uk/onlinegallery/ttp/ttpbooks.html/

For more information on libraries in the United Kingdom and Ireland, see Thompson, Pamela, and Malcolm Lewis. *Access to Music: Music Libraries and Archives in the United Kingdom and Ireland: Current Themes and a Realistic Vision for the Future*. London: International Association of Music Libraries, Archives and Documentation Centres, United Kingdom and Ireland Branch, 2003.

Canada

Library and Archives
www.collectionscanada.gc.ca

Music

The national library of Canada, now known as "Collections Canada" (Library and Archives Canada) has extensive collections of published music, sound recordings, and archival collections. Among the latter are those of pianist Glenn Gould, jazz musicians Paul Bley and Oscar Peterson, and composers Jacques Hétu and Sir Ernest MacMillan. A selected list of collections is available at http://www.collectionscanada.ca/website/topic/index-e.html#h. The Web site of CollectionsCanada also includes an electronic version of the *Encyclopedia of Music in Canada* (see p. 80), which is part of the *Canadian Encyclopedia:* www.thecanadianencyclopedia.com.

Selected Publication

Barriault, Jeannine, Stéphane Jean, and Maureen Nevins. *Music Archives at the National Library of Canada.* Ottawa: National Library of Canada, 2000.

Library of Congress
www.loc.gov

Located in Washington, D.C., the Library of Congress's vast and distinguished collections of music and musical instruments were developed through several important donations and bequests, among them those from the Elizabeth Sprague Coolidge Foundation, the Gertrud Clarke Whittall Foundation (which donated LC's collection of valuable Stradivarius instruments), the Serge Koussevitzky Music Foundation, and the Hans Moldenhauer Archives. Composer archives housed in the Library of Congress include those of Leonard Bernstein and Aaron Copland; both of these collections are available in digital form. Indeed, LC has been a leader in the development of digital collections; an alphabetical list of its digital music collections is available at http://www.loc.gov/resdev/browse/m.html.

Selected Publications

Auman, Elizabeth A., and Raymond A. White. *The Music Manuscripts, First Editions, and Correspondence of Franz Liszt (1811–1886) in the Collections of the Music Division, Library of Congress.* Washington, DC: Library of Congress, 1991.

Library of Congress Music, Theater, Dance: An Illustrated Guide. Washington, DC: Library of Congress, 1993. (Includes list of "Selected Special Collections" in the Music Division, pp. 73–80.)

Newsom, Jon, and Alfred Mann, eds. *The Rosaleen Moldenhauer Memorial: Music History from Primary Sources: A Guide to the Archives.* Washington, DC: Library of Congress, 2000. Also available online: http://memory.loc.gov/ammem/collections/moldenhauer/.

Library of Congress *Z39.50 Gateway to Library Catalogs.* A valuable meta-listing of library catalogs from around the world is found on the Library of Congress Web site at http://lcweb.loc.gov/z3950/gateway.html#J. (see p. 5)

Digital Collections

American Memory project: http://memory.loc.gov/ammem/about/index.html. LC's American Memory Project presents digital collections of sheet music, sound files, maps, photographs, and other materials "that document the American experience." An alphabetical list of specific collections is found at http://memory.loc.gov/ammem/browse/ListAll.php. Among the music collections found through the LC *American Memory* project site are those for *African-American Sheet Music 1850–1920* and the Leonard Bernstein and Aaron Copland archives.

Global Gateway: http://international.loc.gov/intldl/intldlhome.html. The international companion to LC's *American Memory* project is its "Global Gateway," which focuses on international collections and international exhibitions.

Österreichische Nationalbibliothek-Austrian National Library
  http://www.onb.ac.at/index.htm

The Austrian National Library (ANB) Music Department houses more than 50,000 manuscripts, including those of such major composers as Beethoven, Bruckner, Haydn, Mozart, and Schubert. Its collection of printed music (more than 120,000 items) was especially enriched through the donation of Anthony van Hoboken's collection of approximately 8,000 original and early printed editions.[13] Hoboken also donated his *Photogrammarchiv,* which includes photocopies and microfilms of significant manuscripts. The ANB serves as the copyright deposit library for new publications in Austria.

Selected Publications

Brosche, Günther, ed. *Die Musiksammlung der Österreichen Nationalbibliothek und ihr Handschriftenkatalog.* Die Europaische Musik I, Kataloge 1. Vienna: Olms Microform, 1983.

Hilmar, Rosemary. *Katalog der Musikhandschriften, Schriften, und Studien Alban Bergs im Fond Alban Berg und der weitern handschriften Quellen im Besitz der Österreichen Nationalbibliothek.* Wein: Universal Edition, 1980.

Katalog der Sammlung Anthony van Hoboken in der Musiksammlung der Österreichischen Nationalbibliothek: musikalische Erst- und Frühdrucke. Hrsg. vom Inst. für Österr. Musikdokumentation unter d. Leitung von Günter Brosche. 17 vols. Tutzing: Hans Schneider, 1982–98.

Digital Collections

"Composer Autographs" and "Musik und Geschichte": http://www.onb.ac.at/siteseeing/mmedia/musik1/musik1_fr.htm.

Public Libraries with Large Music Collections (arranged alphabetically by city)

Boston
Boston Public Library
  http://www.bpl.org/research/music/spmusic.htm

Boston Public Library's music collections include core collections of books and scores, as well as several distinguished special collections. Among the latter are the Allen A. Brown Music Collection, the Serge Koussevitsky Collection, the Walter Piston Collection, the Handel and Haydn Society Collection, and a Music Program Collection that houses concert and theater programs of events in the Boston area.

Retrospective holdings are documented in: *Dictionary Catalog of the Music Collection of the Boston Public Library,* 20 vols. (Boston: G. K. Hall, 1972); First Supplement, 4 vols. (Boston: G. K. Hall, 1977).

Chicago
Newberry Library
  http://www.newberry.org/general/generalinfo.html

The Newberry Library is an independent research library in Chicago, Illinois, that functions as a public library for researchers. It houses extensive noncirculating collections of rare books, maps, and manuscripts, including more than 200,000 music items (sheet music, manuscripts, theoretical treatises, and early printed editions). For further information, see:

Krummel, Donald W. "The Newberry Library, Chicago." *Fontes Artis Musicae* 16 (1969): 119–24.
Sommerfield, Susan, and JoEllen Dickie. "Music Collections at the Newberry Library." *Fontes Artis Musicae* 48, no. 4 (Oct.–Dec. 2001): 372–75.

New York
New York Public Library
www.nypl.org.

The New York Public Library for the Performing Arts houses distinguished collections of performing arts materials, including circulating and research collections in music, dance, and theater. The Rogers and Hammerstein Archives of Recorded Sound (one of the research divisions), contains more than 500,000 items and is an important repository of historical recordings. Circulating collections are available only to residents of New York. Research collections are available to scholars and researchers from any locale, although an "access card" is required (see http://www.nypl.org/research/general/access.html).

The Research Libraries online catalog, CATNYP, provides access to NYPL's Music Division holdings cataloged since 1972. Retrospective holdings are documented in *Dictionary Catalog of the Music Collection, New York Public Library.* 2nd ed. 44 vols. (Boston: G. K. Hall, 1982).

Pierpont Morgan Library
http://www.morganlibrary.org/;
http://corsair.morganlibrary.org/ (online catalog)

The Pierpont Morgan Library houses an extraordinary collection of music manuscripts and first editions, including autographs by Beethoven, Brahms, Mahler, Mozart, Schubert, Schoenberg, and many other composers. A detailed description of the collection and its history is found in J. Rigbie Turner's two-part article, "Infinite Riches in a Little Room: The Music Collections in the Pierpont Morgan Library," *Notes,* 55, no. 2 (Dec. 1998): 288–326 (part I); *Notes,* 55, no. 3 (March 1999): 547–82 (part II); and his "Music Collections at the Pierpont Morgan Library," *Fontes Artis Musicae* 48, no. 4 (Oct.–Dec. 2001): 367–71.

Philadelphia
Free Library of Philadelphia
http://www.library.phila.gov/

The Free Library of Philadelphia contains significant holdings of music and dance materials, with special collections of orchestral music and chamber music. The latter includes more than 27,000 items that are available for loan to individuals and ensembles with payment of a refundable deposit.

The Edwin A. Fleisher Collection of Orchestral Music, composed of more than 21,000 titles, is considered to be the world's largest lending library of orchestral performance material. Holdings up to 1979 are listed in *The Edwin A. Fleisher Collection of Orchestral Music in the Free Library of Philadelphia: A Cumulative Catalog, 1929–1977* (Boston: G. K. Hall, 1979). Updated information is available at http://libwww.library.phila.gov/collections/collectionDetail.cfm?id=14.

University and College Libraries, Conservatory Libraries

Some of the most significant music collections in the United States are found in university, college, and conservatory music libraries. These libraries obviously serve the school's constituents (students and faculty) and may not be open to the general public. This listing is even more selective than the listing of national libraries, as users are encouraged to identify materials through WorldCat, rather than contacting libraries directly.

Columbia College, Chicago: Center for Black Music Research

http://www.colum.edu/cbmr/

Columbia College in Chicago has developed the Center for Black Music Research (CBMR), which is "devoted to research, preservation, and dissemination of information about the history of black music on a global scale."[14] The center provides extensive resources for those interested in studies of African American and black music. Among its publications are the *International Dictionary of Black Composers* (1999), see p. 78.

Eastman School of Music

http://www.rochester.edu/Eastman/sibley/

The Eastman School of Music's Sibley Library is considered one of the largest university music collections in the United States, presently holding more than 750,000 items.[15] Founded in 1904 by Hiram Sibley as a music library for the citizens of Rochester, New York, in 1922 it became part of the Eastman School of Music, which had been established the prior year.

Selected Publications

Davidson, Mary Wallace. "The Research Collections of the Sibley Music Library of the Eastman School of Music, University of Rochester. *The Library Quarterly* 64, no. 2 (April 1994): 163–92.

Goldberg, Louise, and Charles Lindahl. "Gathering the Sources: A Case History." In *Modern Music Librarianship: Essays in Honor of Ruth Watanabe,* edited by Alfred Mann, 3–26. Festschrift series 8. Stuyvesant, NY: Pendragon Press, 1989.

Rosenthal, Albi. "A Source Survey, Early Music Books in the Sibley Library." In *Modern Music Librarianship: Essays in Honor of Ruth Watanabe,* edited by Alfred Mann, 27–32. Festschrift series 8. Stuyvesant, NY: Pendragon Press, 1989.

Harvard University, Eda Kuhn Loeb Music Library

http://hcl.harvard.edu/loebmusic/text/site-index.html#about

One of the most distinguished university music libraries in the United States, Harvard's Eda Kuhn Loeb Music Library presently holds more than 160,000 books and scores, and more than 60,000 recordings. Its Isham Memorial Library houses the music library's special collections, as well as microfilms and facsimiles of sources in other libraries. Another special collection within the library is the Archive of World Music, which houses archival field recordings and other ethnomusicological materials. Harvard is the home of the U.S. office of RISM (*Répertoire International des Sources Musicales* or *International Inventory of Musical Sources;* see pp. 176–182).

Selected Publications

Howard, John B. "The Eda Kuhn Loeb Music Library at Harvard University." *Library Quarterly* 64, no. 2 (April 1994): 163–76.

Wolff, Barbara Mahrenholz. *Music Manuscripts at Harvard: A Catalogue of Music Manuscripts from the 14th to the 20th Centuries in the Houghton Library and the Eda Kuhn Loeb Music Library.* Cambridge, MA: Harvard University Library, 1992.

Additional publications about the library are listed on its Web site: http://hcl.harvard.edu/loebmusic/about-history.html.

Indiana University (IU)

http://www.music.indiana.edu/muslib.html

Quantitatively competitive with the Eastman School of Music, Indiana University's William and Gayle Cooke Music Library holds more than half a million items: 83,140 books and bound journals, 100,620 scores, 222,3777 performance parts,[16] 134,640 sound recordings, 1,956 videos, and 17,953 microfilms.[17] The Cook Library supports the research and performance needs of a large School of Music on IU's Bloomington campus. This school currently has more than 1,600 students and 160 faculty members.[18]

In addition to its distinction for the demonstrated strength of its collections, IU's Music Library has also been a leader in technology developments among music libraries in the United States. It was one of the founding members of the Associated Music Libraries Group, which fostered cooperative cataloging for music libraries on the OCLC database. Its excellent Internet metasite "Worldwide Internet Music Sources" is referenced on many other music libraries' Web sites because of its comprehensive nature and useful organization.[19] The Cook Library's "Variations" project, launched in 1996, was one of the first digital music initiatives in the United States; it has served as a model for similar projects ever since.[20]

Indiana University's Archives of Traditional Music (http://www.indiana.edu/~libarchm/), Archives of African American Music and Culture (http://www.indiana.edu/~aaamc/), and Latin American Music Center (http://www.music.indiana.edu/som/lamc/) are important research centers in their own right.

Selected Publications

Davidson, Mary Wallace. "Indiana University's William and Gayle Cook Music Library: An Introduction." *Notes* 59, no. 2 (Dec. 2002): 251–63.

Lorenz, Ricardo, Luis Hernández, and Gerardo Dirié, eds. *Scores and Recordings at the Indiana University Latin American Music Center.* Bloomington: Indiana University Press, 1995.

University of California, Berkeley

http://www.lib.berkeley.edu/MUSI/collections.html

University of California (U.C.) Berkeley's Music Library is notable for its extensive holdings, including more than 180,000 volumes of books and scores and 50,000 sound recordings, as well as its distinguished collections of rare materials. The collections were built in part by Vincent H. Duckles, author of the landmark *Music Reference and Research Materials* (see p. 42), who served as librarian from 1947 to 1981.

Selected Publication

Roberts, John H. "The Music Library, University of California, Berkeley." *Library Quarterly* 64, no. 1 (Jan. 1994): 73–84.

Additional publications on the U.C. Berkeley Music Library are found on its Web site: http://www.lib.berkeley.edu/MUSI/bibliography.html.

Conservatory Libraries

Conservatory libraries typically serve schools that educate performers; thus, their library collections may not have the same types of primary source materials found in the university and college libraries that support high-level scholarly research. That said, many conservatory libraries hold significant rare materials and treasures, some of which were donated by their founders or by their faculty. In the United States, conservatories can be further subdivided into those that are connected with larger universities and colleges (such as Cincinnati College Conservatory, which is part of the University of Cincinnati, or the Peabody Conservatory in Baltimore, part of Johns Hopkins University) and those that are independent, such as the Curtis Institute of Music and The Juilliard School. In general, the affiliated conservatories have moved more quickly to develop online catalogs, taking advantage of technology developments in their parent institutions. Today most independent conservatories are members of OCLC, thus making their holdings visible through WorldCat.

Listed here are selected conservatory libraries and their Web site addresses:

Boston Conservatory (Boston, MA) http://www.bostonconservatory.edu/
Cincinnati College-Conservatory (Cincinnati, OH) http://www.ccm.uc.edu/
Curtis Institute of Music (Philadelphia, PA) http://www.curtis.edu/html/10000.shtml
The Juilliard School (New York, NY) http://www.juilliard.edu/ (home of the world-renowned Juilliard Manuscript Collection of 138 original manuscripts, sketches, and annotated editions; selected scores available digitally at www.juilliardmanuscriptcollection.org)
Manhattan School of Music (New York, NY) http://www.msmnyc.edu/
Mannes College The New School for Music (New York, NY) Scherman Music Library http://library.newschool.edu/scherman/

New England Conservatory (Boston, MA) http://www.newenglandconservatory.edu/
Oberlin Conservatory of Music (Oberlin, OH) http://www.oberlin.edu/con/
San Francisco Conservatory of Music (San Francisco, CA) http://www.sfcm.edu/

Church and Monastic Libraries

Many of the early manuscript sources documented in RISM are found in monastery and cathedral libraries. The Vatican Library in Rome is an especially rich repository of manuscripts of polyphonic music. For more detailed information on these collections, see the *Grove Music Online* Libraries article under "Types of Libraries: Monasteries; Cathedrals; Other Ecclesiastical Institutions" as well as individual library descriptions in the *Grove Music Online* article and RISM Series C.

Private Collections

The term *private collections* refers to collections developed by individuals. As discussed in the *Grove Music Online* article "Collections, Private," many of these collections are eventually housed in institutional libraries, either on a deposit basis or as permanent donations. Examples include the Robert Owen Lehmann collection at the Pierpont Morgan Library, the William Schiede Collection of Bach materials at Princeton University Library, and the Ira F. Brilliant Beethoven collection at San Jose State University in California. The *Grove Music Online* article is subdivided into sections on current collections (arranged by country and city) and historical collections (arranged by name of collection).

The following selections provide additional information:

Folter, Siegrun. *Private Libraries of Musicians and Musicologists: A Bibliography of Catalogs.* Buren: F. Knuf, 1987.

Coover, James B. *Private Music Collections: Catalogs and Cognate Literature.* Warren, MI: Harmonie Park Press, 2001.

King, A. Hyatt. *Some British Collectors of Music, c. 1600–1960.* Cambridge, Cambridge University Press, 1963.

Paul Sacher Foundation (Paul Sacher Stiftung)

http://www.paul-sacher-stiftung.ch/e/default.htm.

Swiss conductor Paul Sacher (1906–99) amassed an extraordinary collection of manuscripts and primary source materials of twentieth-century composers. His foundation has published catalogs and inventories of its holdings, as well as facsimile editions of selected publications.

Composers represented in the Paul Sacher Stiftung include Béla Bartók, Conrad Beck, Alban Berg, Luciano Berio, Jean Binet, Harrison Birtwistle, Pierre Boulez, Henry Brant, Fritz Brun, Willy Burkhard, Adolf Busch, Elliott Carter, Henri Dutilleux, Vinko Glokobar, Sofia Gubaidulina, Hans Werner Henze, Arthur Honegger, Mauricio Kagel, Gyorgy Ligeti, Witold Lutoslawski, Bruno Maderna, Frank Martin, Conlon Nancarrow, Goffredo Petrassi, Wolfgang Rihm, George Rochberg, Kaikhosru Shapurji Sorabji, Igor Stravinsky, Viktor Ullmann, Galina Ustvolskaja, Anton Webern, and Stefan Wolpe.[21]

Selected Publications

See http://www.paul-sacher-stiftung.ch/pss/publikationen/ausstellungskataloge.htm.

How to Locate and Access Primary Source Materials

Researchers and performers interested in primary source materials often ask how to find out where a manuscript is located, and how to gain access to materials in private collections. The former question can usually be answered by using a composer thematic catalog (see Chapter 10), if there is one for the composer in question. For pre-1800 works, primary sources can be located using RISM (see pp. 176–182). Access to works in private collections can often be achieved by following the same principles of library etiquette already described: write to the owner of the collection and/or the library that houses the collection, and find out when and where you may gain access to the material.

See also Chapter 8: From Manuscript to Printed Edition.

Music Information Centers

http://www.iamic.net/

Music Information Centers (MICs) document and promote contemporary music in countries around the world, from Australia to Yugoslavia. The International Association of Music Information Centres, (IAMIC) is the umbrella organization for these centers. As of 2006, IAMIC listed 43 centers in 38 countries. Its Web site provides links to MIC member Web sites, which in turn link to their online library catalogs. Many MICs, particularly those in European countries, carry out their mission by publishing and recording music of their native composers. By searching their online catalogs, users may find new works for particular instruments or ensembles. See Figure 1–3.

It should be noted that the American Music Center, which is the U.S. Music Information Center, donated its library of scores to the New York Public Library in 2001. Holdings are found in the CATNYP catalog: http://catnyp.nypl.org/; for further information, see http://www.amc.net/explore/repetoire/library/.

See also O'Kelly, Eve. "Music Information Centres." In *Information Sources in Music,* edited by Lewis Foreman, 26–39 (München: K. G. Saur, 2003).

TIPS ON SEARCHING LIBRARY CATALOGS

The first bibliographic tool in any library is its catalog: whether in old-fashioned card catalog format (rare), book format, or online. Users should note that there are several library system vendors on the market, and interfaces may vary from library to library, depending upon the system each uses.

Library catalogs should provide access to materials by (at a minimum):

NAME of author or composer
TITLE of work (see later explanation of uniform titles)
SUBJECT (usually in the form of Library of Congress subject headings)

FIGURE 1–3   Ireland Music Information Center online catalog.

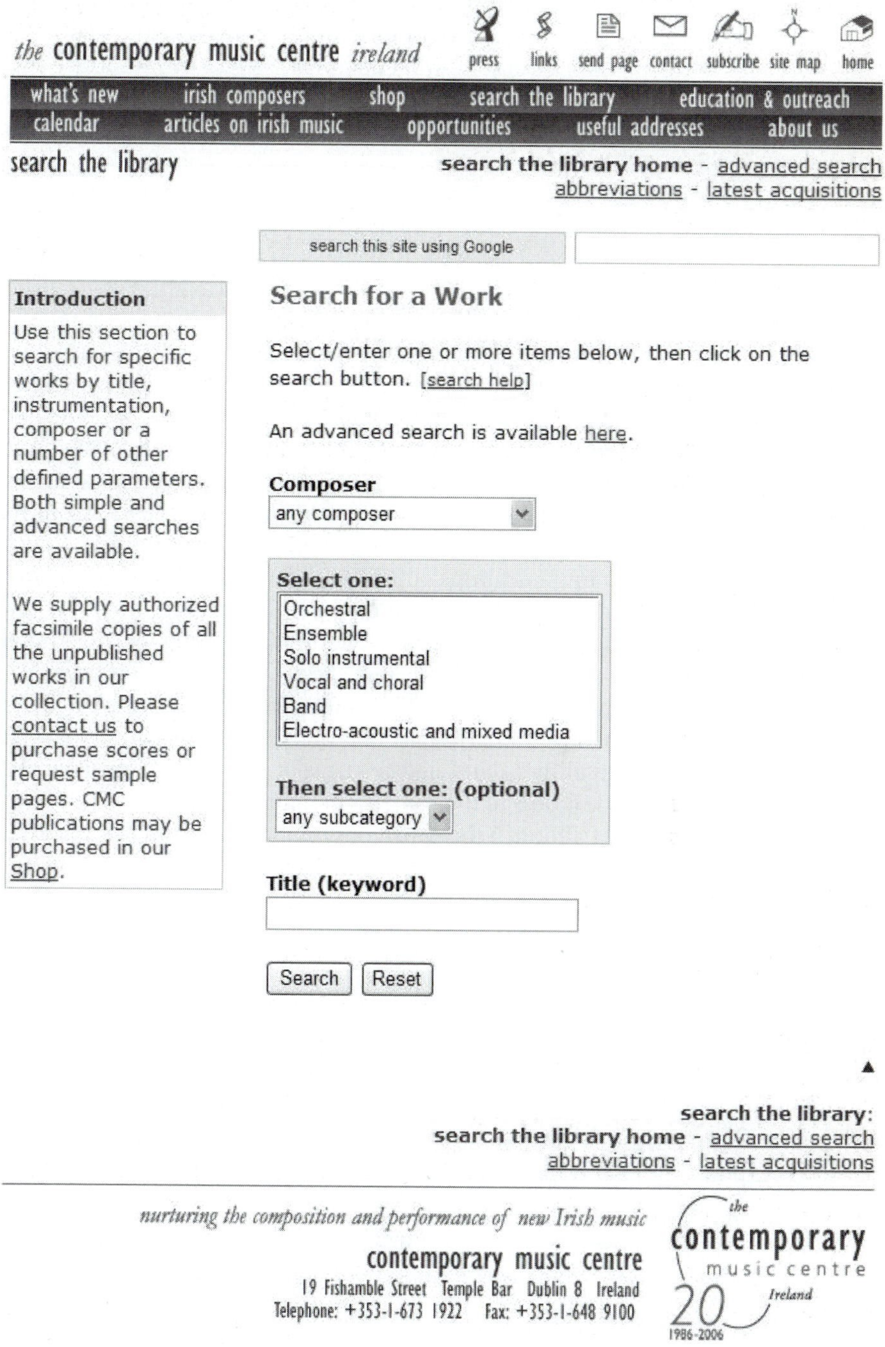

the contemporary music centre *ireland*   press   links   send page   contact   subscribe   site map   home

what's new   irish composers   shop   search the library   education & outreach
calendar   articles on irish music   opportunities   useful addresses   about us

search the library

search the library home - advanced search
abbreviations - latest acquisitions

search this site using Google

Introduction	Search for a Work

Use this section to search for specific works by title, instrumentation, composer or a number of other defined parameters. Both simple and advanced searches are available.

We supply authorized facsimile copies of all the unpublished works in our collection. Please contact us to purchase scores or request sample pages. CMC publications may be purchased in our Shop.

Select/enter one or more items below, then click on the search button. [search help]

An advanced search is available here.

Composer

any composer ▾

Select one:
Orchestral
Ensemble
Solo instrumental
Vocal and choral
Band
Electro-acoustic and mixed media

Then select one: (optional)
any subcategory ▾

Title (keyword)

Search   Reset

▲

search the library:
search the library home - advanced search
abbreviations - latest acquisitions

nurturing the composition and performance of new Irish music

contemporary music centre
19 Fishamble Street Temple Bar Dublin 8 Ireland
Telephone: +353-1-673 1922   Fax: +353-1-648 9100

the
contemporary
music centre
20 *Ireland*
1986-2006

http://cmc.ie/library/index.cfm

In addition, online catalogs usually allow searching by **KEYWORD,** which may seem to be the most natural approach to users more familiar with Google searches, but is not always the most efficient form of searching in library catalogs. This is because library catalogs use somewhat complex systems of "authority control," which direct users from forms of names, titles, or subjects not used in the catalog to those used per established conventions. (See following section, "Uniform Titles.) The "authority file," as it is called, may not be available during a word search. Thus, a search for "Marriage" to find Mozart's *Le Nozze di Figaro* (the form used in library catalogs) may not bring up all of the entries sought.

Similarly, although keyword searches typically search all components of the item's bibliographic record—title, subject, contents notes (if available), and subject headings, the presence of selected words in the bibliographic record does not mean that the item is relevant to the user's search, especially if the search is not carefully constructed. For example, a search under Global Hip Hop in the Library of Congress catalog brings up more than 1,000 entries that have these words in some part of the bibliographic record. Many of these entries are quite relevant to the topic, such as David Toop's *Rap Attack 3: African Rap to Global Hip Hop* (London: Serpent's Tail, 2000). However, it also brings up Jack Canfield's book *Life Lessons for the Way You Live: 7 Essential Ingredients for Finding Balance and Serenity* (Deerfield Beach, FL: Health Communications, 2007), because the words *global* and *hip-hop* are found in different parts of the contents note. The former book is quite relevant to the query; the latter is not. (Placing the term in quotation marks, "Global Hip Hop," or searching it as a phrase would limit the search to relevant titles.)

Catalog entries themselves should provide information on the physical attributes of the item: number of pages, size (usually in centimeters), publication information (place of publication, publisher, date), and language of publication. Ideally, library catalogs should also provide access to the contents of multiauthor or multicomposer collections and anthologies, although this time-consuming work is not always done.

Uniform Titles

Library catalogs use systems for creating *uniform* titles to bring together different manifestations, or versions, of the same work. Uniform titles are especially important in music catalogs because title pages of scores and recordings often use varying forms of a composition's title. Placed below the composer's name and above the title page title (or "title proper"), the uniform title allows users to search for all manifestations or versions of the same work in one alphabetical sequence.

For example, various editions of the score of Beethoven's "Eroica" Symphony (Symphony no. 3 in E flat major, op. 55) have the following title page titles:

Symphony no. 3: Eroica, op. 55, in E flat major (Kalmus miniature score)
Symphonie III, Es dur, op. 55: Eroica (Universal miniature score)
Ludwig van Beethoven: Symphonie Nr. 3 in Es-dur (Bärenreiter critical edition)

If these titles were filed alphabetically under Beethoven's name, one would be under "L" and two under "S."

Use of the uniform title allows all editions of this work to be listed together.

Beethoven, Ludwig van, 1770–1827.
UNIFORM TITLE: Symphonies, no. 3, op. 55, E flat major
TITLE: Symphony no. 3: Eroica, op. 55, in E flat major

Note that the plural form of symphony is used for the uniform title because Beethoven wrote more than one work in this genre.

Other rules governing the creation of uniform titles include the following:

- Use of original language of work: Stravinsky's *Firebird* is listed under *Zhar-ptitsa*
- Use of collective titles for compilations: A collection of various Mozart works for violin and piano is found under the uniform title: Violin, piano music; Similarly, the complete works editions of major composers (described further in chapters 8 and 10), are found under the uniform title: Works.
- Elimination of numbers as initial words: Anton von Webern's eight early songs or *Acht Frühe Lieder* is found under the uniform title *Frühe Lieder.*

Uniform titles also distinguish formats of publication (piano-vocal score or libretto) and language of text and indicate whether the work is an arrangement.

NAME: Puccini, Giacomo, 1858–1924.
UNIFORM TITLE: Madama Butterfly. Vocal Score. Japanese and Italian.
TITLE: Madama Butterfly. Chōchōfujin: opera in due atti.
(a piano-vocal score of Puccini's *Madam Butterfly* in Japanese and Italian)

NAME: Mozart, Wolfgang Amadeus, 1756–1791.
UNIFORM TITLE: Nozze di Figaro. Selections; arr.
TITLE: Marriage of Figaro : for 2 oboes, 2 clarinets, 2 bassoons & 2 horns / W. A. Mozart ; arr. by Wendt ; [edited by Robert Block and Himie Voxman]
(Selections from Mozart's *Marriage of Figaro,* arranged for wind ensemble)

Using the Catalog for Help: Cross-References

Library catalogs use helpful systems of cross-references (or "see" references) to direct users from forms of names or titles that are not used in the catalog to forms that are used.

For example, a search for Mozart, Amadeus will direct the user to Mozart, Wolfgang Amadeus, 1756–1791, because this is the form of his name used in almost all library catalogs.

Similarly, a search for Mozart's *Marriage of Figaro* will direct the user to Mozart's *Nozze di Figaro,* and a search for Stravinsky's *Firebird* will direct the user to *Zhar-ptitsa*.

Subject Headings

Subject headings enable users to search for materials on a particular subject in the library's catalog. Most libraries assign subject headings based on formats published in the latest edition of the *Library of Congress Subject Headings.* Searching by LC subject heading is both more precise and much less intuitive than searching by key word. Google-dependent searchers are too often stumped and frustrated by subject heading searches in library catalogs.

ADVICE

If you are searching for a specific book and know the author or title, it's simpler to look under the most specific information at hand, rather than try to find it via subject. For example, if you recall reading a book with the title *Stomping the Blues*[22] but cannot recall the author's name, it's simpler to search under title or key word, rather than under the broad subject heading "blues."

But, if you are interested in locating additional resources on the subject, once you get to the entry on this book (which is by Albert Murray) in the online catalog, you can click on the subject headings found in the entry to locate similar materials.

Subject Subdivisions

Library of Congress subject headings use subdivisions to provide more refined access to works on specific subjects. For example, users searching for books about Mozart's Piano Concerto, K. 467, might wish to consult both general biographical sources on the composer as well as sources dealing with his piano concertos in general and specifically with K. 467.

Subject headings to search would appear as

MOZART, WOLFGANG AMADEUS, 1756–1791
MOZART, WOLFGANG AMADEUS, 1756–1791 Concertos Piano Orchestra
  General sources on his works for this genre
MOZART, WOLFGANG AMADEUS, 1756–1791. Concertos, piano, orchestra,
  K. 467, C major.
    Specifically about K. 467
    Grayson, David A. *Mozart, Piano Concertos nos. 20 in D minor, K. 466, and no. 21 in C Major, K. 467.* Cambridge Music Handbooks. Cambridge: Cambridge University Press, 1998.

Note: This book also has the subject heading, CONCERTOS (PIANO)—ANALYSIS, APPRECIATION, which would be used when looking for analytical discussions sources of piano concertos in general.

Boolean and Other Types of Search Techniques

Boolean search principles are commonly used in library catalogs and by Web search engines. Named after nineteenth-century mathematician George Boole, Boolean searches use the operators AND, OR, or NOT. Other valuable search techniques include *phrase searching,* or placing words in quotation marks to find incidents when both words are used next to each other, for example, "Aaron Copland," or "Missa Solemnis." *Proximity searches* use terms such as *near, before,* and *after* to find words within a phrase; truncation allows use of wildcards (*) to cover all forms of a word (i.e., fortepiano* will bring up fortepiano, fortepianos, and fortepianists).

Most libraries have "help" screens that explain how these search techniques operate in their catalogs.

More Catalog Help: See Also(s) and Related Subjects

Catalogs also use "see also" references (or directions to "related subjects") that can guide users to additional sources on a particular subject. For example, a search under the very broad term "Popular Music" will direct users to more narrow terms that may locate sources more specific to the topic at hand (Figure 1–4).

Subject Searches for Works for Particular Instruments or Combinations of Instruments

Subject searching can also be helpful when looking for repertoire for a particular instrument or ensemble. Here, too, it may be difficult to guess the appropriate LC subject heading to use, although keyword searches often direct users to the correct heading. For example, an ensemble searching for works for horn, piano, violin, and cello could do a word search under the names of the instruments (but use "violoncello" instead of "cello"). This would direct to the subject heading: QUARTETS (PIANO, HORN, VIOLIN, VIOLONCELLO).

FIGURE 1–4   New York Public Library for the Performing Arts CATNYP Catalog: *see also* references for searches on "Popular music." Credit: The New York Public Library, Astor, Lenox and Tilden Foundations.

☑ SAVE MARKED RECORDS

SUBJECTS (1-39 of 39)
Popular music

1	-- See also the narrower term Bhangra (Music)
2	-- See also the narrower term Big band music
	Here are entered compositions not in a specific form or of a specific type for big band, and collections of compositions in several forms or types for big band
	--headings for forms and types of music that include "big band" and headings with medium of performance that include "big band"; also the subdivisions Methods (Big band) and Studies and exercises (Big band) under individual musical instruments and families of instruments
3	-- See also the narrower term Blues (Music)
	This heading is assigned to blues with voice(s) or for two or more instrumentalists
	--headings for music of individual instruments followed by the qualifier "(Blues)" and the subdivisions Methods (Blues) and Studies and exercises (Blues) under individual musical instruments and families of instruments
4	-- See also the narrower term Cajun music
	Here are entered traditional music of the Cajuns and music containing elements of or inspired by traditional music in the Cajun style
5	-- See also the narrower term Calypso (Music)
6	-- See also the narrower term Celtic music
	Here are entered traditional music of Celtic ethnic groups in general and musical works containing elements of or inspired by traditional music in the Celtic style. Celtic folk music in specific forms is entered under headings such as Strathspeys; Folk songs, Breton; Fiddle tunes--Scotland; Folk music--Ireland; etc
	--headings for music of individual instruments followed by the qualifier "(Celtic)" and the subdivisions Methods (Celtic) and Studies and exercises (Celtic) under individual musical instruments and families of instruments
7	-- See also the narrower term Contemporary Christian music
8	-- See also the narrower term Country music
	This heading is assigned to country music for two or more performers
	--headings for music of individual instruments followed by the qualifier "(Country)" and the subdivisions Methods (Country) and Studies and exercises (Country) under individual musical instruments and families of instruments

http://catnyp.nypl.org/search?/dpopular+music/dpopular+music/1%2C2120%2C30919%2CB/a exact&FF=dpopular+music&1%2C39

However, users should note that the headings will appear as follows:

QUARTETS (PIANO, HORN, VIOLIN, VIOLONCELLO)
Sound recordings of works for this combination
QUARTETS (PIANO, HORN, VIOLIN, VIOLONCELLO)—SCORES
Scores of works for this combination
QUARTETS (PIANO, HORN, VIOLIN, VIOLONCELLO)—SCORES AND PARTS
Scores and parts of works for this combination

Sample Bibliographic Entries for Music Materials

As noted above, several different companies provide library online catalog systems; although these systems utilize the same bibliographic records for individual items and should offer the same minimum search indexes outlined above, the look and specific protocols of these systems vary. The examples below (see Figures 1–5a– 5b – 5c – 5d) are selected from online catalogs at the New York Public Library (Innovative Interfaces Systems), Columbia University (Endeavor Systems), and University of Southern California (SIRSI System).

FIGURE 1–5a Sample bibliographic record for published score, New York Public Library for the Performing Arts CATNYP catalog (Innovative Interfaces Library system)

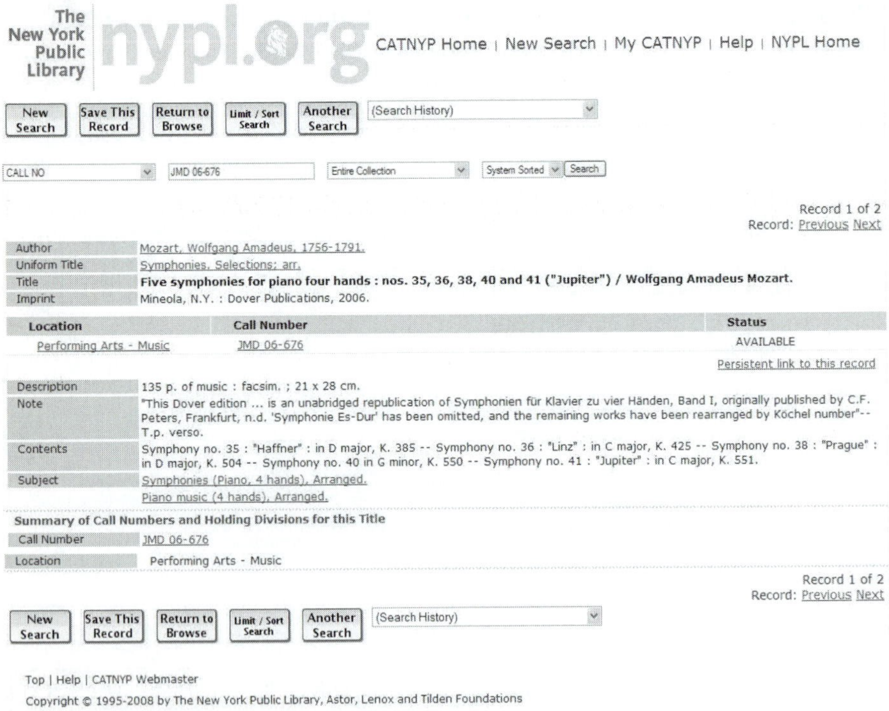
The New York Public Library nypl.org
CATNYP Home | New Search | My CATNYP | Help | NYPL Home

New Search | Save This Record | Return to Browse | Limit / Sort Search | Another Search | (Search History)

CALL NO | JMD 06-676 | Entire Collection | System Sorted | Search

Record 1 of 2
Record: Previous Next

Author	Mozart, Wolfgang Amadeus, 1756-1791.
Uniform Title	Symphonies. Selections; arr.
Title	**Five symphonies for piano four hands : nos. 35, 36, 38, 40 and 41 ("Jupiter") / Wolfgang Amadeus Mozart.**
Imprint	Mineola, N.Y. : Dover Publications, 2006.

Location	Call Number	Status
Performing Arts - Music	JMD 06-676	AVAILABLE

Persistent link to this record

Description	135 p. of music : facsim. ; 21 x 28 cm.
Note	"This Dover edition ... is an unabridged republication of Symphonien für Klavier zu vier Händen, Band I, originally published by C.F. Peters, Frankfurt, n.d. 'Symphonie Es-Dur' has been omitted, and the remaining works have been rearranged by Köchel number"--T.p. verso.
Contents	Symphony no. 35 : "Haffner" : in D major, K. 385 -- Symphony no. 36 : "Linz" : in C major, K. 425 -- Symphony no. 38 : "Prague" : in D major, K. 504 -- Symphony no. 40 in G minor, K. 550 -- Symphony no. 41 : "Jupiter" : in C major, K. 551.
Subject	Symphonies (Piano, 4 hands), Arranged.
	Piano music (4 hands), Arranged.

Summary of Call Numbers and Holding Divisions for this Title

Call Number	JMD 06-676
Location	Performing Arts - Music

Record 1 of 2
Record: Previous Next

New Search | Save This Record | Return to Browse | Limit / Sort Search | Another Search | (Search History)

Top | Help | CATNYP Webmaster
Copyright © 1995-2008 by The New York Public Library, Astor, Lenox and Tilden Foundations

http://clio.cul.columbia.edu/cgibin/Pwebrecon.cgi?v1=1&Search%5fArg=ht1521%20%2Eg524%202000&Search%5FCode=CALL&CNT=50&PID=7UzwUh7gCQZGnav0BibciZj8&SEQ=20080118163140&SID=1

FIGURE 1–5b   Sample bibliographic record for published book from Columbia University CLIO catalog (Endeavor system)

FIGURE 1–5c   Sample bibliographic record for commercial sound recording from University of Southern California HOMER catalog (SIRSI system)

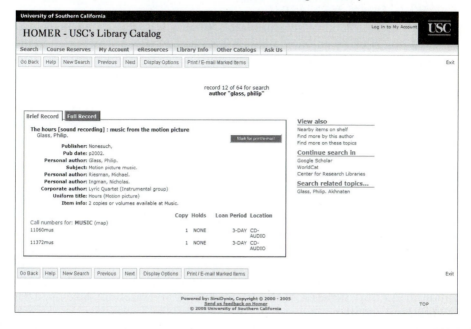

FIGURE 1–5d **Sample bibliographic record for commercial video recording from University of Southeren California HOMER catalog (SIRSI system)**

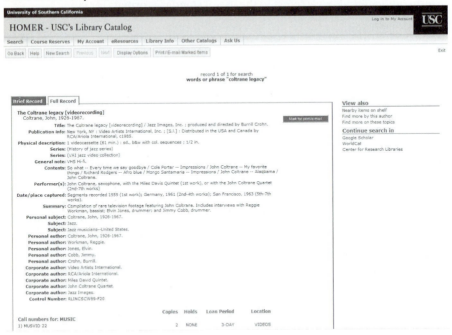

Other Useful Information
ISBN, ISMN, ISSN, ISRC

The ISBN, or International Standard Book Number, is a unique 13-digit number assigned to a book by an internationally authorized ISBN agency, which in the United States is R. R. Bowker. These numbers serve to identify uniquely each book; a separate number is used for hardcover and paperbound versions of individual titles. Because each number is unique, use of ISBNs is advantageous for library catalog searching and online ordering systems.[23] R. R. Bowker is also the agency for the relatively new ISMN, or International Standard Music Number, found on published scores. ISMNs begin with the letter M, followed by a unique 9-digit number.[24]

ISSN = International Standard Serial Number (used for periodicals)[25]
ISRC = International Standard Recording Code (for sound recordings and music video recordings)[26]

It should be noted that all of these numbering systems were developed and authorized by ISO, the International Organization for Standardization.[27] The United States ISO organization is ANSI (American National Standards Institute),[28] which in turn authorizes NISO (National Information Standards Organization).[29] As is evident, all of these conventions are carefully developed for international adoption.

BIBLIOGRAPHIC STYLE AND STYLE MANUALS

The term *bibliographic style* refers to the use of standard formats for citing sources in a research paper. All direct quotes, interpretative ideas of other writers, and factual information beyond commonly known details such as birth and death dates of major composers must be properly cited in a format that enables the reader to track down the source.

There are two primary schools of bibliographic style: *Notes-Bibliography* style, which uses footnotes or endnotes and a bibliography at the end of the paper, and *Author-Date* style, which includes parenthetical references within the text and a reference list at the end of the paper.

These style formats are carefully explained in the two different style format manuals most commonly used in the United States: the *Chicago Manual of Style* and its offshoot, Turabian's *Manual for Writers of Term Papers, Theses, and Dissertations,* and the Modern Language Association's *MLA Style Manual and Guide to Scholarly Publishing,* and its offshoot the *MLA Handbook.* The *Chicago Manual* and the *MLA Style Manual* are detailed compendia that cover all components of book publishing; Turabian and the *MLA Handbook* are condensed versions of the parent sources and are designed for student term papers. Students should check to see which format is required or preferred by their institution and then follow that format consistently. Some institutions have developed their own style manuals or use alternate systems. Again, writers should follow the required format consistently. Citations in this book follow the Chicago format.

This section is subdivided into listings of general style manuals (as just described), style manuals and writing guides specific to music, style manuals dealing with electronic citations, help via software programs, and a selection of general writing and style guides.

Why is bibliographic style important? One of the best ways to demonstrate the importance of following accepted style standards consistently is to show how an incorrect citation in a published article or book can confuse other readers who seek to locate the cited source. For example, let's say you find the following citation in a paper published by a colleague:

Moore, Allan, ed. "The Development of the Blues." *The Cambridge Companion to Blues and Gospel Music.* New York: Cambridge University Press, 2002.

This format does not indicate the name of the author of the article, nor that it is found in a multiauthor collection that is edited by Allan F. Moore, nor the page numbers of the article within the collection. The author of the article is David Evans, the page numbers are 20–43, and the citation format to be followed is Chicago 17.69.

I. General Style Manuals

Gibaldi, Joseph. *MLA Style Manual and Guide to Scholarly Publishing.* 2nd ed. New York: Modern Language Association of America, 1998.

_____. *MLA Handbook for Writers of Research Papers.* 6th ed. New York: Modern
Language Association of America, 2003.
Turabian, Kate L. *A Manual for Writers of Research Papers, Theses and Dissertations:
Chicago Style for Students and Researchers.* 7th ed. Revised by Wayne C. Booth, Gregory
G. Colomb, and Joseph M. Williams. Chicago: University of Chicago Press, 2007.
University of Chicago Press. *The Chicago Manual of Style.* 15th ed. Chicago: University of
Chicago Press, 2003. http://www.press.uchicago.edu/Misc/Chicago/cmosfaq/cmosfaq.html

More about Note/Bibliography Format vs. Author/Date Format

Publications in humanities disciplines, including music, tend to use the note-
bibliography system of citation. In this system, cited passages are indicated by
footnotes at the bottom of the page or endnotes at the end of the chapter. The
bibliography at the end of the paper lists all sources alphabetically by author.

FOOTNOTE

Maynard Solomon, *Late Beethoven: Music, Thought, Imagination* (Berkeley:
University of California Press, 2003), 129.

BIBLIOGRAPHY

Solomon, Maynard. *Late Beethoven: Music, Thought, Imagination.* Berkeley: University
of California Press, 2003.

In a footnote, the first line of the entry is indented; subsequent lines are flush
with the margin. In a bibliography, the first line is flush with the margin; subsequent lines are indented.

The author-date system, which is based on the *Publication Manual of the
American Psychological Association*[30] (frequently abbreviated as APA) is used
more commonly in the sciences and social sciences. Music publications using this
form of citation include those dealing with science or social science–oriented subjects, such as acoustics, psychoacoustics, psychology and music, and music education. Citations are placed in parentheses within the text, using author's last name,
date of publication, and page number. The list of works cited appears at the end
of the paper and is titled "Works cited" or "Reference List."

PARENTHETICAL REFERENCE

(Phelps 1986, 43)

REFERENCES

Phelps, R. P. (1986). *A Guide to Research in Music Education* (3rd ed.) Metuchen: Scarecrow Press.

II. Style Manuals and Writing Guides Specific to Music

Bellman, Jonathan. *A Short Guide to Writing About Music.* 2nd ed. New York: Pearson
Longman, 2007.

Boyle, J. David, Richard K. Fiese, and Nancy Zavac. *A Handbook for Preparing Graduate Papers in Music.* 2nd ed. Houston: Halycon Press, 2004.

Cowdery, James R. *How to Write About Music: The RILM Manual of Style.* 2nd ed. Foreword by Carl A. Skoggard. Introduction by Barbara Dobbs Mackenzie. New York: Répertoire International de Littérature Musicale, 2006.

Helm, E. Eugene, and Albert T. Luper. *Words and Music: Form and Procedure in Theses, Dissertations, Research Papers, Book Reports, Programs, Theses in Composition.* Rev. ed. Totowa, NJ: European American Music Corp, 1982.

Herbert, Trevor. *Music in Words: A Guide to Researching and Writing About Music.* London: Associated Board of the Royal Schools of Music, 2001.

Holoman, D. Kern. *Writing About Music: A Style Sheet from the Editors of 19th-Century Music.* Berkeley: University of California Press, 1988.

Irvine, Delmar. *Irvine's Writing About Music.* 3rd ed. Revised and enlarged by Mark A. Radice. Portland, OR: Amadeus Press, 1999.

Wingell, Richard J. *Writing About Music: An Introductory Guide.* 4th ed. Upper Saddle River, NJ: Prentice Hall, 2007.

Wingell, Richard J., and Silvia Herzog. *Introduction to Research in Music.* Upper Saddle River, NJ: Prentice Hall, 2001.

III. Electronic Citations

(The newest editions of Turabian, Chicago, and MLA include guidelines for citing most types of electronic resources, so it is not always necessary to consult a separate guide for electronic citations.)

Harnack, Andrew, and Eugene Kleppinger. *Online! A Reference Guide to Using Internet Sources, 2003 Update.* Boston: Bedford/St.Martin's, 2003. http://www.bedfordstmartins.com/online/index.html

Li, Xia, and Nancy B. Crane. *Electronic Styles: A Handbook for Citing Electronic Information.* 2nd ed. Medford, NJ: Information Today, 1996.

Walker, Janice R., and Todd Taylor. *The Columbia Guide to Online Style.* 2nd ed. New York: Columbia University Press, 2006.

In general, citations for electronic sources should include the same information in basically the same format as citations for print sources, with the important addition of the **url** (uniform resource locator) and the date accessed:

Why is the date accessed important?

Unlike published books, which can be assumed to be complete as of the date published, the Web is a dynamic resource, and Web sites may be updated or taken down, according to the needs of the author. Indeed, a Web site citation may not exist the next time one looks for it.

EXAMPLE

MacDonald, Ian. "Music Under Soviet Rule: A WWW Resource" http://www.siue.edu/ ~aho/musov/contents.html (accessed August 9, 2007).

IV. Help with Software Programs

Many colleges and universities provide software programs that aid students in formatting references in their papers. These programs typically provide options for formatting citations according to the different style sheets: Turabian/Chicago, MLA, or APA. Some of the most popular programs are

Endnote: http://www.endnote.com/
ProCite: http://www.procite.com
Reference Manager: http://www.refman.com/

Although these programs appear to make citation format easy, students should be cautioned to check the results carefully to make sure that the correct format has been selected and to fill in necessary information properly.

V. A Selection of Other General Writing and Style Guides

Regular visitors to bookstores undoubtedly notice that the onset of every academic year typically brings a wave of new publications to aid students: writing guides, pocket thesauri and dictionaries, and style manuals. The following listing provides a selection of some standard and widely accepted general writing guides. Strunk and White's *Elements of Style* has guided writers at all levels with its simple and straightforward rules for many generations, teaching grammatical principles such as the difference between *that* and *which*.[31] Now in at least its fifth printed edition,[32] the original 1918 edition may be found on the Internet. Historian (and Berlioz scholar) Jacques Barzun has also guided writers and researchers over the years with his landmark books *The Modern Researcher* and *Simple and Direct*. The former deals with general methods of scholarly inquiry and research, while the latter addresses approaches to writing.

Again, the following listings make no attempt at comprehensiveness, and students are advised to check with their departments and their faculties regarding recommended texts.

Barzun, Jacques. *Simple and Direct: A Rhetoric for Writers.* 4th ed. New York: Quill, 2001.
Barzun, Jacques, and Henry F. Graff. *The Modern Researcher.* 6th ed. Belmont, CA: Thompson/Wadsworth, 2004.
Booth, Wayne C., Gregory G. Colomb, and Joseph M. Williams. *The Craft of Research.* Chicago Guides to Writing, Editing, and Publishing. 2nd ed. Chicago: University of Chicago Press, 2003. [Much of the material in this book has been incorporated into Turabian, 7th ed., 2007.]
Elbow, Peter. *Writing With Power: Techniques for Mastering the Writing Process.* 2nd ed. New York: Oxford University Press, 1998.
Frank, Francine Harriet Wattman, and Paula A. Treichler. *Language, Gender, and Professional Writing: Theoretical Approaches and Guidelines for Nonsexist Usage.* New York: Commission on the Status of Women in the Profession, Modern Language Association of America, 1989.

Luey, Beth. *Handbook for Academic Authors.* 4th ed. Cambridge: Cambridge University Press, 2002.

Madsen, David. *Successful Dissertations and Theses: A Guide to Graduate Student Research from Proposal to Completion.* 2nd ed. San Francisco: Jossey-Bass, 1992.

Ritter, R. M., Angus Stevenson, and Lesley Brown. *New Oxford Dictionary for Writers and Editors: The Essential A–Z Guide to the Written Word.* New York: Oxford University Press, 2005.

Shertzer, Margaret D. *The Elements of Grammar.* New York: MacMillan, 1996.

Siegal, Allan M., and William G. Connolly. *New York Times Manual of Style and Usage.* Rev. ed. New York: Times Books, 1999.

Strunk, William, Jr., and E. B. White. *Elements of Style.* 4th ed. Boston: Allyn and Bacon, 1999. (1918 edition is available on the Web at http://www.bartleby.com/141/.)

Troyka, Lynn Quitman, and Douglas Hesse. *Simon and Schuster Handbook for Writers.* 8th ed. Upper Saddle River, NJ: Pearson Prentice Hall, 2007. http://www.prenhall.com/hss_troyka_sshb_8/

Van Leunen, Mary-Claire. *A Handbook for Scholars.* Rev. ed. New York: Oxford University Press, 1992.

USING THE INTERNET FOR MUSIC RESEARCH

There are wonderful resources for music research available on the Internet. There are also Web sites with biased, erroneous, and out-of-date information. How can users best locate relevant Web resources, evaluate them, and use them appropriately for research?

Searching for Information on the Web

It is certainly not difficult to find a Web search engine. Indeed, just as a generation ago Xerox was equivalent to photocopying, today Google has become synonymous with Web searching. (Needless to say, its competitors object to its ubiquitous identity.) With its subsearch universes of Google Book, Google Scholar, Google Patents, and other tools, library users will find much of relevance through carefully crafted Google searches.

Types of Search Engines

Google is a crawler-based search engine, meaning that it searches the Web through technology. Yahoo is a directory-based search engine, loosely defined as one that uses humans to review and compile listings. Metasearch engines search other search engines; examples include www.dogpile.com, www.vivisimo.com, www.kartoo.com, and www.mamma.com. For detailed information about search engines, see www.searchenginewatch.com.

Most search engines have "Help" screens to aid users in the use of Boolean operators and other search techniques on the site. A search for a composer or performer name on the Web is usually best achieved by placing the name in quotation marks: for example, "Leonard Bernstein," "Duke Ellington," "B. B. King," or "Mary J. Blige." Although many of the more established artists have their own "official"

Web sites (www.leonardbernstein.com, www.dukeellington.com, www.bbking.com, www.mjblige.com), less well-known names may only be represented by links to their publisher or record company site. And, the "official" sites just mentioned usually link to publisher and record company sites, with the goal of leading users to places where they may purchase materials.

Definitions and Web site addresses

url = uniform resource locator, or the unique web address for each site.

The last part of the url is used to distinguish the sponsor or creator of the web site:

.edu = educational institution (example: www.harvard.edu)
.gov = government organization (example: www.loc.gov)
.com = commercial (example: www.amazon.com)
.org = organization (example: www.societymusictheory.org)
.net = used for sites that incorporate special types of networking software
    (e.g., www.iamic.net)

Countries around the world also use distinct url suffixes; examples include[33]

.ch = Switzerland
.de = Germany
.fr = France
.it = Italy
.ru = Russian Federation
.uk = United Kingdom

Anyone may set up a Web site: doing so requires registration of a unique domain name, usually done (for a fee) through one of the numerous domain registration companies on the web. ICANN (Internet Corporation of Assigned Names and Numbers: www.icann.org) is the not-for-profit agency charged with managing Web site addresses and the agencies that register them. Its subsidiary InterNic (www.internic.net) provides information on registered Web addresses. Anyone can register a domain with such suffixes as .com, .org, .biz, .info, or .net, but domain names for government agencies (.gov) or educational institutions (.edu) are restricted for use by valid government or educational entities.

SOME BASIC RULES FOR MUSIC RESEARCH ON THE INTERNET

Internet Rule no. 1: Understand the difference between free and subscription-based Web resources

Although much of what is found on the Internet may be accessed for free, many of the more scholarly resources are available only through paid subscriptions. The latter includes *Grove Music Online*, RILM, JSTOR, and content of online journals. When users locate such links on sites from educational institutions, there is often a message stating that access to the site is available only to faculty and students at that institution.

Internet Rule no. 2: Evaluate, evaluate, evaluate

The key to successful use of the Internet for research in music (or in any discipline) is careful evaluation of Web sites. As a self-publishing medium, there is no "editor in chief" of the Internet, and Web sites may contain biased, erroneous, or out-dated information. Criteria that may be used to evaluate internet sources include

1. *Sponsor:*　Who put the site up? Is its url suffix .edu, .gov, .com, or .biz?
2. *Authorship:*　Is the author identified on the site? Is he/she a recognized scholar in the field?
3. *Rationale and content of the site:*　What is the purpose of the site? Does the content appear to be objective, or is there obvious bias?
4. *Currency:*　When was it last updated?

Perhaps the clearest examples of the pitfalls of Web searching may be found when looking for medical information on the Internet. A search for resources on cancer, heart disease, arthritis, or any other condition will typically bring up links to drugs used to treat those diseases, as well as links to more scientific and objective information from organizations such as the U.S. National Institutes of Health (www.nih.gov) or the American Heart Association (www.americanheart.org). Often the searcher will also find links to blogs with postings from people who have symptoms of the disease or have undergone treatment. Obviously none of this information should take the place of consultation with a doctor.

The same warnings apply to music research on the Internet. A search for information on a composer will typically bring up a Wikipedia article, links to books or recordings found on amazon.com, links to sites created by educational institutions or official composer societies (International Gustav Mahler Gesellschaft: http://www.gustav-mahler.org/), and sites created by individuals who may be passionate about the composer and his/her works, such as "Bruckner for Brucknerites" http://www.uv.es/~calaforr/brucknerians.html. Sophisticated researchers will know to be skeptical about such "fan-based" sites and rely instead on information found in scholarly reference tools, such as *Grove Music Online.*

Internet Rule no. 3: Become familiar with music-specific Web portals, also known as gateways or metasites

Collections of links selected and grouped together by experts, gateways or metasites provide guided access to Web sites in specific disciplines. These sites serve as virtual bibliographies for researchers. Selected music-specific gateway sites include

American Musicological Society. WWW Sites of Interest to Musicologists
http://www.ams-net.org/musicology_www.php

Harvard University. Online Resources for Music Scholars
http://hcl.harvard.edu/research/guides/music/resources/index.html

Note category for "Digital Music Collections":
http://hcl.harvard.edu/research/guides/music/resources/digital.html

Indiana University. Worldwide Internet Music Resources
http://library.music.indiana.edu/music_resources/

New York Public Library for the Performing Arts. Selected Internet Resources: Music
http://www.nypl.org/research/lpa/internet/lpa.cfm?trg=1&d1=141&d3=Music

Royal Holloway University of London. Department of Music. The Golden Pages: Links for Musicians on the WWW:
http://www.rhul.ac.uk/Music/Golden-pages/

Sibelius Academy. Music Resources
http://www2.siba.fi/Kulttuuripalvelut/music.html

Yahoo! Entertainment. Music
http://new.music.yahoo.com/

Each of these sites brings together Web links in various categories. Although extremely helpful for guidance in music research on the Web, it should be noted that many of these sites contain outdated or "dead" links.

Internet Rule no. 4: Understand that Web resources represent only a portion of the vast resources available for music researchers. Never assume that what one finds on the Web represents the totality of research on a particular subject!

NOTES

1. American Library Association, "Code of Ethics of the American Library Association" http://www.ala.org/ala/oif/statementspols/codeofethics/codeethics.htm.
2. http://www.worldcat.org/
3. See http://books.google.com/googlebooks/library.html for complete information.
4. "About Google Scholar," http://scholar.google.com/scholar/about.html#search2.
5. Examples of "catalogs in book form" include several published by G. K. Hall, such as the *Dictionary Catalog of the New York Public Library,* and others referenced in the library listing. These catalogs typically include photocopies of the printed cards.
6. See http://www.theeuropeanlibrary.org/portal/organisation/about_us/aboutus_en.html/ for complete information.

7. Librarians and archivists know this technology as EAD, or encoded archival description.
8. For further information on archival etiquette specifically relating to use of music collections, see Ulrich Mosch, "Preliminaries Before Visiting an Archive," and Therese Muxeneder, "Archival Etiquette," in *A Handbook to Twentieth Century Musical Sketches,* ed. Patricia Hall and Friedemann Sallis (Cambridge, NY: Cambridge University Press, 2004), 17–42.
9. "What is IAML," IAML Web site http://www.iaml.info/en/organization/what_is_iaml.
10. Bayerische Staatsbibliothek, Music Department: http://www.bsb-muenchen.de/Department_of_Music.288.0.html?L=3.

11. http://staatsbibliothek-berlin.de/
    english/imageflyer.html.
12. "Staatsbibliothek zu Berlin.
    Musikabteilung mit Mendellssohn-Archiv,"
    in *RISM Series C: Directory of Music
    Research Libraries. Vol. II: Sixteen
    European Countries,* 2d ed. ed. Elizabeth
    Davis (Kassel: Barenreiter, 2001), 100–102.
13. Österreichische Nationalbibliothek,
    Department of Music, Holdings http://www
    .onb.ac.at/ev/collections/music/index.htm.
14. http://www.colum.edu/cbmr/About_the_
    Center.php.
15. "About Sibley Library"
    http://www.rochester.edu/Eastman/sibley/?
    page=about.
16. The term *Performance parts* usually refers
    to orchestral parts and chorus parts. Not all
    libraries include these numbers in their
    published statistics.
17. Mary Wallace Davidson, "Indiana
    University's William and Gayle Cook
    Music Library: An Introduction." *Notes:
    Quarterly Journal of the Music Library
    Association* 59, no. 2 (Dec. 2002): 251.
18. "About the School of Music" http://
    www.music.indiana.edu/about/.
19. http://www.music.indiana.edu/music_
    resources.
20. "Variations" http://variations2.indiana.edu/.
    This page also includes lists of publications
    about the project.
21. http://www.paul-sacher-stiftung.ch/e/
    collections.htm.
22. Albert Murray, *Stomping the Blues* (New
    York: McGraw-Hill, 1976).
23. Additional information on ISBN numbers
    is found on the R. R. Bowker Web site:
    http://www.isbn.org/standards/home/isbn/
    us/isbnqa.asp#Q1.
24. http://www.isbn.org/standards/home/isbn/
    us/ismn/faqs.asp#Q1.
25. http://www.issn.org/.
26. http://www.ifpi.org/content/section_
    resources/isrc.html.
27. http://www.iso.org/iso/en/aboutiso/
    introduction/index.html
28. http://www.ansi.org/
29. http://www.niso.org/
30. *Publication Manual of the American
    Psychological Association,* 5th ed. (Wash-
    ington, DC: American Psychological Asso-
    ciation, 2001).
31. William Strunk Jr. and E. B. White, *The
    Elements of Style,* 4th ed. (Boston: Allyn
    and Bacon), 59.
32. A fifth edition with illustrations by Maira
    Kalman was published in 2005: William
    Strunk Jr. and E. B. White, *The Elements of
    Style.* Illustrated by Maira Kalman (New
    York: Penguin Press, 2005). The title
    Elements of Style was also used by Wendy
    Wasserstein for her last book, which is
    about upper-class women in post 9/11 New
    York.
33. See http://www.webopedia.com/quick_ref/
    topleveldomains/countrycodeF-L.asp for a
    complete list of country domain codes.

CHAPTER

2

Bibliographies
of Music Literature

OVERVIEW

What is a bibliography? In simplest terms, it is a list of sources on a particular subject. Typically found at the end of a book or article, a bibliography lists sources that the author consulted and thus provides guidance for other researchers seeking materials on the same topic. Indeed, the bibliographies included in some scholarly studies are sometimes the most extensive lists of resources on a subject. Examples of these include the detailed bibliographies attached to articles in *Grove Music Online* and found in such books as Gustav Reese's *Music in the Renaissance,* Maynard Solomon's biographies of Mozart and Beethoven, the seventh edition of *A History of Western Music,* and Richard Taruskin's *The Oxford History of Western Music.*[1]

A bibliography may be arranged alphabetically by author's last name, chronologically (as is the case for the bibliographies attached to the articles in *Grove Music Online*), or in a classified manner. If a book-length bibliography is arranged in a classified manner, ideally it should include an index of authors, titles, and more specific subjects. (For example, searching through a classified bibliography of literature on nineteenth-century German song, one would hope to find an index with page references to specific titles of works by Schumann and Brahms, rather than have to check numerous page number references under their names alone.) Similarly, if the entries are arranged alphabetically by authors' last names, there must be an index of subjects. The level of detail in subject indexing is important and often determines the overall success or weakness of a particular source. Finally, *annotated* bibliographies are those that contain brief notes about the sources.

Reference Bibliography vs. Descriptive and Analytical Bibliography

It is important to note the difference between *reference bibliography,* which is the general term for the making of lists of sources as described earlier, and *descriptive and analytical bibliography.* The latter terms refer to the study of books as physical objects, incorporating the precise identification of first editions and/or differences

┌─────────────── **Additional Information** ───────────────┐

See Stanley Boorman's article on "Bibliography of Music" in *Grove Music Online* for more detailed information on reference and descriptive and analytical bibliography. Boorman's article also includes a brief history of music bibliography, as well as selected listings of major bibliographic tools.

└──┘

between particular copies, as well as the history of printing and publishing. Aspects of these studies will be examined briefly in Chapter 8: From Manuscript to Printed Edition. Otherwise, this book focuses primarily on reference bibliography.

Organization of This Section

The first part of this chapter (Part A) identifies selected bibliographies of bibliographies and guides to reference sources, or the metasources that bring together literature about music. (This section is one of the few parts of this book that includes detailed annotations on the sources, in respect to their central role in navigating the reference literature about music.) It is important to distinguish between bibliographies of bibliographies (or lists of lists) and guides to research. Similar to travel guides such as Frommer's, Fodor's, or Lonely Planet, guides to research are designed to *guide* the user through the literature about a subject, just as the best travel guides will tell the reader how many steps the tourist office is from the train station in a particular city, and whether it is closed on Sundays. This book aspires

┌────────────── **Quick Advice for Using
and Evaluating Print Reference Sources** ──────────────┐

It's wise to spend a few minutes with a print reference book before starting to use it:

- Who is the author? Is he/she a recognized scholar in the field?
- Who is the publisher? Is it one that is known for publishing quality music reference books?
- Is the typography suitable for the source? Can you read the print, or does it require a magnifying glass? How will you best remember this book?
- How it the book arranged? Is it arranged in a classified fashion or alphabetically?
- Which types of materials does it include (books, dissertations, articles in periodicals, etc.)?
- What is the cutoff date for inclusion?
- Is there an index (or more than one index) and how is it arranged?
- Does the index refer to item numbers or page numbers?
- Where is the guide to abbreviations located?

└──┘

to be such a resource. Since a thorough search for literature about music must include exploration of *format-specific* sources (books, dissertations, articles in periodicals, Festschriften, and congress reports) as well as *subject-specific* sources, parts B and C of this chapter discuss these areas respectively. Part D of this chapter describes bibliographies of music literature that operate as indexes or guides to other reference sources in which the information is found. Such tools are identified in the classified listing of sources (Part C) by an [I] next to the author's name.

A: BIBLIOGRAPHIES OF BIBLIOGRAPHIES AND GUIDES TO THE LITERATURE ABOUT MUSIC

Duckles, Vincent H., and Ida Reed. *Music Reference and Research Materials.* 5th ed. New York: Schirmer Books, 1997.

First published in 1964, Vincent Duckles's *Music Reference and Research Materials* was, for more than four decades, the gold standard of music bibliographies. Duckles (1913–85) served as music librarian at the University of California at Berkeley from 1947 to 1980. The fourth (1988, rev. 1994) and fifth (1997) editions of his book were revised by Michael Keller and Ida Reed respectively.[2] The fifth edition includes 3,500 annotated entries, 1,500 of which were new to the edition. Duckles is still unsurpassed in its scope and depth, and all music librarians and serious music researchers should consult it.

Duckles is a not, however, a guide to research. Entries are arranged alphabetically by author last name in chapters covering various types of reference sources, including dictionaries and encyclopedias, bibliographies of music and music literature, discographies, and so on. The annotations are descriptive rather than evaluative and include citations to reviews. It should be used alongside this book for its breadth of coverage and extensive descriptions of each source.

Marco, Guy A. *Information on Music: A Handbook of Reference Sources in European Languages.* 3 vols. Littleton, CO: Libraries Unlimited, 1975–84.

Vol. I: Basic and Universal Sources
Vol. II: The Americas
Vol. III: Europe

Originally projected for six volumes, Guy Marco's *Information on Music* was in many ways a model guide to research. His lists of resources in various subject areas were not limited to reference books such as dictionaries and encyclopedias, but also included histories, biographies, and other books typically found in a library's circulating stacks. Marco's entries are annotated and include references to item numbers in the third edition of Duckles. Despite its older date of publication and lack of completion, *Information on Music* still serves as an important guide to the literature about music. Of particular value are the detailed descriptions of sources on music in countries around the world found in volumes II and III.

Brockman, William. *Music: A Guide to the Reference Literature.* Littleton, CO: Libraries Unlimited, 1987.

In the interim between the publication of Duckles's third (1974) and fourth (1988) editions, Brockman's book served as a concise and relatively current bibliography of music reference sources. It includes 841 annotated entries, primarily on sources in English. Its success was perhaps due to its clear goal and limited scope. As stated in its introduction (p. xii), "the present guide does not attempt to compete with international and retrospective scopes of Duckles and Marco. It is offered as a summary guide to the important current and retrospective sources of information on music." Of particular value are its chapters on "Current Periodicals" and "Associations, Research Centers, and Other Organizations."

Mixter, Keith. *General Bibliography for Music Research.* 3rd ed. Warren, MI: Harmonie Park Press, 1996.

First published in 1962, Mixter's book differs from all the other sources described in this section in that it is designed to help music researchers find their way through the general (nonmusic) literature. Organized as a guide to research, the book covers style manuals, general dictionaries and encyclopedias, library catalogs, indexes, and editions of vocal texts. It is especially useful for cross-disciplinary research.

Other Guides to the Literature about Music

Crabtree, Phillip D., and Donald H. Foster. *Sourcebook for Research in Music.* Revised and expanded by Allen Scott. Bloomington: Indiana University Press, 2005.

The authors designed their book as a textbook for their music bibliography course at Cincinnati College-Conservatory of Music. It includes most of the same categories of entries as found in the other sources presented. Relatively few of the entries are extensively annotated, although there are explanatory notes at the beginning of each section. Of particular usefulness are the introductory chapters with definitions of common bibliographical terms, German bibliographical terms, and French bibliographical terms.

Foreman, Lewis, ed. *Information Sources in Music.* Guides to Information Sources. Munich: K. G. Saur Verlag, 2003.

Foreman's book contains 27 articles by music librarians and musicologists about various types of music information resources. Some of the articles include unannotated lists of sources.

Steib, Murray, ed. *Reader's Guide to Music: History, Theory, Criticism.* Chicago and London: Fitzroy Dearborn Publishers, 1999.

Distinct from all of the other sources in this section, Murray Steib's *Reader's Guide* offers just that—guidance in the form of essays by major scholars concerning primarily the monographic literature in English on major topics in music; in other words, it is not limited to discussion of reference literature. For example, the essay on Johann Sebastian Bach is by Bach scholars Daniel R. Melamed and Michael Marissen,[3] the essay on Berlioz is by Peter Bloom. Each essay begins with a list of books on the topic. The subjects included are those that have at least two books in English. For example, Telemann is not included, as the editor did not find sufficient literature in English to meet this criterion.[4] Regrettably, Steib's book is out of print; however, copies can be found in many library collections and through out-of-print services.

Wingell, Richard J., and Silvia Herzog. *Introduction to Research in Music.* Upper Saddle River, NJ: Prentice Hall, 2001.

Professor Wingell (University of Southern California) expanded the third edition of his *Writing About Music: An Introductory Guide,* 3rd ed. (2002) and collaborated with his colleague Silvia Herzog (Wichita State University) to produce this combination research and writing guide. Of particular usefulness is their inclusion of examples of sample pages from selected resources, such as thematic catalogs and RISM. The section on electronic resources is somewhat dated.

See also Chapter 1: Style Manuals, p. 31; Research Handbooks and Writing Guides, p. 32, and Chapter 5: Selected Research on Musicology, pp. 124–125.

B: BIBLIOGRAPHIES OF MUSIC LITERATURE: FORMAT-SPECIFIC SOURCES

Entries in a bibliography usually include different types of materials:

1. books devoted to a single subject
2. collections of essays
   a. essays by different authors on a single subject
   b. Festschriften
   c. congress reports
3. dissertations and theses
4. articles in dictionaries and encyclopedias
5. articles in periodicals (journals and magazines)
6. Web sites or other electronic resources

The researcher seeking to compile extensive bibliographies on a particular subject must therefore bring together materials in a variety of formats. It is not enough to search periodical indexes for current articles, especially in a field such as music, when the most significant research on a subject may have been published in book form, rather than as an article in a periodical, and may have been published decades ago, prior to the development of music periodicals indexes (see Chapter 6: Periodicals, Periodical Indexes, and Databases). And, it is certainly not wise for researchers at any level to assume that what is found on the Internet through a Google search provides an adequate representation of information sources on a subject! (See Chapter 1: Using the Internet for Music Research, pp. 36–38.)

Following is a summary of these formats, along with references to format-specific bibliographies of music literature.

1. Books Devoted to a Single Subject, Often Referred to as Monographs

Examples include biographies of composers or book-length analytical studies of particular works or genres. (See Chapter 1 for guidance on locating materials in library catalogs.)

BOOK-LENGTH BIOGRAPHY OF COMPOSER AMY BEACH BY ONE AUTHOR

Block, Adrienne Fried. *Amy Beach, Passionate Victorian: The Life and Work of an American Composer, 1867–1944.* New York: Oxford University Press, 1988.

BOOK-LENGTH ANALYTICAL STUDY OF JOHN COLTRANE'S RECORDING, "A LOVE SUPREME"

Kahn, Ashley. *A Love Supreme: The Story of John Coltrane's Signature Album.* New York: Viking, 2002.

Tools to access books about music:

- Library catalogs, especially WorldCat.org — the database of libraries worldwide
- *RILM Abstracts of Music Literature*

2. Collections of Essays on a Subject

a. Essays by Different Authors on a Single Subject

It is increasingly common for publishers to bring out book-length scholarly studies of particular composers, works, or genres that are composed of essays by several scholars, rather than written by one author. Examples of these studies include *The Cambridge Companion to Music* series, which covers composers, genres, and instruments.

Ideally, library catalogs should provide access to the contents of these collections in their online catalogs. By searching under key word, for example, the user could locate the individual essays published within these books. These collections are also indexed in RILM [p. 152]

Tools to access contents of multiauthor collections:

- Contents notes in library catalogs
- *RILM Abstracts of Music Literature*

b. Festschriften

Festschriften, or festival writings, are collections of essays by different scholars in honor of a person. The essays are typically on a variety of subjects, usually relating to the honoree's field of study. Examples include titles such as *Beethoven Essays: Studies in Honor of Elliot Forbes,* edited by Lewis Lockwood and Phyllis Benjamin (Cambridge, MA: Harvard University Department of Music, 1984), *Essays Presented to Egon Wellesz,* edited by Jack Westrup (Oxford: Clarendon

Press, 1966); and *New Perspectives on Music: Essays in Honor of Eileen Southern,* edited by Josephine Wright with Samuel A. Floyd (Warren, MI: Harmonie Park Press, 1992.)

For information about Festschriften, see Simeone, Nigel. "Festschriften." *Grove Music Online,* edited by L. Macy. www.grovemusic.com.

Tools to access contents of Festschriften:

- Contents notes in library catalogs
- Gerboth, Walter. *An Index to Musical Festschriften and Similar Publications.* New York: W. W. Norton, 1969. (This source provides author and subject access to 2,710 articles in approximately 400 Festschriften published to 1967.)
- *RILM Abstracts of Music Literature* (see p. 152). With the support of NEH funding, RILM has produced abstracts of some 8,000 articles from 1,240 Festschriften published prior to 1967.[5]

c. Congress Reports

The published proceedings of scholarly conferences are another example of a multi-author format for which users need to gain access to information on the individual essays within the volumes. For information about congress reports and a chronological list of congresses from 1860–1998, see Simeone, Nigel, and David A. Threasher. "Congress Reports." *Grove Music Online,* edited by L. Macy. www.grovemusic.com. (Entries in the list include references to RILM entry numbers).

Tools to access contents of congress reports:

- Contents notes in library catalogs
- Tyrrell, John, and Rosemary Wise. *A Guide to International Congress Reports in Musicology, 1900–1975.* New York: Garland Publishing, 1979. (This book provides access to congress reports published from 1900 to 1975.)
- *RILM Abstracts of Music Literature*
- Cowdery, James R., Zdravko Blazekovic, and Barry S. Brook, eds. *Speaking of Music: Music Conferences, 1835–1966.* RILM Retrospective Series 4. New York: RILM International Center, 2004.

This last volume represents the completion of a project started by Barry Brook in the 1970s to update Marie Briquet's *La musique dans les congrès internationaux (1835–1939)* (Paris: Heugel, 1961) and offers comprehensive and more detailed coverage of congress reports from Briquet's closing date of 1939 to RILM's inception in 1967. Left unfinished at Brook's death in 1997, it was finally completed by the RILM Center in New York with the support of the Andrew W. Mellon Foundation. The book uses RILM-style typography and formatting and includes separate sections for abstracts and indexes. The latter includes indexes of conference locations, conference sponsors, authors, and subjects. Although it overlaps with Tyrrell and Wise for the years from 1900 to 1975, its inclusion of detailed abstracts and indexing provides enhanced access to papers presented at congresses around the world.

3. Dissertations and Theses

Dissertations, theses, and other documents submitted as requirements for graduate degrees in music are often difficult to track comprehensively. As Jeremy Dribble states in his article on "Theses," in Foreman's *Information on Sources in Music,* "The task of searching out academic theses is still one of the most haphazard to be faced by a researcher, and frequently acts as a psychological obstacle to students and scholars who foresee much time being wasted in a hunt for wanted material."[6]

Tools to access dissertations and theses

General

- Library catalogs

- *RILM Abstracts of Music Literature.*

  Selective coverage: As explained in the RILM Scope guidelines, "RILM material includes doctoral level (or highest postgraduate degree level) dissertations in music and in other disciplines when they concern music. Master's level or other student theses are included when they contain significant new information or a new interpretation, and are publicly available."[7]

- *Doctoral Dissertations in Musicology (DDM-Online)*

  http://www.music.indiana.edu/ddm

  This online listing of completed and in-progress dissertations in musicology, music theory, ethnomusicology, and related areas includes the contents of the printed editions of Cecil Adkins and Alis Dickinson, *Doctoral Dissertations in Musicology,* 7th North American ed./2nd international ed. (Philadelphia: American Musicological Society, 1984; with supplements to 1995).

- *Dissertation Abstracts Online/ProQuest Digital Dissertations*

  This is a subscription database of dissertations produced since 1861 by academic institutions in the United States, Canada, Great Britain, and some European countries. It also includes *abstracts* for dissertations published since 1980, and, since 1962, selected master's theses. While music-specific dissertations may be listed in DDM-Online, RILM, and in Dissertation Abstracts, dissertations covering interdisciplinary topics may be listed only in the latter source. Also, documents produced for Doctor of Musical Arts degrees, Music Education degrees, master's theses, and other research-length graduate papers are covered selectively in all of these tools, depending upon whether the college or university submits information on these papers to DDM-Online or Dissertation Abstracts.

- *WorldCat Dissertations and Theses* (available through FirstSearch)

  Included are dissertations and theses cataloged by OCLC member libraries; some overlap with Dissertation Abstracts and RILM.

- *Archive of Dissertation Abstracts in Music*
  http://www.rhul.ac.uk/Music/golden-pages/Archive/Disserts/index.html:
  This source includes abstracts of dissertations, both completed and in
  process, submitted to the site by individual authors. This page also
  includes a useful summary of other dissertation sites, presented as links
  at the bottom of the Web page.
- *Masters Abstracts International (MAI).*
  This service includes citations and abstracts of selected masters theses.

4. Dissertations Produced Outside of the United States and Canada

a. Retrospective

RILM

Adkins and Dickinson, *Doctoral Dissertations in Musicology* (and its online suc-
cessor) have covered non-U.S. and Canada sources since 1977. For coverage of
earlier French and German dissertations, see

Gribenski, Jean. *French Language Dissertations in Music: An Annotated Bibliography.*
RILM Retrospectives 2. New York: Pendragon Press, 1979.
Schaal, Richard. *Verzeichnis Deutschsprachiger Musikwissenschaftler Dissertationen,
1861–1960.* Kassel: Bärenreiter, 1963.
_____. *Verzeichnis Deutschsprachiger Musikwissenschaftler Dissertationen, 1961–1970.*
Kassel: Bärenreiter, 1974.

b. Current

RILM

Dissertationsmeldestelle der Gesellschaft für Musikforschung includes dissertations from
Austria, Switzerland, and Germany; it also includes music education theses since 1998.
http://musikwiss.uni-muenster.de/
*Index to Theses in Great Britain and Ireland: A Comprehensive Listing of Theses with
Abstracts Accepted for Higher Education Degrees in Great Britain and Ireland Since
1716.* http://www.theses.com/

A separate database, *Theses from Ireland,* was launched in 2004.

SPECIALIZED

Anderson, Michael J. *A Classified Index of American Doctoral Dissertations and Disserta-
tion Projects on Choral Music Completed or Currently in Progress Through 1989.* Amer-
ican Choral Directors Association Monograph 6. Lawton, OK: American Choral
Directors Association, 1991.
Heintze, James R. *American Music Studies: A Classified Bibliography of Masters Theses.*
Detroit: Published for the College Music Society [by] Information Coordinators, 1984.
_____. *Igor Stravinsky: An International Bibliography of Theses and Dissertations,
1925–2001.* 2nd ed. Warren, MI: Harmonie Park Press, 2001.
*International Association for the Study of Popular Music: US Branch: PhD Dissertations
in Popular Music.* http://www.iaspm-us.net/resources/dissertations.php

Mead, Rita H. *Doctoral Dissertations in American Music: A Classified Bibliography.* Brooklyn: Institute for Studies in American Music, Brooklyn College of the City University of New York, 1974.

Music Theory Online: Dissertation Index.
http://www.societymusictheory.org/mto/mto-dissertations.php?showall=true
Listings and abstracts of dissertations.

5. Acquiring Dissertations

If you are interested in actually reading the dissertations you find cited in these sources (which you certainly should do before citing them in research papers!), the first step is, as always, to see if your university or college library has a copy of it. If not, check your library's available databases and ask the library to request a copy via interlibrary loan.

Printed (and selected online full-text) copies of many dissertations may be purchased from UMI (University Microforms, Inc; now ProQuest); British dissertations may be ordered from the British Library document supply service.

Proquest Dissertations and Theses
http://wwwlib.umi.com/dissertations/about_pqdd
http://wwwlib.umi.com/dissertations/

British Library Document Supply Service
http://www.bl.uk/reshelp/atyourdesk/docsupply/order/index.html

Center for Research Libraries (CRL),[8] Foreign Doctoral Dissertations
http://www.crl.edu/content.asp?l1=5#dissertations

> *Confused? Well, yes: there are numerous sources that provide access to dissertations and theses, and it's difficult to determine comprehensive coverage.*
>
> *Real Life Scenario:* I'd like to write my dissertation on the music of African American composer Margaret Bonds and need to check if others have written about her.
>
> *Process:* DDM Online lists two DMA dissertations; RILM lists four, with some overlap with the DDM Online list. However, neither source lists all of the dissertations on Bonds found in the bibliography to her article in *The International Dictionary of Black Composers,* edited by Samuel A. Floyd. Chicago: Fitzroy Dearborn Publisher, 1999; see p 78.

6. Articles in Dictionaries and Encyclopedias

Articles in dictionaries and encyclopedias, especially those in "encyclopedic" sources such as *New Grove* and *MGG,* are essential sources of information and important starting points for research. See Chapter 3: Dictionaries and Encyclopedias for a fuller discussion of these types of sources.

The bibliographies attached to these articles are also invaluable to the researcher. They cite materials in a variety of formats: books, dissertations, articles in journals, Festschriften, congress reports, and similar publications.

See Chapter 3: Dictionaries and Encyclopedias, p. 72, for sample bibliography attached to composer article in *Grove Music Online* and the guide to its use.

7. Articles in Journals and Magazines

See Chapter 6: Periodicals, Periodical Indexes, and Databases for discussion of these tools and guidance on using them to locate periodical articles.

8. Web Sites and Other Electronic Resources

See Chapter 1: Using the Internet for Music Research. Web sites relating to particular subjects are listed alongside printed sources in this book.

C: BIBLIOGRAPHIES OF MUSIC LITERATURE: SUBJECT-SPECIFIC SOURCES

> *Seeing the variety of formats in which literature about music is published, it soon becomes clear that it can be to the researcher's advantage to begin a search by using classified bibliographies of music literature that provide access to materials published in a variety of formats.*

The following selected list of bibliographies of music literature is arranged alphabetically by subject. Brief annotations or explanatory notes are provided sparingly, typically when the title of a source may not reveal its coverage, or when the source contains special features that should be mentioned. Otherwise readers are referred to the detailed lists and extensive annotations provided in Duckles, 5th ed. (1997), Chapter 4, "Bibliographies of Music Literature," pp. 163–233, as well as in the guides to research for a particular subject area. There are also many useful descriptions of library source materials developed by librarians for library Web sites.

Within the subject list are titles that function primarily as indexes to the literature — in other words, reference tools that refer the user to other reference tools. These are indicated with an [I] next to the author's name and are explained more fully in Part D (pp. 61–62).

AFRICAN AND AFRICAN-AMERICAN MUSIC

De Lerma, Dominique-Rene. *A Bibliography of Black Music.* 4 vols. Westport, CT: Greenwood Press, 1981–84.

Floyd, Samuel A., and Martha J. Reisser. *Black Music in the United States: An Annotated Bibliography of Selected Reference and Research Materials.* Milwood, NY: Kraus International Publications, 1983.

Gray, John. *African Music: A Bibliographical Guide to the Traditional, Popular, Art, and Liturgical Musics of Sub-Saharan Africa.* Westport, CT: Greenwood Press, 1991.

————. *Blacks in Classical Music: A Bibliographical Guide to Composers, Performers, and Ensembles.* New York: Greenwood Press, 1988.

Jackson, Irene V. *Afro-American Religious Music: A Bibliography and Catalogue of Gospel Music.* Westport, CT: Greenwood Press, 1979.

Bibliography of resources on African American religious music, and catalog of LC holdings of black gospel music copyrighted between 1938 and 1965.

Lems-Dworkin, Carol. *African Music: A Pan-African Annotated Bibliography*. London: Hans Zell, 1991.

AMERICAN MUSIC

Heintze, James R. *American Music Studies: A Classified Bibliography of Masters Theses*. Detroit: Published for the College Music Society [by] Information Coordinators, 1984.

_____. *Early American Music: A Research and Information Guide*. Music Research and Information Guides 13. New York: Garland Publishing, 1990.

[I] District of Columbia Historical Records Survey. *Bio-Bibliographical Index of Musicians in the United States of America Since Colonial Times*. 1956. Reprint, St. Clair Shores, MI: Scholarly Press. 1972.

Horn, David. *The Literature of American Music in Books and Folk Music Collections: A Fully Annotated Bibliography*. Metuchen, NJ: Scarecrow Press, 1977; Supplement 1, 1988. Continued by Marco, Guy A. *Literature of American Music III, 1983–1992*. Lanham, MD: Scarecrow Press, 1996, and Marco, Guy. *Checklist of Writings on American Music 1640-1992*. Lanham, MD: Scarecrow Press, 1996. (index to all of the above sources)

Jackson, Richard. *United States Music: Sources of Bibliography and Collected Biography*. Brooklyn: Institute for American Studies in American Music, Department of Music, Brooklyn College of the City University of New York, 1973.

Krummel, Donald W. *Bibliographical Handbook of American Music*. Urbana: University of Illinois Press, 1987.

Warner, Thomas E. *Periodical Literature on American Music, 1620–1920: A Classified Bibliography With Annotations*. Warren, MI: Harmonie Park Press, 1988.

BAROQUE MUSIC

Baron, John H. *Baroque Music: A Research and Information Guide*. Music Research and Information Guides 16. New York: Garland Publishing, 1993.

BASSOON

Lipori, Daniel G. *A Researcher's Guide to the Bassoon*. Lewiston, NY: E. Mellen Press, 2002.

BLUES

Ford, Robert. *A Blues Bibliography*. 2nd ed. New York: Routledge, 2007.

Hart, Mary L., Brenda M. Eagles and Lisa N. Howorth. *The Blues: A Bibliographic Guide*. Music Reference and Information Guides 7; Garland Reference Library of the Humanities 565. New York: Garland Publishing, 1989.

Sonnier, Austin M. *A Guide to the Blues: History, Who's Who, Research Sources*. Westport, CT: Greenwood Press, 1994.

BORROWING

Burkholder, J. Peter, Andreas Giger, and David C. Birchler. "Musical Borrowing: An Annotated Bibliography." Indiana University. Center for the History of Music Theory and Literature. http://www.chmtl.indiana.edu/borrowing/.

Giger, Andreas. "A Bibliography on Musical Borrowing." *Notes:* 50, no. 3 (March 1994): 871–74.

BRASS MUSIC

Fasman, Mark J. *Brass Bibliography: Sources on the History, Literature, Pedagogy, Performance, and Acoustics of Brass Instruments.* Bloomington: Indiana University Press, 1990.

Lane, G. B. *The Trombone: An Annotated Bibliography.* Lanham, MD: Scarecrow Press, 1999.

Skei, Allen B. *Woodwind, Brass, and Percussion Instruments of the Orchestra: A Bibliographic Guide.* Garland Reference Library of the Humanities 458. New York: Garland Publishing, 1985.

CANADA

Morey, Carl. *Music in Canada: A Research and Information Guide.* Music Research and Information Guides 20. New York: Garland Publishers, 1997.

(See also *Encyclopedia of Music in Canada,* p. 80.)

CHAMBER MUSIC

Baron, John H. *Chamber Music: A Research and Information Guide.* 2nd rev. ed. Routledge Music Bibliographies. New York: Routledge, 2002.

(See also the author's *Intimate Music: A History of Chamber Music.* Stuyvesant, NY: Pendragon Press, 1998.)

CHORAL MUSIC

Orr, N. Lee, and W. Dan Hardin. *Choral Music in Nineteenth-Century America: A Guide to the Sources.* Lanham, MD: Scarecrow Press, 1999.

Sharp, Avery T., and James Michael Floyd. *Choral Music: A Research and Information Guide.* Routledge Music Bibliographies. New York: Routledge, 2002.

CHURCH MUSIC

Sharp, Avery T., and James Michael Floyd. *Church and Worship Music: An Annotated Bibliography of Contemporary Scholarship: A Research and Information Guide.* Routledge Music Bibliographies. New York: Routledge, 2005.

COMPOSER BIOGRAPHIES, BIBLIOGRAPHIES (SEE ALSO ORGAN MUSIC COMPOSERS; MUSICIANS — AUTOBIOGRAPHIES

[I] Bull, Storm. *Index to Biographies of Contemporary Composers.* 3 vols. New York: Scarecrow Press, 1964–87.

[I] Green, Richard D. *Index to Composer Bibliographies.* Detroit: Information Coordinators, 1985.

[I] Nishimura, Mari. *The Twentieth-Century Composer Speaks: An Index of Interviews.* Fallen Leaf Reference Books in Music 28. Berkeley: Fallen Leaf Press; Tokyo: In Association with the Kunitachi College of Music, Library, 1993.

COMPUTER MUSIC/COMPUTER APPLICATIONS IN MUSIC

Davis, Deta S. *Computer Applications in Music: A Bibliography.* Madison, WI: A-R Editions, 1988. Supplement 1: 1992.

Tjepkema, Sandra L. *A Bibliography of Computer Music: A Reference for Composers.* Iowa City: University of Iowa Press, 1981.

(See also *Computer Music Journal, Leonardo Music Journal,* and International Computer Music Association. Resources: http://www.computermusic.org/resourcesf.php.)

CONCERTO

Lindeman, Stephan D. *The Concerto: A Research and Information Guide.* Routledge Music Bibliographies. New York: Routledge, 2006.

CONDUCTORS

[I] Cowden, Robert H. *Concert and Opera Conductors: A Bibliography of Biographical Materials.* New York: Greenwood Press, 1987.

CONTEMPORARY MUSIC NOTATION

Warfield, Gerald. *Writings on Contemporary Music Notation.* MLA Index and Bibliography Series 16. Ann Arbor, MI: Music Library Association, 1976.

DANCE

Bopp, Mary S. *Research in Dance: A Guide to Resources.* New York: G. K. Hall, 1994.

Edsall, Mary E., ed. *A Core Collection in Dance.* Compiled by the Dance Librarians Committee, Association of College and Research Libraries. Chicago: The Association, 2001.

New York Public Library. Dance Collection. *Dictionary Catalog of the Dance Collection. A List of Authors, Titles, and Subjects of Multi-Media Materials in the Dance Collection of the Performing Arts Research Center of the New York Public Library.* 10 vols. Boston: G. K. Hall, 1974.

_____. *Bibliographic Guide to Dance.* Boston: G. K. Hall, 1976–(annual supplements to previous entry).

_____. *Index to Dance Periodicals.* Boston: G. K. Hall, 1992–(data taken from *Dictionary Catalog* and *Bibliographic Guide to Dance*).

New York Public Library. Jerome Robbins Dance Division. CATNYP catalog: http://catnyp .nypl.org/search~b1o1c1i1p1r1a1

New York Public Library. Jerome Robbins Dance Division is one of the world's largest collections of dance materials, both published and unpublished. Its unique holdings include archival collections of such noted choreographers and dancers as Lincoln Kirstein, Isadora Duncan, Doris Humphrey, Merce Cunningham, Rudolph Nureyev, and Jerome Robbins. The Dance Division's catalogs, both printed and online (the latter through CATNYP), index dance-related articles in selected periodicals, thus providing more detailed access to dance materials than what would be normally found in a library catalog.

DANISH MUSIC

McLoskey, Lansing D. *Twentieth Century Danish Music: An Annotated Bibliography and Research Directory.* Westport, CT: Greenwood Press, 1998.

DISSERTATIONS AND THESES

(See previous *discussion under* Part B. Format-Specific Sources.)

ELECTRONIC MUSIC (SEE ALSO COMPUTER MUSIC)

Basart, Ann. *Serial Music: A Classified Bibliography of Writings on 12-Tone and Electronic Music.* Berkeley: University of California Press, 1961.

Cross, Lowell, M. *A Bibliography of Electronic Music.* Toronto: University of Toronto Press, 1967.

Wick, Robert L. *Electronic and Computer Music: An Annotated Bibliography.* Westport, CT: Greenwood Press, 1997.

ETHNOMUSICOLOGY/WORLD MUSIC

Myers, Helen. *Ethnomusicology: Historical and Regional Studies.* New York: W. W. Norton, 1993. See also Myers's companion book: *Ethnomusicology: An Introduction.* New York: W. W. Norton, 1992. Descriptions of both are found in Post, entries 1065, 1066.

Post, Jennifer C. *Ethnomusicology: A Guide to Research.* Routledge Music Bibliographies. New York: Routledge, 2004.

Schuursma, Ann Briegleb. *Ethnomusicology Research: A Select Annotated Bibliography.* Garland Library of Music Ethnology 1; Garland Reference Library of the Humanities 1136. New York: Garland Publishing, 1992. See Post, entry 145.

Stone, Ruth M., ed. *The World's Music: General Perspectives and Reference Tools.* Garland Encyclopedia of World Music, vol. 10. New York: Routledge, 2002.

FILM MUSIC

Marks, Martin. "Film Music: The Material, Literature, and Present State of Research." *Notes:* 36, no. 2 (Dec. 1979): 282–325.

Wescott, Steven D. *A Comprehensive Bibliography of Music for Film and Television.* Detroit: Information Coordinators, 1985. Supplemented by Anderson, Gillian B. *Film Music Bibliography I.* Edited by H. Stephen Wright. Hollywood: Society for the Preservation of Film Music, 1995.

FOLK MUSIC (SEE ALSO WORLD MUSIC, ETHNOMUSICOLOGY)

Bohlman, Philip Vilas. *Central European Folk Music: An Annotated Bibliography of Sources in German.* Garland Library of Music Ethnology 3. Garland Reference Library of the Humanities 1448. New York: Garland Publishing, 1996.

Miller, Terry E. *Folk Music in America: A Reference Guide.* Garland Reference Library of the Humanities 496. Music Research and Information Guides 6. New York: Garland Publishing, 1986.

HYMNS

Schneider, Tina M. *Hymnal Collections of North America.* Studies in Liturgical Musicology 10. Lanham, MD: Scarecrow Press, 2003. (See Bibliography, pp. 163–192.)

INDIANS OF NORTH AMERICA

Keeling, Richard. *North American Indian Music: A Guide to Published Sources and Selected Recordings.* Garland Library of Music Ethnology 5. Garland Reference Library of the Humanities 1440. New York: Garland Publishing, 1997.

INSTRUMENTALISTS

[I] Cowden, Robert H. *Instrumental Virtuosi: A Bibliography of Biographical Materials.* New York: Greenwood Press, 1989.

JAZZ

Carl Gregor, Duke of Mecklenburg. *International Bibliography of Jazz Books, Volumes I, II.* Compiled with the assistance of Norbert Rücker. Baden-Baden: Koerner, 1983–88.
_____. *International Jazz Bibliography: Jazz Books from 1919 to 1968.* Strasbourg: P. H. Heitz, 1969. Supplements, 1970–73.
Carner, Gary. *Jazz Performers: An Annotated Bibliography of Biographical Materials.* New York: Greenwood Press, 1990.
Gray, John. *Fire Music: A Bibliography of the New Jazz, 1959–1990.* New York: Greenwood Press, 1991.
Hoek, D. J. "Jazz Analyses: An Annotated Guide to Periodical Literature." *Bulletin of Bibliography* 57, no. 3 (Sept. 2000): 147–52.
Kennington, Donald, and Danny L. Read. *The Literature of Jazz: A Critical Guide.* 2nd ed. Chicago: American Library Association; London: Library Association, 1980.
Meadows, Eddie S. *Jazz Scholarship and Pedagogy: A Research and Information Guide.* 3rd ed. Routledge Music Bibliographies. New York: Routledge, 2005.
Merriam, Alan P. *A Bibliography of Jazz.* 1954. Reprint, New York: Da Capo Press; New York: Krause Reprint Co., 1970.

JEWISH MUSIC

Heskes, Irene. *The Resource Book of Jewish Music: A Bibliographical and Topical Guide to the Book and Journal Literature and Program Materials.* Westport, CT: Greenwood Press, 1985.

LATIN AMERICAN MUSIC

Chase, Gilbert. *A Guide to the Music of Latin America.* 2nd ed. Rev. and enl., 1962. Reprint, New York: AMS Press, 1972.

Thompson, Annie Figueroa. *An Annotated Bibliography of Writings About Music in Puerto Rico.* Ann Arbor, MI: Music Library Association, 1975.

Thompson, Donald, and Annie F. Thompson. *Music and Dance in Puerto Rico From the Age of Columbus to Modern Times: An Annotated Bibliography.* Metuchen, NJ: Scarecrow Press, 1991.

MEDIEVAL MUSIC

Hughes, Andrew. *Medieval Music: The Sixth Liberal Art.* Rev. ed. Toronto: University of Toronto Press, 1980.

Knighton, Tess, and David Fallows, eds. *Companion to Medieval and Renaissance Music.* New York: Schirmer Books, 1992. (bibliographic references included with each essay)

Leech-Wilkinson, Daniel. *The Modern Invention of Medieval Music: Scholarship, Ideology, Performance.* New York: Cambridge University Press, 2002.

MUSIC ANALYSES

Diamond, Harold. *Music Analyses: An Annotated Guide to the Literature.* New York: Schirmer Books, 1991.

Hoek, D. J. *Analyses of Nineteenth- and Twentieth-Century Music, 1940–2000, Incorporating Material by Arthur Wenk.* Music Library Association Index and Bibliography Series 34. Lanham, MD: Scarecrow Press and Music Library Association, 2007.

Updates Wenk, Arthur. *Analyses of Nineteenth and Twentieth-Century Music, 1940–1985.* MLA Index and Bibliography Series 25. Boston: Music Library Association, 1987.

MUSIC AND WAR

Arnold, Ben. *Music and War: A Research and Information Guide.* New York: Garland Publishing, 1993.

(Also listed under "Bibliographies of Music," p. 231)

MUSIC BIBLIOGRAPHY

Krummel, Donald W. *The Literature of Music Bibliography: An Account of the Writings on the History of Music Printing and Publishing.* Berkeley, CA: Fallen Leaf Press, 1992.

MUSIC EDUCATION

Brookhart, Edward. *Music in American Higher Education: An Annotated Bibliography.* Warren, MI: Harmonie Park Press, 1988.

Kantorski, Vincent. *A Bibliography of Source Readings in Music Education.* Warren, MI: Harmonie Park Press, 1997.

Phelps, Roger P., Ronald H. Sadoff, Edward C. Warbuton, and Lawrence Ferrara. *A Guide to Research in Music Education.* 5th ed. Lanham, MD: Scarecrow Press, 2005.

Not an annotated bibliography or a guide to the literature per se, this book provides instruction in approaching research in music education through chapters titled "Selecting a Research Problem," "The Research Process," "Qualitative Research: Concepts and Techniques," "Philosophical Inquiry: Concepts and Techniques,"

"Nonexperimental Research: Concepts and Techniques," "Quantitative Research: Experimental Methods and Statistical Techniques," "Historical Research: Concepts and Techniqiues," and "Technology and Music Education Research." Each chapter includes a bibliography.

MUSIC LIBRARIANSHIP

Bradley, Carol June. *American Music Librarianship: A Research and Information Guide.* Routledge Music Bibliographies. New York: Routledge, 2005.

MUSIC THEORY (SEE ALSO SCHENKERIAN ANALYSIS)

Center for History of Music Theory and Literature. http://www.music.indiana.edu/chmtl/
Coover, James. "Music Theory in Translation: A Bibliography." *Journal of Music Theory* 3, no. 1 (April 1959): 70–96; updated in *Journal of Music Theory* 13, no. 2 (Winter 1969): 230–48.
Damschroder, David, and David Russell Williams. *Music Theory from Zarlino to Schenker: A Bibliography and Guide.* Stuyvesant, NY: Pendragon Press, 1990.
Perone, James E. *Form and Analysis Theory: A Bibliography.* Westport, CT: Greenwood Press, 1998.
Williams, David Russell. *A Bibliography of the History of Music Theory.* 2nd ed. Athens, OH: Accura Music, 1980.
Williams, David Russell, and C. Matthew Balensuela. *Music Theory from Boethius to Zarlino: A Bibliography and Guide.* Harmonologia 14. Hillsdale, N.Y.: Pendragon Press, 2007.

MUSICIANS' BIOGRAPHIES AND AUTOBIOGRAPHIES

Adams, John L. *Musicians' Autobiographies: An Annotated Bibliography of Writings Available in English, 1800–1980.* Jefferson, NC: McFarland, 1982.
[I] *Internationaler Biographischer Index der Musik: Komponisten, Dirigenten, Instrumentalisten und Sänger = World Biographical Index of Music: Composers, Conductors, Instrumentalists and Singers.* 2 vols. München; New Providence: K. G. Saur, 1995.

OPERA

Grout, Donald J., and Hermine W. Williams. "Bibliographies, Lexicons, Guides, Histories, and Other Works Dealing With Opera." In *A Short History of Opera.* 4th ed. New York: Columbia University Press, 2003.
Marco, Guy A. *Opera: A Research and Information Guide.* 2nd ed. New York: Garland Publishing, 2001.
Parsons, Charles H. *An Opera Bibliography.* The Mellen Opera Reference Index 17–18. Lewiston, NY: The Edwin Mellen Press, 1995.

ORCHESTRATION

Perone, James E. *Orchestration Theory: A Bibliography.* Westport, CT: Greenwood Press, 1996.

Organ Music Composers

Hettinger, Sharon L. *American Organ Music of the Twentieth Century: An Annotated Bibliography of Composers.* Warren, MI: Harmonie Park Press, 1997.

Percussion

Bajzek, Dieter. *Percussion: An Annotated Bibliography, with Special Emphasis on Contemporary Notation and Performance.* Metuchen, NJ: Scarecrow Press, 1988.

Skei, Allen B. *Woodwind, Brass, and Percussion Instruments of the Orchestra: A Bibliographic Guide.* New York: Garland Publishing, 1985.

Performance Practice

Brown, Howard Mayer, et al. "Performing Practice: Western: Bibliography" *Grove Music Online.* Edited by L. Macy. http://www.grovemusic.com.

Jackson, Roland. *Performance Practice, Medieval to Contemporary: A Bibliographical Guide.* New York: Garland Publishing, 1988.

> Annual supplements published in *Performance Practice Review,* 1987–97, (http://ccdl .libraries.claremont.edu/col/ppr/) (See also the author's *Performance Practice: A Dictionary*: Dictionaries and Encyclopedias: Special Subjects.)

Vinquist, Mary and Neal Zaslaw, eds. *Performance Practice: A Bibliography.* New York: W. W. Norton, 1971.

Piano

Hinson, Maurice. *The Pianist's Bookshelf: A Practical Guide to Books, Videos, and Other Resources.* Bloomington: Indiana University Press, 1998.

————. *The Pianist's Reference Guide: A Bibliographical Survey.* Los Angeles: Alfred Publishing, 1987. (See also bibliographical references attached to entries in Hinson's *Guide(s) to the Pianist's Repertoire* [listed in Chapter 9: Bibliographies of Music].)

Palmieri, Robert. *Piano Information Guide: An Aid to Research.* New York: Garland Publishing, 1989.

Wolcott, Michiko Ishiyama. *Piano, the Instrument: An Annotated Bibliography.* Lanham, MD: Scarecrow Press, 2001.

Polish Music

Smialek, William. *Polish Music: A Research and Information Guide.* Music Research and Information Guides 12. New York: Garland Publishing, 1989.

Popular Music

Booth, Mark W. *American Popular Music: A Reference Guide.* Westport, CT: Greenwood Press, 1983.

Cooper, B. Lee. *The Popular Music Handbook: A Resource Guide for Teachers, Librarians, and Media Specialists.* Littleton, CO: Libraries Unlimited, 1984.

Cooper, B. Lee, and Wayne S. Haney. *Rock Music in American Popular Culture III: More Rock 'n' Roll Resources.* New York: Haworth Press, 1999.

[I] Cowden, Robert H. *Popular Singers of the Twentieth Century: A Bibliography of Biographical Materials.* Westport, CT: Greenwood Press, 1999.

Gatten, Jeffrey N. *Rock Music Scholarship: An Interdisciplinary Bibliography.* Westport, CT: Greenwood Press, 1995.

Haggerty, Gary. *A Guide to Popular Music Reference Books: An Annotated Bibliography.* Music Reference Collection 47. Westport, CT: Greenwood Press, 1995.

Hoffmann, Frank W. *The Literature of Rock, 1954–1978.* Metuchen, NJ: Scarecrow Press, 1981. Supplements 1986, 1995.

Iwaschkin, Roman. *Popular Music: A Reference Guide.* Garland Reference Library of the Humanities 642. New York: Garland Publishing, 1986.

Leyser, Brady J., and Pol Gosset. *Rock Stars/Pop Stars: A Comprehensive Bibliography, 1955–1994.* Music Reference Collection 43. Westport, CT: Greenwood Press, 1994.

McCoy, Judy. *Rap Music in the 1980s: A Reference Guide.* Metuchen, NJ: Scarecrow Press, 1992.

Taylor, Paul. *Popular Music since 1955: A Critical Guide to the Literature.* New York: Mansell Publishing; Boston: G. K. Hall, 1985.

See also "Bibliographies" on the Web site of the International Association for Popular Music (IASPM): http://www.iaspm.net/bibliographies.htm.

RECORDER

Griscom, Richard, and David Lasocki. *The Recorder: A Research and Information Guide.* 2nd ed. New York: Routledge, 2003.

RENAISSANCE MUSIC

Reese, Gustave. "Bibliography." In *Music of the Renaissance.* Rev. ed. New York: Norton, 1959.

See also "Bibliographical Notes" appended to each chapter of Allan Atlas's *Renaissance Music: Music in Western Europe, 1400–1600* (New York: Norton, 1998), as well as the bibliography in Leeman L. Perkins's *Music in the Age of the Renaissance* (New York: W.W. Norton, 1999).

SCHENKERIAN ANALYSIS

Ayotte, Benjamin McKay. *Heinrich Schenker: A Guide to Research.* Routledge Music Bibliographies. New York: Routledge, 2004.

Berry, David Carson. *A Topical Guide to Schenkerian Literature: An Annotated Bibliography with Indices.* Hillsdale, NY: Pendragon Press, 2004.

Laskowski, Larry. *Heinrich Schenker: An Annotated Index to His Analyses of Musical Works.* New York: Pendragon Press, 1978.

SERIAL MUSIC

Basart, Ann Phillips. *Serial Music: A Classified Bibliography of Writings on Twelve-Tone and Electronic Music.* Berkeley: University of California Press, 1976.

Vander Weg, John Dean. *Serial Music and Serialism: A Research and Information Guide.* New York: Routledge, 2001.

This source "covers periodical literature published in English during the period from 1955 to 1995 . . . with a small number of citations for books" (p. 6), thus serving more as a fascinating guide to reception history of serial music than a full guide to the literature.

SINGERS AND SONG

[I] Cowden, Robert H. *Classical Singers of the Opera and Recital Stages: A Bibliography of Biographical Materials.* Westport, CT: Greenwood Press, 1994.

[I] _____. *Concert and Opera Singers: A Bibliography of Biographical Materials.* Westport, CT: Greenwood Press, 1985.

[I] _____. *Popular Singers of the Twentieth Century: A Bibliography of Biographical Materials.* Westport, CT: Greenwood Press, 1999.

Farkas, Andrew. *Opera and Concert Singers: An Annotated International Bibliography of Books and Pamphlets.* New York: Garland Publishing, 1985.

McTyre, Ruthann Boles. *Library Resources for Singers, Coaches, and Accompanists: An Annotated Bibliography, 1970–1997.* Westport, CT: Greenwood Press, 1998.

Seaton, Douglass. *The Art Song: A Research and Information Guide.* Music Research and Information Guides 6. Garland Reference Library of the Humanities 673. New York: Garland Publishing, 1987.

STRING INSTRUMENT MAKERS (SEE ALSO VIOLIN)

Regazzi, Roberto. *The Complete Luthier's Library: A Useful International Critical Bibliography for the Maker and Connoisseur of Strings and Plucked Instruments.* Bologna: Florenus Edizioni, 1990.

SYMPHONY

Stedman, Preston. *The Symphony: A Research and Information Guide.* Vol. I: *The Eighteenth Century.* Music Research and Information Guides 14. Garland Reference Library of the Humanities 862. New York: Garland Publishing, 1990.

TUDOR MUSIC

Turbet, Richard. *Tudor Music: A Research and Information Guide.* Music Research and Information Guides 18. Garland Reference Library of the Humanities 1122. New York: Garland Publishing, 1994.

VIOLIN

Heron-Allen, Edward. *De Fidiculis Bibliographia: Being an Attempt Towards a Bibliography of the Violin and All Other Instruments Played with a Bow in Ancient and Modern Times.* London: Griffith, Farran, 1890–94. Reprint, London: Holland Press, 1961.

Katz, Mark. *The Violin: A Research and Information Guide.* Routledge Music Bibliographies. New York: Routledge, 2006.

WOMEN MUSICIANS

Block, Adrienne Fried, and Carol Neuls-Bates. *Women in American Music: A Bibliography of Music and Literature.* Westport, CT: Greenwood Press, 1979.

Ericson, Margaret D. *Women and Music: A Selective Annotated Bibliography on Women and Gender Issues in Music, 1987–1992.* New York: G. K. Hall, 1996.

[I] Hixon, Don L., and Don A. Hennessee. *Women in Music: An Encyclopedic Biobibliography.* 2 vols. 2nd ed. Metuchen, NJ: Scarecrow, 1993.

Pendle, Karin. *Women in Music: A Research and Information Guide.* Routledge Music Bibliographies. New York: Routledge, 2005.

WOODWIND INSTRUMENTS

Skei, Allen B. *Woodwind, Brass, and Percussion Instruments of the Orchestra: A Bibliographic Guide.* Garland Reference Library of the Humanities 458. New York: Garland Publishing, 1985.

D: BIBLIOGRAPHIES OF MUSIC LITERATURE: INDEXES

A number of the bibliographies of music literature listed in Section C function primarily as indexes, with references to where information may be found in other sources.[9] In other words, when using these sources, one finds references to other sources in which the citation/entry may be found, rather than the citation or entry itself. Perhaps the best example of this type of tool is Storm Bull's three-volume set *Index to Biographies of Contemporary Composers* (New York: Scarecrow Press, 1964, 1974, 1987). A typical entry from this source includes birth and death dates of the composer, country of origin, and abbreviations to sources of further information on the composer (abbreviations are written out in the first part of the book). A number of the abbreviations for a particular composer may be references to articles about the composer in *Music Index,* for example.

Useful, you wonder? Yes, in that Bull's coverage of 13,500 composers (in Vol. 3) born after 1900 identifies many that cannot be easily found in other sources. In this case, the references to where information may be found (even through abbreviations) are often the only lead.

Other examples of these types of tools are Robert Cowden's books on conductors, singers, and instrumentalists (listed under the respective subject headings in Part C). In this case, Cowden's primary criterion for inclusion was whether the individual had an entry in a major reference source (Baker's 7 for *Instrumental Virtuosi* and *Concert and Opera Conductors* (1987), Baker's 6 for *Concert and Opera Singers* (1985), and *New Grove*, 6th ed. (1980) for *Classical Singers of the Opera and Recital Stages* (1994). Cowden lists other standard reference sources in his introduction to each book. The entries on individuals include references to their respective entries in the major reference tools (through abbreviations), as well as references to articles in periodicals, published autobiographies, and other sources. Of particular usefulness in all of these sources are the lists of and references to entries in "collective biographies." Such sources include David Ewen's books *Famous Instrumentalists* and *Living Musicians* or Harold Schoenberg's *The Great Pianists*. Few libraries provide access to the contents of these valuable collective biographies, and Cowden's references to them greatly expand the usefulness of his books.

Distinctive among all of these bibliographies/indexes (and one that must be admired for the effort to produce it as well as for its value to future researchers) is the Historical Records Survey *Bio-Bibliographical Index of Musicians in the United States of America Since Colonial Times* (1940). A product of the WPA (Works Progress Administration),[10] the volume lists names of musicians from (as the title says) colonial times to the present (present being ca. 1930 in this case). The project indexers surveyed books about American music (listed in the Bibliography, xvii–xxiii) to extract names of musicians. As explained in the introduction, most of these books did not have indexes. Using this source, one could identify, for example, a singer named Leonora A. Allen, whose work is somehow documented in Phil Adams Otis's book *The Chicago Symphony Orchestra: Its Organization, Growth and Development* (1925). One wonders if we will gain the same sort of access when Google completes its book-scanning projects.

As explained in its introduction, the *World Biographical Index* is an alphabetical list of ca. 60,000 biographical entries on musicians, extracted from a larger K. G. Saur project to index general encyclopedias published between 1700 and 1910, thus providing coverage of musicians from 1500 to 1850.[11]

For example, through this source, one can determine that the singer Emma Bumpus is documented in Brown and Stratton's *British Musical Biography: A Dictionary of Musical Artists, Authors, and Composers Born in Britain and Its Colonies* (Birmingham, 1897).

Although somewhat cumbersome to use, these index tools direct users to information that is often difficult to find in other sources.

NOTES

1. Gustav Reese, *Music in the Renaissance* (New York: Norton, 1959); Maynard Solomon, *Mozart: A Life* (New York: HarperCollins, 1995) and *Beethoven,* 2nd ed. (New York: Schirmer Books, 1998). The bibliographies in Solomon's books are arranged in a classified manner and include his succinct and insightful annotations; J. Peter Burkholder, Donald J. Grout, and Claude V. Palisca, *A History of Western Music,* 7th ed. (New York: W.W. Norton & Co., 2005), A23–A83; Richard Taruskin, *The Oxford History of Western Music,* vol. 6: *Resources, Chronology, Bibliography, Master Index* (New York: Oxford University Press, 2005).

2. The fourth edition was unfortunately riddled with errors. Schirmer Books issued a revised fourth edition in 1994 in an effort to correct these errors.

3. Melamed and Marissen later published *An Introduction to Bach Studies* (see Chapter 4).

4. Murray Steib, ed., *Reader's Guide to Music History, Theory, Criticism* (Chicago and London: Fitzroy Dearborn Publishers, 1999), viii.

5. Press Release, April 2006: "RILM Awarded Major NEH Grant to Index Festschriten." http://www.rilm.org/nehpressrelease.html.

6. Jeremy Dribble, "Theses," in *Information Sources in Music,* ed. Lewis Foreman (München: K. G. Saur, 2003), 168.

7. "RILM Scope Guidelines," and "RILM Coverage" http://www.rilm.org/coverage .html.

8. The Center for Research Libraries is a consortium of North American universities, colleges, and independent research libraries: http://www.crl.edu/.

9. Duckles, 5th ed. uses a broader criteria for these types of works and lists them under "Biographical Dictionaries: Indexes," pp. 47–51. Duckles's listing includes tools such as Gary Carner's *Jazz Performers*, Andrew Farkas's *Opera and Concert Singers*, and John Gray's *Blacks in Classical Music*. I have confined the index designation to those tools that function primarily through entries with references to other tools, rather than with direct information in the entries themselves.

10. The Works Progress Administration (WPA) Federal Music Project was established by Franklin D. Roosevelt in 1935 and ran until 1941. It employed thousands of musicians during the Great Depression in a variety of enterprises. See Metro Voloshin, "Works Progress Administration," *Grove Music Online*, ed. L. Macy http://www.grovemusic.com.

11. Kurt Dorfmüller, "Introduction," *Internationaler Biographischer Index der Musik* (München: K. G. Saur, 1995), xi.

CHAPTER

$$3$$

Dictionaries and Encyclopedias

OVERVIEW AND CHRONOLOGICAL SURVEY OF MUSIC DICTIONARIES

Dictionaries and encyclopedias are often referred to as "ready-reference tools" — sources in which entries are arranged alphabetically, and answers to questions may be found immediately. Unlike the bibliographies of music literature described in the previous chapter, which provide citations to sources on particular subjects and require the user to then locate the sources referred to, dictionary and encyclopedia entries provide factual information firsthand. The details of a composer's life, musical education, compositional output, and other pertinent information are easily found in a dictionary or encyclopedia entry, as are basic definitions of musical terms and topics.

Dictionaries vs. Encyclopedias

While the term *encyclopedic* usually implies exhaustive treatment of a subject and *dictionary* implies more concise treatment, in the case of music sources, publishers and compilers have tended to use these terms almost interchangeably. The *New Grove Dictionary of Music and Musicians,* one of our truly encyclopedic sources, is titled *dictionary,* while the one-volume, 207-page *Thames and Hudson Encyclopedia of Twentieth Century Music* uses the word *encyclopedia* in its title. A more useful categorization of dictionary/encyclopedia sources is found in the articles on "Dictionaries and Encyclopedias" in both the *New Harvard Dictionary of Music* and *Grove Music Online:*

1. Encyclopedic sources (referred to as "Comprehensive" sources in *Grove Music Online*) include both terminological and biographical entries. Examples include *Grove Music Online,* MGG (*Die Musik in Geschichte und Gegenwart*), and Basso's *Dizionario enciclopedico universale della musica e dei musicisti* (often abbreviated as DEUMM). This category may be further subdivided into multivolume sources and concise or single-volume sources.

2. Terminological sources, which include only definitions of terms, such as the *Harvard Dictionary of Music.*
3. Biographical sources, which include only biographical entries, such as *Baker's Biographical Dictionary of Musicians.*
4. Special topic dictionaries and encyclopedias (detailed in the next section).

Selected Sources about Music Dictionaries

Coover, James. *Music Lexicography, Including a Study of Lacunae in Music Lexicography and a Bibliography of Music Dictionaries.* 3rd ed. Rev. and enl. Carlisle, PA: Carlisle Books, 1971.

Coover, James, and John C. Franklin. "Dictionaries and Encyclopedias of Music." In *Grove Music Online.* Edited by L. Macy. www.grovemusic.com.

Duckles, Vincent, and Ida Reed. "Dictionaries and Encyclopedias." In *Music Reference and Research Materials,* 5th ed., 1–114. New York: Schirmer Books, 1997.

Samuel, Harold E. "Dictionaries and Encyclopedias." In *The New Harvard Dictionary of Music.* Edited by Don Michael Randel. Cambridge, MA: Harvard University Press, 1986.

OTHER REFERENCES

Eggebrecht, Hans. *Handwörterbuch der musikalischen Terminologie:* Im Auftrag der Kommission für Musikwissenschaft der Akademie der Wissenschaften und der Literatur zu Mainz. Wiesbaden: F. Steiner, 1972–2007.

Sadie, Stanley. "*The New Grove,* Second Edition." *Notes* 57, no.1 (Sep. 2000): 11–20.

Strahle, Graham. *An Early Music Dictionary: Musical Terms from British Sources 1500–1740.* Cambridge: Cambridge University Press, 1995.

Musicologist and librarian James Coover (1925–2004) was the master researcher on music dictionaries and encyclopedias. Coover authored the article on music dictionaries in both the 1980 and 2001 editions of *New Grove.* His publication *Music Lexicography, Including a Study of Lacunae in Music Lexicography and a Bibliography of Music Dictionaries* (cited earlier) was one of the first detailed studies of music lexicography, or the study of dictionary making. In this book as well as in his *New Grove* articles, Coover discusses the lacunae (or gaps) between Tinctoris's landmark publication *Terminorum musicae diffinitorium* (1495) and the early eighteenth-century publications by Janovcka (1701) and Brossard (1703).[1] He presents evidence that during this 200-year period, musical terms were sometimes defined in general dictionaries as well as in other types of publications on music. This factor is also explored in Graham Strahle's *An Early Music Dictionary: Musical Terms from British Sources, 1500–1740,* which presents definitions of musical terms in chronological order within each entry.

Hans Eggebrecht's *Handwörterbuch der musikalischen Terminologie* examines the etymology of musical terms and their meaning in different historical periods. Articles in the *Handwörterbuch* are published in separate installments and compiled in loose-leaf binders.

The study of early dictionary sources provides important insight into performance practice issues. Knowing how a term was defined in the Renaissance or

Baroque periods helps inform stylistic decisions about performances of music from these periods. Thus we use these historical dictionaries not for defining terms today, but rather for their historical perspectives. Most of the sources listed in the selected chronological outline that follows are available in facsimile or reprint editions. For further information on these writers and their works, see Coover, Duckles, and the *Grove Music Online* articles about dictionary writers.

Coover's article in *Grove Music Online* includes a chronological listing of 1,650 music dictionaries and encyclopedias from 1800 BCE to 2000. (The list appears in the *Appendix* volume [vol. 28] in the print edition.)

Selected Chronological Survey of Music Dictionaries

Fifteenth century through nineteenth century.

1495 Tinctoris, Johannes. *Dictionary of Musical Terms: An English Translation of Terminorum musicae diffinitorium together with the Latin text.* Translated and annotated by Carl Parrish, with a bibliographical essay by James B. Coover. 1495. New York: Free Press of Glencoe, 1963.

Terminorum musicae diffinitorium: A Facsimile of the Treviso Edition (ca.1494). Monuments of music and music literature in facsimile. Second Series Music Literature 26. New York: Broude Brothers, 1966.

Tinctoris was a landmark dictionary of musical terms. Published in 1495, it is also significant as an example of an "incunabulum," a book printed prior to 1501, in the infancy of printing (see also Chapter 8: From Manuscript to Printed Edition). Although Coover points out that it was not the first music dictionary (he cites earlier sources, including the *Dattilam: A Compendium of Ancient Indian Music*, from about 700),[2] it was an important compendium of 299 terms on music theory and practice from the time of the Renaissance.

The English translation by Carl Parrish presents the Latin text and English translations on facing pages. It also includes an essay by Coover on "The Printing of Tinctoris's Dictionary."

1701 Janovka, Tomas Baltazar. *Clavis ad Thesaurum Magnae Artis Musicae.* 1701. Reprint, Amsterdam: Frits Knupf, 1973.

1703 Brossard, Sebastien de. *Dictionnaire de Musique: contenant une explication des Termes Grecs, Latins, Italiens, & François, les plus usitez dans la Musique.* 1703. Reprint, Amsterdam: Frits Knupf, 1965.

1732 Walther, Johann G. *Musikalisches Lexicon oder musikalische Bibliothek.* 1732. Facsimile reprint, hrsg. von Richard Schaal. Documenta Musicologica 1. Reihe: Druckschriften-Faksimiles 3. Kassel: Barenreiter, 1953.

First music dictionary to include both terms and biographies.

1740 Grassineau, James. *A Musical Dictionary, Being a Collection of Terms and Characters, Ancient as Well as Modern, Including the Historical, Theoretical, and Practical Parts of Music.* 1740. Reprint, New York: Broude Brothers, 1966. Adapted from Brossard.

1768 Rousseau, Jean J. *Dictionnaire de Musique.* 1768. English translation by William Waring: *A Complete Dictionary of Music.* Reprint, New York: AMS Press, 1975.

1790 Gerber, Ernst Ludwig. *Historisch-biographisches Lexicon der Tonkünstler . . .* 2 vols. Leipzig: J. G. I. Breitkopf, 1790–92.

_____. *Neues historisch-biographisches Lexicon der Tonkünstler.* 4 vols. Leipzig: A. Kühnel, 1812–14. Reprint of both editions: Wesseley, Othmar, ed. *Historisch-biographisches Lexikon der Tonkünstler (1790–1792) und Neues historisch-biographisches Lexikon der Tonkünstler (1812–1814). Mit den in den Jahren 1792–1834 veröffentlichung Ergänzungen sowie der Erstveröffentlichung handschriftlicher Berichtigungen und Nachträge.* 4 vols. Graz: Akademische Druck-u. Verlagsanstalt, 1966–69.

1810 Choron, Alexandre E. et F. J. M. Fayolle. *Dictionnaire historique des musiciens, artistes et amateurs, morts ou vivans: précédé d'un sommaire de l'histoire de la musique.* 2 vols. 1810–11. Reprint, Hildesheim: G. Olms, 1971.

1835 Fétis, François J. *Biographie Universelle des Musiciens et Bibliographie Generale de la Musique.* 1835–44. 8 vols. Bruxelles: Leroux, 1835–44.

Who was François-Joseph Fétis?

Musicologist, critic, composer and teacher, François-Joseph Fétis (1784–1871) was the librarian at the Paris Conservatoire from 1826–1830. He founded the journal *Revue Musicale* in 1827 and published significant theoretical writings (see list in *Grove Music Online* article) in addition to his landmark biographical dictionary *Biographie Universelle*, which Duckles characterizes as "a work that set the standard for modern biographical research in music."[3] His personal library of books formed an important part of the Bibliothèque Royale in Brussels; his instrument collection was donated to the Brussels Conservatory.

1878 *Grove's Dictionary of Music and Musicians.* 4 vols. London: MacMillan, 1878–89. First edition of Grove's landmark dictionary.

See under "Encyclopedic Sources" for details on current edition.

1882 Riemann, Hugo. *Musik-Lexicon.* Leipzig: Verlag des Bibliographisches Instituts, 1882.

Current editions: *Riemann Musik-Lexicon.* 12th ed., 5 vols. edited by Wilibald Gurlitt. Mainz: B. Schott's Söhne; New York: Schott's Music Corp., 1959–75. Vols. 1–2: *Personenteil;* Vol. 3: *Sachteil;* Vols. 4–5: *Ergänzungsbände.*

Dahlhaus, Carl, and Hans Eggebrecht, eds. *Brockhaus Riemann Musiklexikon: in vier Bänden und einem Ergänzungsband.* 5 vols. Serie Musik Piper-Schott. Mainz: Schott; München: Piper, 1989. (also available on CD-ROM)

The first edition of Riemann's international dictionary was published in 1887. His division of the dictionary into separate volumes addressing terms (*Sachteil*) and biographies (*Personenteil*) became common in later sources, notably the new edition of MGG (edited by Ludwig Finscher) and Albert Basso's *Dizionario enciclopedico universale della musica e dei musicisti* (both described next under "Encyclopedic Sources").

ENCYCLOPEDIC SOURCES (GROVE, MGG, BASSO), CONCISE DICTIONARIES, TERMINOLOGICAL SOURCES, BIOGRAPHICAL SOURCES

Encyclopedic Sources

The following listing is intentionally selective, covering only three of the "giants" among the recent international encyclopedic sources. A more extensive listing of encyclopedic sources is found in Duckles (5th ed.) under "General Works," pp. 1–17, and in Coover's *Grove Music Online* article under "Comprehensive Works."

The New Grove Dictionary of Music and Musicians. 2nd ed., 29 vols. Edited by Stanley Sadie and John Tyrrell. London: Grove's Dictionary, Inc., 2001.

Macy, Laura, ed. *Grove Music Online.* www.grovemusic.com

How did we get from the 1878 edition of *Grove* to *New Grove,* 2nd ed./Grove Music Online?[4]

A bit of history: The very first edition of Sir George Grove's *Dictionary of Music and Musicians* was published in four volumes from 1878 to 1889, with an appendix edited by J. A. Fuller-Maitland and an index by Mrs. Edmond Wodehouse. Sir George Grove, a civil engineer and self-taught musician, began work on his dictionary in 1868 while working as the editor of *Macmillans Magazine.* The second edition of the dictionary was edited by J. A. Fuller Maitland and published in five volumes from 1904 to 1910. The third and fourth editions were edited by H. C. Colles and published in 1927 and 1940 respectively. The fifth edition was edited by Eric Blom and published in nine volumes in 1954; a supplementary volume appeared in 1961. The sixth edition (1980) was edited by Stanley Sadie; it indicated its departure from its predecessors by using the title *The New Grove Dictionary of Music and Musicians.* Hence, the newest edition (which is really the seventh edition of *Grove*) is called *New Grove,* 2nd edition. It was also edited by Mr. Sadie, along with John Tyrrell and a team of consulting editors from around the world; the online edition is edited by Laura Macy, and in 2008 became part of the Oxford Music Online portal. Most references to the dictionary in this book will be to *Grove Music Online.*

Our most important English-language reference source on music, *New Grove,* 2nd edition was the first edition of *Grove* to be available in both electronic and print formats. The availability of the electronic format has arguably transformed the way scholars and students conduct research.[5] The online edition of *New Grove* also incorporates online editions of *The New Grove Dictionary of Opera* (print edition published in 4 volumes in 1992; see p. 86) and *The New Grove Dictionary of Jazz,* 2nd ed. (print edition published in 3 volumes in 2001; see p. 85), as well as selected entries from the *Norton/Grove Dictionary of Women Composers* (see p. 93). Entries are updated periodically (see *Grove Online* home page under "What's New in *Grove Music Online*). Articles include links to external sources such as Web sites, graphical music examples using Sibelius software, and sound files. The electronic edition provides enhanced search capabilities, such as the possibility of searching full texts of articles, composer work lists, and bibliographies.

New Grove, 2nd edition, demonstrated its departure from its predecessors in many other significant ways beyond the availability of an electronic edition. It is all too easy for those who rely solely on electronic searching to assume that dictionaries are conceived primarily as search engines, and therefore judged on whether they include a particular term, biography, or topic that can be brought up electronically. The creation of a new edition of a major reference source such as *Grove* necessitated an entirely new conception of the dictionary, in order to ensure that it reflected modern scholarship and met the needs of contemporary researchers.[6] As Stanley Sadie points out in his preface to the revised edition, *New Grove,* 2nd edition, is approximately 50 percent larger than the 1980 edition of *New Grove,* "its biggest single expansion [is] in the coverage of 20th century composers, some 5,000 of whom are now entered, as compared with 3,000 in the previous edition . . . more composers from every country are entered, more countries are represented, and countries whose representation was hampered in 1980 by political factors are now considered on the same basis . . . as the main Western democracies."[7] *New Grove,* 2nd edition, also expanded its coverage to reflect trends and themes in twentieth-century musicology, with inclusion of articles on "Deconstruction, Post-Structuralism, Postmodernism, Feminism, Gay and Lesbian Music, Gender, Sex, Sexuality, and Women in Music."[8] As well, *New Grove,* 2nd edition, boasted of its inclusion of entries on jazz, rock, pop, and light music, topics that were not covered in prior editions. Reflecting this approach, Vol. 5 of the print set was perhaps not accidentally titled "Canon—Classic Rock." This became somewhat of an embarrassment for the editors, when it was pointed out by critic Greg Sandow and others that the *Grove* definition of *classic rock,* as "a term identifying the incorporation of classical music references into some rock, from the late 1960s onwards"[9] was wrong; the "term means rock from the late '60s through the '70s."[10] While the text of the printed edition is not likely to be corrected, the online edition has been expanded to include two entries, one for each definition.[11]

It is important for users of *Grove* to understand Sadie's comment that

The *Grove* dictionaries never have been, and should never be, cumulative. Material relevant to scholars and inquirers in 1890 or 1927 or 1954, or indeed 1980, may be of very much less interest in 2000, and may no longer be included. This particularly affects entries on performers, of which we have included a much larger number but have been ready to exclude those on performers who have left only a modest mark on musical history. It applies too, though to a lesser extent, to composers whose reputations have faded.[12]

He then refers users to earlier editions of *Grove,* which are available in most music libraries. The editors of *Grove Music Online* have proposed an online historical archive edition, which would make contents of the earlier editions searchable electronically.[13]

And, for those concerned with statistics, at its debut, *New Grove,* 2nd edition, boasted of its 25 million words and 29,000 articles.

Mr. Esrum-Hellrup and other Fictitious Personages

The first printing of the sixth edition of *New Grove* contained two "spurious" (or made-up) entries: Mr. Dag Henrik Esrum-Hellerup (1803–91) and Mr. Gugliemo Baldini (ca.1540–ca.1589). Reading these entries, one is impressed by the clever creation of these virtual composers. The former's name comes from a railroad station in Denmark. These entries were removed from later printings of *New Grove,* 6th edition, but remain legendary in the memories of *Grove* editors and music librarians. For further information on these and other spuriosities, see the *Grove Music Online* article on "Spoof Entries" by David Fallows.

Grove Music Online was relaunched in 2008 as part of a new music portal titled *Oxford Music Online.* The site also includes electronic versions of Colin Larkin's *Encyclopedia of Popular Music, The Oxford Companion to Music, The Oxford Dictionary of Music,* 2nd ed., and Richard Taruskin's *The Oxford History of Western Music.* Users may choose to search all of these resources or limit a search to *Grove.* The portal also features a page of "Learning Resources," with chronologies (time lines) and thematic guides. The "Research Resources" page provides access to the extensive articles found in Vol. 28 (Appendix) of the print edition:

Congress Reports
Dictionaries and Encyclopedias
Editions
Periodicals
Sources, Manuscript
Sources of Instrumental Ensemble Music to 1630
Sources of Keyboard Music to 1660
Sources of Lute Music

Institutions

Collections, Private
Festival

Instruments, Collections of
Libraries
Sound Archives

New Grove Article Bibliographies and Work Lists

The bibliographies attached to articles in *Grove Music Online* are essential sources for research. For lengthier articles, such as those on major composers, the bibliographies are arranged in categories, with entries listed in chronological order from earliest to latest. Entries for published sources include date of publication, but not publisher. Entries for periodicals use abbreviations, which are defined at the beginning of each volume of the print edition and in pop-up boxes in the online edition. The latter system makes it simple to verify sources. When using the bibliographies, researchers should also bear in mind Stanley Sadie's description in the introduction to the 1980 edition of *New Grove:*

> Bibliographies normally include studies on which authors have drawn as well as suggested further reading.... They are not, except in a small number of cases, intended to represent comprehensive lists of literature on the topic. Writings that are trivial or ephemeral, or that have been superseded, are (unless of particular historiographical interest) normally excluded.[14]

This informed selectivity is one of the many reasons why the *Grove* bibliographies are so valuable to researchers.

Following are the subcategories of the bibliography to the *Grove Music Online* Mozart article. This arrangement is similar that of the bibliographies for other major composer articles. (see Figure 3–1.)

Work Lists

The work lists attached to composer articles in *Grove Music Online* are also essential resources for performers and scholars. The work lists typically include composer thematic catalog number (K and K^6 for Mozart) or opus number, date of composition, key, other pertinent remarks, and location of work in new and old composer complete works edition. As will be demonstrated in Chapter 10: Composer Thematic Catalogs, it is helpful to use the *Grove Music Online* works lists alongside composer thematic catalogs to locate an individual work in the composer complete works editions and to quickly determine essential facts about the work, such as date of composition.

Arrangement of Work Lists

The composer works lists are typically arranged in categories "by genre, function or medium, and items are listed chronologically within categories. When dates are not known, items are listed alphabetically by title."[15] Usually, the composer's sacred works are listed first, followed by operas, symphonic works, and instrumental works.

FIGURE 3–1 **Grove Music Online, W. A. Mozart Article Bibliography.**

Bibliography

Search your RILM provider

A Catalogues, bibliographies, letters, documents, iconography. B Compendia, collective works, congress reports, periodicals. C Exhibition catalogues. D Sources, authenticity, chronology, editions. E Sketches, fragments, compositional process. F Biographies, studies of life and works. G Life: particular aspects and episodes. H Works: style, influences, particular aspects. I Sacred works. J Operas. K Arias, songs and other vocal music. L Symphonies, serenades etc. M Concertos. N Chamber music. O Keyboard music. P Performing practice. Q Reception.

A: Catalogues, bibliographies, letters, documents, iconography

L. von Köchel : *Chronologisch-thematisches Verzeichnis sämtlicher Tonwerke Wolfgang Amade Mozarts* (Leipzig, 1862; rev. 2/1905 by P. Graf von Waldersee; rev. 3/1937 by A. Einstein, repr. 4/1958, 5/1963, with suppl. 3/1947; rev. 6/1964 by F. Giegling, A. Weinmann and G. Sievers, repr. 7/1965) ⊘ **Find It!**

C. von Wurzbach : *Mozart-Buch* (Vienna, 1869) [repr. of articles in *WurzbachL*] ⊘ **Find It!**

H. de Curzon : *Essai de bibliographie mozartienne: revue critique des ouvrages relatifs à W.A. Mozart et ses oeuvres* (Paris, 1906) ⊘ **Find It!**

L. Schiedermair, ed.: *Die Briefe W.A. Mozarts und seiner Familie* (Munich, 1914) ⊘ **Find It!**

O. Keller : *Wolfgang Amadeus Mozart: Bibliographie und Ikonographie* (Berlin, 1927) ⊘ **Find It!**

R. Tenschert : *Wolfgang Amadeus Mozart 1756–1791: sein Leben in Bildern* (Leipzig, 1935) ⊘ **Find It!**

E. Anderson, ed.: *The Letters of Mozart and his Family* (London, 1938; rev. 2/1966 by A.H. King and M. Carolan; rev. 3/1985 by S. Sadie and F. Smart) ⊘ **Find It!**

E. Müller von Asow, ed. W.A. Mozart: *Verzeichnis aller meiner Werke* (Vienna, 1943, 2/1956 with L. Mozart: *Verzeichnis der Jugendwerke W.A. Mozarts*) ⊘ **Find It!**

R. Bory : *La vie et l'oeuvre de Wolfgang-Amadeus Mozart par l'image* (Geneva, 1948) [also Eng. edn] ⊘ **Find It!**

O.E. Deutsch : 'Mozart's Portraits', in Landon and Mitchell, B1956, 1–9 ⊘ **Find It!**

O.E. Deutsch : *Mozart: die Dokumente seines Lebens, gesammelt und erläutert* (Kassel, 1961; suppl., 1978, ed. J.H. Eibl; Eng. trans., 1965/R) ⊘ **Find It!**

M. Zenger and O.E. Deutsch : *Mozart und seine Welt in zeitgenössischen Bildern/Mozart and his World in Contemporary Pictures* (Kassel, 1961) ⊘ **Find It!**

The last category of a composer works list is usually miscellaneous works and arrangements. Obviously, each composer works list is distinct, depending upon compositional output and other factors.

Related Sources

Grove's Dictionaries has published a series of off-prints of major composer articles from both the 1980 edition of the *New Grove Dictionary* and the second edition of *New Grove.* The off-prints from the 1980 edition were published in conjunction with W. W. Norton and the *New Grove,* 2nd edition, volumes by Oxford University Press, the current publisher of *New Grove.* For those who cannot afford the entire 26-volume print edition (which, at a cost of $2,200, is beyond the reach of most musicians) or those who do not have access to the electronic edition through a library affiliation, the reasonably priced *New Grove Music Composer Biography Series* titles provide the full text of the dictionary article along with the bibliographies and works lists. Norton also published *The New Grove Musical Instruments Series,* which included reprints of the articles on organ, piano, violin, and early keyboard instruments from the 1980 edition of *New Grove;* citations follow:

Boyden, David. *Violin Family.* Grove Musical Instrument Series. New York: W. W. Norton, 1989.
Ripin, Edwin. *The New Grove Early Keyboard Instruments.* Grove Musical Instrument Series. New York: W. W. Norton, 1989.
_____. *The New Grove Piano.* Grove Musical Instrument Series. New York: W. W. Norton, 1988.
Williams, Peter, and Barbara Owen. *Organ.* New Grove Musical Instrument Series. New York: W. W. Norton, 1988.

Die Musik in Geschichte und Gegenwart: Allgemeine Enzyklopädie der Musik. Edited by Friedrich Blume. 17 vols. Kassel, Germany: Bärenreiter, 1949–86. (Vol. 17: Register).
_____. Zweite, neubearbeitete Ausgabe, hrsg. von Ludwig Finscher. 1994–2007.

The first edition of this German-language comprehensive music encyclopedia, MGG (loosely translated as "Music in History and Time"), was known for its monumental scholarship, its lengthy articles, and its hard-to-read type font. Published over several decades, the later volumes reflected more recent scholarship than the earlier ones. Vols. 15 and 16 are supplemental volumes ("Erganzungs-Bande"), which update selected entries in the earlier volumes. Vol. 17 is the Register or Index to the entire set.

The new edition of MGG, edited by Ludwig Finscher, upholds the same monumental scholarly ideals, with a more readable type font (although the bibliographies may still require a magnifying glass, depending upon one's age). The encyclopedia is divided into sections for *Personenteil* (or biographies) and *Sachteil* (or terms), following the example set by Riemann. It is also published sequentially, so, as with the first edition, volumes with later publication dates reflect more recent scholarship.

MGG1 was a rich source of music iconography. Articles often included full-page plates, with portraits of musicians, extended excerpts from scores (both printed and manuscript), and other valuable illustrations, albeit in back and white. Regrettably, MGG2 does not carry on this tradition.

MGG has published off-prints of selected major composer and genre articles in the dictionary as the *MGGPrisma* series. Published in conjunction with Bärenreiter and Metzler, this series is similar to the New Grove Composer Biography series.

Basso, Alberto, ed. *Dizionario enciclopedico universale della musica e dei musicisti.* 13 vols. Turin: UTET, 1983–90. Vols. 1–4: La lessico (terms); published 1983–84; Vols. 1–8: Le biografie (biographies), published 1985–88; Appendice (1990). (often referred to as DEUMM)

An international encyclopedia published in Italy, DEUMM follows its German-language cousins with separation into terms and biographies, and publication over a multiyear period. In his *Notes* reviews of volumes in the biographical section, Hans Lennenberg mentions that many of the articles refer to *New Grove*, 6th edition, as their source[16] and expresses his regret that Basso is

> too international for its own good. We do not really need more than two cosmopolitan giants in every large library. What we now yearn for are the good old chauvinistic days when reference books covered their own national specialties and personages first and foremost, to complement their equally nationalistic rivals.[17]

(Some of the true "chauvinistic" or nationally focused dictionaries, such as *The New Grove Dictionary of American Music* or the *Encyclopedia of Music in Canada*, are listed in the following section, "Special Subjects.")

Thus, students and researchers are cautioned *not* to necessarily assume national bias when checking one of these encyclopedic sources. For example, the article on "Blues," in MGG2 is longer and has more musical examples than the same article in *Grove Music Online.* Similarly, all three dictionaries have articles on the American jazz icon Louis Armstrong.

So, why, indeed do we need all of these not-inexpensive encyclopedic sources, as well as the numerous special subject sources referenced in the following section? As Harold E. Samuel wrote in his article on "Dictionaries and Encyclopedias" in *The New Harvard Dictionary of Music,* "Although generally derivative, dictionaries often differ in their factual information as well as in their breadth of coverage, so that reference to various dictionaries is advisable."[18]

Finally, the careful researcher will check the bibliographies in *New Grove*, MGG, and DEUMM to obtain thorough coverage of the literature.

Concise Dictionaries and Encyclopedias: Selected List

Even if one could afford the print sets of *New Grove*, 2nd edition; MGG, or Basso, it might be difficult to find shelf space in one's home or office for these giant encyclopedic sources. We are thus grateful for a rich selection of concise or one-volume sources. The following selected list includes concise sources that contain both terms and biographies in one volume. Along with their cost and space efficiency, concise dictionaries often include entries under titles of specific works, something usually absent from the grand encyclopedic sources.

> ### How do I choose which concise dictionary to purchase for home use?
>
> Is it based on a scholarly encyclopedic source, such as *New Grove,* or edited by a recognized scholar? When was it published and how current are the entries? How much does it cost?

The Harvard Concise Dictionary of Music and Musicians. Edited by Don Michael Randel. Cambridge, MA: Belknap Press of Harvard University Press, 1999.

Kennedy, Michael, and Joyce Bourne. *The Oxford Dictionary of Music.* 2nd ed., rev. Oxford, England and New York: Oxford University Press, 2006. (available electronically in Oxford Music Online)

_____. *The Concise Oxford Dictionary of Music.* 5th ed. Oxford, England, and New York: Oxford University Press, 2007.

Latham, Alison, ed. *The Oxford Companion to Music.* New York: Oxford University Press, 2002. (available electronically in Oxford Music Online)

The Norton/Grove Concise Encyclopedia of Music. Edited by Stanley Sadie. New York: W. W. Norton, 1988.

Random House Encyclopedic Dictionary of Classical Music. Edited by David Cummings. New York: Random House, 1997.

Terminological Sources

(Sources that include terms only; no biographies)

Boccagna, David. *Musical Terminology: A Practical Compendium in Four Languages.* Stuyvesant, NY: Pendragon Press, 1999.

Bowman, David. *Rhinegold Dictionary of Music in Sound.* 3 vols. London: Rhinegold Publishing Ltd., 2002. Vol. 1: Alphabetical listing of musical terms with definitions, followed by eight chapters on "Elements of Music"; Vol. 2: Musical examples referred to in Vol. 1; Vol. 3: Recordings of the musical examples.

Eggebrecht, Hans. *Handwörterbuch der musikalischen Terminologie.* Wiesbaden: F. Steiner, 1972–2007.

Latham, Alison, ed. *Oxford Dictionary of Musical Terms.* New York: Oxford University Press, 2004.

_____, ed. *Oxford Dictionary of Musical Works.* New York: Oxford University Press, 2004. (includes entries on particular works)

Leuchtmann, Horst. *Wörterbuch Musik = Dictionary of Terms in Music: English–German/German–English.* 4th ed., rev. and enl. New York: K. G. Saur, 1992.

Randel, Don. *The Harvard Dictionary of Music.* 4th ed. Cambridge, MA: Belknap Press of Harvard University Press, 2003.

Terminorum Musicae Index Septem Lingus Redactus = Polyglot Dictionary of Musical Terms. Budapest: Akadémiai Kiadó, 1978.

Musical terms in English, German, French, Italian, Spanish, Hungarian, Russian.

Biographical Sources

(Biographies only; no terms; see also Dictionaries and Encyclopedias: Special Subjects, p. 78.)

Baker, Theodore. *Baker's Biographical Dictionary of Musicians.* 8th ed. Revised by Nicolas Slonimsky. New York: Schirmer; Toronto: Collier Macmillan; New York: Maxwell Macmillan International, 1992.

_____. *The Concise Edition of Baker's Biographical Dictionary of Musicians.* 8th ed. Revised by Nicolas Slonimsky. New York: Schirmer; Toronto: Collier Macmillan; New York: Maxwell Macmillan International, 1994.

Baker's Biographical Dictionary of Musicians. Centennial Edition. 6 vols. Nicolas Slonimsky, editor emeritus; Laura Kuhn, Baker's Series Advisory Editor. New York: Schirmer Books, 2001.

Baker's Biographical Dictionaries and Nicolas Slonimsky

Perhaps the most well-known biographical dictionary of musicians is *Baker's Biographical Dictionary,* the first edition of which appeared in 1900 under the editorship of its namesake Theodore Baker (1851–1934).[19] The venerable composer and writer Nicolas Slonimsky (1894–1995) was responsible for the editorship of *Baker's,* beginning with its fifth edition in 1958. The centennial (ninth) edition, compiled after his death at the age of 101, was the first to be published without his input. Slonimsky had a unique ability to inject humor into the driest musical discussions, as well as to convey his opinions of artists (sometimes subtly and sometimes not so subtly) in his reference sources.[20] Other Slonimsky reference sources include

Lectionary of Music. New York: McGraw-Hill, 1989.
Lexicon of Musical Invective: Critical Assaults on Composers Since Beethoven's Time. New York: Coleman-Ross, 1953.
Slonimsky, Nicolas, and Laura Diane Kuhn. *Music Since 1900.* 6th ed. New York: Schirmer Reference, 2001. (See also Chronologies and Calendars, p. 139)
Thesaurus of Scales and Melodic Patterns. New York: Charles Scribner's Sons, 1947.

About Nicolas Slonimsky

Kostelanetz, Richard, ed. *Nicolas Slonimsky: The First Hundred Years.* New York: Schirmer Books, 1994. (includes reprints of previously published material)
Slonimsky, Nicolas. *Perfect Pitch: An Autobiography.* Edited by Electra Slonimsky Yourke. New expanded edition. New York: Schirmer Trade Books, 2002.

International Who's Who in Classical Music. Europa Biographical Reference Series. London: Europa Publications, 2002–. (includes *Directory* section, with names and addresses of orchestras, opera companies, festivals, music organizations, major competitions and awards, music libraries, and music conservatories) Also available electronically. (continues *International Who's Who in Music and Musicians' Directory,* published by Cambridge Biographical Centre.)

International Who's Who in Popular Music. London: Europa Publications, 2002–. (biennial)

Don't we find everyone of Importance in *Who's Who?*

Who's Who sources, which exist in most disciplines, generally include biographies of living people. Commonly compiled by sending question-naires to those deemed "notable" in a particular discipline, *Who's Who* vol-umes do not include those who can no longer fill out the questionnaires. The *International Who's Who in Music* (classical and popular) sources cited earlier are indeed who's who of the living. They are not the places to look for biographies of Bach, Beethoven, Brahms, or Nicolas Slonimsky.

What if I'm looking for biographies of notable but deceased nonmusicians?

Other subject disciplines often have their own equivalents of *New Grove* or *Baker's*. Best guidance in this area is of course the available librarian. Librarians themselves often rely on general guides to the reference lit-erature, such as

Kieft, Robert, ed. *Guide to Reference.* Chicago, IL: American Library Associa-tion, 2008. www.guidetoreference.org (online edition)

The largest biographical dictionaries of Americans are

American National Biography (ANB). 24 vols. New York: Oxford University Press, 1999. (also available electronically, as ANB Online.)
Dictionary of American Biography, Under the Auspices of the American Council of Learned Societies. New York: Charles Scribner's Sons, 1928–58. Supple-ments, New York: Scribner, 1973–.
Jackson, Kenneth, Karen Markoe, and Arnold Markoe. *The Scribner Encyclope-dia of American Lives (SEAL).* New York: Charles Scribner's Sons, 1998–.

So, what about Wikipedia? It's just so easy to use. When I look something up on the Web, I'm quickly directed to the Wikipedia entry.

Established in 2001, *Wikipedia* is an online, interactive collaborative ency-clopedia in which entries may be edited or changed by anyone using "Wiki" technology.[21] Its democratic, interactive and Web-ubiquitous nature help make it both an easily accessible source of information and a mini-mally supervised reference source. Educated users are wise to not rely on *Wikipedia* as a sole source of information, but rather to check entries against *Grove Music Online* and other more scholarly edited sources.[22]

SPECIAL SUBJECT SOURCES

Even though comprehensive or encyclopedic sources are expected (perhaps unrealistically so) to document all that one expects to know about the discipline of music, it is obvious that specific topics can be covered in much more depth in focused special subject sources. The abundance of these sources and their increased rate of publication in recent years (especially in the areas of popular music) demonstrate just how vast our "universe of information on music" has become.

Special subjects include national sources, with titles such as the *Encyclopedia of Music in Canada, New Grove Dictionary of American Music,* and the *Oxford Companion to Australian Music.*[23] Given the broad international scale of the three "giant" encyclopedic sources (*New Grove,* MGG, and DEUMM), it is especially useful to have these nationally focused tools. All of these sources include biographical entries, as well as general discussions of particular topics, such as the development of opera in Canada or Jewish music in Australia.

Within these special topic distinctions, some tools are strictly biographical in nature *(Biographical Dictionary of Russian/Soviet Composers),* others cover terms exclusively (*The Language of Twentieth-Century Music: A Dictionary of Terms*), and others endeavor to be "encyclopedic" in their coverage.

Although many of the entries in these tools include bibliographic references, the bibliographies are generally not as extensive as those found in *Grove Music Online.* It is, however, always advisable to check the bibliographic references in the special subject dictionaries for comprehensiveness.

The following list is arranged by subject. It is selective in nature; additional sources are listed in Duckles, 5th ed., Chapter 1: Dictionaries and Encyclopedias. Composer-specific dictionaries, such as Clive Brown's *Beethoven and His World: A Biographical Dictionary* and his *Schubert and His World* are listed in Chapter 4: Composers, Performers, and Composer-Performers.

AFRICAN AND AFRICAN-AMERICAN MUSIC AND MUSICIANS

Floyd, Samuel A., ed. *International Dictionary of Black Composers.* 2 vols. Chicago: Fitzroy Dearborn, 1999.

Handy, D. Antoinette. *Black Conductors.* Lanham, MD: Scarecrow Press, 1995.

_____. *Black Women in American Bands and Orchestras.* 2nd ed. Lanham, MD: Scarecrow Press, 1998.

Nettles, Darryl Glenn. *African American Concert Singers Before 1950.* Jefferson, NC: McFarland, 2003.

Smith, Eric Ledell. *Blacks in Opera: An Encyclopedia of People and Companies, 1873–1993.* Jefferson, NC: McFarland, 1995.

Southern, Eileen. *Biographical Dictionary of Afro-American and African Musicians.* Westport, CT: Greenwood Press, 1982.

AMERICAN MUSIC

Anderson, E. Ruth. *Contemporary American Composers: A Biographical Dictionary.* 2nd ed. Boston: G. K. Hall, 1982.

Butterworth, Neil. *Dictionary of American Classical Composers.* 2nd ed. New York: Routledge, 2005.

DuPree, Mary. *Musical Americans: A Bibliographical Dictionary, 1918–1926.* Fallen Leaf Reference Books in Music 23. Berkeley: Fallen Leaf Press, 1997.
    Contains brief biographical entries on 414 American musicians (composers, performers, teachers, scholars) that were published in the periodical *Musical America* from 1918 to 1926. The musicians included were born between ca. 1850 and 1906.

Hitchcock, H. Wiley, and Stanley Sadie, eds. *The New Grove Dictionary of American Music.* 4 vols. New York: Grove's Dictionaries of Music, 1986. (New edition in process, will also be available electronically through Oxford Music Online)

ASCAP MEMBERS

American Society of Composers, Authors, and Publishers. *ASCAP Biographical Dictionary of Composers, Authors, and Publishers.* Compiled for the American Society of Composers, Authors, and Publishers by Jacques Catell Press. 4th ed. New York: R. R. Bowker, 1980.

AUDIO

Cary, Tristam. *Dictionary of Musical Technology.* New York: Greenwood Press, 1992.

Wadhams, Wayne. *Dictionary of Music Production and Engineering Terminology.* New York: Schirmer Books, 1988.

White, Glenn D., and Gary J. Louie. *The Audio Dictionary.* 3rd ed. Seattle: University of Washington Press, 2005.

AUSTRALIAN MUSIC

Bebbington, Warren. *A Dictionary of Australian Music.* Melbourne and New York: Oxford University Press, 1998.

_____. *The Oxford Companion to Australian Music.* Melbourne and New York: Oxford University Press, 1997.

AVANT-GARDE MUSIC

Kostelanetz, Richard. *A Dictionary of the Avant-Gardes.* 2nd ed. New York: Schirmer Books, 2000.

Sitsky, Larry, ed. *Music of the Twentieth-Century Avant-Garde: A Biocritical Sourcebook.* Westport, CT: Greenwood Press, 2002.

BAND MUSIC

Rehrig, William H. *The Heritage Encyclopedia of Band Music: Composers and Their Music.* Edited by Paul E. Bierley. 2 vols. Westerville, OH: Integrity Press, 1991.

BLUES (SEE ALSO JAZZ, POPULAR MUSIC)

DeSalvo, Debra. *The Language of the Blues: From Alcorub to Zuzu.* New York: Billboard Books, 2006.

Harris, Sheldon. *Blues Who's Who: A Biographical Dictionary of Blues Singers.* New Rochelle, NY: Arlington House, 1979.

Herzhaft, Gérard. *Encyclopedia of the Blues.* Translated by Brigitte Debord. Fayetteville: University of Arkansas Press, 1992.

Komara, Edward, ed. *Encyclopedia of the Blues.* 2 vols. New York: Routledge, 2006.

Stambler, Irwin, and Lyndon Stambler. *Folk and Blues: The Encyclopedia.* New York: Thomas Dunne Books, 2001.

Weissman, Dick. *Blues: The Basics.* New York: Routledge, 2005.

Bowing Terms

Berman, Joel, Barbara G. Jackson, and Kenneth Sarch. *Dictionary of Bowing and Pizzicato Terms.* Bloomington, IN: American String Teachers Association with the National School Orchestra Association, 1999. (There are three earlier editions of this dictionary—1968, 1976, and 1987—that begin with title *A.S.T.A. Dictionary of . . .*)

Brass Players

Meckna, Michael. *Twentieth Century Brass Players.* Westport, CT: Greenwood Press, 1994.

British Composers

Poulton, Alan J. *A Dictionary-Catalog of British Composers.* 3 vols. Westport, CT: Greenwood Press, 2000.

Canada

Kallman, Helmut, Gilles Potvin, Mark Miller, and Robin Elliott, eds. *Encyclopedia of Music in Canada.* 2nd ed. Toronto: University of Toronto Press, 1992. Also available electronically: http://www.collectionscanada.ca/emc/index-e.html.

Chamber Music

Cobbett, Walter W., ed. *Cobbett's Cyclopedic Survey of Chamber Music.* With supplementary material edited by Colin Mason. 2nd ed. 3 vols. London: Oxford University Press, 1963.

Cohn, Arthur. *The Literature of Chamber Music.* 4 vols. Chapel Hill, NC: Hinshaw Music, 1997.

Both of these sources provide much needed guidance in selecting and surveying chamber music. Cobbett (originally published in 1929–30) includes surveys of chamber music by particular composers, articles about specific genres or instrumental combinations (piano trio, duets for strings, etc.), articles about performing groups and festivals, as well as general articles discussing the development of chamber music in particular countries.

Arthur Cohn's four-volume compendium covers chamber music for all instrumental combinations, with the exception of works with voice, works for piano duet, or works for two pianos. His coverage begins with the Baroque and continues to modern times (the book was completed in 1995); it is especially strong in its coverage of twentieth-century music. An accomplished composer and conductor, Mr. Cohn served as Head of Serious Music at MCA Publishers from 1966–72 and in the same role at Carl Fischer from 1972 until his death in 1987. Entries in his book are arranged by composer. Cohn's analytical descriptions of works provide a good sense of the composer's musical style. Had this book included information on publishers of works and durations, it would have been an ideal bibliography of chamber music (it is listed in Duckles under "Bibliographies of Music"). Without these features, it should be used alongside bibliographies of chamber music (see Chapter 9) to gain both insights into the composition and information on how to locate the work.

Each volume also includes related essays by Cohn on subjects such as "Microtonal Music," "The Chronology of Mendelssohn's String Quartets," and "The Dedications of Elie Siegmeister's Chamber Music."

CHURCH MUSIC

(See also Duckles, 5th ed., pp. 104–111 and Leaver, Robin A. "Hymnals, Hymnal Collections and Collection Development" *Notes* 47, no. 1 (Sept. 1990): 331–54.)

Cross, F. L., ed. *Oxford Dictionary of the Christian Church.* 3rd ed. Edited by E. A. Livingstone. New York: Oxford University Press, 1997.

Hughes, Dom Anselm. *Liturgical Terms for Music Students: A Dictionary.* 1940. Reprint, St. Clair Shores, MI: Scholarly Press, 1972.

Julian, John. *A Dictionary of Hymnology, Setting Forth the Origin and History of Christian Hymns of All Ages and Nations.* 2 vols. London: J. Murray, 1907. Reprint, New York: Dover Publications, 1957; Grand Rapids, MI: Kregel Publications, 1985.

Poultney, David. *Dictionary of Western Church Music.* Chicago: American Library Association, 1991.

Stubbings, George W. *A Dictionary of Church Music.* London: Epworth Press, 1949.

Swain, Joseph P. *Historic Dictionary of Sacred Music.* Lanham, MD: Scarecrow Press, 2006.

COMPUTER MUSIC

Cary, Tristram. *Dictionary of Musical Technology.* New York: Greenwood Press, 1992.

Dobson, Richard. *Dictionary of Electronic and Computer Music Technology: Instruments, Terms, Techniques.* Oxford: Oxford University Press, 1992.

CONDUCTORS

Handy, D. Antoinette. *Black Conductors.* Metuchen, NJ: Scarecrow Press, 1995.

Holmes, John L. *Conductors on Record.* Westport, CT: Greenwood Press, 1982.

CONTEMPORARY MUSIC (SEE TWENTIETH- AND TWENTY-FIRST-CENTURY/CONTEMPORARY MUSIC)

COUNTRY MUSIC (SEE ALSO POPULAR MUSIC)

The Encyclopedia of Country Music: The Ultimate Guide to the Music. Compiled by the Staff of the Country Music Hall of Fame and Museum. Edited by Paul Kingsbury with the assistance of Laura Garrard, Daniel Cooper, and John Rumble. New York: Oxford University Press, 1998.

CREMONA, ITALY

Sommi Picenardi, Giorgio. *Dizionario Biografico dei Musicisti e Fabbricatori di Strumenti Musicali Cremonesi.* Edizione annotate da Cesare Zambelloni. Turnhout, Belgium: Brepols, 1997.

CUBAN MUSIC (SEE ALSO LATIN-AMERICAN MUSIC)

Orovio, Helio. *Cuban Music from A to Z.* Durham, NC: Duke University Press, 2004.

DANCE

International Dictionary of Ballet. Edited by Martha Bremser and Larraine Nicholas; picture editor, Leanda Shrimpton. 2 vols. Detroit: St. James Press, 1993.
International Dictionary of Modern Dance. Edited by Taryn Benbow-Pfalzgraf and Glynis Benbow-Niemier; with a preface by Don McDonagh. Detroit: St. James Press, 1998.
International Encyclopedia of Dance. 6 vols. New York: Oxford University Press, 1998.

DUTCH MUSIC

van der Klis, Jolande. *The Essential Guide to Dutch Music: 100 Composers and Their Works.* Translated by Robert Avak, Robert Benjamin, and Ian Gaukroger. Amsterdam: Amsterdam University Press: Musiekgroep Nederland, 2000.

EARLY MUSIC

Pulver, Jeffrey. *A Biographical Dictionary of Old English Music.* 1927. Reprinted with a new introduction and a bibliography of the writings of Jeffrey Pulver by Gilbert Blount. New York: Da Capo Press, 1973.
Roche, Jerome, and Elizabeth Roche. *A Dictionary of Early Music, from the Troubadors to Monteverdi.* New York: Oxford University Press, 1981.
Strahle, Graham. *An Early Music Dictionary: Musical Terms from British Sources 1500–1740.* Cambridge: Cambridge University Press, 1995.
   Not a dictionary of early music per se; see description on p. 65.

ENGLAND

A Biographical Dictionary of English Court Musicians, 1485–1714. Compiled by Andrew Ashbee and David Lasocki, with the assistance of Peter Holman and Fiona Kisby. 2 vols. Aldershot, Hants, England: Ashgate, 1998.

ETHNOMUSICOLOGY (SEE ALSO WORLD MUSIC)

Kaufmann, Walter. *Selected Musical Terms of Non-Western Cultures: A Notebook-Glossary.* Warren, MI: Harmonie Park Press, 1990.

ELECTRONIC MUSIC

Dobson, Richard. *Dictionary of Electronic and Computer Music Technology: Instruments, Terms, Techniques.* Oxford: Oxford University Press, 1992.

Tomlyn, Bo, and Steve Leonard. *Electronic Music Dictionary: A Glossary of the Specialized Terms Relating to the Music and Sound Technology of Today.* Milwaukee, WI: H. Leonard Books, 1988.

FILM MUSIC

Beaver, Frank Eugene. *Dictionary of Film Terms: The Aesthetic Companion to Film Art.* Rev. ed. New York: Peter Lang, 2006.

Craggs, Stewart R. *Soundtracks: An International Dictionary of Composers on Film.* Aldershot, Hants, England and Brookfield, VT: Ashgate, 1998.

Film Music Society. "Resources & Links: Composers & Songwriters": http://www.filmmusicsociety.org/resources_links/resources_links.html

FINLAND

Hillila, Ruth-Esther, and Barbara Blanchard Hong. *Historical Dictionary of the Music and Musicians of Finland.* Westport, CT: Greenwood Press, 1997.

FLUTE

Busch-Salmen, Gabriele, and Adelheid Krause-Pichler, eds. *Handbuch Querflöte: Instrument, Lehrwerke, Aufführungspraxis, Musik, Ausbildung, Beruf.* Kassel: Barenreiter, 1999.

FOLK MUSIC (SEE ALSO POPULAR MUSIC)

Cohen, Ronald. *Folk Music: The Basics.* New York: Routledge, 2006.

Stambler, Irwin, and Lyndon Stambler. *Folk and Blues: The Encyclopedia.* New York: St. Martin's Press, 2001.

FRANCE

Fauquet, Joël-Marie, ed. *Dictionnaire de la Musique en France au XIXe Siècle.* Paris: Fayard, 2003.

GOSPEL MUSIC (SEE ALSO *POPULAR MUSIC*)

Anderson, Robert, and Gail North. *Gospel Music Encyclopedia.* New York: Sterling Publishing, 1979.

GUITAR

Summerfield, Maurice J. *The Classical Guitar: Its Evolution, Players, and Personalities Since 1800.* 5th ed. Newcastle-upon-Tyne: Ashley Mark, 2002.

HARPISTS

Govea, Wenonah Milton. *Nineteenth- and Twentieth-Century Harpists: A Bio-Critical Sourcebook.* Westport, CT: Greenwood Press, 1995.

HORN

Pizka, Hans. *Hornisten-Lexicon = Dictionary for Hornists.* Munich: Hans Pizka Edition, 1986.

INSTRUMENTS (SEE ALSO SECTIONS ON KEYBOARD INSTRUMENTS, PIANO MAKERS, AND VIOLIN MAKERS ON THIS LIST, AND DUCKLES'S (5TH ED.) SECTION ON DICTIONARIES OF "MUSICAL INSTRUMENTS, MAKERS, PERFORMERS, AND TERMINOLOGY" PP. 87–104.)

Baines, Anthony. *The Oxford Companion to Musical Instruments.* Oxford: Oxford University Press, 1992.

Marcuse, Sybil. *Musical Instruments: A Comprehensive Dictionary.* Garden City, NY: Doubleday, 1964.

The New Grove Dictionary of Musical Instruments. Edited by Stanley Sadie. 3 vols. London: Macmillan Press, 1984.

Praetorius, Michael. *Syntagma Musicum. II, De organographia.* Wolfenbüttel, 1618–20.
> *De Organographia,* part two of Praetorius's theoretical treatise *Syntagma Musicum,* is one of the earliest dictionaries of musical instruments. Included with Praetorius's text is a "Sciagraphia," with diagrams of instruments of his time. (These are presented to scale, with a ruler beside the diagrams.) The book is of great importance to an understanding of Renaissance and early Baroque performance practice. It has been published in facsimile edition as well as in several translations:
> *Syntagma Musicum. Bd. II: De Organographia.* Faksimile-Nachdruck herausgegeben von Willibald Gurlitt. Documenta Musicologica. 1. Reihe: Druckschriften-Faksimiles XIV. Kassel: Barenreiter, 1958–59.
> *The Syntagma Musicum of Michael Praetorius. Vol. II: De Organographia, First and Second Parts, Plus All Forty-Two Original Woodcut Illustrations From Theatrum Instrumentorum.* Translated by Harold Blumenfeld. New York: Da Capo Press, 1980.
> *Syntagma Musicum, II, De Organographia, Parts I and II,* by Michael Praetorius. Translated and edited by David Z. Crookes. Early Music Series. Oxford: Clarendon Press, 1986.

Waterhouse, William. *The New Langwill Index: A Dictionary of Musical Wind-Instrument Makers and Inventors.* London: Tony Bingham, 1993.

JAZZ

Carr, Ian, Digby Fairweather, and Brian Priestly. *Jazz: The Essential Companion.* New York: Prentice Hall Press, 1987.

Chilton, John. *Who's Who of Jazz: Storyville to Swing Street.* 4th ed. Foreword by Johnny Simmen. London: Macmillan; New York: Da Capo Press, 1985.

Cook, Richard. *Richard Cook's Jazz Encyclopedia.* London: Penguin Books, 2005.

Feather, Leonard, and Ira Gitler. *The Biographical Encyclopedia of Jazz.* Oxford: Oxford University Press, 1999. (Updated revision of Feather's *Encyclopedia of Jazz; Encyclopedia of Jazz in the Sixties, Encyclopedia of Jazz in the Seventies.*)

Gold, Robert S. *A Jazz Lexicon.* New York: Knopf, 1964.

Jenkins, Todd S. *Free Jazz and Free Improvisation: An Encyclopedia*. 2 vols. Westport, CT: Greenwood Press, 2004.

Mandel, Howard, ed. *The Billboard Illustrated Encyclopedia of Jazz and Blues*. New York: Billboard Books, 2005.

Meeder, Christopher. *Jazz: The Basics*. New York: Routledge, 2005.

The New Grove Dictionary of Jazz. Edited by Barry Kernfeld. 2nd ed. 3 vols. London: Macmillan, 2002.
> Included in *Grove Music Online*.

JEWISH MUSIC

Nulman, Macy. *Concise Encyclopedia of Jewish Music*. New York: McGraw-Hill, 1975.

KEYBOARD INSTRUMENTS (SEE ALSO ORGAN, PIANOS AND PIANISTS)

Encyclopedia of Keyboard Instruments. 2nd ed. Edited by Robert Palmieri. 3 vols. New York: Routledge, 2003–7.

1. *The Piano*.   Edited by Robert Palmieri and Margaret W. Palmieri. New York: Routledge, 2003.
2. *The Harpsichord and Clavichord*.   Edited by Igor Kipnis and Robert Zappulla. New York: Routledge, 2007.
3. *The Organ*.   Edited by Douglas E. Bush. New York: Routledge, 2005.

LATIN AMERICAN MUSIC

Diccionario de la música Cubana: biográfico y técnico. 2nd ed. La Habana, Cuba: Editorial Letras Cubanas, 1992.

Diccionario de la música española e hispanoamericana. 10 vols. Spain: Sociedad General de Autores y Editores, 1999–2000.

Ficher, Miguel, Martha Furman Schleifer, and John M. Furman. *Latin American Classical Composers: A Biographical Dictionary*. 2nd ed. Lanham, MD: Scarecrow Press, 2002.

MUSIC TECHNOLOGY (SEE ALSO AUDIO, SOUND RECORDINGS)

The Routledge Guide to Music Technology. Edited by Thom Holmes. New York: Routledge, 2006.

MUSICAL THEATER

Benjamin, Ruth, and Arthur Rosenblatt. *Who Sang What on Broadway, 1886–1996*. 2 vols. Jefferson, NC: McFarland, 2005. (biographies of singers)

Bloom, Ken. *American Song: The Complete Musical Theatre Companion*. 2nd ed. 2 vols. New York: Schirmer Books, 1996.

Gänzl, Kurt. *The Encyclopedia of the Musical Theatre*. 2 vols. New York: Schirmer Books; Toronto: Maxwell Macmillan Canada, 1994.

Green, Stanley. *Encyclopedia of the Musical Theatre*. New York: Dodd, Mead, 1976.

Suskin, Steven. *Show Tunes: The Songs, Shows, and Careers of Broadway's Major Composers*. 3rd ed. New York: Oxford University Press, 2000.

NOTATION

Risatti, Howard. *New Music Vocabulary: A Guide to Notational Signs for Contemporary Music.* Urbana: University of Illinois Press, 1975.

OPERA/SINGERS (SEE ALSO MUSICAL THEATER, SONG, VOCAL TERMINOLOGY)

The Billboard Illustrated Encyclopedia of Opera. General editor, Stanley Sadie; foreword by Philip Langridge. New York: Billboard Books, 2004.

Bourne, Joyce. *Who's Who in Opera: A Guide to Opera Characters.* Oxford: Oxford University Press, 1998.

Enciclopedia dello Spettacolo. 9 vols. Rome: Casa editrice Le Maschere, 1954–62; Supplements: 1963, 1966.

Gallo, Denise. *Opera: The Basics.* New York: Routledge, 2006.

Griffel, Margaret Ross. *Operas in English: A Dictionary.* Westport, CT: Greenwood Press, 1999.

———. *Operas in German: A Dictionary.* New York: Greenwood Press, 1990.

The Grove Book of Operas. 2nd ed. Edited by Stanley Sadie; revised by Laura Macy. New York: Oxford University Press, 2006.

International Dictionary of Opera. Edited by C. Steven LaRue. 2 vols. Detroit: St. James Press, 1993.

Kuhn, Laura. *Baker's Dictionary of Opera.* New York: Schirmer Books, 2000.

Kutsch, K. J., Leo Riemens, and Hansjörg Rost. *Grosses Sangerlexicon.* 3rd rev. ed. 7 vols. Bern: K. G. Saur, 1997–2000. (also available on CD-ROM)

The Mellen Opera Reference Index. Compiled by Charles H. Parsons. 23 vols. Lewiston, NY: Edwin Mellen Press, 1986–2003.

The Metropolitan Opera Encyclopedia: A Comprehensive Guide to the World of Opera. Edited by David Hamilton. New York: Simon and Schuster, Metropolitan Opera Guild, 1987.

The New Grove Dictionary of Opera. Edited by Stanley Sadie and Christina Bashford. 4 vols. New York: Grove's Dictionaries of Music, 1998. First published 1992 by Macmillan Press, London.

　Included in *Grove Music Online.*

The New Kobbe's Opera Book. 11th ed. Edited by the Earl of Harewood and Antony Peattie. New York: G. P. Putnam's Sons, 1997.

Osborne, Charles. *The Dictionary of Opera.* New York: Simon and Schuster, 1983.

Pipers Enzyklopädie des Musiktheaters: Opera, Operette, Musical, Ballett. Hrsg. von Carl Dahlhaus und Sieghart Dohring. 8 vols. Munich: Piper, 1986–97.

Rosenthal, Harold, and John Warrack. *The Concise Oxford Dictionary of Opera.* 2nd ed. London: Oxford University Press, 1980.

Smith, Eric Ledell. *Blacks in Opera: An Encyclopedia of People and Companies, 1873–1993.* Jefferson, NC: McFarland, 1995.

Stieger, Franz. *Opernlexicon.* 11 vols. Tutzing: Hans Schneider, 1975–83.

Towers, John. *Dictionary Catalogue of Opera and Operettas Which Have Been Performed on the Public Stage.* Morgantown, WV: Acme Publishing Company, 1910.

　Lists 28,015 operas by title and composer, an amazing achievement considering its date of publication; little other information is included.

The Viking Opera Guide. Edited by Amanda Holden, with Nicholas Kenyon and Stephen Walsh. London: Viking, 1993.

Warrack, John, and Ewan West. *The Concise Oxford Dictionary of Opera.* 3rd ed. Oxford: Oxford University Press, 1996.

_____. *The Oxford Dictionary of Opera.* Oxford: Oxford University Press, 1992.

Wlaschin, Ken. *Encyclopedia of American Opera.* Jefferson, NC: McFarland, 2006.

Why so many opera dictionaries, and which one should I use?

Good question. Opera dictionaries have been published to meet the needs of both scholars and amateur music lovers. The latter tend to look for a one-volume, easy-to-use source in which to read a quick synopsis prior to attending that evening's opera. The music lover may also want to know some quick facts about a singer or conductor. Books that serve this function include David Hamilton's *The Metropolitan Opera Encyclopedia: A Comprehensive Guide to the World of Opera,* Charles Osborne's *The Dictionary of Opera, Concise Oxford Dictionary of Opera,* and *The Oxford Dictionary of Opera.* The legendary *Kobbe's Opera Book* (now in its 11th edition), is found in the homes of many opera lovers; its focus is on opera synopses.

Specialized opera dictionaries, such as Margaret Griffel's *Operas in English* and *Operas in German* provide more in-depth coverage of particular repertoire. Griffel's books also include discographies and references to editions of music. Discographies and edition information are also found in *Pipers* and the *Viking Opera Book.*

Although they also may function as dictionaries, chronologies of opera, including Lowenberg's *Annals of Opera* and the *Metropolitan Opera Annals,* are listed in this book under "Chronologies" (see Chapter 5).

Finally, we have encyclopedic opera sources, notably *The New Grove Dictionary of Opera, Pipers Enzyklopadie des Musiktheaters: Opera, Operette, Musical, Ballett,* and *Enciclopedia dello Spettacolo.* These sources cover all aspects of opera in scholarly detail. As noted earlier, *The New Grove Dictionary of Opera* is available electronically through *Grove Music Online.*[24]

ORGAN

Praet, Wilfried. *Orgelwoordenboek = Organ Dictionary.* Zwijndrecht, Belgium: CEOS vzw, 1989.

PERCUSSION

Barnhart, Stephen L. *Percussionists: A Biographical Dictionary.* Westport, CT: Greenwood Press, 2000.

Beck, John H., ed. *Encyclopedia of Percussion.* 2nd ed. New York: Routledge, 2007.
Holland, James. *Practical Percussion: A Guide to the Instruments and Their Sources.* Rev. ed. Lanham, MD: Scarecrow Press, 2005.
The Percussionist's Dictionary: Translations, Descriptions and Photographs of Percussion Instruments from Around the World. Compiled and edited by Joseph Adato and George Judy. Melville, NY: Belwin-Mills Publishing Corporation, 1984.

PERFORMERS (GENERAL)

Jacobs, Arthur. *The Penguin Dictionary of Musical Performers.* London: Viking, 1990.

PERFORMING ARTS

Library of Congress. *Performing Arts Encyclopedia:* http://www.loc.gov/performingarts/encyclopedia/.

PIANOS AND PIANISTS (SEE ALSO KEYBOARD INSTRUMENTS)

American Keyboard Artists. 2nd ed. Chicago: Chicago Biographical Center, 1992–93.
Dubal, David. *The Art of the Piano: Its Performers, Literature, and Recordings.* 3rd ed. Pompton, NJ: Amadeus Press, 2004.
Gillespie, John, and Anna Gillespie. *Notable Twentieth-Century Pianists: A Bio-Critical Sourcebook.* 2 vols. Westport, CT: Greenwood Press, 1995.
Hinson, Maurice. *The Pianist's Dictionary.* Bloomington Indiana University Press, 2004.
Kehler, George. *The Piano in Concert.* 2 vols. Metuchen, NJ: Scarecrow Press, 1982.
A unique tool that provides brief biographies and lists of concert programs by 2,000 pianists. Arranged alphabetically, one can peruse concert programs presented by Brahms, Clara Schumann, and many other artists. Unfortunately, the book lacks an index of works performed. Such a tool would have made it possible to research performance histories of particular works.

Lexicon des Klaviers: Baugeschichter, Spielpraxis, Komponisten und ihre Werke, Interperten. Herausgegeben von Christoph Kammertöns und Siegfried Mauser, mit einem Geleitwort von Daniel Barenboim. Instrumente-Lexica 2. Laaber: Laaber Verlag, 2006.

PIANO MAKERS

Boalch, Donald H. *Makers of the Harpsichord and Clavichord 1440-1840.* 3rd ed. Oxford: Clarendon Press, 1995.
Clinkscale, Martha Novak. *Makers of the Piano, 1700–1820.* Oxford: Oxford University Press, 1993.
_____. *Makers of the Piano.* Vol. II: *1820–1860.* Oxford: Oxford University Press, 1999.

PIANO MUSIC

Hollfelder, Peter. *Klaviermusik: Internationales chronologisches Lexikon: Geschichte, Komponisten, Werke.* Rev. ed. Wilhelmshaven: F. Noetzel, 1999.

Popular Music (See also Blues, Country Music, Folk Music, Gospel, Rock Music)

American Popular Music. 8 vols. New York: Facts on File, 2006.

Vol. 1: *Blues,* edited by Dick Weissman
Vol. 2: *Classical,* edited by Brad Hill
Vol. 3: *Country,* edited by Richard Carlin
Vol. 4: *Folk,* edited by Richard Carlin
Vol. 5: *Jazz,* edited by Thom Holmes
Vol. 6: *Rhythm and Blues, Rap, and Hip-Hop,* edited by Frank W. Hoffmann
Vol. 7: *Rock and Roll,* edited by Craig Morrison
Vol. 8: *Comprehensive Index*

Experience Music Project: http://www.emplive.org/index.asp

Not a dictionary per se, but a valuable resource for information on popular music. Founded by Microsoft guru Paul G. Allen and his collaborator Jody Patton, Seattle's Experience Music Project "is dedicated to the exploration of creativity and innovation in popular music. By blending interpretive, interactive exhibitions with cutting-edge technology, EMP captures and reflects the essence of rock 'n' roll, its roots in jazz, soul, gospel, country and the blues, as well as rock's influence on hip-hop, punk and other recent genres. Visitors can view rare artifacts and memorabilia and experience the creative process by listening to musicians tell their own stories."[25] The Experience Music Project's collection is composed of more than 80,000 artifacts, including musical instruments, recordings, photographs, sheet music, and fanzines. Its Web site features online exhibits with valuable historical information, such as "Yes, Yes, Y'All: The First Decade of Hip Hop" and "Disney: The Music Behind the Magic."

Gammond, Peter. *The Oxford Companion to Popular Music.* Oxford: Oxford University Press, 1991.

The Guinness Encyclopedia of Popular Music. Edited by Colin Larkin. 2nd ed. 6 vols. Enfield, Middlesex, England: Guinness Publications; New York: Stockton Press, 1995.

Hardy, Phil, and Dave Laing. *The Da Capo Companion to 20th-Century Popular Music.* Revised and updated. New York: Da Capo Press, 1995.

The Harmony Illustrated Encyclopedia of Rock. Consultant editor, Mike Clifford. 7th ed. New York: Harmony, 1992.

Kinkle, Roger D. *The Complete Encyclopedia of Popular Music and Jazz 1900–1950.* 4 vols. New Rochelle, NY: Arlington House, 1974.

Larkin, Colin, ed. *The Encyclopedia of Popular Music.* 4th ed. 10 vols. New York: Oxford University Press, 2006. (also available through Oxford Music Online)

Lissauer's Encyclopedia of Popular Music in America: 1888 to the Present. New York: Paragon House, 1991.

MusicWeb Encyclopaedia of Popular Music. Edited by Donald Clarke. London: MusicWeb, 2005: http://www.musicweb-international.com/encyclopaedia/index.htm. (also available as a CD-ROM.)

Nite, Norm N., and Ralph M. Newman. *Rock On: The Illustrated Encyclopedia of Rock n Roll.* Special introduction by Dick Clark. 2 vols. New York: T.Y. Crowell Co., 1974–78.

The Penguin Encyclopedia of Popular Music. Edited by Donald Clarke. 2nd ed. London: Penguin Books, 1998.

Robins, Wayne. *Rock: The Basics.* New York: Routledge, 2007.

Rock and Roll Hall of Fame and Museum. http://www.rockhall.com
Not a dictionary per se, but a valuable resource for information on popular music. Since its founding in 1983, the Rock and Roll Hall of Fame and Museum has honored major popular music artists and industry figures as "inductees" into the Hall of Fame. The 2008 inductees were Leonard Cohen, The Dave Clark Five, Gamble & Huff, Little Walter, Madonna, John Mellencamp and The Ventures. Its Web site includes biographical information on each inductee, as well as online exhibits. In general, this source is most useful for information on classic rock artists.

The Rolling Stone Encyclopedia of Rock & Roll. Edited by Holly George-Warren and Patricia Romanowski; consulting editor, Jon Pareles. 3rd ed. Revised and updated for the twenty-first-century. New York: Fireside, 2001.

Rosalsky, Mitch. *Encyclopedia of Rhythm and Blues and Doo-Wop Vocal Groups.* Lanham, MD: Scarecrow, 2000.

Roxon, Lillian, and Ed Naha. *Lillian Roxon's Rock Encyclopedia.* Rev. ed. New York: Grosset & Dunlap, 1978.

Shaw, Arnold. *Dictionary of American Pop/Rock.* New York: Schirmer Books, 1982.

Stambler, Irwin. *Encyclopedia of Pop, Rock and Soul.* Rev. ed. New York: St. Martin's Press, 1989.

Stambler, Irwin, and Grelun Landon. *The Encyclopedia of Folk, Country & Western Music.* 2nd ed. New York: St. Martin's Press, 1983.

Stambler, Irwin, and Lyndon Stambler. *Folk and Blues: The Encyclopedia.* New York: St. Martin's Press, 2001.

Vaché, Warren W. *The Unsung Songwriters: America's Masters of Melody.* Lanham, MD: Scarecrow, 2000.

> **There are so many dictionaries of popular music and its various genres. How do I know which one to use, and how do I keep current with information on new performers and genres?**

Good question. Some of the sources listed here contain primarily biographical information on individuals and ensembles; other sources also cover genres and styles. As is evident from glancing at publication dates, few are up-to-date. For example, it would be difficult to find information on the acclaimed group "TV on the Radio," which was founded in 2001. Popular music magazines and the Internet are the best ways to keep up with information on the newest artists. See also Chapter 7: Discographies.

QUOTATIONS

Crofton, Ian, and Donald Fraser. *A Dictionary of Musical Quotations.* New York: Schirmer Books, 1985.

Shapiro, Nat. *An Encyclopedia of Quotations About Music.* New York: Da Capo Press, 1981. First published in 1978 by Doubleday.

Rock Music (See Popular Music)

RUSSIAN/SOVIET COMPOSERS

Ho, Allan, and Dmitry Feofanov, eds. *Biographical Dictionary of Russian/Soviet Composers.* New York: Greenwood Press, 1989.

Song

Emmons, Shirley, and Wilbur Watkin Lewis. *Researching the Song: A Lexicon.* New York: Oxford University Press, 2006.

Sound Recordings

Marco, Guy A., and Frank Andrews. *Encyclopedia of Recorded Sound in the United States.* New York: Garland Publishing, 1993.

Spain (See Latin American Music)

SUBJECT INDEXES TO MUSICAL WORKS

These sources list musical works by various subject criteria.

Reischert, Alexander. *Kompendium der musikalischen Sujets: ein Werkkatalog.* 2 vols. Kassel: Bärenreiter, 2001.
> Lists musical works based on characters and events from history, literature, classical mythology, and the Judeo-Christian tradition.

Schneider, Klaus. *Lexikon Programmusik.* Rev. ed. Bd. I: *Stoffe und Motiv.* Bd. II: *Figuren und Personen.* Bd. III: *Musik über Musik: Variationen, Transkriptionen, Hommagen, Stilimitationen, B-A-C-H.* Kassel: Bärenreiter, 2000–2004.

Themes

Barlow, Harold, and Sam Morgenstern. *Dictionary of Musical Themes.* Rev. ed. New York: Crown Publishers; London: E. Benn, 1975. First published 1948 by Crown.
_____. *A Dictionary of Opera and Song Themes, Including Cantatas, Oratorios, Lieder, and Art Songs.* Rev. ed. New York: Crown Publishers; London: E. Benn, 1976. Originally published as *A Dictionary of Vocal Themes* (New York: Crown Publishers, 1950).

Twentieth- and Twenty-First-Century Music; Contemporary Music

Anderson, E. Ruth. *Contemporary American Composers: A Biographical Dictionary.* 2nd ed. Boston: G. K. Hall, 1982.

Contemporary Composers. Edited by Brian Morton and Pamela Collins. Chicago: St. James Press, 1992.

Fink, Robert, and Robert Ricci. *The Language of Twentieth-Century Music: A Dictionary of Terms.* New York: Schirmer Books, 1975.

Griffiths, Paul. *The Thames and Hudson Encyclopaedia of 20th-Century Music.* London: Thames and Hudson, 1986.

Poulton, Alan J. *A Dictionary-Catalog of Modern British Composers*. Foreword by Vernon Handley. 3 vols. Westport, CT: Greenwood Press, 2000.

Slonimsky, Nicolas. *Baker's Biographical Dictionary of Twentieth-Century Classical Musicians*. Edited by Laura Kuhn; associate editor, Dennis McIntyre. New York: Schirmer Books, 1997.

Thompson, Kenneth. *A Dictionary of Twentieth-Century Composers, 1911–1971*. London: Faber & Faber; New York: St. Martin's Press, 1973.

> Includes Bartók, Berg, Bloch, Busoni, Debussy, Delius, Elgar, Falla, Fauré, Hindemith, Holst, Honegger, Ives, Janáček, Kodály, Mahler, Martinů, Nielsen, Poulenc, Stravinsky, Prokofiev, Puccini, Rachmaninoff, Roussel, Satie, Schoenberg, Sibelius, R. Strauss, Stravinsky, Varèse, Vaughan Williams, and Webern.

Vinton, John. *Dictionary of Contemporary Music*. New York: E. P. Dutton, 1974.

Beware of misleading titles

It is all too easy to assume that reference books with titles such as *Dictionary of Twentieth-Century Composers* (Kenneth Thompson) or *A Dictionary Catalog of Modern British Composers* (Alan Poulton) provide information on *all* composers from the twentieth century. In fact, as is evident from scope note on Thompson, his book and Poulton's focus selectively on composers from the earlier part of the century (Poulton's book covers many of the early twentieth-century "established" British composers, such as Malcolm Arnold, Lennox Berkeley, Iain Hamilton, Elisabeth Lutyens, Elizabeth Maconchy, Phyllis Tate, Michael Tippett, William Walton, among others). However, these two books include the valuable feature of dates and places of performances of the composers' works, information not easily found in other sources.

In fact, coverage of twentieth-century and contemporary composers is selective in all of these books. *Contemporary Composers,* edited by Brian Morton and Pamela Collins, includes biographical information on approximately 500 composers from all regions of the world.

Information on some contemporary composers may also be found in *International Who's Who in Music* (listed under Biographical Dictionaries, p. 76). The *Who's Who* entries often include addresses—either for the individual or his/her manager—something not easily found elsewhere.

UKRAINIAN COMPOSERS

Sonevyts'kyi, Ihor and Natalia Palidvor-sonevyts'ka. *Dictionary of Ukrainian Composers*. L'viv: Union of Ukrainian Composers, 1997.

VIOLIN, VIOLIN MAKERS, AND VIOLIN MUSIC

Bachmann, Alberto. *An Encyclopedia of the Violin*. Original introduction by Eugène Ysaÿe. Preface to the Da Capo edition by Stuart Canin. Translated by Frederick H.

Martens. New York: D. Appleton and Company, 1925. Reprint, New York: Da Capo Press, 1966.

Henley, William. *Universal Dictionary of Violin and Bow Makers.* 2d ed. Brighton, England: Amati Publishing, 1973.

Jalovec, Karel. *Encyclopedia of Violin-Makers.* Edited by Patrick Hanks. Translated by J. B. Kozak. 2 vols. London: Paul Hamlyn, 1965. (See Duckles, 5th ed., entry 1.565 for information on other sources by Jalovec.)

Kolneder, Walter. *The Amadeus Book of the Violin: Construction, History, and Music.* Translated and edited by Reinhard S. Pauly. Portland, OR: Amadeus Press, 1998.

Lexicon der Violine: Baugeschichte, Spielpraxis, Komponisten und ihre Werke, Interpreten. Herausgegeben von Stefan Drees. Mit einem Geleitwort von Gidon Kremer. Instrumenten-Lexica 1. Laaber: Laaber-Verlag, 2004.

Morris, W. Meredith. *British Violin Makers: A Biographical Dictionary of British Makers of Stringed Instruments and Bows, and a Critical Description of Their Work with Introductory Chapters, and Numerous Portraits and Illustrations.* 3rd ed. Gretna, LA: Pelican Publishing, 2006.

Pedigo, Alan. *International Encyclopedia of Violin-Keyboard Sonatas and Composer Biographies.* 2nd ed. Rev. and enl. Booneville, AR: Arriaga Publications, 1995.

VOCAL TERMINOLOGY

Reid, Cornelius L. *A Dictionary of Vocal Terminology.* New York: Joseph Patelson Music House, 1983.

WOMEN MUSICIANS

Burns, Kristine H. *Women and Music in America Since 1900: An Encyclopedia.* 2 vols. Westport, CT: Greenwood Press, 2002.

Claghorn, Charles Eugene. *Women Composers and Hymnists: A Concise Biographical Dictionary.* Metuchen, NJ: Scarecrow Press, 1984.

———. *Women Composers and Songwriters: A Concise Biographical Dictionary.* Lanham, MD: Scarecrow Press, 1996.

Cohen, Aaron I. *International Encyclopedia of Women Composers.* 2nd ed. 2 vols. New York: Books & Music USA, 1987.

Handy, D. Antoinette. *Black Women in American Bands and Orchestras.* 2nd ed. Lanham, MD: Scarecrow Press, 1998.

The Norton/Grove Dictionary of Women Composers. Edited by Julie Ann Sadie and Rhian Samuel. New York: W. W. Norton, 1995.

   Selected entries from this dictionary are incorporated into *Grove Music Online.*

WORLD MUSIC

The Garland Encyclopedia of World Music. Advisory editors, Bruno Nettl and Ruth M. Stone; founding editors, James Porter and Timothy Rice. New York: Garland Publishing, 1998–2002.

   Vol. 1. *Africa.* Edited by Ruth M. Stone. 1998.

   Vol. 2. *South America, Mexico, Central America and the Caribbean.* Edited by Dale A. Olsen and Daniel E. Sheehy. 1998.

Vol. 3. *The United States and Canada.* Edited by Ellen Koskoff. 2001.

Vol. 4. *Southeast Asia.* Edited by Terry E. Miller and Sean Williams. 1998.

Vol. 5. *South Asia, The Indian Subcontinent.* Edited by Alison Arnold. 2000.

Vol. 6. *The Middle East.* Edited by Virginia Danielson, Scott Marcus, and Dwight Reynolds. 2002.

Vol. 7. *East Asia: China, Japan, and Korea.* Edited by Robert C. Provine, Yoshiko Tokumaru, and J. Lawrence Witzleben. 2002.

Vol. 8. *Europe.* Edited by Timothy Rice, James Porter, and Chris Goertzen. 1999.

Vol. 9. *Australia and the Pacific Islands.* Edited by Adrienne L. Kaeppler and J. W. Love. 1998.

Vol. 10. *The World's Music: General Perspectives and Reference Tools.* Edited by Ruth M. Stone. 2002.

> Also available on-line via paid subscription service.
>
> Entries in this wide-ranging dictionary of world music are not arranged alphabetically. Rather, under the direction of a general editor, each volume follows a basic three-part structure:
>
> Part I: An introduction to the region, its culture, and its music, as well as a survey of previous music scholarship and research
>
> Part II: Major issues and processes that link the musics of the region
>
> Part III: Detailed accounts of individual music cultures[26]

Shepherd, John, et al. *Continuum Encyclopedia of Popular Music of the World.* 7 vols. London: Continuum, 2003–5.

Nidel, Richard O. *World Music: The Basics.* New York: Routledge, 2005.

TITLES, AKAS, AND CROSS-REFERENCES

Ever wonder what makes librarians so smart? How can we know, for example, which Boccherini Quintet is known as "Night Music on the Streets of Madrid" (it's G. 324), or that B.B. King's real name is Riley B. King and one of his nicknames was Blues Boy King? These details and others are found in some of the sources listed here. Some nicknames and subtitles may be found through cross-references in library catalogs (e.g., searching for Blues Boy King in a library catalog will direct the user to B.B. King); others must be uncovered through searching these sources. The books listed are neither dictionaries or bibliographies (although some may be titled as such); rather, they fall into the specialized category of "finding aids" to titles and subtitles of musical works, abbreviations, pseudonyms of composers, and other curiosities.

Berkowitz, Freda. *Popular Titles and Subtitles of Musical Compositions.* 2nd ed. Metuchen, NJ: Scarecrow Press, 1975.

Cudworth, Charles. "Ye Olde Spuriosity Shoppe, or, Put It in the Anhang." *Notes* 12 (1954–55): 25–40, 533–53.

> A two-part article documenting what Cudworth terms *spuriosities* (adopted from the term coined by Otto Erich Deutsch that combines "spurious" and "curiosity," and is used for "spurious, doubtful, and mis-attributed compositions," or the ones usually found in the *Anhang* or appendix to thematic catalogs).[27]

The listing itself is divided into three sections: (1) spuriosities proper, misattributed compositions, and so forth; (2) nicknamed and falsely named compositions; and (3) pseudonyms, altered forms of names, and nicknames.[28]

Chwialkowski, Jerzy. *The Da Capo Catalog of Classical Compositions.* New York: Da Capo Press, 1996.

Drone, Jeanette Marie. *Musical AKAs: Assumed Names and Sobriquets of Composers, Songwriters, Librettists, Lyricists, Hymnists, and Writers on Music.* Lanham, MD: Scarecrow Press, 2007.

Hixson, Donald L. *Music Abbreviations: A Reverse Dictionary.* Lanham, MD: Scarecrow Press, 2005.

Hodgson, Julian. *Music Titles in Translation: A Checklist of Musical Compositions.* London: Clive Bingley; Hamden, CT: Linnet Books, 1976.

Pallay, Steven G. *Cross Title Guide to Opera and Operetta.* New York: Greenwood Press, 1989.

_____. *Cross Title Index to Classical Music.* New York: Greenwood Press, 1987.

Room, Adrian. *A Dictionary of Music Titles: The Origins of the Names and Titles of 3,500 Musical Compositions.* Jefferson, NC: McFarland, 2000.

NOTES

1. See Coover's essay, "Lacunae in Music Lexicography," in *Music Lexicography,* 3rd ed. (Denver, CO: Bibliographical Center for Music Research, 1971), xi–xxv. Following this discussion are four lists: "Some 17th century works with Appended Music Dictionaries; Some 18th Century Works with Appended Music Dictionaries; General Music Dictionaries to 1700 Which Contain Music Terms; and General Music Dictionaries to 1700 Which May Contain Music Terms." Coover's article in *Grove Music Online* (revised by John C. Franklin) presents an expanded discussion of this same phenomenon.

2. James Coover, "Dictionaries and Encyclopedias of Music: To the 15th Century," *Grove Music Online,* ed. L. Macy http://www.grovemusic.com.

3. Vincent Duckles and Ida Reed, *Music Reference and Research Materials: An Annotated Bibliography,* 5th ed. (New York: Schirmer Books, 1997), 21.

4. For further information on Sir George Grove, see Michael Musgrave, *George Grove, Music and Victorian Culture* (Houndmills, Basingstoke, Hampshire; New York: Palgrave Macmillan, 2003).

5. The decision to publish simultaneously in print and electronic form did not result in immediate acclaim. As with all major reference sources, *New Grove,* 2nd edition was the subject of numerous reviews, among them, Charles Rosen, "Within a Budding Grove," *The New York Review of Books* XLVIII, no. 10 (June 21, 2001): 29–32; Mark Germer, "The New Grove Dictionary of Music and Musicians, 2nd ed.," *Notes* 58, no. 2 (Dec. 2001): 320–25; Lenore Coral (on the electronic version), "Grove Music," *Notes* 58, no. 2 (Dec. 2001): 406–8; and Greg Sandow and Anne Midgette, "Grove Sees Trees, But Not Forests," *Wall Street Journal* (July 3, 2001): http://www.gregsandow.com/wsj.htm.

6. For additional information on music lexicography, and the process of creating revised editions of standard reference works, see Vincent Duckles, "Some Observations on Music Lexicography," *College Music Symposium* xi (Fall 1971): 115–22; Don Michael Randel, "Defining Music," *Notes* 43, no. 4 (June 1987): 751–66; Stanley Sadie, "The New Grove," *Notes* 32, no. 2 (Dec. 1975): 259–268; H. Wiley Hitchcock, "On the Path to the U.S. Grove," *Notes* 41, no. 3 (March 1985): 467–70; and other references in the bibliography of "Dictionaries and Encyclopedias" in *Grove Music Online.*

7. Stanley Sadie, "Preface to the Revised Edition," *The New Grove Dictionary of Music and Musicians,* 2nd ed., ed. Stanley Sadie, and John Tyrrell (London: Macmillan Publishers, Ltd., 2001), vol. 1, viii.

8. Ibid.

9. "Classic Rock," *Grove Music Online,* ed. L. Macy. www.grovemusic.com.

10. Greg Sandow and Anne Midgette, "Grove: Sees Trees but not Forests," http://www .gregsandow.com/grove.htm.

11. Allan F. Moore, "Classic Rock 1, 2," *Grove Music Online,* ed. L. Macy. http://www .grovemusic.com.

12. Stanley Sadie, "Preface to the Revised Edition," *The New Grove Dictionary of Music and Musicians* 2nd ed., ed. S. Sadie and J. Tyrrell (London: Macmillan, 2001), vol. 1, viii.

13. This idea is still in the proposal stage.

14. Stanley Sadie, "Introduction," in *The New Grove Dictionary of Music and Musicians,* 2nd ed., ed. S. Sadie and J. Tyrrell (London: Macmillan Publishing, Inc., 2001), vol. 1, xxi.

15. Ibid., xxix.

16. Hans Lennenberg, review of Alberto Basso, ed. *Dizionario Enciclopedico Universale Della Musica e Dei Musicisti. Le Biographie. Notes* 45, no. 1 (Sept. 1988): 72–74; and *Notes* 46, no. 1 (Sept. 1989): 83–84.

17. Lenneberg, *Notes* 45, 1 (Sept. 1988): 72.

18. Harold E. Samuel, rev. Lenore Coral, "Dictionaries and Encyclopedias, in *"The Harvard Dictionary of Music,* 4th ed., ed. Don Randel (Cambridge, MA: Belknap Press of Harvard University Press, 2003), 240.

19. Baker also compiled a *Dictionary of Musical Terms* (1895).

20. Some examples of Slonimsky's approach to biographical entries are reprinted in Richard Kostelanetz, *Nicholas Slonimsky: The First Hundred Years* (New York: Schirmer Books, 1994), in a chapter titled "Entries from Baker's," pp. 175–303.

21. The most detailed information on *Wikipedia,* including its history and mission, may be found on its Web site: http://en.wikipedia.org/wiki/Main_Page.

22. *Wikipedia* has also generated some spin-offs that are designed to be more scholarly in their approach, among them *Citizedium* (http://www.citizendium.org/) and *Scholarpedia* (http://www.scholarpedia.org/).

23. Duckles, 5th edition, provides a more extensive list of national dictionaries under heading "Nationally Oriented Dictionaries," pp. 27–47.

24. For further discussion of history of opera dictionaries, see Nigel Simeone, "Dictionaries and Guides," (opera) *Grove Music Online,* ed. L. Macy. http://www.grovemusic.com; an interesting discussion of more recent opera dictionaries, including *The New Grove Dictionary of Opera, International Dictionary of Opera, Viking's Opera Guide,* and *The Oxford Dictionary of Opera,* is found in David Littlejohn, "Everything You Ever Wanted to Know About Opera: A Review-Essay of Recent Reference Works." *Notes* 51, no. 3 (March 1995): 843–64.

25. Experience Music Project, "About EMP": http://www.emplive.org/aboutEMP/index. asp.

26. "About *The Garland Encyclopedia of World Music,*" in *The Garland Encyclopedia of World Music,* vol. 1 (New York: Garland Publishing, 1998), ix–x.

27. Charles L. Cudworth, "Ye Olde Spuriosity Shoppe, or, Put It in the *Anhang." Notes* 12, 1 (Dec. 1954): 25.

28. Cudworth, "Ye Olde Supriosity Shoppe, or Put It in the Anhang (Conclusion)." *Notes* 12, 3 (June 1955): 534.

CHAPTER

4

Composers, Performers, and Composer-Performers

Selected Bibliographic and Dictionary Sources

This chapter brings together bibliographical compendia and dictionary sources (both print and online) on selected individual composers, performers, and composer-performers. Such resources are important starting points for research on musicians and their works, and should be used in conjunction with the article on the individual in *Grove Music Online,* the bibliographies accompanying that article, the composer thematic catalog (when one exists), and, when available, a discography.

There are two notable publisher series among the titles in this section: Greenwood Press's *Bio-Bibliography in Music* series, and Routledge's (formerly Garland's) *Composer Resource Manual* series. Titles in the former series typically include sections devoted to a brief biography of the individual, lists of works and performances, discography, and bibliography of source materials, with brief descriptive annotations on each source. The Routledge/Garland titles are truly guides to research. Titles in this series often include important summaries of existing literature about the composer, with discussion of major source materials and lacunae. The bibliographies of resources are selective in nature, and annotations provide critical commentary about the value of the source in research on the composer.

ADAM, ADOLPHE

Studwell, William E. *Adolphe Adam and Léo Delibes: A Guide to Research.* Garland Composer Resource Manuals 5. New York: Garland Publishing, 1987.

Albéniz, Isaac

Clark, Walter Aaron. *Isaac Albéniz: A Guide to Research.* Garland Composer Resource Manuals 45. New York: Garland Publishing, 1998.

Andersen, Joachim

Dzapo, Kyle J. *Joachim Andersen: A Bio-Bibliography.* Bio-Bibliographies in Music 73. Westport, CT: Greenwood Press, 1999.

Archer, Violet

Hartig, Linda. *Violet Archer: A Bio-Bibliography.* Bio-Bibliographies in Music 41. New York: Greenwood Press, 1991.

Arnold, Malcolm

Craggs, Stewart R. *Malcolm Arnold: A Bio-Bibliography.* Bio-Bibliographies in Music 69. Westport, CT: Greenwood Press, 1998.

Bach, Carl Philipp Emanuel

Powers, Doris Bosworth. *Carl Philipp Emanuel Bach: A Guide to Research.* Routledge Music Bibliographies. New York: Routledge, 2002.

Bach, Johann Sebastian

Boyd, Malcolm, ed. *J. S. Bach.* Oxford Composer Companions. Oxford: Oxford University Press, 1999.

Haselböck, Lucia. *Bach Textlexikon: ein Wörterbuch der religiösen Sprachbilder im Vokalwerk von Johann Sebastian Bach.* Kassel: Barenreiter, 2004.

Heinemann, Michael, ed. *Bach-Handbuch.* Bd. 6. *Das Bach-Lexikon.* Laaber: Laaber-Verlag, 2000.

Melamed, Daniel R., and Michael Marissen. *An Introduction to Bach Studies.* New York: Oxford University Press, 1998.

Tomita, Yo. *Bach Bibliography: For the Global Community of Bach Scholars.* http://www.music.qub.ac.uk~tomita/bachbib.html.

Wolff, Christoph. *Bach-Bibliographie: Nachdruck der Verzeichnisse des Schrifttums über Johann Sebastian Bach (Bach-Jahrbuch 1905–1984): mit einem supplement und Register.* Kassel: Merseburger, 1985.

Baez, Joan

Fuss, Charles J. *Joan Baez: A Bio-Bibliography.* Bio-Bibliographies in the Performing Arts 70. Westport, CT: Greenwood Press, 1996.

Ballou, Esther Williamson

Heintze, James R. *Esther Williamson Ballou: A Bio-Bibliography.* Bio-Bibliographies in Music 5. New York: Greenwood Press, 1987.

Barber, Samuel

Hennessee, Don A. *Samuel Barber: A Bio-Bibliography.* Bio-Bibliographies in Music 3. New York: Greenwood Press, 1985.

Wentzel, Wayne. *Samuel Barber: A Guide to Research.* Routledge Music Bibliographies. New York: Routledge, 2001.

Bartók, Béla

Antokoletz, Elliott. *Béla Bartók: A Guide to Research.* Garland Composer Resource Manuals 40. New York: Garland Publishing, 1997.

Bassett, Leslie

Johnson, Ellen S. *Leslie Bassett: A Bio-Bibliography.* Bio-Bibliographies in Music 52. Westport, CT: Greenwood Press, 1994.

Bazelon, Irwin

Cox, David Harold. *Irwin Bazelon: A Bio-Bibliography.* Bio-Bibliographies in Music 80. Westport, CT: Greenwood Press, 2000.

The Beatles (selected list)

Bratfisch, Rainer. *The Fab Four: das grosse Beatles-Lexikon: John, Paul, George & Ringo —aus Liverpool in die Welt: Namen, Fakten, Daten zum berühmtesten Quartett der Sixties.* Berlin: Lexikon Imprint Verlag, 2002.

Harry, Bill. *The Beatles Encyclopedia.* Rev. ed. London: Virgin, 2000.

_____. *Paperback Writers: The History of the Beatles in Print.* London: Virgin Books, 1984.

Heuger, Markus. *Beabibliography: Mostly Academic Writings About the Beatles.* http://www.icce.rug.nl/~soundscapes/BEAB/index.shtml.

Lewisohn, Mark. *The Beatles Live!: The Ultimate Reference Book.* London: Pavilion Books, 1986.

_____. *The Complete Beatles Chronicles.* New York: Harmony Books, 1992.

McKeen, William. *The Beatles: A Bio-Bibliography.* Popular Culture Bio-Bibliographies. New York: Greenwood Press, 1989.

Terry, Carol D. *Here, There, & Everywhere: The First International Beatles Bibliography, 1962–1982.* Ann Arbor, MI: Pierian Press, 1985.

Beethoven, Ludwig van

Beethoven Bibliography (San Jose State University). http://www.sjsu.edu/depts/beethoven/database/database.html

Beethoven Digital. http://beethoven.staatsbibliothek-berlin.de/. Berlin Staatsbibliothek digital copy of Symphony no. 9.

Clive, Peter. *Beethoven and His World: A Biographical Dictionary.* New York: Oxford University Press, 2001.

Cooper, Barry, ed. *The Beethoven Compendium: A Guide to Beethoven's Life and Music.* London: Thames and Hudson, 1992.

Nettl, Paul. *Beethoven Encyclopedia.* New York: Philosophical Library, 1956.

Bellini, Vincenzo

Willier, Stephen A. *Vincenzo Bellini: A Guide to Research.* Routledge Music Bibliographies. New York: Routledge, 2002.

Bennett, Richard Rodney

Craggs, Stewart R. *Richard Rodney Bennett: A Bio-Bibliography.* Bio-Bibliographies in Music 24. New York: Greenwood Press, 1990.

Bennett, Robert Russell

Ferencz, George Joseph. *Robert Russell Bennett: A Bio-Bibliography.* Bio-Bibliographies in Music 29. New York: Greenwood Press, 1990.

Berg, Alban

Alban Berg Stiftung. http://www.albanbergstiftung.at/.

Simms, Bryan R. *Alban Berg: A Guide to Research.* Garland Composer Resource Manuals 38. New York: Garland Publishing, 1996.

Berlioz, Hector

Citron, Pierre, and Cécile Reynaud. *Dictionnaire Berlioz.* Paris: Fayard, 2003.

Langford, Jeffrey Alan. *Hector Berlioz: A Guide to Research.* Garland Composer Resource Manuals 22. New York: Garland, 1989.

Bernstein, Leonard

Laird, Paul. *Leonard Bernstein: A Guide to Research.* Routledge Music Bibliographies. New York: Routledge, 2001.

Bliss, Arthur

Craggs, Stewart R. *Arthur Bliss: A Bio-Bibliography.* Bio-Bibliographies in Music 13. New York: Greenwood Press, 1988.

Blitzstein, Marc

Lehrman, Leonard. *Marc Blitzstein: A Bio-Bibliography.* Bio-Bibliographies in Music 99. Westport, CT: Praeger, 2005.

Bloch, Ernest

Kushner, David Z. *Ernest Bloch: A Guide to Research.* Garland Composer Resource Manuals 14. New York: Garland, 1988.

BRAHMS, JOHANNES

Clive, Peter. *Brahms and His World: A Biographical Dictionary.* Lanham, MD: Scarecrow Press, 2006.

Platt, Heather. *Johannes Brahms: A Guide to Research.* Routledge Music Bibliographies. New York: Routledge, 2003.

Quigley, Thomas. *Johannes Brahms: An Annotated Bibliography of the Literature through 1982.* Metuchen, NJ: Scarecrow Press, 1990.

_____. *Johannes Brahms: An Annotated Bibliography of the Literature from 1982 to 1996 with an Appendix on Brahms and the Internet.* Lanham, MD: Scarecrow Press, 1998.

BRIDGE, FRANK

Little, Karen R. *Frank Bridge: A Bio-Bibliography.* Bio-Bibliographies in Music 36. New York: Greenwood Press, 1991.

BRITAIN, RADIE

Bailey, Walter B., and Nancy Gisbrecht Bailey. *Radie Britain: A Bio-Bibliography.* Bio-Bibliographies in Music 25. New York: Greenwood Press, 1990.

BRITTEN, BENJAMIN

Banks, Paul, ed. *Benjamin Britten: A Catalogue of the Published Works.* Aldeburgh, Suffolk, England: The Britten-Pears Library for The Britten Estate Limited, 1999.

Britten-Pears Library. Research Resources. Bibliography. http://www.brittenpears.org/?page=research/bibliography/.

Craggs, Stewart R. *Benjamin Britten: A Bio-Bibliography.* Bio-Bibliographies in Music 87. Westport, CT: Greenwood Press, 2002.

Evans, John, Philip Reed, and Paul Wilson. *A Britten Source Book.* Aldeburgh: Published for the Britten Pears Library by the Britten Estate Limited, 1987; reprinted, Winchester: St. Paul's Bibliographies, 1988.

Hodgson, Peter J. *Benjamin Britten: A Guide to Research.* New York: Garland Publishing, 1996. (Relies heavily on *A Britten Source Book*)

BRUCKNER, ANTON

Grasberger, Renate. *Bruckner-Bibliographie (bis 1974).* Anton Bruckner Dokumente und Studien 4. Graz, Austria: Akademische Druck-und-Verlagsanstalt, 1985.

BUSH, ALAN

Craggs, Stewart R. *Alan Bush: A Source Book.* Aldershot, England: Ashgate, 2007.

BUSONI, FERRUCCIO

Roberge, Marc-André. *Ferruccio Busoni: A Bio-Bibliography.* Bio-Bibliographies in Music 34. New York: Greenwood Press, 1991.

BYRD, WILLIAM

Turbet, Richard. *William Byrd: A Guide to Research.* 2nd ed. Routledge Music Bibliographies. London: Routledge, 2006.

CARPENTER, JOHN ALDEN

O'Connor, Joan. *John Alden Carpenter: A Bio-Bibliography.* Bio-Bibliographies in Music 54. Westport, CT: Greenwood Press, 1994.

CARTER, ELLIOTT

Doering, William T. *Elliott Carter: A Bio-Bibliography.* Bio-Bibliographies in Music 51. Westport, CT: Greenwood Press, 1993.

Link, John F. *Elliott Carter: A Guide to Research.* Garland Composer Resource Manuals 52. New York: Garland Publishing, 2000.

CHADWICK, GEORGE WHITEFIELD

Faucett, Bill F. *George Whitefield Chadwick: A Bio-Bibliography.* Bio-Bibliographies in Music 66. Westport, CT: Greenwood Press, 1998.

CHAMINADE, CÉCILE

Citron, Marcia J. *Cécile Chaminade: A Bio-Bibliography.* Bio-Bibliographies in Music 15. New York: Greenwood Press, 1988.

CHÁVEZ, CARLOS

Parker, Robert L. *Carlos Chávez: A Guide to Research.* Garland Composer Resource Manuals 46. New York: Garland Publishing, 1998.

CHOPIN, FRÉDÉRIC

Smialek, William. *Frédéric Chopin: A Guide to Research.* Garland Composer Resource Manuals 50. New York: Garland Publishing, 2000.

COPLAND, AARON

Robertson, Marta, and Robin Armstrong. *Aaron Copland: A Guide to Research.* Composer Resource Manual 53. New York: Routledge, 2001.

Skowronski, JoAnn. *Aaron Copland: A Bio-Bibliography.* Bio-Bibliographies in Music 2. Westport, CT: Greenwood Press, 1985.

CRESTON, PAUL

Slomski, Monica J. *Paul Creston: A Bio-Bibliography.* Bio-Bibliographies in Music 55. Westport, CT: Greenwood Press, 1994.

Crosby, Bing

Osterholm, J. Roger. *Bing Crosby: A Bio-Bibliography*. Bio-Bibliographies in the Performing Arts 58. New York: Greenwood Press, 1994.

Crumb, George

Cohen, David. *George Crumb: A Bio-Bibliography*. Bio-Bibliographies in Music 90. Westport, CT: Greenwood Press, 2002.

Davies, Peter Maxwell

Craggs, Stewart R. *Peter Maxwell Davies: A Source Book*. Aldershot, England: Ashgate, 2002.

Smith, Carolyn J. *Peter Maxwell Davies: A Bio-Bibliography*. Bio-Bibliographies in Music 57. Westport, CT: Greenwood Press, 1995.

Debussy, Claude

Abravanel, Claude. *Claude Debussy: A Bibliography*. Detroit: Information Coordinators, 1974.

Briscoe, James R. *Claude Debussy: A Guide to Research*. Garland Composer Resource Manuals 27. New York: Garland Publishing, 1990.

Delibes, Leo

Studwell, William E. *Adolphe Adam and Léo Delibes: A Guide to Research*. Garland Composer Resource Manuals 5. New York: Garland Publishing, 1987.

Delius, Frederick

Huismann, Mary Christison. *Frederick Delius: A Guide to Research*. Routledge Music Bibliographies. New York: Routledge, 2005.

Diamond, David

Kimberling, Victoria. *David Diamond: A Bio-Bibliography*. Metuchen, NJ: Scarecrow Press, 1987.

Diemer, Emma Lou

Schlegel, Ellen Grolman. *Emma Lou Diemer: A Bio-Bibliography*. Bio-Bibliographies in Music 84. Westport, CT: Greenwood Press, 2001.

Dohnányi, Ernö

Grymes, James A. *Ernst von Dohnányi: A Bio-Bibliography*. Bio-Bibliographies in Music 86. Westport, CT: Greenwood Press, 2001.

DONIZETTI, GAETANO

Cassaro, James P. *Gaetano Donizetti: A Guide to Research*. Garland Composer Resource Manuals 51. New York: Garland Publishing, 2000.

DYLAN, BOB

McKeen, William. *Bob Dylan: A Bio-Bibliography*. Popular Culture Bio-Bibliographies. Westport, CT: Greenwood Press, 1993.

Wissolik, Richard David, ed. *Bob Dylan, American Poet and Singer: An Annotated Bibliography and Study Guide to Sources and Background Materials, 1961–1991: With a Supplemental Checklist of Studies on the 1960s and the Folk Revival*. Greensburg, PA: Eadmer Press, 1991.

ELGAR, EDWARD

Kent, Christopher. *Edward Elgar: A Guide to Research*. Garland Composer Resource Manuals 37. New York: Garland Publishing, 1993.

FALLA, MANUEL DE

Chase, Gilbert. *Manuel de Falla: A Bibliography and Research Guide*. Garland Composer Resource Manuals 4. New York: Garland Publishing, 1986.

Harper, Nancy Lee. *Manuel de Falla: A Bio-Bibliography*. Bio-Bibliographies in Music 68. Westport, CT: Greenwood Press, 1998.

FAURÉ, GABRIEL

Phillips, Edward R. *Gabriel Fauré: A Guide to Research*. Garland Composer Resource Manuals 49. New York: Garland Publishing, 2000.

FELDMAN, MORTON

Villars, Chris. "Morton Feldman Page." http://www.cnvill.net/mfhome.htm.

FINE, VIVIAN

Cody, Judith. *Vivian Fine: A Bio-Bibliography*. Bio-Bibliographies in Music 88. Westport, CT: Greenwood Press, 2001.

FINNEY, ROSS LEE

Hitchens, Susan Hayes. *Ross Lee Finney: A Bio-Bibliography*. Bio-Bibliographies in Music 63. Westport, CT: Greenwood Press, 1996.

FINZI, GERALD

Dressler, John C. *Gerald Finzi: A Bio-Bibliography*. Bio-Bibliographies in Music 64. Westport, CT: Greenwood Press, 1997.

Foss, Lukas

Perone, Karen L. *Lukas Foss: A Bio-Bibliography.* Bio-Bibliographies in Music 37. New York: Greenwood Press, 1991.

Foster, Stephen

Elliker, Calvin. *Stephen Collins Foster: A Guide to Research.* Garland Composer Resource Manuals 10. New York: Garland Publishing, 1988.

Frescobaldi, Girolamo

Hammond, Frederick. *Girolamo Frescobaldi: A Guide to Research.* Garland Composer Resource Manuals 9. New York: Garland Publishing, 1988.

Gershwin, George

Carnovale, Norbert. *George Gershwin: A Bio-Bibliography.* Bio-Bibliographies in Music 76. Westport, CT: Greenwood Press, 2000.

Gilbert, Henry F.

Martin, Sherrill, V. *Henry F. Gilbert: A Bio-Bibliography.* Bio-Bibliographies in Music 93. Westport, CT: Praeger, 2004.

Glanville-Hicks, Peggy

Hayes, Deborah. *Peggy Glanville-Hicks: A Bio-Bibliography.* Bio-Bibliographies in Music 27. New York: Greenwood Press, 1990.

Gluck, Christoph Willibald

Howard, Patricia. *Christoph Willibald Gluck: A Guide to Research.* 2nd ed. Routledge Music Bibliographies. New York: Routledge, 2003.

Gottschalk, Louis Moreau

Perone, James E. *Louis Moreau Gottschalk: A Bio-Bibliography.* Bio-Bibliographies in Music 91. Westport, CT: Greenwood Press, 2002.

Gounod, Charles

Flynn, Timothy. *Charles-François Gounod: A Guide to Research.* Routledge Music Bibliographies. New York: Routledge, 2008.

Granados, Enrique

Hess, Carol A. *Enrique Granados: A Bio-Bibliography.* Bio-Bibliographies in Music 42. New York: Greenwood Press, 1991.

GRATEFUL DEAD

Dodd, David G., and Robert G. Weiner. *The Grateful Dead and the Deadheads: An Annotated Bibliography.* Music Reference Collection 60. Westport, CT: Greenwood Press, 1997.
Trager, Oliver. *The American Book of the Dead: The Definitive Grateful Dead Encyclopedia.* New York: Simon and Schuster, 1997.

HANDEL, GEORGE FRIDERIC

Parker, Mary Ann. *G. F. Handel: A Guide to Research.* 2d ed. Routledge Music Bibliographies. New York: Routledge, 2005.
Sasse, Konrad. *Händel Bibliographie.* Zusammengestellt von Konrad Sasse unter Verwendung des im Händel-Jahrbuch 1933 von Kurt Taut veröffentlichten Verzeichnisses des Schrifttums über Georg Friedrich Händel. Abgeschlossen im Jahr 1961. Leipzig: VEB Deutscher Verlag für Musik, 1963.
_____. *Händel Bibliographie.* Zusammengestellt unter Verwendung des im Händel-Jahrbuch 1933 von Kurt Taut veröffentlichten Verzeichnisses des Schrifttums über Georg Friedrich Händel. Abgeschlossen im Jahr 1961. 2nd ed. Leipzig: VEB Deutscher Verlag für Musik, 1967.

HANSON, HOWARD

Perone, James E. *Howard Hanson: A Bio-Bibliography.* Bio-Bibliographies in Music 47. Westport, CT: Greenwood Press, 1993.

HARRIS, ROY

Stehman, Dan. *Roy Harris: A Bio-Bibliography.* Bio-Bibliographies in Music 40. New York: Greenwood Press, 1991.

HAYDN, JOSEPH

Brown, A. Peter, James T. Berkenstock, and Carol Vanderbilt Brown. *Joseph Haydn in Literature: A Bibliography.* Haydn-Studien Bd. 3, Heft 3/4. Munich: G. Henle, 1974.
Grave, Floyd K. *Franz Joseph Haydn: A Guide to Research.* Garland Composer Resource Manuals 31. New York: Garland Publishing, 1990.
Haydn Bibliography. http://www.haydn-institut.de/Bibliographie/bibliographie.html.
Wyn Jones, David. *Oxford Composer Companions: Haydn.* Oxford: Oxford University Press, 2002.

HILL, EDWARD BURLINGAME

Tyler, Linda L. *Edward Burlingame Hill: A Bio-Bibliography.* Bio-Bibliographies in Music 21. New York: Greenwood Press, 1989.

HINDEMITH, PAUL

Luttmann, Stephen. *Paul Hindemith: A Guide to Research.* Routledge Music Bibliographies. New York: Routledge, 2005.

Hoddinott, Alun

Craggs, Stewart R. *Alun Hoddinott: A Bio-Bibliography*. Bio-Bibliographies in Music 44. Westport, CT: Greenwood Press, 1993.
_____. *Alun Hoddinott: A Source Book*. Aldershot, England: Ashgate, 2007.

Husa, Karel

Hitchens, Susan Hayes. *Karel Husa: A Bio-Bibliography*. Bio-Bibliographies in Music 31. New York: Greenwood Press, 1991.

Ireland, John

Craggs, Stewart R. *John Ireland: A Catalogue, Discography, and Bibliography*. 2nd ed. Aldershot, England: Ashgate, 2007.

Isaac, Heinrich

Picker, Martin. *Henricus Isaac: A Guide to Research*. Garland Composer Resource Manuals 35. New York: Garland Publishing, 1991.

Ives, Charles

Block, Geoffrey. *Charles Ives: A Bio-Bibliography*. Bio-Bibliographies in Music 14. New York: Greenwood Press, 1988.
Sherwood, Gayle. *Charles Ives: A Guide to Research*. Routledge Music Bibliographies. New York: Routledge, 2002.

Janáček, Leoš

Janáček Bibliography. http://www.leos-janacek.org.

Jolson, Al

Fisher, James. *Al Jolson: A Bio-Bibliography*. Bio-Bibliographies in the Performing Arts 48. Westport, CT: Greenwood Press, 1994.

Joplin, Scott

Ping-Robbins, Nancy R. *Scott Joplin: A Guide to Research*. Garland Composer Resource Manuals 47. New York: Garland Publishing, 1998.

Josquin des Prez

Charles, Sydney Robinson. *Josquin des Prez: A Guide to Research*. Garland Composer Resource Manuals 2. New York: Garland Publishing, 1983.

Kay, Ulysses

Hobson, Constance Tibbs, and Deborra A. Richardson. *Ulysses Kay: A Bio-Bibliography*. Bio-Bibliographies in Music 53. Westport, CT: Greenwood Press, 1994.

KING, CAROLE

Perone, James E. *Carole King: A Bio-Bibliography*. Bio-Bibliographies in Music 71. Westport, CT: Greenwood Press, 1999.

KODÁLY, ZOLTÁN

Houlahan, Micheál, and Philip Tacka. *Zoltán Kodály: A Guide to Research*. Garland Composer Resource Manuals 44. New York: Garland Publishing, 1998.

KRENEK, ERNST

Bowles, Garrett H. *Ernst Krenek: A Bio-Bibliography*. Bio-Bibliographies in Music 22. New York: Greenwood Press, 1989.

LANGLAIS, JEAN

Thomerson, Kathleen. *Jean Langlais: A Bio-Bibliography*. Bio-Bibliographies in Music 10. New York: Greenwood Press, 1988.

LASSO, ORLANDO DI

Erb, James. *Orlando di Lasso: A Guide to Research*. Garland Composer Resource Manuals 25. New York: Garland Publishing, 1990.

LEIGHTON, KENNETH

Smith, Carolyn J. *Kenneth Leighton: A Bio-Bibliography*. Bio-Bibliographies in Music 94. Westport, CT: Praeger, 2004.

LIGETI, GYÖRGY

Richart, Robert W. *György Ligeti: A Bio-Bibliography*. Bio-Bibliographies in Music 30. New York: Greenwood Press, 1990.

LISZT, FRANZ

Arnold, Ben, ed. *The Liszt Companion*. Westport, CT: Greenwood Press, 2002.
Saffle, Michael Benton. *Franz Liszt: A Guide to Research*. 2nd ed. Routledge Music Bibliographies. New York: Routledge, 2004.

LUENING, OTTO

Hartsock, Ralph. *Otto Luening: A Bio-Bibliography*. Bio-Bibliographies in Music 35. New York: Greenwood Press, 1991.

LUTOSLAWSKI, WITOLD

Bedkowski, Stanislaw, and Stanislaw Hrabia. *Witold Lutoslawski: A Bio-Bibliography*. Bio-Bibliographies in Music 83. Westport, CT: Greenwood Press, 2001.

MACHAUT, GUILLAUME DE

Earp, Lawrence Marshburn. *Guillaume de Machaut: A Guide to Research.* Garland Composer Resource Manuals 36. New York: Garland Publishing, 1995.

MADONNA

Rettenmund, Matthew. *Encyclopedia Madonnica: Madonna — The Woman and the Icon — From A to Z.* New York: St. Martin's Press, 1995.

MAHLER, GUSTAV

Filler, Susan Melanie. *Gustav and Alma Mahler: A Research and Information Guide.* 2nd ed. Routledge Music Bibliographies. New York: Routledge, 2008.

Freytag, Veronika, ed. *Zweiter Ergänzungsband zur Gustav Mahler Dokumentation, Sammlung Eleonore Vondenhoff: Materialien zu Leben und Werk.* Publikationen des Instituts für Österreichische Musikdokumentation 21. Tutzing: Schneider, 1997.

Internationale Gustav Mahler Gesellschaft. http://www.gustav-mahler.org/.

Médiathèque Musicale Mahler. http://www.bgm.org/.

Namenwirth, Simon Michael. *Gustav Mahler: A Critical Bibliography.* 3 vols. Wiesbaden: O. Harrassowitz, 1987.

Vondenhoff, Bruno, und Eleonore Vondenhoff. *Gustav Mahler Dokumentation: Sammlung Eleonore Vondenhoff: Materialien zu Leben und Werk.* Publikationen des Instituts für Österreichische Musikdokumentation 4. Tutzing: Schneider, 1978.

_____. *Ergänzungsband zur Gustav Mahler Dokumentation. Sammlung Eleonore Vondenhoff: Materialien zu Leben und Werk.* Publikationen des Instituts für Österreichische Musikdokumentation 9. Tutzing: Schneider, 1983.

MARTIN, FRANK

King, Charles W. *Frank Martin: A Bio-Bibliography.* Bio-Bibliographies in Music 26. New York: Greenwood Press, 1990.

MASCAGNI, PIETRO

Flury, Roger. *Pietro Mascagni: A Bio-Bibliography.* Bio-Bibliographies in Music 82. Westport, CT: Greenwood Press, 2001.

MASON, LOWELL

Pemberton, Carol A. *Lowell Mason: A Bio-Bibliography.* Bio-Bibliographies in Music 11. New York: Greenwood Press, 1988.

MATHIAS, WILLIAM

Craggs, Stewart R. *William Mathias: A Bio-Bibliography.* Bio-Bibliographies in Music 58. Westport, CT: Greenwood Press, 1995.

McCabe, John

Craggs, Stewart R. *John McCabe: A Bio-Bibliography.* Bio-Bibliographies in Music 32. New York: Greenwood Press, 1991.

McKinley, William Thomas

Sposato, Jeffrey S. *William Thomas McKinley: A Bio-Bibliography.* Bio-Bibliographies in Music 56. Westport, CT: Greenwood Press, 1995.

Mendelssohn-Bartholdy, Felix

Cooper, John Michael. *Felix Mendelssohn Bartholdy: A Guide to Research, with an Introduction to Research Concerning Fanny Hensel.* Composer Resource Manuals 54. New York: Routledge, 2001.

Seaton, Douglass, ed. *The Mendelssohn Companion.* Westport, CT: Greenwood Press, 2001.

Menotti, Gian Carlo

Hixon, Donald L. *Gian Carlo Menotti: A Bio-Bibliography.* Bio-Bibliographies in Music 77. Westport, CT: Greenwood Press, 2000.

Messager, André

Wagstaff, John. *André Messager: A Bio-Bibliography.* Bio-Bibliographies in Music 33. New York: Greenwood Press, 1991.

Messiaen, Olivier

Benitez, Vincent. *Olivier Messiaen: A Guide to Research.* Routledge Music Bibliographies. New York: Routledge, 2008.

Morris, David. *Olivier Messiaen: A Comparative Bibliography of Material in the English Language.* Ulster: University of Ulster, 1991.

Meyerbeer, Giacomo

Lettellier, Robert Ignatius, and Marco Clemente Pellegrini. *Giacomo Meyerbeer: A Guide to Research.* Middlesex, England: Cambridge Scholars Press, 2007.

Milner, Anthony

Siddons, James. *Anthony Milner: A Bio-Bibliography.* Bio-Bibliographies in Music 20. New York: Greenwood Press, 1989.

Monteverdi, Claudio

Adams, K. Gary. *Claudio Monteverdi: A Guide to Research.* Garland Composer Resource Manuals 23. New York: Garland Publishing, 1989.

MOZART, WOLFGANG AMADEUS

Dimond, Peter. *A Mozart Diary: A Chronological Reconstruction of the Composer's Life*. Music Reference Collection 58. Westport, CT: Greenwood Press, 1997.

Du Mont, Mary. *The Mozart-Da Ponte Operas: An Annotated Bibliography*. Music Reference Collection 81. Westport, CT: Greenwood Press, 2000.

Eisen, Cliff, and Simon P. Keefe, eds. *The Cambridge Mozart Encyclopedia*. Cambridge: Cambridge University Press, 2006.

Gruber, Gernot, Joachim Brügge, and Dieter Borchmeyer, eds. *Das Mozart-Lexikon*. Vol. 6 of *Das Mozart-Handbuch*. Edited by Gernot Gruber and Dieter Borchmeyer. Laaber: Laaber Verlag, 2005.

Hastings, Baird. *Wolfgang Amadeus Mozart: A Guide to Research*. Garland Composer Resource Manuals 16. New York: Garland Publishing, 1989.

Leopold, Silke, ed. *Mozart Handbuch*. Kassel: Bärenreiter; Stuttgart: Metzler, 2005.

Robbins Landon, H. C. *The Mozart Compendium: A Guide to Mozart's Life and Music*. New York: Schirmer Books, 1990.

Salzburger Mozart Lexikon. Hrsg. Land Salzburg und Internationale Salzburg Association: Redaktion: Gerhard Ammerer und Rudolph Angermüller unter Mitarbeit von Andrea Blöchl-Köstner. Bad Honnef: Bock, 2006.

See also lists of Mozart organizations and Web sites in *The Cambridge Mozart Encyclopedia*, Appendices 4 and 5.

MUSGRAVE, THEA

Hixon, Donald L. *Thea Musgrave: A Bio-Bibliography*. Bio-Bibliographies in Music 1. Westport, CT: Greenwood Press, 1984.

NIELSEN, CARL

Miller, Mina F. *Carl Nielsen: A Guide to Research*. Garland Composer Resource Manuals 6. New York: Garland Publishing, 1987.

NONO, LUIGI

Archivio Luigi Nono. www.luiginono.it.

OBRECHT, JACOB

Picker, Martin. *Johannes Ockeghem and Jacob Obrecht: A Guide to Research*. Garland Composer Resource Manuals 13. New York: Garland Publishing, 1988.

OCHS, PHIL

Cohen, David. *Phil Ochs: A Bio-Bibliography*. Bio-Bibliographies in Music 74. Westport, CT: Greenwood Press, 1999.

OCKEGHEM, JOHANNES

Picker, Martin. *Johannes Ockeghem and Jacob Obrecht: A Guide to Research*. Garland Composer Resource Manuals 13. New York: Garland Publishing, 1988.

PALESTRINA, GIOVANNI PIERLUIGI DA

Marvin, Clara. *Giovanni Pierluigi da Palestrina: A Guide to Research.* Routledge Music Bibliographies. New York: Routledge, 2002.

PENDERECKI, KRZYSZTOF

Bylander, Cindy. *Krzysztof Penderecki: A Bio-Bibliography.* Bio-Bibliographies in Music 98. Westport, CT: Praeger, 2004.

PERGOLESI, GIOVANNI BATTISTA

Paymer, Marvin E., and Hermine Weigl Williams. *Giovanni Battista Pergolesi: A Guide to Research.* Garland Composer Resource Manuals 26. New York: Garland Publishing, 1989.

PERSICHETTI, VINCENT

Patterson, Donald L., and Janet L. Patterson. *Vincent Persichetti: A Bio-Bibliography.* Bio-Bibliographies in Music 16. New York: Greenwood Press, 1988.

PINKHAM, DANIEL

Deboer, Kee, and John B. Ahouse. *Daniel Pinkham: A Bio-Bibliography.* Bio-Bibliographies in Music 12. New York: Greenwood Press, 1988.

PONCE, MANUEL MARÍA

Barrón Corvera, Jorge. *Manuel María Ponce: A Bio-Bibliography.* Bio-Bibliographies in Music 95. Westport, CT: Praeger Press, 2004.

POULENC, FRANCIS

Keck, George R. *Francis Poulenc: A Bio-Bibliography.* Bio-Bibliographies in Music 28. New York: Greenwood Press, 1990.

PRESLEY, ELVIS

Hammontree, Patsy Guy. *Elvis Presley: A Bio-Bibliography.* Popular Culture Bio-Bibliographies. Westport, CT: Greenwood Press, 1985.

Hinds, Mary Hancock. *Infinite Elvis: An Annotated Bibliography.* Chicago: A Capella, 2001.

Opdyke, Steven. *The Printed Elvis: The Complete Guide to Books About the King.* Music Reference Collection 75. New York: Greenwood Press, 1999.

Sauers, Wendy. *Elvis Presley, a Complete Reference: Biography, Chronology, Concerts List, Filmography, Discography, Vital Documents, Bibliography, Index.* Jefferson, NC: McFarland, 1984.

Whisler, John A. *Elvis Presley: Reference Guide and Discography.* Metuchen, NJ: Scarecrow Press, 1981.

Puccini, Giacomo

Fairtile, Linda Beard. *Giacomo Puccini: A Guide to Research.* Garland Composer Resource Manuals 48. New York: Garland Publishing, 1999.

Purcell, Henry

Zimmerman, Franklin B. *Henry Purcell: A Guide to Research.* Garland Composer Resource Manuals 18. New York: Garland Publishing, 1989.

Rachmaninoff, Sergei

Cunningham, Robert. *Sergei Rachmaninoff: A Bio-Bibliography.* Bio-Bibliographies in Music 81. Westport, CT: Greenwood Press, 2001.

Palmieri, Robert. *Sergei Vasil'evich Rachmaninoff: A Guide to Research.* Garland Composer Resource Manuals 3. New York: Garland Publishing, 1985.

Rameau, Jean-Philippe

Foster, Donald H. *Jean-Philippe Rameau: A Guide to Research.* Garland Composer Resource Manuals 20. New York: Garland Publishing, 1989.

Ravel, Maurice

Zank, Stephen. *Maurice Ravel: A Guide to Research.* Routledge Music Bibliographies. New York: Routledge, 2005.

Rawsthorne, Alan

Dressler, John C. *Alan Rawsthorne: A Bio-Bibliography.* Bio-Bibliographies in Music 97. Westport, CT: Praeger, 2001.

Read, Gardner

Dodd, Mary Ann, and Jayson Rod Engquist. *Gardner Read: A Bio-Bibliography.* Bio-Bibliographies in Music 60. Westport, CT: Greenwood Press, 1996.

Reed, Alfred

Jordan, Douglas M. *Alfred Reed: A Bio-Bibliography.* Bio-Bibliographies in Music 72. Westport, CT: Greenwood Press, 1999.

Reger, Max

Grim, William E. *Max Reger: A Bio-Bibliography.* Bio-Bibliographies in Music 7. New York: Greenwood Press, 1988.

REICH, STEVE

Hoek, D. J. *Steve Reich: A Bio-Bibliography.* Bio-Bibliographies in Music 89. Westport, CT: Greenwood Press, 2002.

RESPIGHI, OTTORINO

Barrow, Lee G. *Ottorino Respighi: An Annotated Bibliography.* Lanham, MD: Scarecrow Press, 2004.

RIMSKY-KORSAKOV, NIKOLAY

Seaman, Gerald R. *Nikolai Andreevich Rimsky-Korsakov: A Guide to Research.* Garland Composer Resource Manuals 17. New York: Garland Publishing, 1988.

RODGERS, RICHARD

Hischak, Thomas S. *The Rodgers and Hammerstein Encyclopedia.* Westport, CT: Greenwood Press, 2007.

ROLLING STONES (SELECTED LIST)

Dimmick, Mary Laverne. *The Rolling Stones: An Annotated Bibliography.* Rev. and enl. Pittsburgh: University of Pittsburgh Press, 1979.
MacPhail, Jessica Holman Whitehead. *Yesterday's Papers: The Rolling Stones in Print, 1963–1984.* Ann Arbor, MI: Pierian Press, 1986.
Weiner, Sue, and Lisa Howard. *The Rolling Stones A to Z.* New York: Grove Press, 1983.

ROREM, NED

McDonald, Arlys L. *Ned Rorem: A Bio-Bibliography.* Bio-Bibliographies in Music 23. New York: Greenwood Press, 1989.

ROSBAUD, HANS

Evans, Joan. *Hans Rosbaud: A Bio-Bibliography.* Bio-Bibliographies in Music 43. New York: Greenwood Press, 1992.

ROSSINI, GIOACHINO

Gallo, Denise P. *Gioachino Rossini: A Guide to Research.* Routledge Music Bibliographies. New York: Routledge, 2002.

ROUSSEL, ALBERT

Follet, Robert. *Albert Roussel: A Bio-Bibliography.* Bio-Bibliographies in Music 19. New York: Greenwood Press, 1988.

RUGGLES, CARL

Green, Jonathan D. *Carl Ruggles: A Bio-Bibliography*. Bio-Bibliographies in Music 59. Westport, CT: Greenwood Press, 1995.

SAINT-SAËNS, CAMILLE

Flynn, Timothy. *Camille Saint-Saëns: A Guide to Research*. Routledge Music Bibliographies. New York: Routledge, 2003.

SAPP, ALLEN

Green, Alan. *Allen Sapp: A Bio-Bibliography*. Bio-Bibliographies in Music 62. Westport, CT: Greenwood Press, 1996.

SAUGUET, HENRI

Austin, David L. *Henri Sauguet: A Bio-Bibliography*. Bio-Bibliographies in Music 39. New York: Greenwood Press, 1991.

SCARLATTI, ALESSANDRO/SCARLATTI, DOMENICO

Vidali, Carole Franklin. *Alessandro and Domenico Scarlatti: A Guide to Research*. Garland Composer Resource Manuals 34. New York: Garland Publishing, 1993.

SCHENKER, HEINRICH

Ayotte, Benjamin McKay. *Heinrich Schenker: A Guide to Research*. Routledge Music Bibliographies. New York: Routledge, 2004.

SCHICKELE, PETER

Ravas, Tammy. *Peter Schickele: A Bio-Bibliography*. Bio-Bibliographies in Music 92. Westport, CT: Greenwood Press, 2004.

SCHOENBERG, ARNOLD

Christensen, Jean and Jesper Christensen. *From Arnold Schoenberg's Literary Legacy: A Catalog of Neglected Items*. Detroit Studies in Music Bibliography 59. Warren, MI: Harmonie Park Press, 1988.

Kimmey, John A., Jr., comp. *The Arnold Schoenberg-Hans Nachod Collection*. Detroit Studies in Music Bibliography 41. Detroit: Information Coordinators, 1979. (catalog of Schoenberg materials in North Texas State University Music Library)

SCHUBERT, FRANZ

Clive, H. P. *Schubert and His World: A Biographical Dictionary*. Oxford: Clarendon Press, 1997.

Hilmar, Ernst, and Margret Jestremski. *Schubert-Enzyklopädie.* 2 vols. Rev. ed. of *Schubert-Lexikon,* 1997. Tutzing: H. Schneider, 2004.

SCHÜTZ, HEINRICH

Skei, Allen B. *Heinrich Schütz: A Guide to Research.* Garland Composer Resource Manuals 1. New York: Garland Publishing, 1981.

SCHULLER, GUNTHER

Carnovale, Norbert. *Gunther Schuller: A Bio-Bibliography.* Bio-Bibliographies in Music 6. New York: Greenwood Press, 1987.

SCHUMAN, WILLIAM

Adams, K. Gary. *William Schuman: A Bio-Bibliography.* Bio-Bibliographies in Music 67. Westport, CT: Greenwood Press, 1998.

SCOTT, CYRIL

Sampsel, Laurie J. *Cyril Scott: A Bio-Bibliography.* Bio-Bibliographies in Music 79. Westport, CT: Greenwood Press, 2000.

SCULTHORPE, PETER

Hayes, Deborah. *Peter Sculthorpe: A Bio-Bibliography.* Bio-Bibliographies in Music 50. Westport, CT: Greenwood Press, 1993.

SIBELIUS, JEAN

Goss, Glenda Dawn. *Jean Sibelius: A Guide to Research.* Garland Composer Resource Manuals 41. New York: Garland Publishing, 1998.

SIMON, PAUL

Perone, James E. *Paul Simon: A Bio-Bibliography.* Bio-Bibliographies in Music 78. Westport, CT: Greenwood Press, 2000.

SINATRA, FRANK

Mustazza, Leonard. *Sinatra: An Annotated Bibliography, 1939–1998.* Music Reference Collection 74. Westport, CT: Greenwood Press, 1999.

SITSKY, LARRY

Holmes, Robyn, et al. *Larry Sitsky: A Bio-Bibliography.* Bio-Bibliographies in Music 65. Westport, CT: Greenwood Press, 1997.

Sousa, John Philip

Danner, Phyllis. *Sousa at Illinois: The John Philip Sousa and Herbert L. Clarke Manuscript Collections at the University of Illinois at Urbana-Champaign.* Detroit Studies in Music Bibliography. Warren, MI: Harmonie Park Press, 2005.

Still, William Grant

Still, Judith Anne, et al. *William Grant Still: A Bio-Bibliography.* Bio-Bibliographies in Music 61. Westport, CT: Greenwood Press, 1996.

Strauss, Richard

Schmid, Mark-Daniel, ed. *The Richard Strauss Companion.* Westport, CT: Praeger, 2003.

Stravinsky, Igor

Heintze, James R. *Igor Stravinsky: An International Bibliography of Theses and Dissertations, 1925–2000.* 2nd ed. Detroit Studies in Music Bibliographies. Warren, MI: Harmonie Park Press, 2001.

Sullivan, Arthur, Sir

Benford, Harry. *The Gilbert and Sullivan Lexicon in Which Is Gilded the Philosophic Pill: Featuring New Illustrations and New Insights.* 3rd ed. Houston: Queensbury Press, 1999.
Dillard, Philip H. *How Quaint the Ways of Paradox!: An Annotated Gilbert & Sullivan Bibliography.* Metuchen, NJ: Scarecrow Press, 1991.

Tailleferre, Germaine

Shapiro, Robert. *Germaine Tailleferre: A Bio-Bibliography.* Bio-Bibliographies in Music 48. Westport, CT: Greenwood Press, 1994.

Takemitsu, Toru

Siddons, James. *Toru Takemitsu: A Bio-Bibliography.* Bio-Bibliographies in Music 85. Westport, CT: Greenwood Press, 2001.

Tcherepnin, Alexander

Arias, Enrique Alberto. *Alexander Tcherepnin: A Bio-Bibliography.* Bio-Bibliographies in Music 8. New York: Greenwood Press, 1989.

Thompson, Randall

Benser, Caroline Cepin, and David Francis Urrows. *Randall Thompson: A Bio-Bibliography.* Bio-Bibliographies in Music 38. New York: Greenwood Press, 1991.

THOMSON, VIRGIL

Meckna, Michael. *Virgil Thomson: A Bio-Bibliography.* Bio-Bibliographies in Music 4. New York: Greenwood Press, 1986.

TIPPETT, MICHAEL

Theil, Gordon. *Michael Tippett: A Bio-Bibliography.* Music reference Collection 21. New York: Greenwood Press, 1989.

TOWER, JOAN

Grolman, Ellen K. *Joan Tower: The Comprehensive Bio-Bibliography.* Lanham, MD: Scarecrow Press, 2007.

USSACHEVSKY, VLADIMIR

Hartsock, Ralph, and Carl Rahkonen. *Vladimir Ussachevsky: A Bio-Bibliography.* Bio-Bibliographies in Music 75. Westport, CT: Greenwood Press, 2000.

VAUGHAN WILLIAMS, RALPH

Butterworth, Neil. *Ralph Vaughan Williams: A Guide to Research.* Garland Composer Resource Manuals 21. New York: Garland Publishing, 1990.

VERDI, GIUSEPPE

Harwood, Gregory. *Giuseppe Verdi: A Guide to Research.* Garland Composer Resource Manuals 42. New York: Garland Publishing, 1998.

VICTORIA, TOMÁS LUIS DE

Cramer, Eugene. *Tomás Luis de Victoria: A Guide to Research.* Garland Composer Resource Manuals 43. New York: Garland Publishing, 1998.

VILLA-LOBOS, HEITOR

Appleby, David P. *Heitor Villa-Lobos: A Bio-Bibliography.* Bio-Bibliographies in Music 9. New York: Greenwood Press, 1988.

VIVALDI, ANTONIO

Talbot, Michael. *Antonio Vivaldi: A Guide to Research.* Garland Composer Resource Manuals 12. New York: Garland Publishing, 1988.

WAGNER, RICHARD

Bauer, Hans-Joachim. *Richard Wagner Lexikon.* Bergisch Gladbach: G. Lübbe, 1988.
Millington, Barry, ed. *The Wagner Compendium: A Guide to Wagner's Life and Music.* New York: Schirmer Books, 1992.

Müller, Ulrich, and Peter Wapnewski, eds. *Wagner Handbook.* Translation edited by John Deathridge. Cambridge, MA: Harvard University Press, 1992.

Saffle, Michael. *Richard Wagner: A Guide to Research.* Routledge Music Bibliographies. New York: Routledge, 2002.

Terry, Edward M. *A Richard Wagner Dictionary.* 1939. Reprint, Westport, CT: Greenwood Press, 1971.

WALTON, WILLIAM

Craggs, Stewart R. *William Walton: A Source Book.* Aldershot, England: Scolar Press; Brookfield, VT: Ashgate Publishing, 1993.

Smith, Carolyn J. *William Walton: A Bio-Bibliography.* Bio-Bibliographies in Music 18. New York: Greenwood Press, 1988.

WARD, ROBERT

Kreitner, Kenneth. *Robert Ward: A Bio-Bibliography.* Bio-Bibliographies in Music 17. New York: Greenwood Press, 1988.

WARREN, ELINOR REMICK

Borton, Virginia. *Elinor Remick Warren: A Bio-Bibliography.* Bio-Bibliographies in Music 46. Westport, CT: Greenwood Press, 1993.

WEBER, CARL MARIA VON

Henderson, Donald G. *Carl Maria von Weber: A Guide to Research.* Garland Composer Resource Manuals 24. New York: Garland Publishing, 1990.

WEBERN, ANTON

Roman, Zoltan. *Anton von Webern: An Annotated Bibliography.* Detroit Studies in Music Bibliography 48. Detroit: Information Coordinators, 1983.

THE WHO

Wolter, Stephen and Karen Kimber. *The Who in Print: An Annotated Bibliography, 1965 through 1990.* Jefferson, NC: McFarland, 1992.

WILDER, ALEC

Demsey, David, and Ronald Prather. *Alec Wilder: A Bio-bibliography.* Bio-Bibliographies in Music 45. Westport, CT: Greenwood Press, 1993.

WILLAERT, ADRIAN

Kidger, David. *Adrian Willaert: A Guide to Research.* Routledge Music Bibliographies. New York: Routledge, 2005.

WOLF, HUGO

Ossenkop, David. *Hugo Wolf: A Guide to Research.* Garland Composer Resource Manuals 15. New York: Garland Publishing, 1988.

WUORINEN, CHARLES

Burbank, Richard D. *Charles Wuorinen: A Bio-Bibliography.* Bio-Bibliographies in Music 49. Westport, CT: Greenwood Press, 1994.

5

Histories of Music and Related Subjects

INTRODUCTION

Published histories of music are essential sources of information for all musicians. It is through these histories that we learn about composers and their works, genres and style periods, and the cultural and sociological factors surrounding musical developments. Although music history books may be more likely found in the circulating stacks than in the reference rooms of music libraries, they should not be overlooked in the research process. That said, each music history title must also be understood in terms of its own historical approach. Music histories of the nineteenth or early twentieth century differ markedly from more recently published sources. In order to understand the changing perspectives and approaches of music histories, it is necessary to understand the concept of *historiography,* or the study of music history, as well as development of musicology as a discipline.

This chapter presents information on histories of music and related areas, as follows:

> Historiography of Music and Landmark Music Histories
> Musicology
> Ethnomusicology
> Popular Music Studies
> Jazz Research
> German Musicologists in Perspective
> Teaching of Music History and Music History Textbooks
> Specific Music Histories Published since 1990
> Source Readings
> Oral History
> Music Iconography
> Organology
> Chronologies and Calendars
> Biographies

HISTORIOGRAPHY OF MUSIC AND LANDMARK MUSIC HISTORIES

Historiography of Music

Allen, Warren Dwight. *Philosophies of Music History: A Study of General Histories of Music 1600–1900.* New York: American Book Company, 1939. Reprint, New York: Dover Publications, 1962.

Duckles, Vincent H. "Patterns in the Historiography of 19th-Century Music." *Acta Musicologica* 42, fasc. 1/2 Special Issue. Preliminary Papers of the Colloque de Saint-Germain-en-Laye (September 1970): 75–82.

_____. "Johann Nicolaus Forkel: The Beginning of Music Historiography." *Eighteenth-Century Studies,* i (1967–68): 277–90.

Stanley, Glenn. "Historiography." *Grove Music Online.* Edited by L. Macy. http://www.grovemusic.com.

Treitler, Leo. *Music and the Historical Imagination.* Cambridge, MA: Harvard University Press, 1989.

Landmark Music Histories

Burney, Charles. *A General History of Music, from the Earliest Time to the Present Period.* 4 vols. London: Printed for the author and sold by T. Becket, Strand; J. Robson, New Bond-Street; and G. Robinson, Paternoster-Row, 1776–1789. Reprint, ed. Frank Mercer in 2 vols. with the 1789 text of the orig. Vol. 1. Reprint, New York: Harcourt, Brace, 1935.

Hawkins, Sir John. *A General History of the Science and Practice of Music.* 5 vols. London: Printed for T. Payne and son, 1776. A new ed., with the author's posthumous notes. London: Novello, Ewer & Co.; New York: J. L. Peters, 1875; Vol. 3, 1853. Reprint of 1853 ed. 2 vols. New York: Dover, 1963.

Music historiography refers to the study of music history. These sources provide perspectives on the writing of music histories over time. Warren Allen's *Philosophies of Music History,* although first published in 1939, remains perhaps one of the most detailed resources on music historiography. An important feature of the book is its bibliography of "Literature Concerning the History of Music in Chronological Order," which covers sources to 1931.

Although there were writings about music even in ancient times, it was not until the eighteenth century's "Age of Enlightenment" and its interest in empirical thought that writers sought to present sweeping chronological histories of music using primary sources as evidence. The two landmark sources that represent the beginning of music histories of this type are Charles Burney's *A General History of Music, from the Earliest Time to the Present Period* and Sir John Hawkins's *A General History of the Science and Practice of Music.* Both sources appeared in the same year, 1776, although Burney's four-volume history was published over a multiyear period from 1776 to 1789, while Hawkins published his five-volume source all at once. Much has been written about their respective strengths and weaknesses. It is said that Burney evidenced a higher literary quality in his work, while Hawkins emphasized more of the theoretical and technical aspects of music. Such sweeping comparisons can be misleading, however. For further information and perspectives, see the *Grove Music Online* articles by Kerry S. Grant and Percy A. Scholes on Burney and Hawkins respectively.

Interest in large-scale music histories in the eighteenth century was not limited to England. Among other notable sources published in this period were Padre Martini's three-volume, but incomplete, *Storia della musica* (Bologna: 1757–81), Jean-Benjamin de La Borde's four-volume *Essai sur la musique ancienne et moderne* (Paris: 1780), and Johann Nicolaus Forkel's two-volume *Allgemeine Geschichte der Musik* (Leipzig: 1790, 1801).

It should be noted that with the exception of Forkel (1749–1818), most of these eighteenth-century writers of music histories did not utilize the techniques of musicological research that were developed around the middle of the nineteenth century.

MUSICOLOGY

Research about music is indelibly tied to the discipline of musicology. Without this discipline and the work of musicologists, we would lack sophisticated writings about music, and such essential tools as thematic catalogs and composer critical editions.

What Is Musicology?

In the *Grove Music Online* article on musicology (updated from the earlier article in the sixth edition of *New Grove*), Vincent Duckles cites the definition of the discipline that had been developed by the American Musicological Society in 1955: "Musicology is a field of knowledge having as its object the investigation of the art of music as a physical, psychological, aesthetic, and cultural phenomenon."[1] *Webster's Eleventh Collegiate Dictionary* defines musicology as "a study of music as a branch of knowledge or field of research as distinct from composition or performance;" similarly, the *Oxford English Dictionary* defines the term as "the branch of knowledge that deals with music as a subject of study rather than as a skill or performing art; academic research in or scholarly study of music. More generally: writing about music; musicography." The *Harvard Dictionary of Music* defines it more broadly as "the scholarly study of music, wherever it is found historically or geographically."[2] The German equivalents of the term are perhaps more specific in their emphasis on scientific process: *Musikwissenschaft* (music science) and *Musikforschung* (music research).

Musicology as a discipline developed in Germany in the latter part of the nineteenth century. Among its first proponents were the Handel scholar Friedrich Chrysander (1826–1901), historian and bibliographer Johann Nicolaus Forkel (1749–1818), Bach scholar Philip Spitta (1841–94), and the Austrian theorist Guido Adler (1855–1941). It was Adler who proposed the distinction between historical and systematic musicology in a paper printed in the first issue of *Vierteljahrsschrift für Musikwissenschaft,* a journal he founded with Chrysander and Spitta in 1885. As presented in the *Grove Music Online* article on "Musicology," the areas of historical and systematic musicology were defined as follows:

I. **The historical field**   (the history of music arranged by epochs, peoples, empires, countries, provinces, towns, schools, individual artists): A. Musical palaeography (semiography) (notations). B. Basic historical categories (groupings of musical forms). C. Laws: (1) as embodied in the compositions of each epoch; (2) as conceived and taught by the theorists; (3) as they appear in the practice of the arts. D. Musical instruments.

II. **Systematic:**   The systematic field (tabulation of the chief laws applicable to the various branches of music): A. Investigation and justification of these laws in: (1) harmony (tonal); (2) rhythm (temporal); (3) melody (correlation of tonal and temporal). B. Aesthetics and psychology of music: comparison and evaluation in relation to the perceived subjects, with a complex of questions related to the foregoing. C. Music education: the teaching of (1) music in general; (2) harmony; (3) counterpoint; (4) composition; (5) orchestration; (6) vocal and instrumental performance. D. Musicology (investigation and comparative study in ethnography and folklore).[3]

This distinction had important implications for the subsequent development of the discipline. Adler and his followers elevated historical musicological research (which concerned mostly Western art music) over systematic musicological research, thus marginalizing study of music of non-Western cultures.

Late twentieth-century musicologists have gone beyond these now somewhat archaic distinctions and embraced the study of the cultural and sociological factors that provide context for understanding composers and their works. Genres of popular music and world music are studied with the same scholarly rigor formerly applied only to the study of Western art music. Similarly, studies of gender and sexuality in music have allowed scholars to examine Western art music from interesting new perspectives. The so-called Western musical canon of "great" composers, once limited to Bach, Beethoven, Brahms, Haydn, Mozart, Schubert, Schumann and Stravinsky, has now been broadened to include women composers and others from outside the realm of dead German males.[4]

And, the writings of musicologists such as Susan McClary, Joseph Kerman, Richard Taruskin, Carolyn Abbate, Pamela Potter, and the late Philip Brett have transformed the literature and inspired new generations of scholars.

SELECTED RESOURCES

Beard, David, and Kenneth Gloag. *Musicology: The Key Concepts.* Routledge Key Guides. London and New York: Routledge, 2005.

Brett, Philip, Elizabeth Wood, and Gary C. Thomas, eds. *Queering the Pitch: The New Gay and Lesbian Musicology.* 2nd ed. New York: Routledge, 2004.

Brook, Barry, Edward E. D. Downes, and Sherman Van Solkema, eds. *Perspectives in Musicology: The Inaugural Lectures of the Ph.D. Program in Music at the City University of New York.* New York: W. W. Norton, 1972.

Clarke, Eric, and Nicholas Cook, eds. *Empirical Musicology: Aims, Methods, Prospects.* New York: Oxford University Press, 2004.

Crist, Stephen A., and Roberta Montemorra Marvin, eds. *Historical Musicology: Sources, Methods, Interpretations.* Rochester, NY: University of Rochester Press, 2004.

Duckles, Vincent, et al. "Musicology." *Grove Music Online.* Edited by L. Macy. www.grovemusic.com.

Ewans, Michael, Rosalind Halton, and John A. Phillips, eds., *Music Research: New Directions for a New Century*. Cambridge: Cambridge Scholars Press, 2004.

Gibson, Sophie. *Aristoxenus of Tarentum and the Birth of Musicology*. London: Routledge, 2005.

Grout, Donald Jay. "Current Historiography and Music History." In *Studies in Music History: Essays for Oliver Strunk*, edited by Howard Powers, 23–40. Princeton, NJ: Princeton University Press, 1968.

Haydon, Glen. *Introduction to Musicology: A Survey of the Fields, Systematic and Historical, of Musical Knowledge and Research*. Prentice Hall Music Series. New York: Prentice Hall, 1941.

Higgins, Paula. "Women in Music, Feminist Criticism, and Guerilla Musicology: Reflections on Recent Polemics." *Nineteenth Century Music* 17, no. 2 (Autumn 1993): 174–92.

Holoman, D. Kern, and Claude V. Palisca, eds. *Musicology in the 1980s: Methods, Goals, Opportunities*. Da Capo Press Music Series. New York: Da Capo Press, 1982.

Kerman, Joseph. "American Musicology in the 1990s." *Journal of Musicology* 9, no. 2 (Spring 1991): 131–44.

———. *Contemplating Music: Challenges to Musicology*. Cambridge, MA: Harvard University Press, 1985.

Lang, Paul Henry. *Musicology and Performance*. Edited by Alfred Mann and George J. Buelow. New Haven and London: Yale University Press, 1997.

Pruett, James W., and Thomas P. Slavens. *Research Guide to Musicology*. Sources of Information in the Humanities 4. Chicago: American Library Association, 1985.

Solie, Ruth, ed. *Musicology and Difference: Gender and Sexuality in Music Scholarship*. Berkeley: University of California Press, 1993.

Steinzor, Curt Efram. *American Musicologists, c. 1890–1945: A Bio-Bibliographical Sourcebook to the Formative Period*. Music Reference Collection 17. Westport, CT: Greenwood Press, 1989.

Stevens, Denis. *Musicology: A Practical Guide*. Yehudi Menuhin Music Guides. New York: Schirmer Books, 1980.

Van den Toorn, Pieter C. "Politics, Feminism, and Contemporary Music Theory." *Journal of Musicology* 9, no. 3 (Summer 1991): 275–99.

ETHNOMUSICOLOGY

The opening of the canon in the twentieth century has also allowed increased attention to the field of ethnomusicology, or the study of music from a cross-cultural perspective. In *Ethnomusicology: An Introduction,* Helen Myers defines ethnomusicology as

> the study of music in its cultural context—the anthropology of music [the field] includes the study of folk music, Eastern art music and contemporary music in oral tradition as well as conceptual issues such as the origins of music, musical change, music as symbol, universals in music, the function of music in society, the comparisons of musical systems and the biological basis of music and dance.[5]

Multidisciplinary in nature, ethnomusicology often involves work of anthropologists, sociologists, and others who examine music from perspectives other than those used in study of Western art music. Ethnomusicologists conduct fieldwork to gain firsthand information on how music operates in a particular community. Documents produced by fieldwork include diaries, interviews, photographs, and, perhaps most important, audio and video recordings of musical performances. The latter are especially important when documenting music that lacks written notation.

SELECTED PUBLICATIONS

(See also Chapter 2: Bibliographies of Music Literature: Ethnomusicology, p. xx.)

Danielson, Virginia. "The Canon of Ethnomusicology: Is There One?" *Notes* 64, no. 2 (Dec. 2007): 223–31.

Myers, Helen. *Ethnomusicology: An Introduction.* The Norton/Grove Handbooks in Music. New York: W. W. Norton, 1992.

Shelemay, Kay, ed. *Ethnomusicological Theory and Method.* Garland Library of Readings in Ethnomusicology 2. New York: Garland Publishing, 1991.

Stone, Ruth M. *Theory for Ethnomusicology.* Upper Saddle River, NJ: Pearson Prentice Hall, 2008.

POPULAR MUSIC STUDIES

The so-called "new" musicology has also embraced the study of popular music, encouraging scholarly papers on genres from reggae to rap. The German philosopher Theodore Adorno (1903–69) is often cited as one of the catalysts for serious study of popular music, even though he was quite critical of it in his writings.[6] He did, however, advocate the type of sociological perspective on music that would open up possibilities for later research of popular music, as well as studies of gender and sexuality in music. As Susan McClary says of Adorno in her path-breaking book *Feminine Endings: Music, Gender, and Sexuality,*

> His work, while parochially grounded in the German canon of great composers from Bach to Schoenberg, provides the means for understanding how compositions of the tonal repertory are informed by the fundamental social tensions of their time. His conceptual framework opens up that sacrosanct canon to questions of great social and political urgency . . . Without my study of Adorno, I could not have undertaken any of the projects presented in this volume, for I would have had no way of getting beyond formalism.[7]

The formalization of popular music studies as a scholarly discipline in its own right took place in the last decades of the twentieth century, as evidenced by the establishment of the scholarly journal *Popular Music* in 1981, and the creation of the International Association for the Study of Popular Music (ISPAM) that same year.[8]

SELECTED PUBLICATIONS

Frith, Simon. *Performing Rites: On the Value of Popular Music.* Cambridge, MA: Harvard University Press, 1996.

Frith, Simon, and Andrew Goodwin. *On Record: Rock, Pop, and the Written Word.* New York: Pantheon Books, 1990.

Frith, Simon, Will Straw, and John Street, eds. *Cambridge Companion to Pop and Rock.*
   Cambridge Companions to Music. New York: Cambridge University Press, 2001.
Middleton, Richard, and Peter Manuel. "Popular Music," *Grove Music Online.* Edited by
   L. Macy. www.grovemusic.com. See also bibliography for this article.
Middleton, Richard. *Studying Popular Music.* Philadelphia: Open University Press, 1990.
Moore, Allan F., ed. *Analyzing Popular Music.* Cambridge: Cambridge University Press, 2003.
Moore, Allan F. *Rock: The Primary Text; Developing a Musicology of Rock.* 2nd ed.
   Aldershot, England: Ashgate Publishing, 2001.

JAZZ RESEARCH

As noted by Sherrie Tucker in her article on "Historiography: Jazz" in *Grove Music Online,* writings about jazz emerged alongside the development of the art form itself. Some of the earliest jazz histories, biographies, and discographies were published in the 1920s and 1930s. Eileen Southern delves even further back into jazz historiography in her examination of sources on the prehistory of jazz, including compilations and writings about slave songs, spirituals, and blues in her important article "A Study in Jazz Historiography: *The New Grove Dictionary of Jazz.*"[9]

Jazz scholarship has been greatly influenced by research into African American music and black music. It is also indelibly tied to discographical research and studies of early jazz recordings.

Important centers for jazz research include the Center for Black Music Research in Chicago (http://www.colum.edu/cbmr/), the Rutgers University Institute of Jazz Studies (http://newarkwww.rutgers.edu/IJS/), and the International Society for Jazz Research (Internationale Gesellschaft für Jazzforschung) in Graz, Austria (http://www.kug.ac.at/ijf/website_directory/society/overview.html). Each of these sites maintains useful pages on jazz resources.

SELECTED PUBLICATIONS

Floyd, Samuel A. *The Power of Black Music: Interpreting Its History from Africa to the
   United States.* New York: Oxford University Press, 1995.
Porter, Lewis. *Jazz: A Century of Change: Readings and New Essays.* New York: Schirmer
   Books, 1997.
Ramsey, Guthrie P., Jr. "Cosmopolitan or Provincial?: Ideology in Early Black Music
   Historiography." *Black Music Research Journal* 16, no. 1 (Spring 1996): 11–42.
Schiff, David. "Riffing the Canon." *Notes* 62, no. 2 (Dec. 2007): 216–22.
Southern, Eileen. "A Study in Jazz Historiography: *The New Grove Dictionary of Jazz.*"
   College Music Symposium 29 (1989): 123–33.
Tucker, Sherrie. "Historiography: Jazz." *Grove Music Online.* Edited by L. Macy. www
   .grovemusic.com.

GERMAN MUSICOLOGISTS IN PERSPECTIVE

Twentieth-century musicologists have approached the delicate subject of the relationship between German musicology and the Nazi regime. Pamela Potter has written extensively on this subject. Her work reveals the not-so-benign Nazi connections of some prominent musicologists, among them Karl Gustav Fellerer, Heinrich Besseler, Friederich Blume, and Heinrich Gerigk.

In a related area, recent scholarship has also shed new light on the careers of the musicians and musicologists who were forced to flee Germany under the Nazi regime.

SELECTED PUBLICATIONS

Brinkmann, Reinhold, and Christoph Wolff, eds. *Driven Into Paradise: The Musical Migration from Nazi Germany to the United States.* Berkeley: University of California Press, 1999.

Gerhard, Anselm. "Musicology in the Third Reich: A Preliminary Report." *Journal of Musicology* 18, no. 4 (Fall 2001): 517–43.

Potter, Pamela. *Most German of the Arts: Musicology and Society from the Weimar Republic to the End of Hitler's Reich.* New Haven: Yale University Press, 1998.

Vries, Willem de. *Sonderstab Musik: Music Confiscations by the Einsatzstab Reichsleiter Rosenberg under the Nazi Occupation of Western Europe.* Amsterdam: Amsterdam University Press, 1996.

SUMMARY

It is clear that the discipline of musicology has undergone a profound transformation in the last century. Its nineteenth-century German founders surely would have been surprised had they found themselves at the 2007 American Musicological Society conference, which featured sessions such as "Hip-Hop: Identity, Geography, and Voice" and "Posing the Question: Queer Performances and Popular Culture" alongside more traditional sessions such as "Collecting French Polyphony" or "Making Meaning in French Baroque Opera."

TEACHING OF MUSIC HISTORY AND MUSIC HISTORY TEXTBOOKS

Changes in the discipline of musicology and broadening of the so-called canon are also evidenced in the music history textbooks that are used to teach undergraduate and graduate courses in music. Whereas the 3rd edition of Donald Jay Grout's *A History of Western Music* (New York: W. W. Norton, 1973) included one mention, albeit a laudatory one, of Clara Schumann,[10] virtually all of the recently published music history textbooks include discussions of women composers alongside their male contemporaries.

Comparisons of the third edition of Grout and the seventh edition of the same title by J. Peter Burkholder, Grout, and Claude V. Palisca (New York: W. W. Norton, 2006)[11] reveal other changes in approach. As Burkholder summarizes in his preface:

> *A History of Western Music* is a story about where music in the Western tradition came from and how it has changed over the centuries from ancient times to the present. This new edition remains an account of

musical styles and genres, as Donald Jay Grout and Claude V. Palisca envisioned the book through the first six editions. But in retelling the tale, I have tried to bring several other themes to the fore: the people who created, performed, heard, and paid for this music; the choices they made and why they made them; what they valued most in the music; and how these choices reflected both tradition and innovation. I have also broadened the story to encompass more music from the Americas, including jazz and popular music, while preserving an emphasis on art music.[12]

The later edition is also much more user-friendly: whereas the 1973 edition had text, illustrations, and musical examples printed entirely in black and white, the 2006 edition has illustrations in color and a more attractive layout. Burkholder/Grout and similar one-volume music histories (see following section) used by music history classes typically come with companion score and recording anthologies.

Another significant twentieth-century music history text was Paul Henry Lang's *Music in Western Civilization,* first published in 1941.[13] A refugee from Nazi-occupied Europe, Lang (1901–91) became one of the most influential musicologists in America. He served as editor of *The Musical Quarterly* from 1945 to 1973 and taught legions of musicologists, among them Richard Taruskin, as a professor at Columbia University from 1939 to 1969. *Music in Western Civilization* was a monumental study of music within the broader context of Western culture. As Leon Botstein writes in his foreword to the 1997 reprint,

There are few books that are as comprehensive, as provocative, and as convincing about the importance of music as *Music in Western Civilization.* Even fewer can serve both the general reader and the educated reader in search of fresh insight and further knowledge. Whoever reads all or part of this imposing volume cannot fail to be inspired by it. The book engenders curiosity and, above all, the desire to listen. There can be no greater tribute to the work and life of a musician who devoted his career to teaching and writing.[14]

Music History in Series

Responding to the obvious challenges of describing thousands of years of music history in a single textbook, several publishers have also produced *series* of music history texts in which individual volumes cover a particular time period or style. Among those of particular importance from a musicological perspective was the six-volume *Norton History of Music Series* (1940–66), which included individual contributions by Gustav Reese (*Music in the Middle Ages,* 1940, and *Music in the Renaissance,* 1959), Manfred Bukofzer (*Music in the Baroque Era from Monteverdi to Bach,* 1947), Alfred Einstein (*Music in the Romantic Era,* 1947), and William W. Austin (*Music in the 20th Century, from Debussy through Stravinsky,* 1966).

Norton has issued a new series of texts in the *Norton Introduction to Music History Series,* which began in 1978. Other important music history series have been published by Prentice Hall, Oxford University Press, and Cambridge University Press. Each volume in the series published by Oxford (*The New Oxford History of Music*) and Cambridge (*The Cambridge History of Music*) is composed of essays by various scholars. Volumes in the *New Oxford* series are also renowned for the strength of their bibliographies, which include references to editions of music, as well as references to books and articles on a topic. Also of special note is the Prentice Hall *Music and Society* series: each volume in this series consists of essays by scholars about the cultural and societal factors that influenced music during the time period.[15]

Twenty-First Century Landmark?

Richard Taruskin's *Oxford History of Western Music* (New York: Oxford University Press, 2005) represents an extraordinary exception to the approaches taken by standard music history texts. In six hefty volumes, the *Oxford History of Western Music* is not the type of source that can be placed in a student's backpack or used easily with a companion score anthology. Its value as a reference tool is evidenced by its inclusion in the *Oxford Music Online* portal, which also includes *Grove Music Online*. Volume 6 of the print set serves as a resource guide to the entire book and includes a detailed chronology, bibliography (of books in English), and index of musical examples.

Susan McClary describes Taruskin's achievement in her review article "The World According to Taruskin":

> It should seem clear to anyone who has followed the course of musicology since the late 1980s that Taruskin's *Oxford History of Western Music* stands as nothing less than the triumph of the New Musicology (if we must continue to use that term of abuse). For here we find a comprehensive narrative history with all those hard-fought issues—political accounts of canon formation, the contributions and silencing of women throughout music history, the identification of composers as gay, and readings of scores that address their ideological content (a project Adornean in all but acknowledgement)—offered as if entirely reasonable.[16]

And she concludes, "If the OHWM does not lend itself to easy adoption as a text book, it certainly ought to become the principal guide for all instructors of the 'history survey.' Nowhere else can one find such a compelling way of weaving together the development of Western music within the larger framework of cultural history."[17]

SPECIFIC MUSIC HISTORIES PUBLISHED SINCE 1990

The list of titles in this section is quite selective. As any listing will inevitably become out of date, it is advisable to rely on library catalogs to locate sources. Relevant subject headings to locate music histories in library catalogs are

For general music histories:

MUSIC—HISTORY AND CRITICISM

For music histories of specific periods:

MUSIC—17TH CENTURY—HISTORY AND CRITICISM
MUSIC—18TH CENTURY—HISTORY AND CRITICISM

For music histories of specific countries and/or specific periods:

MUSIC—FRANCE—PARIS—19TH CENTURY—HISTORY
AND CRITICISM

SELECTED GENERAL SURVEY HISTORIES SINCE 1990 SINGLE AUTHOR

Bonds, Mark Evan. *A History of Music in Western Culture.* 2nd ed. Upper Saddle River, NJ: Prentice Hall, 2006.

Burkholder, J. Peter, Donald J. Grout, and Claude V. Palisca. *A History of Western Music.* 7th ed. New York: W. W. Norton, 2005.

Poultney, David. *Studying Music History: Learning, Reasoning, and Writing About Music History and Literature.* 2nd ed. Englewood Cliffs, NJ: Prentice Hall, 1996.

Seaton, Douglass. *Ideas and Styles in the Western Musical Tradition.* 2nd ed. Boston, MA: McGraw-Hill, 2007.

Stolba, Marie. *The Development of Western Music: A History.* 3rd ed. Boston, MA: McGraw-Hill, 1998.

Taruskin, Richard. *The Oxford History of Western Music.* 6 vols. New York: Oxford University Press, 2005.

INDIVIDUAL VOLUMES WITHIN SERIES

Atlas, Allan. *Renaissance Music: Music in Western Europe, 1400–1600.* The Norton Introduction to Music History. New York: W. W. Norton, 1998.

Buelow, George J., ed. *The Late Baroque Era: From the 1680s to 1740.* Music and Society. Englewood Cliffs, NJ: Prentice Hall, 1993.

Carter, Tim, and John Butt, eds. *The Cambridge History of Seventeenth-Century Music.* The Cambridge History of Music. Cambridge: Cambridge University Press, 2005.

Christensen, Tom, ed. *The Cambridge History of Western Music Theory.* The Cambridge History of Music. Cambridge: Cambridge University Press, 2002.

Cook, Nicholas, and Anthony Pople, eds. *The Cambridge History of Twentieth-Century Music.* The Cambridge History of Music. Cambridge: Cambridge University Press, 2004.

Crocker, Richard, and David Hiley, eds. *The Early Middle Ages to 1300.* 2nd ed. New Oxford History of Music 2. Oxford: Oxford University Press, 1990.

McKinnon, James, ed. *Antiquity and the Middle Ages: From Ancient Greece to the 15th Century.* Music and Society. Englewood Cliffs, NJ: Prentice Hall, 1991.

Morgan, Robert P., ed. *Modern Times.* Music and Society. Englewood Cliffs, NJ: Prentice Hall, 1993.

Nicholls, David, ed. *The Cambridge History of American Music.* The Cambridge History of Music. Cambridge: Cambridge University Press, 1998.

Perkins, Leeman L. *Music in the Age of the Renaissance.* New York: W. W. Norton, 1999.

Price, Curtis A., ed. *The Early Baroque Era: From the Later 16th Century to the 1660s.* Music and Society. Englewood Cliffs, NJ: Prentice Hall, 1992.

Ringer, Alexander, ed. *The Early Romantic Era: Between Revolutions: 1789 and 1848.* Music and Society. Englewood Cliffs, NJ: Prentice Hall, 1991.

Samson, Jim, ed. *The Cambridge History of Nineteenth-Century Music.* The Cambridge History of Music. Cambridge: Cambridge University Press, 2001.

_____. *The Late Romantic Era: From the Mid-19th Century to World War I.* Music and Society. Englewood Cliffs, NJ: Prentice Hall, 1991.

Strohm, Reinhard, and Bonnie J. Blackburn, eds. *Music as Concept and Practice in the Late Middle Ages.* 2nd ed. The New Oxford History of Music 3, part 1. Oxford: Oxford University Press, 2001.

SELECTED PERIOD SOURCEBOOKS

Sadie, Julie Ann, ed. *Companion to Baroque Music.* New York: Schirmer, 1991.

Knighton, Tess, and David Fallows, eds. *Companion to Medieval and Renaissance Music.* New York: Schirmer Books; Maxwell Macmillan International, 1992.

SOURCE READINGS

Source readings are collections of primary source documents, such as correspondence and musicians' writings, which are brought together in a volume to shed light on a particular topic or historical period. Although usually published in translation and with explanatory notes or comments, these historical documents present history in its most objective form. Source reading collections should be used alongside standard music history texts, so students may gain contemporaneous perspectives from primary source documents written in a particular historical period.

Oliver Strunk's *Source Readings in Music History from Classical Antiquity Through the Romantic Era* (New York: W. W. Norton, 1950) was the standard source reading text in music history classes for many years; it was revised and updated in a new edition by Leo Treitler in 1998. Piero Weiss and Richard Taruskin compiled their 1984 source reading collection, *Music in the Western World: A History in Documents* as a tool for both nonspecialists (i.e., students in music appreciation classes) and specialists (i.e., music majors).

Following is a selected list of general and special topic source reading collections:

Albright, Daniel. *Modernism and Music: An Anthology of Sources.* Chicago: University of Chicago Press, 2004.

Alexander, J. Heywood, ed. *To Stretch Our Ears: A Documentary History of America's Music.* New York: W. W. Norton, 2002.

Bent, Ian. *Music Analysis in the Nineteenth Century.* 2 vols. Cambridge: Cambridge University Press, 1994.

Haskell, Harry, ed. *The Attentive Listener: Three Centuries of Music Criticism.* Princeton, NJ: Princeton University Press, 1996.

MacClintock, Carol, ed. *Readings in the History of Music in Performance.* Bloomington: Indiana University Press, 1979.

Mark, Michael L., ed. *Music Education: Source Readings form Ancient Greece to Today.* 2nd ed. New York: Routledge, 2002.

Music, David W. *Hymnology: A Collection of Source Readings.* Lanham, MD: Scarecrow Press, 1996.

Neuls-Bates, Carol, ed. *Women in Music: An Anthology of Source Readings from the Middle Ages to the Present.* New York: Harper & Row, 1982.

Southern, Eileen. *Readings in Black American Music.* 2nd ed. New York: W. W. Norton, 1983.

Strunk, W. Oliver, ed. *Source Readings in Music History.* Rev. ed. by Leo Treitler. New York: W. W. Norton, 1998. Individual chapters also published separately as

   Mathiesen, Thomas J., ed. *Greek Views of Music.*

   McKinnon, James, ed. *The Early Christian Period and the Latin Middle Ages.*

   Tomlinson, Gary, ed. *The Renaissance.*

   Murata, Margaret, ed. *The Baroque Era.*

   Allanbrook, Wye Jamison, ed. *The Late Eighteenth Century.*

   Solie, Ruth, ed. *The Nineteenth Century.*

   Morgan, Robert P., ed. *The Twentieth Century.*

Weiss, Piero. *Opera: A History in Documents.* New York and Oxford: Oxford University Press, 2002.

Weiss, Piero, and Richard Taruskin. *Music in the Western World: A History in Documents.* 2d ed. Australia; Belmont, CA: Thomson/Schirmer, 2008.

ORAL HISTORY

Among Thomas Edison's 1878 list of 10 uses for his new invention of sound recording was "The Family Record — registering sayings, reminiscences, etc., by members of a family in their own voices, and the last words of dying persons."[18] When the tape recorder was invented half a century later, musicologists found a way to preserve music's own family record through the practice of oral history.

Vivian Perlis has led this charge, first with her published oral history of Charles Ives[19] and then with the establishment of the Oral History American Music Center at Yale University: http://www.yale.edu/oham/frameabout.html. For additional information about this project and oral history of American music in general, see

Perlis, Vivian, and Libby Van Cleve. *Composers' Voices from Ives to Ellington: An Oral History of American Music.* New Haven: Yale University Press, 2005.

MUSIC ICONOGRAPHY

"A Picture Is Worth a Thousand Words"

Music iconography is the study of representations of music in works of art. Iconographical evidence provides important insights into performance practices of earlier periods through depiction of instruments and ensembles. It is closely related to organology (the study of musical instruments, see pgs. 136–138) and is an important tool for ethnomusicologists studying music of non-Western cultures.

The *Grove Music Online* article on "Iconography" by Tillman Seebass provides an overview of the field, its historical development, and its methodology. Iconographical evidence must be carefully used in the context of the artist's reason for creating the work: a representation of a musical instrument or ensemble in a painting may not necessarily be an accurate portrayal. As pioneering iconography specialist Emanuel Winternitz wrote,

> Before the invention of photography, most visual depictions occurred in works of art. Since an artistic portrayal of an object may differ in many ways from a realistic sketch or a snapshot, familiarity with the idiosyncrasies of the individual artists is necessary in order to translate its altered image, its style-bound rendering, into information that the music historian can accept as reliable "visual evidence" for his own purposes. . . . We have to think of the various forms of perspective as practiced in various artistic climates, from Egyptian wall paintings to Renaissance intarsias to Baroque cupola frescoes, to immediately become aware of some of the basic differences in rendering instruments or players.[20]

Winternitz then goes on to extol the value of iconographical research when done carefully: "It helps to free musicology from that isolation into which so many specialized branches of research have fallen in our overspecializing times. It makes us study music within its socio-cultural context, uniting it with its sister arts, particularly the visual arts."[21]

The following list includes a selection of some of the numerous book-length sources that serve as resources for the *general* study of music iconography. It includes sources with illustrations (such as Kinsky, Besseler and Schneider, Bowles, and Montagu), as well as sources *about* the study of the discipline (such as Crane's bibliography, Heck, McKinnon, Seebass, and the periodicals *Imago Musicae* and *Music in Art*). Additional resources on the general subject of music iconography may be found in library catalogs under the subject heading MUSIC IN ART.

Other book-length sources of music iconography not mentioned in the list include iconographical studies of individual composers, such as Ernst Burger's *Franz Liszt: A Chronicle of His Life in Pictures and Documents* or *Arnold Schönberg, 1874–1951: Lebensgeschichte in Begegnungen.*[22] These sources may be located in library catalogs under the subject heading for the composer followed by subdivision PICTORIAL WORKS, for example, Lizst, Franz, 1811–1866 — Pictorial Works.

The international project RIdIM (Répertoire International d'Iconographie Musicale) was founded in 1971 to assist in the systematic study of music iconography through classification of music images in works of art found in museum collections around the world. A sister project of RISM and RILM, RIdIM is a joint project of the International Association of Music Libraries (IAML), the International Musicological Society (IMS), and the International Council of Museums (ICM). The RIdIM database was developed to provide access to information on musical images via searches by artist, year of creation, object, and museum location. It will also link to other image databases, such as ARTstor.[23]

Besseler, Heinrich, and Max Schneider. *Musikgeschichte in Bildern.* 18 vols. Leipzig: Deutscher Verlag für Musik, 1961–90.

Blažekovic, Zdravko, ed. *Music in Art: Iconography as a Source for Music History. Ninth Annual Conference of the Research Center for Music Iconography, Commemorating the*

20th Anniversary of the Death of Emmanuel Winternitz (1898–1983), New York City 5–8 November 2003. New York: The Research Center for Music Iconography, 2003.

Bowles, Edmund A. *Music Ensembles in Festival Books 1500–1800: An Iconographical and Documentary Survey.* Ann Arbor, MI: UMI Research Press, 1989.

————. "Music in Court Festivals of State: Festival Books as Sources for Performance Practices." *Early Music* 28, no. 3 (August 2000): 421–43.

Crane, Frederick. *A Bibliography of the Iconography of Music.* Iowa City: University of Iowa School of Music, 1971. Also available online: http://web.gc.cuny.edu/rcmi/CraneBIbliography1971.pdf.

Gratl, Franz. "Iconography of Music, 1976–1995: A Bibliography" *Imago Musicae* XIV/XV (1997/98); Natter, Martina, and Franz Gratl, "Bibliographia 1995–2000" *Imago Musicae* XVIII/XIX (2001/02): 155–242.

Heck, Thomas. *Picturing Performance: The Iconography of the Performing Arts in Concept and Practice.* Rochester, NY: University of Rochester Press, 1999.

Imago Musicae. Basel: Bärenreiter-Verlag; Durham, NC: Duke University Press, 1985–.

Kinsky, Georg. *A History of Music in Pictures.* London: J. M. Dent, 1937.

McKinnon, James W. "Iconography." In *Musicology in the 1980s: Methods, Goals, Opportunities.* Edited by D. Kern Holoman and Claude V. Palisca, 79–93. New York: Da Capo Press, 1982.

Montagu, Jeremy, and Gwen Montagu. *Minstrels & Angels: Carvings of Musicians in Medieval English Churches.* Fallen Leaf Reference Books in Music 33. Berkeley, CA: Fallen Leaf Press, 1998.

Music in Art: International Journal for Music Iconography 1999–. (Continuation of *RIdIM/RCMI Newsletter*)

RIdIM/RCMI Inventory of Music Iconography. 1986–.

(RCMI = Research Center for Music Iconography at the City University of New York; see also other publications at http://web.gc.cuny.edu/rcmi/ridim.htm.)
  no. 1. National Gallery of Art, Washington
  no. 2. Art Institute of Chicago
  no. 3. Pierpont Morgan Library: Medieval and Renaissance Manuscripts
  no. 7. The Frick Collection, New York.
  no. 8. The Cleveland Museum of Art
(Inventories of music iconography located in respective museum collections.)

RIdIM (Répertoire International d'Iconographie Musicale): http://www.ridim.org/.

Seebass, Tilman. "Iconography," *Grove Music Online.* Edited by L. Macy. www.grovemusic.com.

————. "Iconography." In *Ethnomusicology: An Introduction,* edited by Helen Myers, 238–44. The Norton/Grove Handbooks in Music. New York: W. W. Norton, 1992.

Slim, H. Colin. *Painting Music in the Sixteenth Century: Essays in Iconography.* Variorum Collected Studies Series. Aldershot, England; Brookfield, VT: Ashgate Publishing, 2002.

Winternitz, Emanuel. *Musical Instruments and Their Symbolism in Western Art.* New York: W. W. Norton, 1967.

————. "The Iconology of Music: Potentials and Pitfalls." In *Perspectives in Musicology: The Inaugural Lectures of the Ph.D. Program in Music at the City University of New York,* edited by Barry S. Brook, Edward O. D. Downes, and Sherman Van Solkema, 80–90. New York: W. W. Norton, 1972.

ORGANOLOGY

Defined by Laurence Libin in *Grove Music Online* as "The study of musical instruments in terms of their history and social function, design, construction and relation to performance,"[24] *organology* is the general term used for the classification and study of musical instruments. Its cousin term *organography* refers more specifically to the description of musical instruments. Both terms are derived from the Latin *organum*, which, in turn, is derived from the Greek *organon*, or "instrument." A fuller description of the etymology and use of these terms is found in *Grove Music Online* in Libin's article and in the article "Instruments, Classification of" by Klaus P. Wachsmann, Margaret J. Kartomi, and others.

Another valuable source on the historical development of organology as a discipline is Geneviève Dornon's article "Organology" in *Ethnomusicology: An Introduction*, ed. Helen Myers (New York and London: W. W. Norton, 1992), 245–300. Myers's book also includes a reprint of the English translation of Hornbostel-Sachs's original treatise (pp. 444–61).

One of the earliest dictionaries of musical instruments was Michael Praetorius's *De Organographia*, part two of *Syntagma Muscium*, 1618. A fuller description of this source is found under "Dictionaries and Encyclopedias: Special Subjects—Musical Instruments," p. 84.

The New Grove Dictionary of Musical Instruments (1984), our major English-language reference tool on musical instruments, is sometimes referred to as "OrganaGrove." Most of the articles from this source are found in *Grove Music Online*.

Classification Systems: Hornbostel-Sachs

Study of musical instruments worldwide requires the use of classification systems to describe instruments in their own terms, rather than through comparisons with familiar Western instruments. Victor-Charles Mahillon (1841–1924), curator of the instrument museum of the Brussels Conservatory, was an early developer of such a system. The system most in use today (and based in part on Mahillon's work) is the Hornbostel-Sachs classification system. Developed in 1914 by musicologists Erich M. von Hornbostel (1877–1935) and Curt Sachs (1881–1959),[25] this system classifies musical instruments according to how sound is produced. In doing so, it removes hierarchical comparisons that may be made when describing, for example, a non-Western stringed instrument in terms of how it compares to a familiar Western stringed instrument, such as a violin or cello.

Hornbostel-Sachs divides instrument groups into four categories:[26] Within each category, instruments are further subdivided via use of the Dewey Decimal system.

1. Idiophones: "General term for musical instruments that produce their sound by setting up vibrations in the substance of the instrument itself."
2. Membranophones: "General term for musical instruments that produce their sound by setting up vibrations in a stretched membrane"
3. Chordophones: "General term for musical instruments that produce their sound by setting up vibrations in stretched strings"

4. Aerophones: "General term for musical instruments that produce their sound by setting up vibrations in a body of air."[27]

Some scholars have proposed a new category for electronically produced sounds titled *Electrophones,* or "General term for instruments that produce vibrations that must be passed through a loudspeaker before they are heard as sound."[28]

An excellent Web site with definitions and illustrations of Hornbostel-Sachs classification is found online in the *Virginia Tech Multimedia Music Dictionary:* http://www.music.vt.edu/musicdictionary/appendix/instruments/instrumentmain .html.[29]

SOURCES OF INFORMATION

Brown, Howard Mayer, with Frances Palmer. "Aerophone," "Chordophone," "Idiophone," "Membranophone." *Grove Music Online.* Edited by L. Macy. www.grovemusic.com.

Campbell, Murray, Clive Greated, and Arnold Myers. *Musical Instruments: History, Technology, and Performance of Instruments of Western Music.* Oxford: Oxford University Press, 2004.

Cole, Richard, and Ed Schwartz. "Comprehensive Table of Musical Instrument Classifications." *Virginia Tech Multimedia Music Dictionary.* http://www.music.vt.edu/musicdictionary/appendix/instruments/instrumentmain.html.

Dornon, Geneviève. "Organology." In *Ethnomusicology: An Introduction,* edited by Helen Myers. 245–300. The Norton/Grove Handbooks in Music. New York and London: W. W. Norton, 1992.

Hornbostel, Erich, and Curt Sachs. "Systematic der Musikinstrumente" *Zeitschrift für Ethnologie* xlvi (1914): 553–90; English translation by Anthony Baines and K. P. Wachsmann, "Classification of Musical Instruments." *Galpin Society Journal* xiv (1961): 3–29. Reprint, *Ethnomusicology: An Introduction,* edited by Helen Myers, 444–61. The Norton/Grove Handbooks in Music. London and New York: W. W. Norton, 1992.

Libin, Laurence, "Organology." *Grove Music Online.* Edited by L. Macy. www .grovemusic.com.

Wachsmann, Klaus P., Margaret J. Kartomi, et al. "Instruments, Classification of," *Grove Music Online.* Edited by L. Macy. www.grovemusic.com.

Collections of Musical Instruments

Detailed study of musical instruments obviously requires access to the instruments themselves. Many libraries and museums have extensive collections of musical instruments, encompassing Western historic instruments or modern replicas, and/or

Why Is It Important to Study Musical Instruments of the Past?

Study of musical instruments is a critical component of historic performance practice. One cannot accurately re-create works of the past without an understanding of the instruments for which they were written.

non-Western instruments. Sources of information on musical instrument collections include

American Musical Instrument Society (AMIS). http://www.amis.org/.

Coover, James B. *Musical Instrument Collections: Catalogs and Cognate Literature.* Detroit Studies in Music Bibliography 47. Detroit: Information Coordinators, 1981.

Duckles, Vincent H., and Ida Reed. "Catalogs of Music Instrument Collections." In *Music Reference and Research Materials: An Annotated Bibliography,* 5th ed., 497–514. New York: Schirmer Books, 1997.

International Committee of Musical Instrument Museums and Collections (CIMCIM). http://www.music.ed.ac.uk/euchmi/cimcim/. Includes "CIMCIM International Directory of Musical Instrument Collections."

Libin, Laurence, "Instruments, Collections of." *Grove Music Online.* Edited by L. Macy. www.grovemusic.com.

Studies of individual instruments frequently have the most extensive information about the instrument's history and development. Such titles include Walter Kolneder's *Amadeus Book of the Violin: Construction, History and Music* (Portland, OR: Amadeus Press, 1998), Nancy Toff's, *The Flute Book: A Complete Guide for Students and Performers* (New York: Charles Scribner's Sons, 1985), or Will Jansen's five-volume, *The Bassoon: Its History, Construction, Makers, Players, and Music* (Buren: Frits Knuf, 1978). Cambridge University Press has published several collections on instruments within its *Cambridge Companion to Music Series,* including *The Cambridge Companion to the Cello, The Cambridge Companion to the Clarinet, The Cambridge Companion to the Guitar, The Cambridge Companion to the Piano, The Cambridge Companion to the Recorder, Saxophone, Violin,* and similar titles. References to these sources may be found in library catalogs under the name of the instrument as subject [VIOLIN] or [VIOLIN—HISTORY], as well as in the bibliographies attached to the *Grove Music Online* article on the respective instrument. See also dictionary sources under names of individual instruments in Chapter 3: Dictionaries and Encyclopedias: Special Subjects, pp. 78–94. Of particular note in this genre of sources are pictorial studies of instruments with lavish color reproductions of the instruments, especially important for identification of rare stringed instruments. Examples include the book by Karel Jalovec listed in Chapter 3, p. 93.

CHRONOLOGIES AND CALENDARS

"Just the facts, ma'am, just the facts"

Chronologies and calendars present listings of events in some sort of chronological order, year by year or day by day. As such, they serve as outline, or skeletal, histories of a subject. Loewenberg's *Annals of Opera, 1597–1940* demonstrates how history may be understood from listings of events. Information on each opera is presented under the year in which it was premiered, which allows readers to gain a sense of contextual history. For example, under 1791, the year that Mozart's last operas *La Clemenza di Tito* and *Die Zauberflöte* were premiered, we also see premieres of operas by Stephen Storace (*The Siege of Belgrade*),

Dittersdorf (*Der Gutsherr*), and Grétry (*Guillaume Tell*). It is then up to historians to arrive at any conclusions from this confluence of events.

Although chronologies are assumed to be an objective presentation of facts, it must be stressed that they are compiled by editors who select these facts for inclusion and sometimes present biased editorial opinions on them. The master of this technique was, of course, the venerable Nicholas Slonimsky (1894–1995; see also p. 76), compiler of *Music Since 1900,* one of our most important chronologies of twentieth-century music. See, for example, Slonimsky's entry on the death of French composer Cécile Chaminade on April 13, 1944: "Cécile Chaminade, French composeress of ingratiatingly harmonious piano pieces adorned with endearingly sentimental titles, possessing a perennial appeal to frustrated spinsters and emotional piano teachers, dies in war-darkened Monte Carlo at the hopeless age of 86."[30]

It is also important to see musical events in the context of world events and other significant cultural activities. Charles Hall's books present this information along with chronologies of musical events. *A History of Western Music,* 7th ed., by Burkholder, Grout, and Palisca, includes time lines of concurrent events in each chapter.

Following is a selection of music-specific chronologies and calendars published in book form. There are many chronologies and time lines available on the Web, both general and music specific; as they change frequently, users are advised to locate them via Web searches.

Annals of the Metropolitan Opera: The Complete Chronicle of Performances and Artists.
 Gerald Fitzgerald, Editor-in-Chief. New York: Metropolitan Opera Guild; Boston: G. K.
 Hall, 1989. Available online, Metropolitan Opera Web site: www.metopera.org under
 "Archives": http://66.187.153.86/archives/frame.htm.
Burbank, Richard. *Twentieth Century Music.* New York: Facts on File, 1984.
Gangwere, Blanche. *Music History during the Renaissance Period, 1425–1520: A Documented Chronology.* New York: Greenwood Press, 1991.
_____. *Music History During the Renaissance Period, 1520–1550: A Documented Chronology.* Music Reference Collection 85. Westport, CT: Praeger, 2004.
_____. *Music History from the Later Roman through the Gothic Periods, 313–1425: A Documented Chronology.* Westport, CT: Greenwood Press, 1986.
Hall, Charles J. *A Chronicle of American Music, 1600–1995.* New York: Schirmer Books;
 London: Prentice Hall International, 1996.
_____. *Chronology of Western Classical Music.* Vol. 1: *1751–1900.* Vol. 2: *1901–2000.*
 New York: Routledge, 2002.
_____. *An Eighteenth Century Musical Chronicle: Events 1750–1799.* New York:
 Greenwood Press, 1990.
_____. *A Nineteenth Century Musical Chronicle: Events 1800–1899.* New York:
 Greenwood Press, 1989.
_____. *A Twentieth Century Musical Chronicle: Events 1900–1988.* New York:
 Greenwood Press, 1989.
 Each of Hall's books presents listings of musical events year by year, along
  with subsections on "World Events" and "Cultural Highlights" for the year.
Hoffmann, Frank W. *Chronology of American Popular Music, 1900–2000.* New York:
 Routledge, 2008.

Johnson, H. Earle. *First Performances in America to 1900: Works with Orchestra.* Detroit: Published for the College Music Society by Information Coordinators, 1979.

Loewenberg, Alfred. *Annals of Opera 1597–1940.* 3rd rev. ed. Genève: Societas Bibliographica, 1978.

Manson, Adele P. *Calendar of Music and Musicians.* Metuchen, NJ: Scarecrow Press, 1981.

> Manson presents a day-by-day chronology of musical events. One may see, for example, that on February 17, composer Archangelo Corelli was born (1653), as was singer Marian Anderson (1902). Verdi's *Un Ballo in Maschera* was premiered (1859), as was Franck's Symphony in D minor. Such a chronology is especially useful for those seeking to program concerts or broadcasts in connection with specific events or anniversaries. It should be noted that one may now locate such information through a full text search of *Grove Music Online.*

Mattfeld, Julius. *Variety Music Cavalcade, 1620–1969: A Chronology of Vocal and Instrumental Music Popular in the United States.* 3rd ed. Englewood Cliffs, NJ: Prentice Hall, 1971.

Schering, Arnold. *Tabellen zur Musikgeschichte, ein Hilfsbuch beim Studium der Musikgeschichte.* 4th ed. Leipzig: Breitkopf & Härtel, 1934.

Selfridge-Field, Eleanor. *New Chronology of Venetian Opera and Related Genres, 1660–1760.* Calendar of Venetian Opera. Stanford: Stanford University Press, 2007.

Slonimsky, Nicolas, and Laura Kuhn. *Music Since 1900.* 6th ed. New York: Schirmer Reference, 2001.

Sokol, Martin L. *The New York City Opera: An American Adventure, With the Complete Annals (1944–1981) compiled by George Mayer and Martin Sokol.* New York: Macmillan, 1981.

Warner, Jay. *On This Day in Black Music History.* Milwaukee: Hal Leonard, 2006.

BIOGRAPHIES

We read life stories of musicians to learn about their lives and to gain insight into their works. Biographies of musicians are found in many places in the literature, from entries in dictionaries and encyclopedias to extensive multivolume studies of individual composers. Although thousands of book-length biographies of composers have been published since the first such biographical monograph, John Mainwaring's 1760 *Life of Handel,* it is only in recent years that scholars have examined the art of music biography itself. *The New Grove Dictionary of Music and Musicians,* 2nd edition (2001), was the first *Grove* to include a separate entry on Biography in its article by Maynard Solomon.

There are several distinct categories of biographical literature on musicians:

- *Documentary:* Documentary biographies reveal the life of a person through the compilation of original source documents. Examples include Otto Erich Deutsch's documentary biographies of Handel, Mozart, and Schubert; *The New Bach Reader: A Life of Johann Sebastian Bach in Letters and Documents;* or H. C. Robbins-Landon's five-volume *Haydn: Chronicle and Works.*[31] Similar to the Source Readings described on pp. 132–133, these books provide facts about the composer through presentation of primary source documents.

Letters: Collections of composer letters may be categorized as documentary biographies. The documentary biographies previously noted may provide excerpts from selected letters; however, complete correspondence collections for composers, whether published in translation (e.g., Emily Anderson's English-language translations of Beethoven and Mozart letters) or in the original language (e.g., Deutsch and Bauer's complete edition of Mozart correspondence *Mozart: Briefe und Aufzeichnungen*)[32] are important primary source documents for study of composers and their works.

- **Life-Work, Work-Life Studies:** Most musician biographies fall into the largest category of life and work studies, with varying degrees of musicological detail. Biographers have taken different approaches to the challenge of presenting an artist's work in the context of his or her life, from the more traditional separation of a discussion of "Life" following a discussion of "Works" seen in sources such as Alfred Einstein's biography of Mozart, *Mozart: His Character, His Work,*[33] with presentation of Mozart "The Man" followed by "The Musician," to the integrated approaches taken by more recently published biographies in which works are discussed within the full context of the subject's life. (It should be noted that *Grove Music Online* composer biography entries usually separate discussion of life from that of works.)

  Some of the integrated discussions of life and works have also incorporated psychoanalytical approaches to their subjects. This can be seen in Maynard Solomon's biographies of Beethoven and Mozart; in psychoanalyst Dr. Stuart Feder's biography of Ives; and in Peter Oswald's biographies of Robert Schumann, Vaclav Nijinsky, and Glenn Gould.[34]

  Biographical literature published in the late twentieth and early twenty-first centuries is also filled with multiauthor collections of essays on the subject's life and works. Among these are the published proceedings of Bard Music Festivals such as *Brahms and His World* and *Bartók and His World;* the *Cambridge Companion to Music Series;* and, Greenwood Press compilations such as *The Mendelssohn Companion, The Liszt Companion,* and the *Richard Strauss Companion.*[35] In all of these cases, the composer's life and works are illuminated through contributions by a number of different scholars.

- **Autobiographies:** When she took a line from one of her most famous songs in titling her book *Between Each Line of Pain and Glory: My Life Story* (New York: Hyperion, 1997), Gladys Knight joined generations of musicians who chose to tell their own stories in the form of autobiography.[36] Certainly valuable as research sources, autobiographies must always be used with caution, as the subject is the least objective observer of his or her own life. Music literature is filled with examples of ghostwritten autobiographies, when the storyteller is not really the subject, but rather an individual seeking to cast the subject in a certain light. Legendary examples of this phenomenon may be seen in Igor Stravinsky's autobiographical writings, cowritten (and largely influenced) by Robert Craft, and the controversial *Testimony* of Shostakovich by Simon Volkov.[37]

The works cited here provide intellectual commentary on the art of musical biography.

Selected Sources about Biography

Lenneberg, Hans. *Witnesses and Scholars: Studies in Musical Biography.* Musicology 5. New York: Gordon and Breach, 1988.

Pekacz, Jolanta T. *Musical Biography: Towards New Paradigms.* Aldershot, England; Burlington, VT: Ashgate Publishing, 2006.

Solomon, Maynard. "Biography." *Grove Music Online.* Edited by L. Macy. www.grovemusic.com.

Locating and Evaluating Composer Biographies

It would be impossible to provide even a selected listing of composer biographies, and such a list would go out of date almost immediately. Biographical studies may be located via the following tools:

- Search library catalogs under composer name as SUBJECT; also browse through subject subdivisions to locate more focused studies on individual works or genres. For example, studies of Schubert and his works may be found under some of the following subject headings:

  SCHUBERT, FRANZ, 1797–1828
  SCHUBERT, FRANZ, 1797–1828 — CRITICISM AND INTERPRETATION
  SCHUBERT, FRANZ, 1797–1828 — PIANO MUSIC
  SCHUBERT, FRANZ, 1797–1828 — SCHÖNE MULLERIN
  SCHUBERT, FRANZ, 1797–1828 — SCHWANENGESANG
  SCHUBERT, FRANZ, 1797–1828 — SONG CYCLES

  (See Chapter 1, pp. 25–26 for further discussion of subject searching in library catalogs.)
- *Grove Music Online* bibliographies
- Composer resource manuals, guides to research, and other composer-specific tools, listed in Chapter 4. In some cases these resources contain valuable information about the biographical literature on a composer. See, for example, the chapter on "Biographies of J. S. Bach" in Daniel Melamed and Michael Marissen, *An Introduction to Bach Studies* (New York: Oxford University Press, 1988), or Michael Saffle's commentary on Liszt biographies in his *Franz Liszt: A Guide to Research,* 2nd ed. (New York: Routledge, 2004).

Evaluation

There are numerous biographical studies on most of the major composers of Western art music. It is therefore important for researchers to understand the role and special nature of each biography. As noted earlier, composer resource guides and other bibliographic tools provide guidance from scholars, as do book reviews, especially those published in scholarly journals.

NOTES

1. "Report of the Committee on Graduate Studies." *Journal of the American Musicological Society* 8, no. 2 (Summer 1955), 153. The rest of this quote reads: "The musicologist is a research scholar, and he aims primarily at knowledge about music. With this primacy he differs from the composer, who is an artist concerned primarily with the creation of music, and from the performer, who is an artist primarily concerned with its practical realization."

2. Don Michael Randel, "Musicology," *Harvard Dictionary of Music,* 4th ed. (Cambridge, MA: Harvard University Press, 2003), 542.

3. Vincent Duckles, et al, "Musicology: iv. Historical and Systematic Musicology," *Grove Music Online,* ed. L. Macy. www.grovemusic.com.

4. For further discussion on the subject of musical canons, see Jim Samson, "Canon," *Grove Music Online,* ed. L. Macy. www.grovemusic.com; Marcia Citron, *Gender and the Musical Canon* (Cambridge: Cambridge University Press, 1993); Citron's "Women and the Western Art Canon: Where Are We Now"; David Schiff, "Rifting the Canon"; Virginia Danielson, "The Canon of Ethnomusicology: Is There One?"; Edward Komara, "Culture Wars, Canonicity, and *A Basic Music Library;*" in *Notes* 64, no. 2 (December 2007): 209–247. The latter articles were based on papers presented at the February 2007 joint meeting of the Music Library Association and Society for American Music in Pittsburgh.

5. Helen Myers, *Ethnomusicology: An Introduction.* The Norton/Grove Handbooks in Music (New York: W. W. Norton, 1992), 3.

6. See Theodore Adorno, "On Popular Music" (with the assistance of George Simpson), in *Essays on Music.* Selected, with Introduction, Commentary, and Notes by Richard Leppert. New translations by Susan H. Gillespie (Berkeley: University of California Press, 2002), 437–69. For commentary on Adorno, see Max Paddison, *Adorno,*

Modernism, and Mass Culture: Essays on Critical Theory and Music (London: Kahn & Averill, 2004) and his *Adorno's Aesthetics of Music* (Cambridge: Cambridge University Press, 1993).

7. Susan McClary, *Feminine Endings: Music, Gender, and Sexuality* (Minneapolis: University of Minnesota Press, 1991), 28–29. Among the essays in her book are "Constructions of Gender in Monteverdi's Dramatic Music," "Sexual Politics in Classical Music," "Excess and Frame: The Musical Representation of Madwomen," and "Living to Tell: Madonna's Resurrection of the Fleshy."

8. Richard Middleton, "Popular Music, §1: Popular Music in the West, 6. The study of popular music," *Grove Music Online,* ed. L. Macy. www.grovemusic.com.

9. Eileen Southern, "A Study in Jazz Historiography: *The New Grove Dictionary of Jazz." College Music Symposium* 29 (1989): 123–33. The article is a review of the 1988 edition of *The New Grove Dictionary of Jazz.*

10. Donald Jay Grout, "The best composers and players of piano music in the nineteenth century made constant efforts to avoid the two extremes of sentimental salon music and pointless technical display. Among those whose style and technique were primarily determined by the musical substance, without superfluous ornament or bravura, were Schubert, Schumann, Clara Wieck Schumann (1819–96), and the composer-pianists Mendelssohn and Brahms." *A History of Western Music,* rev. ed. (New York: W. W. Norton, 1973), 560.

11. Revised by Burkholder and published after the deaths of both Grout and Palisca.

12. J. Peter Burkholder, *A History of Western Music,* 7th ed. (New York: W. W. Norton, 2006), xxiii.

13. Paul Henry Lang, *Music in Western Civilization* (New York: W. W. Norton, 1941); reprinted with foreword by Leon Botstein (New York: W.W. Norton, 1997).

14. Leon Botstein, foreword, Paul Henry Lang, *Music in Western Civilization* (New York: W. W. Norton, 1997), x.

15. The series, under the general editorship of Stanley Sadie, was originally titled *Man and Music* and based on a television series with the same title. See Stanley Sadie and Arthur Jacobs, "Man and Music: An Introduction and a Preview." *Musical Times* 127, no. 1715 (Jan. 1986): 24–26.

16. Susan McClary, "The World According to Taruskin," *Music & Letters* 87, no. 3 (2006): 412.

17. Ibid., 414.

18. Thomas Alva Edison, "The Phonograph and Its Future," *North American Review,* June 1878; reproduced in James R. Smart and Jon W. Newsom, *"A Wonderful Invention": A Brief History of the Phonograph from Tinfoil to the LP* (Washington, DC: Library of Congress, 1977), 8. Also online at http://memory.loc.gov/ammem/edhtml/edcyldr.html.

19. Vivian Perlis, *Charles Ives Remembered: An Oral History* (New Haven: Yale University Press, 1974).

20. Emanuel Winternitz, "The Iconology of Music: Potentials and Pitfalls," in *Perspectives in Musicology: The Inaugural Lectures of the PhD Program in Music at the City University of New York,* ed. Barry S. Brook, Edward O.D. Downes, and Sherman Van Solkema (New York: W. W. Norton, 1972), 81.

21. Ibid., 90.

22. Ernest Burger, *Franz Liszt: A Chronicle of His Life in Pictures and Documents.* Translated by Stewart Spencer (Princeton: Princeton University Press, 1989); Nuria Nono-Schoenberg, Catherine Lorenz, and Anita Luginbuehl, *Arnold Schönberg, 1874–1951: Lebensgeschichte in Begegnungen* (Klagenfurt: Ritter Klagenfurt, 1992).

23. www.ridim.org. For information on the ARTstor interdisciplinary database of images, see www.artstor.org. This database is available in many library collections.

24. Laurence Libin, "Organology," *Grove Music Online,* ed. L. Macy. www.grovemusic.com.

25. Hornbostel and Sachs originally published their treatise in *Zeitschrift für Ethnologie* in 1914 (Eng. trans. in *Galpin Society Journal,* xiv (1961): 3–29, repr. in Myers, *Ethnomusicology: An Introduction,* 444–61.

26. *Grove Music Online* article "Instruments, Classification of" includes Appendix "Introduction to the Hornbostel-Sachs classification system," from the English translation of Hornbostel-Sachs 1914 treatise. The dictionary also includes separate articles on each instrument category. The entire classification system is reproduced in Dornon's article in Myers, *Ethnomusicology: An Introduction,* 444–61.

27. Howard Mayer Brown and Francis Palmer, "Idiophone, Membranophone, Chordophone, Aerophone," *Grove Music Online,* ed. L. Macy. http://www.grovemusic.com.

28. Hugh Davies, "Electrophone," *Grove Music Online,* ed. L. Macy. http://www.grovemusic.com.

29. Richard Cole and Ed Schwartz, "Comprehensive Table of Musical Instrument Classifications," in *Virginia Tech Multimedia Music Dictionary.* http://www.music.vt.edu/musicdictionary/appendix/instruments/instrumentmain.html.

30. Nicolas Slonimsky, *Music Since 1900,* 5th ed. (New York: Schirmer Books, 1994), 494.

31. Otto Erich Deutsch, *Handel: A Documentary Biography* (New York: W. W. Norton, 1955); *Mozart: A Documentary Biography,* trans. Eric Blom, Peter Branscombe, and Jeremy Noble (Stanford: Stanford University Press, 1965); *The Schubert Reader: A Life of Schubert in Letters and Documents,* trans. Eric Blom (New York: W. W. Norton, 1947); *The New Bach Reader: A Life of Johann Sebastian Bach in Letters and Documents,* ed. Hans T. David and Arthur Mendel, rev. Christoph Wolff (New York: W. W. Norton, 1998); H. C. Robbins Landon, *Haydn: Chronicle and Works,* 5 vols. (Bloomington: Indiana University Press, 1976–77).

32. Emily Anderson, trans., ed. *The Letters of Mozart and His Family,* chronologically arranged, translated, edited, and with an introduction by Emily Anderson, 3rd ed. (New York: Norton, 1985); *The Letters of Beethoven,* collected, translated, and edited with an introduction and notes by Emily Anderson, 3 vols (New York: W. W. Norton, 1985); Otto Erich Deutsch and Wilhelm A. Bauer, *Mozart: Briefe und Aufzeichnungen.* 7 vols. (Kassel: Bärenreiter, 1962–75).

33. Alfred Einstein, *Mozart: His Character, His Work,* trans. Arthur Mendel and Nathan Broder (London: Oxford University Press, 1945).

34. Maynard Solomon, *Beethoven,* 2nd ed. (New York: Schirmer Books, 1998), *Mozart: A Life* (New York: HarperCollins, 1995); Stuart Feder, *Charles Ives: My Father's Song: A Psychoanalytic Biography* (New Haven: Yale University Press, 1992); Peter Ostwald, *Schumann: The Inner Voices of a Musical Genius* (Boston: Northeastern University Press, 1985), *Vaslav Nijinsky: A Leap Into Madness* (New York: Carol Publishing 1991), *Glenn Gould: The Ecstasy and Tragedy of Genius* (New York: W. W. Norton, 1997).

35. Walter Frisch, ed., *Brahms and His World* (Princeton, NJ: Princeton University Press, 1990); Peter Laki, ed., *Bartók and His World* (Princeton, NJ: Princeton University Press, 1995); *Cambridge Companion to Music Series:* http://www.cambridge.org/series/sSeries.asp?code=CCMC; Douglass Seaton, ed. *The Mendelssohn Companion* (Westport, CT: Greenwood Press, 2001); Ben Arnold, ed., *The Liszt Companion* (Westport, CT: Greenwood Press, 2002); Mark-Daniel Schmid, ed., *The Richard Strauss Companion* (Westport, CT: Praeger, 2003).

36. See also John L. Adams's *Musicians' Autobiographies: An Annotated Bibliography of Sources Available in English, 1800–1900.* (Jefferson, NC: McFarland, 1982), listed on p. 57, under Bibliographies of Music Literature.

37. Igor Stravinsky and Robert Craft, *Conversations With Igor Stravinsky* (London: Faber and Faber, 1959), *Dialogues and a Diary* (London: Faber and Faber, 1968), *Expositions and Developments* (London: Faber and Faber, 1962), *Memories and Commentaries: New One Volume Edition* (London: Faber and Faber, 2002); Dmitri Shostakovich, *Testimony: The Memoirs of Dmitri Shostakovich, As Related to and Edited by Solomon Volkov,* trans. Antonina W. Bouis (New York: Harper & Row, 1979).

CHAPTER

6

Periodicals, Periodical Indexes, and Databases

INTRODUCTION

Periodicals are publications that appear with some periodicity, or some established frequency: daily, weekly, monthly, bimonthly, quarterly, or annually; some are published on irregular schedules. Music periodicals may also be informally distinguished as falling into two broad categories: *journals* and *magazines*. The former typically include lengthy, scholarly articles; the latter contain articles aimed at a more popular audience, albeit one of musicians and music lovers. Scholarly journals are also distinguished by their inclusion of peer-reviewed articles, meaning that an article must be reviewed by scholars before it is accepted for publication.

Many of these periodicals, particularly the magazines, also contain "news and notes" columns that provide brief updates of appointments, changes, or important events in the field. Also within the category of magazines are *fanzines* and their electronic versions, *e-fanzines* (or *e-zines*): informal publications circulated among fans of particular artists or genres, such as punk rock. These publications are especially important for popular music research topics, when the artist is not well documented in more formally published sources; given their somewhat ephemeral nature, they are also somewhat difficult for libraries to collect and preserve.

SELECTED MUSIC PERIODICAL TITLES

The following selected list contains periodicals in all of the categories just mentioned:

A. Selected Scholarly Journals: General and Special Subject

19th Century Music
Acta Musicologica

American Music
Asian Music
Black Music Research Journal
Cambridge Opera Journal
Computer Music Journal
Contemporary Music Review
Early Music
Early Music History
Eighteenth Century Music
Ethnomusicology
Galpin Society Journal
International Jazz Archives Journal
International Review of the Aesthetics and Sociology of Music
Journal of Music Theory
Journal of Musicological Research
Journal of Musicology
Journal of Popular Music Studies
Journal of Seventeenth Century Music (electronic only)
Journal of the American Musicological Society (JAMS)
Journal of the Royal Music Association
Journal of the Society for American Music
Latin American Music Review
Leonardo
Medical Problems of Performing Artists
Music & Letters
Music Analysis
Music Perception
Music Theory Spectrum
Musica Disciplina
Musical Quarterly
Musical Times
Opera Quarterly
Perspectives of New Music
Popular Music
Popular Music and Society
Psychology of Music
Tempo
World of Music
Yearbook for Traditional Music

B. Selected Magazines: General and Special Subject

American Organist
American String Teacher
Brass Bulletin
Chamber Music Magazine
Choir and Organ
Clarinet
Classical Singer

Clavier
Cue Sheet: The Newsletter of the Society for the Preservation of Film Music
Diapason
Downbeat
Early Keyboard Journal
Flute Talk
Flutist Quarterly
Guitar Review
Historical Brass Society Journal
Horn Call
International Piano Quarterly
Music Educators Journal
Opera News
Opernwelt
Das Orchester
Piano and Keyboard
The Strad
Symphony Magazine
21st Century Music
Violin Society of America Journal

C. Selected Composer-Specific Periodicals (Journals and Magazines)

(See also Chapter 4: Composer Resources, pp. 97–120.)

BACH

Bach: Journal of the Riemenschneider Bach Institute, Baldwin-Wallace College

BEETHOVEN

The Beethoven Journal. Published by the Ira F. Brilliant Center for Beethoven Studies, San Jose State University. See also *Beethoven Bibliography Database:* http://www.sjsu.edu/depts/beethoven/database/database.html.

BRAHMS

American Brahms Society Newsletter

LISZT

Journal of the American Liszt Society

SCHOENBERG

Journal of the Arnold Schoenberg Center. Published by the Arnold Schoenberg Center, Vienna: http://schoenberg.at/7_research/publications_subscription_e.htm.

WEILL

Kurt Weill Newsletter

D. Music Librarianship (Journals and Magazines)

Brio
Fontes Artis Musicae
Music Reference Services Quarterly
Notes: Quarterly Journal of the Music Library Association

E. Sound Recording Periodicals

American Record Guide
Billboard
Black Grooves: www.blackgrooves.org
BBC Music Magazine
Fanfare
Gramophone

F. Selected Fanzines

Note: The availability of the Internet has led many fanzine publishers to set up fan-based Web sites rather than publish paper magazines. Examples include *Madonna Fanzine*: http://www.madonnafanzine.com/ and *JustRadioHead Fanzine:* http://www.justradiohead.com/fanzine1.html. There are numerous listings of fanzine sites on the Web. Selected articles *about* fanzines include

Atton, Chris. "'Living in the Past?' Value Discourses in Progressive Rock Fanzines." *Popular Music* 20, no. 1 (2001): 29–46.
Pruter, Robert. "History of Doowop Fanzines." *Popular Music and Society* 21, no. 1 (Spring 1997): 11–41.

Where to Find Out More about Periodicals

The *Grove Music Online* article on "Periodicals" by Imogen Fellinger and others provides a history of music periodicals, from their first appearance in the early eighteenth century to the present day. This article also includes a list of periodicals, arranged geographically, with an alphabetical index.

Other *lists* of periodicals include

Basart, Ann P. *Writing About Music: A Guide to Publishing Opportunities for Authors and Reviewers.* Fallen Leaf Reference Books in Music 11. Berkeley, CA: Fallen Leaf Press, 1989. (Provides basic information on 430 music periodicals from 21 countries that accept unsolicited material for possible publication.)

Brockman, William S. "Current Periodicals." In *Music: A Guide to the Reference Literature*, 161–85. Littleton, CO: Libraries Unlimited, 1987. (Includes brief information on each title.)

Crabtree, Phillip D., and Donald H. Foster. "Current Research Journals in Music." In *Sourcebook for Research in Music*. 2nd ed., 152–59. Revised and expanded by Allen Scott. Bloomington: Indiana University Press, 2005. (Classified title list only with selected Web addresses.)

Fellinger, Imogen, et al. "Periodicals." *Grove Music Online*. Edited by L. Macy. www.grovemusic.com.

Fidler, Linda M., and Richard S. James, eds. *International Music Journals*. Historical guides to the world's periodicals and newspapers. New York: Greenwood Press, 1990. (Includes very detailed profiles of ca. 200 music periodicals, both current and historical; also includes an introductory essay on the development of periodicals.)

Publist.com: http://www.publist.com/ (Free site with information on more than 150,000 periodicals from around the world; registration required for use; also links to databases for ordering of specific articles.)

Robinson, Doris. *Music and Dance Periodicals: An International Directory and Guidebook*. Voorheesville, NY: Peri Press, 1989. (Lists 1,867 periodicals.)

Ulrich's Periodicals Directory. New York: R. R. Bowker, 1932– . Ulrichsweb.com: http://www.ulrichsweb.com/. (Information on more than 300,000 periodicals in all disciplines, including journals, magazines, fanzines, and electronic resources; subscription-based online version has links to full text of articles through other services.)

See also lists of periodicals in *Music Index Online* and *International Index of Music Periodicals*. These lists contain basic information about the title, including publisher, frequency of publication, and subscription price.

Notes: The Quarterly Journal of the Music Library Association features a regular column with reviews of new periodicals.

MUSIC PERIODICAL INDEXES AND DATABASES

The sources previously cited include information *about* journals and magazines; they do not, however, provide access to their contents. As virtually all periodicals include articles by a variety of authors on different subjects, it is necessary to have *indexes* that provide access to the contents of the publications.

Researchers in law, the sciences, and social sciences take it for granted that an electronic database search will yield quick results on a topic, with links to abstracts and full text; however, music researchers did not have the advantage of dedicated, music-specific, online indexes until the late 1970s. The currently available online databases provide at best a patchwork quilt of indexing to music periodicals, with some provision of abstracts and full text.

It should be stressed that many of the bibliographic tools cited previously, such as the bibliographies of music literature (Chapter 2), dictionaries and encyclopedias (Chapter 3), and composer-performer resources (Chapter 4) also provide access to articles in periodicals. It is often more efficient to locate articles through a subject-oriented reference tool for which the author(s) have preselected relevant sources in a variety of formats.

Real Life Scenario

In our previously mentioned search for information on Beethoven's String Quartet, op. 131, the bibliography attached to the Grove Music Online Beethoven article notes the following sources in subcategory f: Studies of the Works, iii. Chamber Music (listed chronologically, as per form in Grove Music Online bibliographies):

Winter, Robert. "Plans for the Structure of the String Quartet in C sharp minor." In *Beethoven Studies* 2, edited by Alan Tyson, 106–37. London: Oxford University Press, 1977.

Glauert, Amanda Lisa. "The Double Perspective in Beethoven's Opus 131." *19th Century Music* 4, no. 2 (November 1980): 113–20.

Winter, Robert. *Compositional Origins of Beethoven's Opus 131.* Ann Arbor, MI: UMI Research Press, 1982.

These sources may be found in RILM, with a link to the full text of Glauert's article in *JSTOR*. (Winter's 1982 book should also have been found during a subject search of a library catalog under the heading: Beethoven, Ludwig van, 1770–1827. Quartets, strings, no. 14, op. 131, C# minor.) In this case, it was much more efficient to locate these sources in the *Grove Music Online* bibliography rather than in the various databases.

Concepts

Effective use of periodical indexes requires some understanding of several concepts:

Indexes provide access to the contents of periodicals (and other literature, in the case of RILM), via author, title, subject, or key word. They do not necessarily link to full texts of the articles themselves.

Abstract is a brief summary of an article.

Full text is the complete text of an article, available through some, but not all, index sources.

Vendors for full text are agencies that provide libraries with full text of their subscribed periodicals.

Access to full texts of articles is frequently dependent upon the vendor resources available in the library. Subscriptions to full-text databases can be quite costly, and public libraries, small college libraries, and conservatory libraries may not have the breadth of full-text resources that are available in a large university library. Users of Google Scholar, which is free, will often locate citations to articles that are only available through fee-based full text databases, such as Project Muse or JSTOR; however, these articles may be requested via interlibrary loan.

Chronological Survey of Music Periodical Indexes

Although the first music periodicals appeared in the early part of the eighteenth century, indexes to their contents were not available for another two centuries.[1]

Established in 1949, *Music Index* was the first dedicated index to music periodicals. It was published monthly with annual cumulations, and users needed to plow through issues by date in order to locate articles, an activity that likely seems quite alien to researchers in the electronic age. Online access to *Music Index* did not become available until the early 1990s; *Music Index Online* currently covers the years from 1975 to 2007, with indexing of 800 music periodicals, both journals and magazines. The database does not offer full text, although users may obtain selected articles through other full-text databases, such as JSTOR.

RILM Abstracts of Music Literature (Répertoire International de Littérature Musicale) began in 1966 as a joint project of the International Musicological Society (IMS) and the International Association of Music Libraries (IAML). A visionary project of the master musicologist Barry S. Brook, RILM (one of the 4 Rs),[2] was designed to offer broad international coverage of scholarly literature about music. It differs from other music periodical indexes in several important ways:

- Coverage includes books (both monographs and collections of essays), articles in Festschriften and congress reports, dissertations and theses, editions of music with scholarly prefaces and Web sites, as well as articles in periodicals.
- Entries include brief abstracts that describe the source.
- Each RILM entry includes detailed, hierarchical subject indexing of concepts, topics, names, and geographic locations.
- It is broadly international and yet selective in coverage. Entries are compiled by RILM committees in more than 55 countries. These committees survey their area's scholarly literature about music and submit entries to a central office at the City University of New York.
- Although some journal titles ("core journals") are indexed in their entirety, other periodicals are covered only selectively, when an article meets RILM's criteria for coverage. Complete coverage guidelines, including listings of core and primary journals, are available on the RILM Web site: www.rilm.org.

RILM is available electronically via several vendors. Although it does not include full text itself, it does provide links to full-text journal articles in JSTOR and other databases. *Grove Music Online* also links to RILM entries.

As noted in Chapter 2, RILM has also undertaken projects to index and abstract retrospective materials prior to 1966: these include James Cowdery's *Speaking of Music: Music Conferences, 1835–1966* (see p. 46) and a current project to cover music Festschriften prior to 1966. Abstracts from these retrospective projects are added to the RILM database, thus enhancing its coverage of the literature.

International Index of Music Periodicals (IIMP) and International Index of Music Periodicals Full Text (IIMPFT)

IIMP, which first appeared in 1996, indexes articles in ca. 430 international music periodicals, both journals and magazines. It includes abstracts for some entries, as well as retrospective coverage (back to 1874) for selected titles. Its companion, IIMPFT, offers full text for selected journals, as well as links to full text provided by other sources, such as JSTOR. The only way to determine the exact coverage of a title in IIMP or IIMPFT is to use "BROWSE JOURNALS." Users should be cautioned that its subject search modes only cover articles published after 1996.

JSTOR and JSTOR Music Collection

JSTOR (acronym for "journal storage") began as a project of the Andrew W. Mellon Foundation in the early 1990s. It offers full texts of complete back issues of journals from a broad range of disciplines. Coverage is usually up to between two and five years of the journal's most recent publications. It is distinct from the other databases in several key areas:

- It is a not-for-profit organization, so subscription prices are less costly for libraries.
- As noted earlier, it limits coverage to back issues in a system referred to as a "moving wall." Through its negotiations with publishers, the date of coverage moves forward periodically to coverage of more recent issues. It is therefore *not* the tool to use for access to the most recent issues of journals.
- JSTOR offers libraries subscriptions through its various subject areas, both multidisciplinary and subject-specific. The Music Section of JSTOR currently includes 32 scholarly music journals; a complete list is available at http://www.jstor.org/action/showJournals?browseType=collectionInfoPage &selectCollection=music.

These music titles are also offered through other JSTOR sets, such as "Arts & Sciences." Users should check to see which JSTOR set is offered by their library.

RIPM

(*Retrospective Index to Music Periodicals, 1800–1950*) [originally *Répertoire international de la presse musicale*]. A collaborative project of the International Musicological Society, the International Association of Music Libraries, and Unesco's International Council for Philosophy and Humanistic Studies (and one of the 4 Rs), the RIPM project was established to provide access to the significant quantity of music periodical literature published in the nineteenth century. By extending coverage to 1950, it fills the gap in music periodical indexing prior to the establishment of *Music Index* in 1949. In addition, RILM and RIPM are collaborating to ensure complete coverage of major music journals through this period by distributing titles between these sister organizations.

The RIPM database is available electronically through several vendors; a plan to link to the full text of the journals is currently underway.[3]

Other Electronic Music-Specific Periodical Indexes
Canadian Music Periodical Index
http://www.collectionscanada.ca/cmpi-ipmc/index-e.html

Other Electronic Databases for Performing Arts (Dance and Theatre)

International Bibliography of Theatre and Dance
International Index to Performing Arts (IIPA)
North American Theatre Online

Selected General Periodical and Full-Text Databases

Music research projects that are multidisciplinary in nature require searching general periodical and literature databases. These sources are numerous and complex in nature and provide sometimes overlapping coverage of various subject areas, some with full text. Following is a very selective list of general periodical indexes:

Academic Search Premier

Full-text database of more than 3,200 scholarly databases in a variety of humanities and scientific disciplines.

Arts & Humanities Citation Index (AHCI)

Modeled on scientific databases, AHCI provides access to articles and their citations in nearly 1,130 humanities journals.[4] Searching citations allows researchers to build upon work done by other authors and to trace sources.

FirstSearch

OCLC's FirstSearch, the centerpiece of which is WorldCat.org, also links to dozens of databases and full-text resources; listing is available at http://www.oclc.org/firstsearch/content/databases/databaselist.htm.

Google Scholar

http://scholar.google.com/. One of Google's digital projects, Google Scholar provides links to a range of materials from the scholarly literature, including journal articles, theses and dissertations, books, and conference papers. Similar to Google Book, the extent of digital access is sometimes limited by copyright issues. Google Scholar also provides links to library resources in WorldCat.

LexisNexis

Database of legal, news, and business resources, this database is heavily used by lawyers and business professionals.

MLA International Bibliography

This database of scholarly resources on modern languages, literature, folklore, and linguistics is compiled under the auspices of the Modern Language Association of America.

Project Muse

Project Muse provides full text of 350 journals in the humanities and social sciences. In a reciprocal collaboration with JSTOR, Project Muse provides contents of current issues, with links to back issues in JSTOR.

Readers Guide to Periodical Literature 1901–

Readers Guide Abstracts. 1983–
Readers Guide Full Text, Mega Edition. 1994–

Indexes to popular magazines and journals. See descriptions: http://www.hwwilson.com/Databases/Readersg.htm.

Social Sciences Citation Index

This is a database of scholarly resources on the social sciences.

SUMMARY AND PRACTICAL APPLICATIONS

This all seems so confusing.

Why isn't everything available in full text?

How can I know if I've done a thorough search through the periodical literature?

ANSWERS: Yes, it is confusing. We have overlapping coverage of some titles in Music Index, IIMP, and RILM, and spotty coverage of other titles. The economic realities of the music database world make it unlikely that all music periodicals will be available in full text anytime soon. Although it is nearly impossible to do a comprehensive search through the periodical literature, with the reminder that periodical articles represent only one format of music research literature, here are some hints on best tools to use for different types of searches:

- RILM has the broadest coverage of *scholarly* literature about music, since it includes other formats (books, dissertations, etc.) in addition to periodical articles; however, its coverage is *selective*. Use RILM before using JSTOR, as the latter is limited to back issues of selected periodicals.
- Music Index or IIMP are sometimes preferable tools to use when searching for reviews of recent performances, especially reviews that may be less scholarly in nature, as RILM's coverage is limited to reviews that include substantial analytical information.
- Make note of which articles may be from peer-reviewed journals, thus representing more worthy scholarly research. IIMP allows limits of search by "peer-reviewed articles only."

NOTES

1. For further information, see Linda M. Fidler and Richard S. Jones, "Appendix B.: Music Periodical Indexes," in *International Music Journals* (New York: Greenwood Press, 1990), 471–81.

2. The other Rs are: RISM (*Répertoire International des Sources Musicale*, see pp. 176–182;

RIDIM (*Répertoire International d'Iconographie Musicale*, see p. 134; and RIPM, *Retrospective Index to Music Periodicals*, see p. 153).

3. For further information, see www.ripm.org.

4. http://scientific.thomson.com/products/ahci/.

CHAPTER

7

Discographies

INTRODUCTION: DISCOGRAPHIC TOOLS AND THE HISTORY OF RECORDING

As defined by Jerome F. Weber in his article on "Discography" in *Grove Music Online, discography* is simply a "systematic listing of recordings."[1] In current practice, this term is used for listings of all formats of sound recordings: discs, tapes, wire recordings, wax cylinders, piano and organ rolls, and digital files; it has also been extended to video recordings, although the term *videography* is sometimes used.

Discographers are challenged to document information beyond what would normally be relevant to descriptions of a book or score. In addition to documentation of the recorded work (composer, title, opus number, author of text), discographies must also document the performance itself, with information on performer(s), date and place of recording, session, and matrix number. The latter refers to a number etched onto a disc recording near the label, which often includes coded information on session or take number. As well, discographies document the physical properties of the recorded medium (78 rpm disc, wax cylinder, 33 $1/3$ lp) and the mechanical means used to produce it (analog, digital). Researchers use discographies to locate specific performances, such as Maria Callas's 1954 performance of Bellini's *Norma,* conducted by Tulio Serafin, or Louis Armstrong's recording of "Heebie Jeebies" with his Hot Five band in the early 1920s. Connoisseurs will also want to know how the original disc was remastered (e.g., Armstrong's recording was originally released by OKeh records on 78 rpm discs), or which exact session was recorded (especially important for jazz recordings).

The information desired in a discography includes

- composer
- title
- opus number
- text author
- duration
- performer(s)
- type of recording
- recording label

- manufacturer
- name of series
- issue number
- matrix number
- session or take number
- patent and copyright information
- date and place of recording

An understanding of the practice of discography is inseparable from an understanding of the history of recording. In order to have some perspective on the sources that document this relatively recent and ever-changing technology, a brief outline of landmark events in sound recording history, along with references to discographical tools, is presented here. This is an intentionally brief overview of audio recording, with few of the specialist details found in some of the more technically oriented resources. Additional information on the development of recording may be found in sources on the "About Recordings" list, pp. 173–174.

1877[2]   Simultaneous discovery of the process of recording by Charles Cros in France and Thomas Alva Edison in New Jersey. In a scientific decision with long-term implications, Cros proposed recording on lamp-blackened glass and Edison used tin foil. Cros was geared more toward the theoretical implications of his invention rather than the practical, and thus Thomas Edison is credited as the inventor of the phonograph. It was, however, up to others—notably Emil Berliner, who devised the flat disc in 1888—to modify the technology and make it practical for mass production.

1877–   Acoustic or preelectric period. Recordings were made on cylinders
1925   and discs entirely by mechanical means (the microphone had not yet been invented). Musicians had to gather around the acoustic recording horn (see Figure 7–1), which was obviously simpler for singers and solo instrumentalists, and much more awkward for recording large ensembles. In spite of this difficulty, the Berlin Philharmonic recorded Beethoven's Symphony no. 5 in 1913 (without double basses or timpani), and Stokowski, the Philadelphia Orchestra, and Toscanini all took advantage of the new technology in its earliest years. Claude Arnold's book *The Orchestra on Record, 1896–1926,* details orchestral recordings made during this technologically primitive time.

The predominance of vocal recording during the acoustic period is evident in Robert Bauer's book, *The New Catalogue of Historical Records, 1898–1908/09,* in which singers are documented on pages 15–482 and instrumentalists on pages 483–87. Notable among the latter are recordings by violinists Pablo de Sarasate, Joseph Joachim, Fritz Kreisler, Jan Kubelik, Maud Powell, and Jacques Thibaud, and pianists Wilhelm Backhaus, Edward Grieg, and Josef Hofmann.

Among the many singers who took particular advantage of recording technology to advance their careers was the legendary tenor Enrico Caruso (1873–1921). He made his first recordings in 1902, after which he was engaged by the Metropolitan Opera Company for appearances in

FIGURE 7–1   **Acoustic recording session.**

Source: Centre for History and Analysis of Recorded Music, "A Brief History of Recording."

the 1903–04 season. His recording of "Vesti la giubba" from *I Pagliacci* was one of the first discs to sell more than one million copies.

In another technological feat, the Metropolitan Opera House Librarian Lionel Mapelson recorded live Met opera performances from the prompter's box on a rather primitive early recording device between the years of 1900 and 1904. These recordings were reissued in a special collectors' set by the New York Public Library Rogers and Hammerstein Archive of Recorded Sound in 1986.[3]

1904   Welte-Mignon's reproducing piano appears. Distinct from its close cousin the player piano, a reproducing piano could replicate the expressive marks, tempo, and dynamics of its performer. Until its demise around 1930, reproducing pianos by Welte-Mignon, Duo-Art, Ampico, and other companies marketed recordings by an extraordinary roster of pianists, including Eugene d'Albert, Ferruccio Busoni, Teresa Carreño, Claude Debussy, Josef Hofmann, Wanda Landowska, and Josef Lhévinne. The heritage of reproducing piano rolls is documented in Larry Sitsky's two-volume book *The Classical Reproducing Piano Roll: A Catalogue-Index,* and in Smith and Howe's *The Welte-Mignon: Its Music and Musicians.*

1925   Electrical recording begins with the invention of the microphone. Many 78 rpm discs were released between 1925 and 1948, although the duration of a "side" remained under five minutes. Again demonstrating the desire to record performances despite technological limitations, many complete operas were produced during this time, including lengthy operas by Verdi and Wagner.[4] The rich heritage of 78 rpm recordings from these years is documented in Clough and Cuming, *World's Encyclopedia of Recorded Music, Gramophone Shop Encyclopedia of Recorded Music, Rigler and Deutsch Index,* as well as the specialized genre discographies listed under "Historical" on the attached list.

1948   Columbia introduced the long-playing disc, which held up to 20 minutes of music on a 12-inch side, and 15 minutes on a 10-inch side. The following year RCA Victor responded by introducing the 45 rpm disc, which was adopted primarily for popular music songs, since it had a playing time of a little more than five minutes (Figure 7–2). In a marketing technique that perhaps presaged the iPod, some 45 rpm players could play up to 10 discs at a time via a special "changer" that dropped one disc on top of another.

1958   Introduction of stereophonic recording.

1983   Compact disc (CD) recordings appear on the market. Measuring $4\frac{3}{4}$ inches in diameter, each CD holds up to 80 minutes of music.

FIGURE 7–2   **45 rpm player.**

Source: Eric Long, Smithsonian © 1993.

1986   Digital audiotape (DAT) introduced.
1996   United States patent for MP3 audio compression format; its development began in Europe in the late 1980s.
2001   Apple introduces the iPod portable music player.

The rest, as they say, is and will likely continue to be history. Most music today is transmitted digitally via the Internet. Libraries provide access to recordings via licensed digital sound databases, such as Naxos Music Library, Classical Music Library, and DRAM, although most also retain the physical recording media (78, LP, CD) they spent many acquisition dollars acquiring. Many listeners acquire music via legal or illegal file-sharing services such as Napster, Kazaa, or Lime Wire.

The only apparent constant in media technology is its continuing evolution. Or, as Will Crutchfield wrote in a 1986 article about the introduction of digital audiotapes, "In 1904 the Gramophone & Typewriter Company was telling people that equipment for the reproduction of sound had reached the highest state of perfection. It wasn't true then and it isn't true yet."[5]

Perspectives and Possibilities for Research

As Robert Philip states in his important study of recordings and their influence on performance,

> It is impossible to overemphasize the extent to which the growing availability of recordings over the last hundred years has changed the ways in which musicians and audiences experience music. If we could transport ourselves back to the late nineteenth-century, before the existence of recordings, we would find ourselves in a deeply unfamiliar world. Brahms and his contemporaries never heard a note of music unless they were in the presence of someone performing it.[6]

Before the advent of recording, individuals in all classes had a much higher level of musical literacy. If an enthusiastic audience member attended an opera performance and enjoyed a particular aria, the only way to reexperience the tune would be to sing it oneself or purchase a sheet music arrangement of it and re-create it at home.

Philip and others cited on the list "About Recordings" have delved into the fruitful and fascinating areas of research through recorded performances. As noted earlier, Edison's invention was quickly adopted by performing artists and their audiences. Composers such as Debussy, Mahler, Prokofiev, Rachmaninoff, Ravel, Richard Strauss, and Stravinsky have left historic recordings that provide clues into their own interpretation of their works. For example, piano rolls made by Debussy were used as secondary sources for some of his piano works published in the *New Debussy Edition,* when they appeared to present sufficient evidence of his interpretation.[7]

In their book *Edison, Musicians, and the Phonograph: A Century in Retrospect,* John Harvith and Susan Edwards Harvith interview a number of artists about their experience in the recording studio. The great singer Lotte Lehmann (1888–1976) was asked if she thought future generations would pay attention to her recordings. Lehmann answered, "I don't think so. . . . I sang my *Lieder* or my aria, what I do. I live in the present." The Harviths responded, "That's fascinating, because we feel we know you through your recordings." Lehmann: "That's very nice. It always surprises me very much. I have not performed since 1951, and I get so many flowers and letters, even from you younger people. They hear how grandma tells of Lehmann."[8]

SPECIFIC DISCOGRAPHIES

I. Bibliographies of Discographies

Bibliography of Discographies. 3 vols. New York: R. R. Bowker, 1977–83.

> Vol. 1: *Classical Music, 1925–1975.* Edited by Michael H. Gray and Gerald D. Gibson. 1977.
> Vol. 2: *Jazz.* Edited by Daniel Allen. 1981.
> Vol. 3: *Popular Music.* Edited by Michael H. Gray. 1983.

Cooper, David Edwin. *International Bibliography of Discographies: Classical Music and Jazz & Blues, 1962–1972; A Reference Book for Record Collectors, Dealers, and Librarians.* Littleton, CO: Libraries Unlimited, 1975.

Gray, Michael H. *Classical Music Discographies, 1976–1988: A Bibliography.* New York: Greenwood Press, 1989.

Rust, Brian A. L. *Brian Rust's Guide to Discography.* Discographies 4. Westport, CT: Greenwood Press, 1980.

II. Encyclopedia

Hoffmann, Frank W., ed., and Howard Ferstler, technical ed. *Encyclopedia of Recorded Sound in the United States.* 2nd ed. 2 vols. New York: Routledge, 2005.

III. Discographies

A. Historical

1. Classical

Arnold, Claude G. *The Orchestra on Record, 1896–1926: An Encyclopedia of Orchestral Recordings Made by the Acoustical Process.* Discographies 73. Westport, CT: Greenwood Press, 1997.

Bauer, Robert. *The New Catalogue of Historical Records, 1898–1908/09.* 2nd ed. London: Sidgwick and Jackson, 1947.

Clough, Francis F., and G. J. Cuming. *The World's Encyclopedia of Recorded Music.* London: Sidgwick & Jackson, 1952. (Includes First Supplement: 1950–51.) Second (1951–52) and third (1953–55) supplements: 1957.

Girard, Victor, and Harold M. Barnes. *Vertical-Cut Cylinder and Discs: A Catalogue of all "Hill-&-Dale" Recordings of Serious Worth Made and Issued Between 1897 and 1932 circa.* London: British Institute of Recorded Sound, 1964.

Gramophone Shop Encyclopedia of Recorded Music. 3rd ed. Revised and enlarged. Westport, CT: Greenwood Press, 1970. First published 1948 by Crown Publishers.

Rigler, Lloyd E., and Lawrence E. Deutsch. *Rigler and Deutsch Record Index.* Syracuse, NY: Mi-kal County-Matic, 1986. Also available in FirstSearch.

> Computer-generated index to ca. 615,000 78 rpm sound recordings in the collections of the Associated Audio Archives (Syracuse University, Library of Congress, Rodgers and Hammerstein Archives of the New York Public Library of the Performing Arts, Stanford University, and Yale University) 1250 microfiche. Copyright held by the Association for Recorded Sound Collections, Inc. See Richard Koprowski's review in *Notes* 42, no. 3 (March 1986): 535–37.

Sitsky, Larry. *The Classical Reproducing Piano Roll: A Catalogue-Index.* 2 vols. New York: Greenwood Press, 1990.

Smith, Charles Davis, and Richard James Howe. *The Welte-Mignon: Its Music and Musicians.* Vestal, NY: Published by Vestal Press for the Automatic Musical Instrument Collector's Association, 1994.

2. Jazz and Related Genres (Historical and Current)

Albin, Steve, and Michael Fitzgerald. *The Jazz Discography.* www.jazzdiscography.com. (The authors have developed the "Brian" software [named for jazz discographer Brian Rust] to include session information in their discographies. See "Why Session-Based Discography?" on their Web site.)

Bruyninckx, Walter, and Domi Truffandier. *Jazz Discography: 85 Years of Recorded Jazz.* CD-ROM. 2004.

Crawford, Richard, and Jeffrey Magee. *Jazz Standards on Record: 1900–1942: A Core Repertory.* Chicago: Center for Black Music Research, Columbia College, Chicago, 1992.

Delaunay, Charles. *New Hot Discography: The Standard Dictionary of Recorded Jazz.* Edited by Walter E. Schaap and George Avakian. New York: Criterion, 1948.

Fancourt, Leslie, and Bob McGrath. *Blues Discography, 1943–1970: A Selective Discography of Post-War Blues Records.* West Vancouver, Canada: Eyeball Productions, 2006.

Godrich, John, and Robert M.W. Dixon. *Blues and Gospel Records: 1902–1943.* 3rd rev. ed. Essex, England: Storyville Publications, 1982.

Jepsen, Jorgen Grunnet. *Jazz Records, 1942–1965: A Discography.* 11 vols. in 8. Holte, Denmark: K.E. Knudsen, 1963–1970.

Kernfeld, Barry, and Howard Rye. "Comprehensive Discographies of Jazz, Blues, and Gospel." *Notes* 51, no. 2 (December 1994): 501–47 and 51, no. 3 (March 1995): 865–91.

Leadbitter, Mike, and Neil Slaven. *Blues Records, 1943–1970: A Selective Discography.* Rev. ed. 2 vols. London: Record Information Services, 1987–94.

Leder, Jan. *Women in Jazz: A Discography of Instrumental Music, 1913–1968.* Westport, CT: Greenwood Press, 1985.

Lord, Tom. *The Jazz Discography.* West Vancouver, British Columbia, Canada: Lord Music Reference, 1992– . Also available on CD-ROM and on-line via paid subscription: www.lordisco.com/tjdonline.html.

Lotz, Rainer E. *Deutsche Hot Discographie: Cakewalk, Ragtime, Hot Dance & Jazz: Ein Handbuch.* Bonn: B. Lotz, 2006.

Raben, Erik. *Jazz Records, 1942–1980: A Discography.* CD-ROM. Copenhagen: Stainless/Wintermoon, 1987. (update of Jepsen)

Rust, Brian. *Jazz and Ragtime Records: 1897–1942.* 6th ed. 3 vols. Denver, CO: Mainspring Press, 2002.

Rust, Brian, and Allen G. Debus. *The Complete Entertainment Discography, from 1897 to 1942.* 2nd ed. New York: Da Capo Press, 1989.

Sutton, Allan. *Cakewalks, Rags, and Novelties: The International Ragtime Discography (1894–1930).* Denver, CO: Mainspring Press, 2003.

Togashi, Nobuaki. *Jazz Discography Project.* http://www.jazzdisco.org/.

Yanow, Scott. *Jazz on Record: The First Sixty Years.* San Francisco: Backbeat Books, 2003.

B. Current Discographies

Bielefelder Katalog Jazz; Verzeichnis der Jazz-Schallplatten. (with CD-ROM) 1962– . http://www.bielefelderkataloge.de/ (authorization required for online versions).

Bielefelder Katalog Klassik. (with CD-ROM) 1979– . http://www.bielefelderkataloge.de/ BKK_neu.htm.

Diapason Catalogue General Classique. 1956– .

MUZE. (Only available to commercial enterprises)

Phonolog Reporter. 1948–1995. (Replaced by *Billboard/Phonolog Music Reference Library,* CD-ROM format)

R. E. D. Classical Catalogue. 1996– . (Formerly *Gramophone Classical Catalogue*)

Schwann. 1949–1999.

> Compiled by the master discographer William Schwann (1913–98), the Schwann catalogs were *the* source that librarians and consumers would consult to determine if a recording was currently available. The publication went through various name and scope changes over the years; its near-final guise as a print source was through three specialized publications: *Opus* (1990–99?) for classical recordings, *Spectrum* (1990–99) for popular recordings, and *In Music* (1990–91) for new releases.[9]

Schwann Online. 2001. http://www.paratext.com/schwann.htm.

C. Selected Collector Guides

1. Series

Designed to provide guidance to consumers, "collector guides" typically offer reviewer comments and recommendations on recordings in various genres (classical, jazz, blues, reggae, etc). As these guides are updated frequently to reflect new releases, the following list includes the primary collector guide series, rather than specific editions.

All Music Guide(s). See http://www.allmusic.com/ (covers various genres)

Gramophone. http://www.gramophone.co.uk/publications.asp

> From editors of *Gramophone* magazine; classical only.

Penguin Guides. (various genres)

> See Duckles and Reed (1997), entry 10.11, on the *Penguin Guide to Compact Discs and Cassettes* (1994), for a history of this source.

Rough Guides: www.roughguides.com/

> Cover various genres as well as individual performers and performing groups. Books typically contain articles about the subject along with lists of recommended recordings. Selected titles include

Broughton, Simon, Jon Lusk, and Duncan Clark. *Africa and the Middle East.* Vol. 1: *The Rough Guide to World Music.* 3rd ed. London: Rough Guides, 2006.

Broughton, Simon. *Latin and North America, Caribbean, India, Asia and Pacific.* Vol. 2: *The Rough Guide to World Music.* 2nd ed. London: Rough Guides, 2006.

Egan, Sean. *The Rough Guide to the Rolling Stones.* London: Rough Guides, 2006.

Ingham, Chris. *The Rough Guide to the Beatles.* 2nd ed. London: Rough Guides, 2006.

Manning, Toby. *The Rough Guide to Pink Floyd.* London: Rough Guides, 2006.

Shapiro, Peter. *The Rough Guide to Soul and R & B.* London: Rough Guides, 2006.

Spicer, Al. *The Rough Guide to Punk.* London: Rough Guides, 2006.

Staines, Joe. *The Rough Guide to Classical Music.* 4th ed. London: Rough Guides, 2005.

Williamson, Nigel. *The Rough Guide to Bob Dylan.* 2nd ed. London: Rough Guides, 2006.

_____. *The Rough Guide to the Blues.* London: Rough Guides, 2007.

Wolff, Kurt, and Orla Duane. *Rough Guide to Country Music.* London: Rough Guides, 2000.

2. Collector Guides: Selected Individual Titles

Basic Music Library: Essential Scores and Sound Recordings. 3rd ed. Compiled by Elizabeth Davis, Pamela Bristah, Jane Gottlieb, Kent Underwood, and William Anderson. Chicago: American Library Association, 1997.

Cohn, Arthur. *Recorded Classical Music: A Critical Guide to Compositions and Performances.* New York: Schirmer Books, 1981.
The Essential Jazz Records. Edited by Max Harrison, Eric Thacker, Charles Fox, and Stuart Nicholson. Vol. 1: *Ragtime to Swing.* Vol. 2: *Modernism to Postmodernism.* London: Mansell Publishing, 2000.
MacTaggart, Garaud, ed. *The Omnibus Essential Guide to Classical CDs.* New York: Schirmer Trade Books, 2004.
Morton, Brian. *The Blackwell Guide to Recorded Contemporary Music.* Oxford, UK: Blackwell Publishing, 1996.

D. Special Subject Discographies and Collectors' Guides

1. African American Music (see also Jazz)

Center for Black Music Research. "Discography of Music by Black Composers." http://www.colum.edu/cbmr/Library_and_Archives/Discography_of_Music_by_Black_Composers.php.
Turner, Patricia. *Dictionary of Afro-American Performers: 78 RPM and Cylinder Recordings of Opera, Choral Music, and Song, c. 1900–1949.* Garland Reference Library of the Humanities 590. New York: Garland Publishing, 1990.

2. American Music

Heintze, James R. *American Music Before 1865 in Print and on Records: A Biblio-Discography.* Brooklyn: Institute for Studies in American Music, Conservatory of Music, Brooklyn College of the City University of New York, 1990.
Oja, Carol. *American Music Recordings: A Discography of 20th-Century U.S. Composers.* Brooklyn: Institute for Studies in American Music, Conservatory of Music, Brooklyn College of the City University of New York, 1982.

3. Art in Music

Evans, Gary. *Music Inspired by Art: A Guide to Recordings.* Music Library Association. Index and Bibliography Series 30. Lanham, MD: Scarecrow Press, 2002. (Lists recordings of musical compositions inspired by the work of visual artists.)

4. Early Music

Coover, James, and Richard Colvig. *Medieval and Renaissance Music on Long-Playing Records.* Detroit Studies in Music Bibliographies 6. Detroit: Information Service, 1964.
———. *Medieval and Renaissance Music on Long-Playing Records: Supplement, 1962–1971.* Detroit Studies in Music Bibliographies 26. Detroit: Information Coordinators, 1973.
Croucher, Trevor. *Early Music Discography: From Plainsong to the Sons of Bach.* 2 vols. Phoenix: Oryx Press, 1981.
Weber, Jerome F. *A Gregorian Chant Discography.* 2 vols. Utica, NY: J.F. Weber, 1990.

5. Individual Composers, Performers, Performing Ensembles

ARMSTRONG, LOUIS

Brooks, Edward. *The Young Louis Armstrong on Records: A Critical Survey of the Early Recordings, 1923–1928.* Studies in Jazz 39. Lanham. MD: Scarecrow Press, 2002.
Willems, Jos. *All of Me: The Complete Discography of Louis Armstrong.* Studies in Jazz 51. Lanham, MD: Scarecrow Press, 2006.

Bach, Johann Sebastian

Elste, Martin. *Meilensteine der Bach-Interpretation 1750–2000: Eine Werkgeschichte im Wandel.* Kassel: Bärenreiter, 2000. (Includes CD of excerpts from performances originally recorded 1908–1948.)

Beatles

Terry, Carol D. *Here, There & Everywhere: The First International Beatles Discography, 1962–1982.* Ann Arbor, MI: Pierian Press, 1985.
Wiener, Allen J. *The Beatles: A Recording History.* Jefferson, NC: McFarland, 1986. (See also *Popular Music* 6, no. 3 [October 1987], "Beatles Issue.")

Bruckner, Anton

Lovallo, Lee T. *Anton Bruckner: A Discography.* Fallen Leaf Reference Books in Music 6. Berkeley: Fallen Leaf Press, 1991.

Callas, Maria

Ardoin, John. *The Callas Legacy: The Complete Guide to Her Recordings on Compact Disc.* 4th ed. Portland, OR: Amadeus Press, 1995.

Caruso, Enrico

Bolig, John R. *Caruso Records: A History and Discography.* Denver, CO: Mainspring Press, 2002.

Cash, Johnny

Smith, John L. *The Johnny Cash Record Catalog.* Music Reference Collection 44. Westport, CT: Greenwood Press, 1994.

Coltrane, John

DeVito, Chris, and Lewis Porter. *The John Coltrane Reference.* New York: Routledge, 2008.
Fujioka, Yasuhiro, Lewis Porter, and Yoh-ichi Hamada. *John Coltrane: A Discography and Musical Biography.* Studies in Jazz 20. Metuchen, NJ: Scarecrow Press, 1995.

Davis, Miles

Lohmann, Jan. *The Sound of Miles Davis: The Discography; A Listing of Records and Tapes, 1945–1991.* Copenhagen: JazzMedia Aps, 1992. Updated on http://www.jan-lohmann.com/.
Losin, Peter. *Miles Ahead: A Miles Davis Website.* http://www.plosin.com/milesAhead/.
Tingen, Paul. *Miles Beyond: Electric Explorations of Miles Davis, 1967–1991.* New York: Billboard Books, 2001.
(See also other references on Peter Losin Web site: http://www.plosin.com.)

DELIUS, FREDERICK

Jenkins, Lyndon. *While Spring and Summer Sang: Thomas Beecham and the Music of Frederick Delius*. Aldershot, England: Ashgate Publishing, 2005.

DORATI, ANTAL

Hunt, John. *Antal Dorati, 1906–1988: Discography and Concert Register*. John Hunt Discographies. London: John Hunt, 2004.

DVOŘÁK, ANTONÍN

Yoell, John H. *Antonin Dvořák on Records*. New York: Greenwood Press, 1991.

DYLAN, BOB

Krogsgaard, Michael. *Postively Bob Dylan: A Thirty-Year Discography, Concert & Recording Session Guide, 1960–1991*. Ann Arbor, MI: Popular Culture, 1991.

ELLINGTON, DUKE

Lambert, Eddie. *Duke Ellington: A Listener's Guide*. Studies in Jazz 26. Lanham, MD: Scarecrow Press, 1999.
Timmer, W. E. *Ellingtonia: The Recorded Music of Duke Ellington and His Sideman*. 5th ed. Studies in Jazz 54. Lanham, MD: Scarecrow Press, 2007.

GETZ, STAN

Churchill, Nicholas. *Stan Getz: An Annotated Bibliography and Filmography, with Song and Session Information for Albums*. Jefferson, NC: McFarland, 2005.

GOODMAN, BENNY

Connor, D. Russell. *Benny Goodman: Wrappin' It Up*. Lanham, MD: Scarecrow Press, 1996.

GOULD, GLENN

Canning, Nancy. *A Glenn Gould Catalog*. Westport, CT: Greenwood Press, 1992.

KARAJAN, HERBERT VON

Hunt, John, and Stephen J. Pettitt. *From Adam to Webern: The Recordings of Von Karajan*. John Hunt Discograpahies. London: J. Hunt, 1987.

LONDON PHILHARMONIC

Stuart, Philip. *The London Philharmonic Discography*. Westport, CT: Greenwood Press, 1997.

MAHLER, GUSTAV

Fülöp, Peter, ed. *Mahler Discography.* New York: The Kaplan Foundation, 1995.
Smoley, Lewis M. *The Symphonies of Gustav Mahler: A Critical Discography.* New York:
Greenwood Press, 1986.
_____. *Gustav Mahler's Symphonies: Critical Commentary on Recordings Since 1986.*
Westport, CT: Greenwood Press, 1996.

MARLEY, BOB

Steffens, Roger, and Leroy Jodie Pierson. *Bob Marley and the Wailers: The Definitive
Discography.* Cambridge, MA: Rounder Records, 2005.

MITROPOULOS, DIMITRI

Arfanis, S.A. *The Complete Discography of Dimitri Mitropoulos.* 2nd ed. Athens:
Potamos, 2000.

MONROE, BILL

Rosenberg, Neil V. *Music of Bill Monroe.* Music in American Life. Urbana: University of
Illinois Press, 2007.

NEW YORK PHILHARMONIC

North, James H. *New York Philharmonic: The Authorized Recordings, 1917–2005; A
Discography.* Lanham, MD: Scarecrow Press, 2006.

PET SHOP BOYS

Hoare, Philip, and Chris Heath. *Pet Shop Boys, Catalogue.* London: Thames & Hudson, 2006.

RACHMANINOFF, SERGEI

Harrison, Max. *Rachmaninoff: Life, Works, Recordings.* New York: Continuum, 2005.

RICHTER, SVIATOSLAV

Hunt, John. *Sviatoslav Richter: Pianist of the Century Discography.* London: J. Hunt, 1999.

SCHOENBERG, ARNOLD

Shoaf, R. Wayne. *The Schoenberg Discography.* 2nd ed. Berkeley: Fallen Leaf Press, 1994.
http://www.usc.edu/libraries/archives/schoenberg/asi.htm.

SCHUBERT, FRANZ

Weber, Jerome F. *Schubert's Great C Major Symphony, D. 944: A Discography.* Utica, NY:
Weber, 2000.

SHAW, ARTIE

Simosko, Vladimir. *Artie Shaw: A Musical Biography and Discography*. Studies in Jazz 29. Lanham, MD: Scarecrow Press, 2000.

SOUSA, JOHN PHILIP

Bierley, Paul. *The Incredible Band of John Philip Sousa*. Music in American Life. Urbana: University of Illinois Press, 2006.

SOUZAY, GÉRARD

Morris, Manuel. *The Recorded Performances of Gérard Souzay: A Discography*. New York: Greenwood Press, 1991.

STEVENS, CAT

Brown, George. *Cat Stevens: The Complete Illustrated Biography and Discography*. Leish-on-Sea, England: George Brown, 2006.

STOKOWSKI, LEOPOLD

Hunt, John. *Leopold Stokowski*. 2nd ed. John Hunt Discographies. Exeter: J. Hunt, 2006.

STRAVINSKY, IGOR

Stuart, Philip. *Igor Stravinsky—The Composer in the Recording Studio: A Comprehensive Discography*. New York: Greenwood Press, 1991.

WAGNER, RICHARD

Brown, Jonathan. *Parsifal on Record: A Discography of Complete Recordings, Selections, and Excerpts of Wagner's Music Drama*. New York: Greenwood Press, 1992.
_____. *Tristan und Isolde on Record: A Comprehensive Discography of Wagner's Music Drama with a Critical Introduction to the Recordings*. Westport, CT: Greenwood Press, 2000.
Hunt, John. *Wagner im Festspielhaus: Discography of the Bayreuth Recordings*. John Hunt Discographies. Exeter: J. Hunt, 2006.

WALLER, FATS

Taylor, Stephen. *Fats Waller on the Air: The Radio Broadcasts and Discography*. Studies in Jazz 50. Lanham, MD: Scarecrow Press, 2006.

6. Conductors (Collective)

Holmes, John L. *Conductors on Record*. Westport, CT: Greenwood Press, 1982.
Hunt, John. *A Gallic Trio: Charles Munch, Paul Paray, Pierre Monteux; Discographies*. John Hunt Discographies. London: John Hunt, 2003.

_____. *Gramophone Stalwarts: Bruno Walter, Erich Leinsdorf, Georg Solti; 3 Separate Discographies.* London: J. Hunt, 2001.

7. Instruments

Basart, Ann. *The Sound of the Fortepiano: A Discography of Recordings on Early Pianos.* Berkeley: Fallen Leaf Press, 1985.

Creighton, James. *Discopaedia of the Violin.* 2nd ed. 4 vols. Burlington, Ontario: Records Past Publishing, 1994.

Elste, Martin. *Modern Harpsichord Music: A Discography.* Westport, CT: Greenwood Press, 1995.

Hunt, John. *Great Violinists: David Oistrakh, Wolfgang Schneiderhan, Arthur Grumiaux; Three Separate Discographies.* John Hunt Discographies. [Great Britain]: J. Hunt, 2004.

_____. *Pianists for the Connoisseur: Michelangeli, Cortot, Weissenberg, Curzon, Solomon, Ney; Discographies.* [Great Britain]: J. Hunt, 2002.

Kratzenstein, Marilou, and Jerald Hamilton. *Four Centuries of Organ Music: From the Robertsbridge Codex through the Baroque Era; An Annotated Discography.* Detroit: Information Coordinators, 1984.

Lowrey, Alvin. *Lowrey's International Trumpet Discography.* 2 vols. Columbia, SC: Camden House, 1990.

McBeth, Amy. *A Discography of 78 rpm Era Recordings of the Horn: Solo and Chamber Literature with Commentary.* Westport, CT: Greenwood Press, 1997.

Meza, Fernando A. *Percussion Discography: An International Compilation of Solo and Chamber Percussion Music.* New York: Greenwood Press, 1990.

Nelson, Susan. *The Flute on Record: The 78 rpm Era; A Discography.* Lanham, MD: Scarecrow Press, 2006.

8. Native American Music

Wright-McLeod, Brian. *The Encyclopedia of Native Music: More Than a Century of Recordings from the Wax Cylinder to the Internet.* Tucson: University of Arizona Press, 2005.

9. Popular Music (Various Styles)

Allen, Bob. *The Blackwell Guide to Recorded Country Music.* Oxford, UK: Blackwell Publishers, 1994.

Cowley, John, and Paul Oliver. *The New Blackwell Guide to Recorded Blues.* Cambridge, MA: Blackwell Publishers, 1996.

Duxbury, Janell R. *Rockin' the Classics and Classicizin' the Rock: A Selectively Annotated Discography.* Westport, CT: Greenwood Press, 1985. First supplement, 1991.

Edwards, John W. *Rock 'n' Roll through 1969: Discographies of All Performers Who Hit the Charts, Beginning in 1955.* Jefferson, NC: McFarland, 1992.

_____. *Rock 'n' Roll, 1970 through 1979: Discographies of All Performers Who Hit the Charts.* Jefferson, NC: McFarland, 1993.

Gänzl, Kurt. *The Blackwell Guide to the Musical Theatre on Record.* Oxford, UK: Blackwell Reference, 1990.

Kernfeld, Barry. *The Blackwell Guide to Recorded Jazz.* 2nd ed. Cambridge, MA: Blackwell Publishers, 1995.

Kocandrle, Mirek. *The History of Rock and Roll: A Selective Discography.* Boston: G. K. Hall, 1988.

Pruter, Robert. *The Blackwell Guide to Soul Recordings.* Oxford, UK: Blackwell Publishers, 1993.

Russell, Tony, and Bob Pinson. *Country Music Records: A Discography, 1921–1942.* New York: Oxford University Press, 2004.

Strong, M. C. *The Great Rock Discography.* 6th ed. Edinburgh: Canongate, 2000.

Tudor, Dean. *Popular Music: An Annotated Guide to Recordings.* Littleton, CO: Libraries Unlimited, 1983.

10. Vocal Music: Opera, Song, and Musical Theatre

Blyth, Alan. *Choral Music on Record.* Cambridge: Cambridge University Press, 1991.

_____ *Opera on Record.* Discographies compiled by Malcolm Walker. New York: Harper & Row, 1982.

_____. *Song on Record.* 2 vols. Cambridge: Cambridge University Press, 1986.

Fellers, Frederick P. *The Metropolitan Opera on Record: A Discography of the Commercial Recordings.* Westport, CT: Greenwood Press, 1984.

Gruber, Paul, ed. *The Metropolitan Opera Guide to Recorded Opera.* New York: Metropolitan Opera Guild; W. W. Norton, 1993.

Hummel, David. *The Collector's Guide to the American Musical Theatre.* 2 vols. Metuchen, NJ: Scarecrow Press, 1984.

Lynch, Richard Chigley. *TV and Cast Studio Musicals on Record: A Discography of Television Musicals and Studio Recordings of Stage and Film Musicals.* New York: Greenwood Press, 1990.

McCants, Clyde T. *American Opera Singers and Their Recordings: Critical Commentaries and Discographies.* Jefferson, NC: McFarland, 2004.

Raymond, Jack. *Show Music on Record: The First One Hundred Years.* New rev. ed. Washington, DC: J. Raymond, 1998.

11. Women Composers

Cohen, Aaron. *International Discography of Women Composers.* Westport, CT: Greenwood Press, 1984.

12. World Music: A Selected List

"Current Discography" and reviews of audio and video materials in *Ethnomusicology.* 1953– .

Dols, Nancy, ed. *Musics of the World: A Selective Discography.* 4 vols. Los Angeles: Ethnomusicology Archive, UCLA Music Library, 1977–85.

Harvard University. Loeb Music Library. Archive of World Music. http://hcl.harvard.edu/libraries/loebmusic/collections/archive.html.

    Harvard University's Archive of World Music contains significant collections of field recordings and other unique materials for ethnomusicological research.

Seeger, Anthony, and Louise S. Spear. *Early Field Recordings: A Catalogue of Cylinder Collections at the Indiana University Archives of Traditional Music.* Bloomington: Indiana University Press, 1987. http://www.indiana.edu/~libarchm/.

    Indiana University's Archives of Traditional Music houses a significant collection of commercial and noncommercial recordings of music from all regions of the world.

University of California, Los Angeles (UCLA). Ethnomusicology Archive. http://www.ethnomusic.ucla.edu/archive/.

    Since its founding in 1961, UCLA's Ethnomusicology Archive has amassed more than 100,000 noncommercial and commercial recordings in all formats.

See also the listings in Jennifer Post, *Ethnomusicology: A Guide to Research* (New York: Routledge, 2004), 70–75. There are also specialized listings in Ruth M. Stone, *The World's Music: General Perspectives and Reference Tools. Garland Encyclopedia of World Music,* vol. 10 (New York: Routledge, 2002), and Helen Myers, *Ethnomusicology: Historical and Regional Studies* (New York: W. W. Norton, 1993).

E. Selected Media Periodicals and Indexes to Reviews

Librarians and consumers rely on reviews to aid in the selection of recordings and other media materials. In addition to the collector's guides noted, the following periodicals focus on reviews of recordings:

American Record Guide
BBC Music Magazine
Fanfare
Gramophone

It should be noted that recording and video reviews are also found in special subject periodicals, such as *American Music, Early Music, Ethnomusicology,* and *Notes,* as well as in major newspapers, such as the *New York Times.* The following sources *index* these reviews, as an aid to access:

Media Review Digest. Ann Arbor, MI: Pierian Press, 1977– . (print + subscription database)

Myers, Kurtz, and Richard LeSueur. "Index to Record Reviews, with Symbols Indicating Opinions of Reviewers"; continued as "Index to CD Reviews," compiled by Paul Cauthen and Mark Palkovic. *Notes* 1948–97. (quarterly)

CUMULATIONS

Myers, Kurtz. *Index to Record Reviews; Based on Material Originally Published in* Notes, *the Quarterly Journal of the Music Library Association Between 1949 and 1977.* 5 vols. Boston: G. K. Hall, 1978–80.

_____. *Index to Record Reviews, 1978–1983.* Boston: G. K. Hall, 1985.

_____. *Index to Record Reviews 1984–1987.* Boston: G. K. Hall, 1989.

UPDATED BY

Palkovic, Mark, Paul Cauthen, Richard LeSueur, and Kurtz Myers. *Index to CD and Record Reviews, 1987–1997: Based on Material Originally Published in* Notes, *Quarterly Journal of the Music Library Association, Between 1987 and 1997.* 3 vols. New York: G. K. Hall, 1999.

F. Price Guides

Moses, Julian. *Collectors' Guide to American Recordings, 1900–1925.* 1949. Reprint, New York: Dover Publications, 1977.

Osborne, Jerry, and Bruce Hamilton. *The Official Price Guide to Records.* 18th ed. New York: House of Collectibles, 2007.

G. Label Discographies

Although quite specialized, discographies of recording companies ("label discographies") are essential sources of information for documentation of recordings. Indeed, many discographies are compiled from recording company archives. It would be impossible to list even a selection of the numerous published record label discographies. Duckles & Reed (1997) includes several under the heading "Discographies by Label" (entries 10.228–10.252). The *ARSC Journal* (Association for Recorded Sound Collections) is a good source of information on new discographies.

H. Videos

Almquist, Sharon. *Opera Mediagraphy: Video Recordings and Motion Pictures.* Westport, CT: Greenwood Press, 1993.

_____. *Opera Singers in Recital, Concert, and Feature Film: A Mediography.* Westport, CT: Greenwood Press, 1999.

Croissant, Charles E. *Opera Performances in Video Format: A Checklist of Commercially Available Recordings.* MLA Index and Bibliography Series 26. Canton, MA: Music Library Association, 1991.

Gillespie, John, and Anna Gillespie. *Piano Performance Video Recordings on VHS: A Selected Catalog.* Lanham, MD: Scarecrow Press, 2003.

Gruber, Paul. *The Metropolitan Opera Guide to Opera on Video.* New York: Metropolitan Opera Guild; W. W. Norton, 1997.

Levine, Robert. *Guide to Opera and Dance on Videocassette.* Mount Vernon, NY: Consumers Union, 1989.

Spain, Louise. *Dance on Camera: A Guide to Dance Films and Videos.* Lanham, MD: Scarecrow Press, 1998.

Towers, Deirdre. *Dance Film and Video Guide.* Princeton, NJ: Dance Horizons/Princeton Book Co., 1991.

Wlaschin, Ken. *Gian Carlo Menotti on Screen: Opera, Dance, and Choral Works on Film, Television, and Video.* Jefferson, NC: McFarland & Company, 1999.

_____. *Encyclopedia of Opera on Screen: A Guide to More Than 100 Years of Opera Films, Videos, and DVDs.* New Haven, CT: Yale University Press, 2004.

_____. *Opera on Screen: A Guide to 100 Years of Films and Videos Featuring Operas, Opera Singers, and Operettas.* Los Angeles: Beachwood Press, 1997.

I. SELECTED WEB SITES

ArchivMusic
http://www.archivmusic.com/

Association for Recorded Sound Collectors (ARSC)
http://www.arsc-audio.org/

CDConnection
http://www.cdconnection.com

CD Information Center
http://www.cd-info.com/

CDUniverse
http://www.cduniverse.com

H & B Recordings Direct
http://www.hbdirect.com/

Muze
http://www.muze.com

Tower Records
www.tower.com

ABOUT RECORDINGS: A SELECT BIBLIOGRAPHY

Badal, James. *Recording the Classics: Maestros, Music, & Technology.* Kent, OH: Kent State University Press, 1996.

Beardsley, Roger, and Daniel Leech-Wilkinson. "A Brief History of Recording." Center for the History and Analysis of Recorded Music (CHARM). http://www.charm.rhul.ac .uk/content/KCL_resources/beardsley_brief_history.html.

Brooks, Tim. *Lost Sounds: Blacks and the Birth of the Recording Industry 1890–1919.* Urbana: University of Illinois Press, 2004.

Center for the History and Analysis of Recorded Music (CHARM). http://www.charm .rhul.ac.uk/index.html.

> Directed by John Rink, this project was created to "promote the study of music as performance through a specific focus on recordings. Its activities include a major discographic project, seminars, and research projects."[10] Projects include "Analyzing motif in performance"; "Expressive gesture and style in Schubert song performance"; "Style, performance, and meaning in Chopin's Mazurkas"; and "Recording and performance style"[11]

Chanan, Michael. *Repeated Takes: A Short History of Recording and Its Effects on Music.* London: Verso, 1995.

Coleman, Mark. *Playback: From the Victrola to MP3: 100 Years of Music, Machines, and Money.* Cambridge, MA: Da Capo Press, 2003.

Cook, Nicholas, Peter Johnson, and Hans Zender, eds. *Theory Into Practice: Composition, Performance, and the Listening Experience.* Leuven, Belgium: Leuven University Press, 1999.

Copeland, Peter. *Sound Recordings.* London: British Library, 1990.

Day, Timothy. *A Century of Recorded Music: Listening to Musical History.* New Haven, CT: Yale University Press, 2000.

Eisenberg, Evan. *The Recording Angel: Explorations in Phonography.* New York: McGraw-Hill, 1987.

_____. *The Recording Angel: Music, Records and Culture from Aristotle to Zappa.* 2nd ed. New Haven, CT: Yale University Press, 2005.

Fabian, Dorottya. *Bach Performance Practice, 1945–1975: A Comprehensive Review of Sound Recordings and Literature.* Burlington, VT: Ashgate Publishing, 2003.

Gelatt, Roland. *The Fabulous Phonograph, from Edison to Stereo.* Rev. ed. New York: Appleton-Century, 1966.

Harvith, John, and Susan Edwards Harvith. *Edison, Musicians and the Phonograph: A Century in Retrospect.* New York: Greenwood Press, 1987.

Johnson, Peter. "The Legacy of Recordings." In *Musical Performance: A Guide to Understanding,* edited by John Rink, 197–212. Cambridge, England: Cambridge University Press, 2002.

Katz, Mark. *Capturing Sound: How Technology Has Changed Music.* Berkeley: University of California Press, 2004.

Kenney, William Howland. *Recorded Music in American Life: The Phonograph and Popular Memory, 1890–1945.* New York: Oxford University Press, 1999.

Lebrecht, Norman. *Maestros, Masterpieces, and Madness: The Secret Life and Shameful Death of the Classical Record Industry.* London: Allen Lane, 2007.

Millard, A. J. *America on Record: A History of Recorded Sound.* 2nd ed. Cambridge, England: Cambridge University Press, 2005.

Philip, Robert. *Early Recordings and Musical Style: Changing Tastes in Instrumental Performance, 1900–1950.* Cambridge, England: Cambridge University Press, 1992.

_____. *Performing Music in the Age of Recording.* New Haven, CT: Yale University Press, 2004.

Read, Oliver, and Walter L. Welch. *From Tin Foil to Stereo: Evolution of the Phonograph.* Indianapolis: H. W. Sams, 1959.

Smart, James Robert, and Jon W. Newsom. *"A Wonderful Invention": A Brief History of the Phonograph from Tinfoil to the LP: An Exhibition in the Great Hall of the Library of Congress in Celebration of the 100th Anniversary of the Invention of the Phonograph.* Washington, DC: Library of Congress, 1977.

Starr, Larry, and Christopher Waterman. *American Popular Music: From Minstrelsy to MP3.* 2nd ed. New York: Oxford University Press, 2007.

Steffen, David J. *From Edison to Marconi: The First Thirty Years of Recorded Music.* Jefferson, NC: McFarland, 2005.

Symes, Colin. *Setting the Record Straight: A History of Classical Recording.* Middleton, CT: Wesleyan University Press, 2004.

Weber, Jerome F., et al. "Recorded Sound" in *Grove Music Online.* Edited by Laura Macy. www.grovemusic.com.

NOTES

1. Jerome F. Weber, "Discography," *Grove Music Online,* ed. L. Macy http://www.grovemusic.com.

2. In March 2008, researchers announced discovery of an 1860 spoken-word recording made by Paris inventor Édouard-Léon Scott de Martinville. See Jody Rosen, "Researchers Play Tune Recorded Before Edison," *New York Times,* March 27, 2008.

3. For further information, see "Mapelson Cylinders," *Encyclopedia of Recorded Sound,* 2nd ed. Frank W. Hoffmann and Howard Ferstler (New York: Routledge, 2004), 654–55.

4. William Ashbrook, "Opera Recordings," *Encyclopedia of Recorded Sound,* 2nd ed. Frank W. Hoffmann and Howard Ferstler (New York: Routledge, 2004), 771–77.

5. Will Crutchfield, "Next Home Stereo Advance: Digital Tape Cassettes in 1987," *New York Times,* October 24, 1986.

6. Robert Philip, *Performing Music in the Age of Recording* (New Haven: Yale University Press, 2004), 4–5.

7. See Roy Howat, *Oeuvres Complètes de Claude Debussy, Series I, Volume 5: Préludes* (Paris: Durand-Costallat, 1985), 159–60.

8. John Harvith and Susan Edwards Harvith, *Edison, Musicians, and the Phonograph: A Century in Retrospect.* Contributions to the Study of Music and Dance 11 (New York: Greenwood Press, 1987), 75.

9. Leonard Burkat and George Boziwick, "Schwann, William (Joseph)," *Grove Music Online,* ed. L. Macy. www.grovemusic.com.

10. CHARM website: http://www.charm.rhul.ac.uk/index.html.

11. Ibid.

CHAPTER 8

From Manuscript to Printed Edition

INTRODUCTION

For the last 600 years, information has been disseminated through techniques of mass production: as we have seen in the last chapter, the recorded sound technologies developed at the turn of the twentieth century have enabled multiple copies of the same performance to reach millions. Similarly, printing has facilitated the mass production of books, periodicals, and music scores. The digital copies we rely on today are largely replicas of materials originally produced in other media; even "born digital" resources were created for mass dissemination.

Prior to the invention of printing, information could be conveyed only via a handwritten manuscript, which, by its very nature, is unique. As the study of manuscript sources and their relationship to printed editions can be rather complex, a review of some basic definitions may be helpful:

MANUSCRIPT: handwritten document
AUTOGRAPH OR HOLOGRAPH: handwritten document in the hand of the creator
MANUSCRIPT COPY: copy of another manuscript
COPYIST MANUSCRIPT: manuscript prepared from the autograph by an authorized copyist, usually under the supervision of the composer
PRINTED: document created using a printing technology (printing from type, lithography, or computer methods), for the purpose of mass dissemination
PUBLISHED: document (either printed or in manuscript form) managed by a business enterprise for the purpose of sale to other parties; the verb *publish* means "to make public." Composers may self-publish their works. Not all published music is offered in printed editions for sale: some music scores (particularly large ensemble works) are issued only on a *rental* basis. In these cases, a copy of the work (full score and performance parts) is provided only for a specific performance.
COPYRIGHT: government-authorized legal protection of creator rights for original works, either published or unpublished. Under the terms of the current U.S. copyright law, material is protected for the life of the creator plus 70 years.

OUT-OF-PRINT: term generally used when copies are no longer available from a publisher; does not imply that work is *out of copyright/public domain,* meaning no longer eligible for legal protection. For further information on copyright, see pp. 213–217.

MANUSCRIPT SOURCES AND RISM

The *Grove Music Online* articles on "Sources" provide detailed information on manuscript sources and their significance for music research. The general article under "Sources" by Stanley Boorman and others is followed by specific articles on "Sources of Instrumental Ensemble Music to 1630," "Sources of Keyboard Music to 1660," and "Sources of Lute Music." Each section also includes lists of significant manuscript sources and their library locations.

The term *sources,* as it relates to the study of manuscripts, is further subdivided into categories of primary sources and secondary sources, defined as follows:

Primary sources: sources that are closest to the creator, such as autographs or holographs; composer-supervised manuscript copies; first editions with annotations by the composer; or autograph letters.

Secondary sources: sources that are one or more steps removed from the creator, such as copyist manuscripts without connection to the composer or editions published after the composer's death.

Scholars examine primary sources, such as manuscripts and early editions, both to understand musical repertoire from earlier periods and to create scholarly/ critical editions of works by individual composers.

RISM

RISM (Répertoire International des Sources Musicales = International Inventory of Musical Sources) is the music community's *inventory* of primary sources. Founded in Paris in 1952 with joint sponsorship of the International Musicological Society (IMS) and International Association of Music Libraries (IAML), RISM represented a unique post–World War II effort at world harmony.[1] It is important to note that RISM is an *inventory* of manuscripts and early printed editions (both books and scores) from ca. 1500 to 1800 held by libraries worldwide. The RISM system of library locations (or siglia), which uses a pattern of country letter followed by library abbreviation, has been adopted by many other scholarly tools in music, such as *Grove Music Online.* For example, A-Wn is the symbol for the Österreichische Nationalbibliothek, Musik-Sammlung in Austria; US-Wc represents the U.S. Library of Congress in Washington, DC.

RISM is published in three distinct series: Series A, or the alphabetical catalog, lists works under the names of individual composers, in separate series for printed editions (A/I) and manuscripts (A/II); Series B includes specialized catalogs of printed and manuscript music; and, Series C is a guide to information on music libraries and archives worldwide. A complete publications listing is found on the RISM Web site: http://rism.stub.uni-frankfurt.de/index1_e.htm.

A (or alphabetical catalog) lists works under names of individual composers, in separate sections for printed music (A/I) and manuscript music (A/II).

A/I = Printed Editions Before 1800

Published in 15 volumes (1971–2003); vol. 15: *Index of Publishers, Printers and Engravers and Index of Places to volumes 1–9 and 11–14.* Also available on CD-ROM. Documents ca. 200,000 printed editions by 8,000 composers published from 1500 to 1800. The RISM founders allowed that composers such as Haydn whose most productive periods fell before 1800 would have their post-1800 works included, but they did not extend coverage to composers such as Beethoven, whose most productive periods were after 1800.[2]

Entries in the A/I volumes tend to be rather bare boned, with information limited to composer name, title of work as it appeared on the title page, imprint, and holding libraries, reflecting RISM's primary mission as an inventory of sources, rather than a dictionary or bibliographical study.

This limitation is often confusing to new users of RISM. For example, the entries under Handel's *Messiah* (vol. 4, nos. 718–805) have information on where to find editions of the work published before 1800, but RISM does not indicate which of these editions is the *first* edition. Indeed, the availability of location information in RISM is what enables scholars to locate sources and do the type of comparative study that helps to determine a first edition. Once this information is determined, it is usually recorded in the composer thematic catalog.

It can also be challenging to locate individual works within the RISM A/I volumes, as they are typically arranged in a classified manner similar to arrangements in complete works editions. The first entry under the composer's name provides a guide to the arrangement (Figure 8–1).

A/II = Music Manuscripts 1600–1800 (available on CD-ROM and online)

Lists close to 600,000 works by nearly 30,000 composers; entries continue to be added as libraries report holdings. Its inclusive date coverage of 1600–1800 means that Beethoven works are found in A/II, while, as noted earlier, they are not found in A/I. The entries in RISM A/II are much more detailed than those in A/I and include bibliographic references to literature about the work along with basic information, such as composer, title, and library location. As well, RISM A/II entries include musical incipits, the opening notes, of each work. This unique feature allows users to search for works by musical notation, using the "Plaine and Easie Code" developed by Barry S. Brook in 1960 for transcribing musical notation using computer keyboard codes.[3] (See also p. 246 and Figure 8–2.)

Series B = Specialized Catalogs of Manuscripts and Printed Editions

(For complete listing, see http://rism.stub.uni-frankfurt.de/index1_e.htm.) The volumes in RISM Series B provide access to a variety of printed and manuscript sources in various subseries, summarized as follows: collections or anthologies of works printed before 1800 (B/I and B/II); music theory manuscripts before 1500 (B/III); manuscripts

FIGURE 8–1 Arrangement of entries for Handel works in RISM A/I, *Einzeldrucke vor 1800,* Bd. 4 (Kassel: Bärenreiter, 1974), 4

Hadrava, Norbert   *H 38–H 48*

HADRAVA Norbert

La partenza. Sonata per cembalo, o piano-forte dedicata al Sig. D. Federico-Luigi Moritz. – *Napoli, s. n.*   [H 38
CH E – I Nc

Sonata per il clavicembalo o piano-forte dedicata a Sua Eccellenza il Sig. D. Onorato Gaetani. – *Napoli, Luigi Marescalchi.*   [H 39
A Wn – US NYp

Nenia funebre (Sit tibi terra levis) alla memorie dell' infelice Cavaliere Alessandro Roos . . . dedicata all . . . Sig. Brun. – *s. l., s. n.* – KLA.   [H 40
I Nc

HAEFTEN Benedictus van

Den lust-hof der christelycke leeringhe beplant met gheestelycke liedekens [a 2 v, niederländisch und lateinisch], tot verklaringhe van den cathecismus des Artsbischdoms van Mechelen. – *Antwerpen, Hieronymus Verdussen, 1622.*   [H 41
B Amp, Br – GB Lbm (2 Ex.) – NL DHk – US AA

HÄNDEL Georg Friedrich

Die Redaktion dankt Herrn Dr. Bernd Baselt für seine Beratung. – Die verschiedenen Ausgaben eines Werkes sind in der Regel chronologisch geordnet; Serien sind überwiegend in einzelne Ausgaben aufgelöst worden.

Gliederung:

I. Vokalmusik:

1. Opern ([H 42 – [H 378). – 2. Oratorien und Masques ([H 379 – [H 985). – 3. Serenaden ([H 986 – [H 993). – 4. Oden ([H 994 – [H 1045). – 5. Kammerduette und -trios ([H 1046 – [H 1050). – 6. Arien und Lieder ([H 1051 – [H 1142). – 7. Kirchenmusik ([H 1143 – [H 1211).

II. Instrumentalmusik:

1. Orchesterwerke (Konzerte für 1 – 2 Solo-Instrumente und Orchester [H 1212 –

[H 1240; Concerti grossi [H 1241 – [H 1262; Ouverturen [H 1263 – [H 1317; Water music [H 1318 – [H 1335; Fireworks music [H 1336 – [H 1339). – 2. Kammermusik (Sonaten für 1 Solo-Instrument und Basso continuo [H 1340 – [H 1345; Trio-Sonaten [H 1346 – [H 1355; Menuette, Märsche und andere Stücke [H 1356 – [H 1365; Solos for a german flute [H 1366 – [H 1387; Sonatas or chamber airs [H 1388 – [H 1429). – 3. Musik für Tasteninstrumente ([H 1430 – [H 1492).

III. Arnold-Edition   ([H 1493 – [H 1571).

I. VOKALMUSIK

1. OPERN

Admeto

Admetus. An opera, compos'd by Mr Handel. – *London, J. Cluer.* – P.   [H 42
B Bc, Br – D-brd Bhm, F, Hs – F Pc (2 Ex.), Pn – GB BENcoke, Ckc, En, Er, Lbm, Lcm, Lgc, Ob – I Bc, BGi, Rsc – US CA, NYp, Wc, Ws

— *ib., [nach 1727].*   [H 43
A Wn – D-brd Hs – D-ddr LEm – PL Wu – S St – US Wc

— Admetus. An opera compos'd by Mr. Handel. – *ib., J. Walsh.*   [H 44
F Pc – GB BENcoke, En, T

The favourite songs in the opera call'd Admetus. – *London, J. Walsh & J. Hare.* – P.   [H 45
F Pc

— *ib., [nach 1728].*   [H 46
GB BENcoke, Lam

— The favourite songs in the opera call'd Admeto by Mr Handel. – *ib., J. Walsh.*   [H 47
A Wgm – GB BENcoke, Cfm, Lcm

Mr. Handel's opera of Admetus transposed for the flute, . . . published by authority of the patentee. – *London, Benjamin Cooke (Thomas Cross).* – P.   [H 48
GB BENcoke – US Wc

Admetus, for a flute, the ariets with their symphonys for a single flute and the duet

FIGURE 8–2   Entry for Haydn manuscript from RISM A/II database (NISC Biblioline)

Used by permission.

of polyphonic music from the eleventh to the sixteenth centuries (B/IV); manuscripts of tropes and sequences (B/V); printed writings about music (B/VI); manuscripts of lute and guitar music in tablature (B/VII); printed sources of German hymns (B/VIII); Hebrew manuscript sources (B/IX); Arabic manuscript sources (B/X); manuscripts of Ancient Greek music theory (B/XI); Persian manuscript sources (B/XII); manuscripts of liturgical processional books (B/XIV); and printed and manuscript sources of polyphonic masses in Spain, Portugal, and Latin America (B/XV). Among the forthcoming volumes is a study of Slovak hymn sources (B/XIII).

RISM Series B volumes provide detailed bibliographical and historical information on sources and fall more in the category of musicological surveys, rather than basic inventories. The arrangement and features of each volume vary depending upon the subject of study. Selected titles are described here:

B/I AND B/II: *RECUEILS IMPRIMÉS XVIE-XVIIIE SIÈCLES* (2 BÄNDE)

B/I: Lesure, François. *Recueils Imprimés XVIe-XVIIe Siècles*. Munich: G. Henle, 1960.
Modeled on Eitner's *Bibliographie der Musik Sammelwerke des XVI und XVII Jahrhunderts* (see later entry), Lesure's book documents ca. 2,700 collections published in the sixteenth and seventeenth centuries, arranged chronologically beginning with Petrucci's *Odhecaton*.

Zappala, Pietro, et al. *The Index of Composers to RISM B/I (Recueils imprimés XVI-XVII siécles)*. Available online as PDF file: http://philomusica.unipv.it/materiali/rism/IndexB1.pdf.

B/II: Lesure, François. *Recueils Imprimés XVIIIe Siècles*. Munich: G. Henle, 1964.
Documents ca. 1,800 collections published between 1701 and 1800, arranged alphabetically, rather than chronologically as in B/I, because most of these publications were not dated.

B/IV/5. Bridgman, Nanie: *Manuscrits de Musique Polyphonique XVe et XVIe Siècles. Italie*. Munich: G. Henle, 1991.
Documenting manuscripts of polyphonic music from approximately 1425 to 1530 preserved in Italian libraries, this volume presents a fine example of the amount of scholarly detail provided by some of the volumes in RISM Series B. Arranged by library location, each manuscript is described in enormous detail, with information on physical characteristics (size, number of folios); composer and work found on each folio; references to modern editions, facsimiles, and scholarly literature; and codes for the musical incipits. (Other volumes within series B/IV have actual musical notation for the incipits.)

Similarly, Thomas Mathiesen's RISM B/XI volume, *Ancient Greek Music Theory: A Catalogue Raisonné of Manuscripts* (München: G. Henle, 1988), provides folio-by-folio descriptions of texts in manuscript sources of ancient Greek Music theory. (Mathiesen has also created the online *Thesaurus Musicarum Latinarum* under the auspices of the Center for Music Theory and Translation—see under "Bibliographies of Early Music," pp. 184–185.)

C = Directory of Music Research Libraries

The "Baedeckers" for music research, RISM Series C volumes provide detailed information on music libraries worldwide. Series C initially covered only those libraries with holdings in RISM Series A and B, but it now includes music libraries with a wide range of collections and types of materials. In addition to essential information such as hours and protocols for libraries, some volumes include useful visitor information, such as "Guide to the Japanese Language and Its Romanization" (found in vol. C/IV).

- C/I: Kahn, Marian, Helmut Kallmann, and Charles Lindahl. *Directory of Music Research Libraries*. Volume 1: *Canada and the United States*. 2nd rev. ed. Kassel: Bärenreiter, 1983.
- C/II: Davis, Elizabeth. *Directory of Music Research Libraries*. Volume 2: *Sixteen European Countries (Austria, Belgium, Switzerland, Germany, Denmark, Spain)*. 2nd rev. ed. Kassel: Bärenreiter, 2001.
- C/III/1: Davis, Elizabeth. *Directory of Music Research Libraries*. Volume 3,1: *Sixteen European Countries (France, Finland, United Kingdom. Ireland, Luxembourg, Norway, Netherlands, Portugal, Sweden)*. 2nd rev. ed. Kassel: Bärenreiter, 2001.

- C/III/2: *Directory of Music Research Libraries.* Volume 3,2: *Italy* (in preparation).
- C/IV: Hill, Cecil, Katya Manor, James Siddons, and Dorothy Freed. *Directory of Music Research Libraries.* Volume 4: *Australia, Israel, Japan, New Zealand.* Kassel: Bärenreiter, 1979.
- C/V: Moldovan, James B., and Lilian Pruett. *Directory of Music Research Libraries.* Volume 5: *Czechoslovakia, Hungary, Poland, Yugoslavia.* Kassel: Bärenreiter, 1985.

The predecessors to RISM were two tools by the German bibliographer Robert Eitner (1832–1905):

Biographisch-bibliographisches Quellen-Lexikon der Musiker und Musikgelehrten der christlichen Zeitrechnung bis zur Mitte des neunzehnten Jahrhunderts. 10 vols. Leipzig: Breitkopf & Härtel, 1900–04.
Bibliographie der Musik-Sammelwerke des XVI. und XVII. Jahrhunderts. Berlin: Liepmannssohn, 1877. Reprint, Hildesheim: G. Olms, 1977.

Eitner's "Quellen-Lexicon," or source-lexicon, was a biographical-bibliographical dictionary of composers born before 1771; entries included brief biographical information and listings of the composer's works (both printed and manuscript) with library locations in more than 200 European libraries. This served as the model for RISM series A. The *Bibliographie der Musik-Sammelwerke* is a chronological listing of 795 collections of music published between 1501 (Petrucci's *Odhecaton*) and 1700; it served as the model for RISM B/I. Eitner's achievement in producing these books is remarkable, considering that he compiled this information before the advent of photocopying, fax, the telephone, and, of course, the Internet.

Interest in documenting musical sources coincided with the development of musicology as a discipline, especially compilation of composer critical editions and thematic catalogs (explained more fully in Chapter 5: Histories of Music and Related Subjects). By 1950, much of the information in Eitner's books was obsolete due to the devastation of two European world wars, which led to displacement of many of the sources he so carefully documented. Born as an effort to update Eitner, RISM is now recognized as a model tool for scholarly research in the humanities.

SUMMARY

RISM enables scholars to locate primary sources, specifically manuscripts and early editions (prior to 1800) held in libraries worldwide.

- USE RISM A/I (which covers printed editions) or RISM A/II (which covers manuscripts in an online database) when searching for sources by individual composers. For composers with scholarly thematic catalogs, there may be some overlap in the information found in RISM and the thematic catalog. For composers without scholarly thematic catalogs, RISM may be the only place in which to locate information on sources of their works.

- USE RISM Series B volumes (which include specialized catalogs for manuscripts and printed editions) or one of the bibliographies of music before 1800 (listed on pp. 184–185) as needed if searching for detailed information on particular repertoire, such as manuscripts of polyphonic masses, manuscripts of Greek music theory, or seventeenth-century British keyboard music.
- USE RISM Series C to learn more about individual libraries.

Question: Why do I need to bother using RISM when so many manuscripts are available digitally on the Internet?

Answer: Only a very small portion of the hundreds of thousands of manuscripts documented by RISM have been digitized.

BIBLIOGRAPHIES OF EARLY MUSIC (MUSIC BEFORE 1800)

In addition to RISM, many other valuable reference tools seek to document "early music," specifically music before 1800, following RISM's cutoff date. As RISM is primarily an inventory (or locator tool) of sources, the books cited here usually provide more detailed descriptions of individual sources.

See, for example, the entry for Petrucci's landmark *Odhecaton* (discussed in more detail on pp. 186–187), RISM 1501 in Howard Mayer Brown's *Instrumental Music Printed Before 1600: A Bibliography* (Figure 8–3).

Similar to RISM, Brown lists a library location (I: Bc, which is the abbreviation for the Biblioteca communale annessa al Conservatorio musicale in Bologna, Italy) and notes that it is an imperfect copy. However, going much further than RISM B/I, Brown provides a detailed description of the source, with focus on its instrumental works. Of special note are his indications of where facsimile and modern editions of particular works may be found. For example, a modern edition of Heinrich Isaac's "La morra," located on folio 49 verso in the *Odhecaton,* may be found in the historical series *Denkmaler Tonkunst der Osterreiche,* vol. XIV/29, p. 90. (This reference includes more precise detail than could be extracted by using Hill, Heyer, or other indexes to historical series, described on pp. 203–206).

Brown's book is itself a landmark music bibliography, as it provides the bibliographical data from which the history of instrumental music in the Renaissance may be understood. As he states in his introduction,

Before a comprehensive survey of the field can be made, however, the music must be assembled, sorted, and studied. Using the bibliographical techniques developed mainly by Emil Vogel, Alfred Einstein, Claudio Sartori, and, most recently, by the compilers of the first volume of *Répertoire International des sources musicales (RISM),* my aim has been

10 $148?_1$

41	B5	*Alenchon*
42	B5	*La portingaloyse*[3]
43	B5	*Vatem mon amoureux desir*[1]
44	B5v	*Joyeusement*
45	B5v	*Passe rose*
46	B5v	*La basine*
47	B5v	*Ma souverayne* (compare PlamF, p. 6, no. 102)
48	B6	*La marguerite*
49	B6	*Vyses*

[1] Facs. of fol. A5 in BukMR, opp. p. 128.
[2] Mod. ed. in KinDT, p. 102. Facs. of fol. B1 in PN, p. 63.
[3] Apparently not related to Dufay's "Portugaler" (mod. ed. in BorD, pp. 297–302).
[4] Apparently not related to "Va tost mon amoureux desir," in I:Fr, MS 2356; see PlamSC, no. 30.

1501_1

PETRUCCI, OTTAVIANO, PUBLISHER

Harmonice Musices / Odhecaton / A[1]

104 fols. Mensural notation. Dedication to Girolamo Donato on fol. 1v headed "Octavianus petrutius forosemproniensis Hieronymo Donato patricio Veneto Felicitatem," and dated "Venetiis decimo octavo cal. iuias. Salutis anno. MDI." (May 15, 1501). On fol. 2: a letter from Bartolomeo Budrio to Girolamo Donato, headed "Bartholomaeus Budrius Justinopolita Hieronymo donato patricio Veneto. S." On fol. 2v: table of contents. All of the prefatory material is reprinted in SartP, pp. 34–37. PetrO is a facsimile reprint (made from 1504_2) of the entire collection, Petrucci's first publication, and the first volume of polyphonic music ever printed. HewO is a modern edition of the entire collection, with an extensive introduction, several facsimile pages, and complete concordances. For further information, see also ReO and SartP, pp. 34–42. The volume contains 96 compositions, most of them with text incipits only. At least four of these were almost certainly originally conceived for instruments (see the statement of policy in the Introduction, above, and also CauO, CauT, and HewO, pp. 74–78, where seven such pieces from this volume are listed and discussed). Contents = 1503_1 and 1504_2.
Copy in: I:Bc (imperfect).

	fol.			
1	20v	*Dit le burguygnon*		a4
2	49v	*La morra*[2]	Yzac	a3
3	54v	*La stangetta*[3]	Werbach [or Obrecht?]	a3
4	87v	*La alfonsina*[4]	Jo. ghiselin	a3

[1] Facs. of title page in GrandT, p. 7. Facs. of title page and one other page in MagniSM I, 239. Facs. of several pages in AbbS I, 331; PN, p. 66; ReO; and VernO, fig. 3.
[2] Mod. ed. also in DTO XIV/28, p. 90, and RieM, no. 18.
[3] Mod. ed. also in ObrWW, p. 45.
[4] Mod. ed. also in AmbG V, 190, and GiesS, p. 92.

1502_1

PETRUCCI, OTTAVIANO, PUBLISHER

Motetti. A. numero. / .trentatre. / A

56 fols. Mensural notation. On fol. 1v: table of contents. Colophon on fol. 56: "Impressum Venetiis per Octavianum Petrutium Forosemproniensem die 9 Madii Salutis anno 1502. Cum privilegio invictissimi Dominii Venetiarum quod nullus possit cantum Figuratum Imprimere sub pena in ipso privilegio contenta," followed by the register of signatures. For further information see SartP, pp. 44–46. The volume contains 32 compositions with Latin text, two vocal compositions ("O flores rosa" and "De tous biens") with text incipit only, and one composition for instruments. SartP gives a complete list of the contents.
Copy in: I:Bc.[1]

	fol.			
1	32	*La spagna*[2]	Ghiselin	a4

[1] A copy was in E:S; see SartN, no. 11.
[2] The beginning is pr. in GomVC, p. 1.

1503_1

PETRUCCI, OTTAVIANO, PUBLISHER

Harmonice Musices / Odhecaton / A

104 fols. Mensural notation. The prefatory material is identical with that in the first edition (1501_1). Colophon on fol. 104: "Impressum Venetiis per Octavianum Petrutium Forosemproniensem 1502 die 14 Januarii. Cum privilegio invictissimi Dominii

Source: Reprinted by permission of the publisher from *Instrumental Music Printed Before 1600: A Bibliography,* by Howard Mayer Brown, p. 10. Cambridge, MA: Harvard University Press, copyright © 1965 by the President and Fellows of Harvard College.

to gather in one place information relevant to a study of this repertoire, describing each volume, making an inventory of its contents, and listing modern editions and studies of the music.[4]

He does this in a magnificent volume that lists some 400 collections of instrumental music chronologically, beginning with a 148? collection published by Michel de Toulouze and concluding with several collections published in 1599. There is an appendix of "Editions with Basso Continuo Parts Not Listed Elsewhere in the Bibliography" and indexes: List of Libraries and Their Holdings; Volumes Described, Arranged by Types of Notation; Volumes Described, Arranged by Performing Medium; Names; and First Lines and Titles.

Similarly, the other early music bibliographies listed here provide more focused studies of particular repertoire, albeit with varying levels of detail and distinct approaches.

Apel, Willi. *Italian Violin Music of the Seventeenth Century.* Edited by Thomas Binkley. Bloomington: Indiana University Press, 1990.

Bailey, Candace. *Seventeenth-Century British Keyboard Sources.* Detroit Studies in Music Bibliography 83. Warren, MI: Harmonie Park Press, 2003.

Britton, Allen Perdue, Irving Lowens, and Richard Crawford. *American Sacred Music Imprints 1698–1810: A Bibliography.* Worcester, MA: American Antiquarian Society, 1990.

Brookes, Virginia. *British Keyboard Music to c. 1600: Sources and Thematic Index.* Oxford, England: Clarendon Press, 1996.

Brown, Howard Mayer. *Instrumental Music Printed Before 1600: A Bibliography.* Cambridge, MA: Harvard University Press, 1965.

Call, Jerry, and Herbert Kellman. *Census-Catalogue of Manuscript Sources of Polyphonic Music, 1400–1550.* Compiled by the University of Illinois, Musicological Archives for Renaissance Manuscript Studies. Renaissance Manuscript Studies 1. 5 vols. (vol. 1 edited by Charles Hamm with Herbert Kellman; vols. 2–5 edited by Herbert Kellman). Rome: American Institute of Musicology, 1979–1988.

Center for the History of Music Theory and Literature. *Theasurus Musicarum Latinarum.* http://www.chmtl.indiana.edu/tml/start.html: "an evolving database of the entire corpus of Latin music theory written during the Middle Ages and the Renaissance."

Charteris, Richard. *Johann Georg von Werdenstein (1542–1608): A Major Collector of Early Music Prints.* Detroit Studies in Music Bibliography 87. Sterling Heights, MI: Harmonie Park Press, 2006.

Eitner, Robert. *Biographisch-Bibliographisches Quellen-Lexicon der Musiker und Musikgelehrten der Christlichen Zeitrechnung bis Zur Mitte des Neunzehnten Jahrhunderts.* 10 vols. Leipzig: Breitkopf & Härtel, 1898–1904.

Eitner, Robert, and F. X. Haberl. *Bibliographie der Musik-Sammelwerke des XVI und XVII Jahrhunderts.* Berlin: Liepmannssohn, 1877. Reprint, Hildesheim; Olms, 1977.

Fallows, David. *A Catalogue of Polyphonic Songs, 1415–1480.* Oxford: Oxford University Press, 1999.

Gustafson, Bruce. *French Harpsichord Music of the 17th Century: A Thematic Catalog of the Sources with Commentary.* 3 vols. Ann Arbor, MI: UMI Research Press, 1979.

Gustafson, Bruce, and David Fuller. *A Catalogue of French Harpsichord Music 1699–1780.* Oxford: Oxford University Press, 1990.

Hagopian, Viola Luther. *Italian Ars Nova Music: A Bibliographic Guide to Modern Editions and Related Literature.* Berkeley: University of California Press, 1964.

Hartzell, K.D. *Catalogue of Manuscripts Written or Owned in England Up to 1200 Containing Music.* Woodbridge, Suffolk, England: The Boydell Press in association with the Plainsong and Medieval Music Society, 2006.

Hunter, David. *Opera and Song Books Published in England 1703–1726: A Descriptive Bibliography.* London: Bibliographical Society, 1997.

Jackson, Barbara Garvey. *"Say You Can Deny Me": A Guide to Surviving Music by Women from the 16th through the 18th Centuries.* Fayetteville: University of Arkansas Press, 1994. (RISM for women composers)

Lincoln, Harry B. *The Italian Madrigal and Related Repertories: Indexes to Printed Collections 1500–1600.* New Haven: Yale University Press, 1988.

_____. *The Latin Motet: Indexes to Printed Collections, 1500–1600.* Musicological Studies LIX. Ottawa, Canada: The Institute of Medieval Music, 1993.

Massip, Catherine and Cécile Grand, eds. *Catalogue des manuscrits musicaux antérieurs á 1800: conserves au Département de la musique, A et B.* Paris: Bibliothéque nationale de France, 1999.

RISM = Repertoire International des Sources Musicales. (See pp. 176–182.) http://rism.stub .uni-frankfurt.de/index1_e.htm under "Publications"

Sartori, Claudio. *Bibliografia della Musica Strumentale Italiana Stampata in Italia fino all 1700.* 2 vols. Firenze: L. S. Olschki, 1952–68.

Silbiger, Alexander. *Italian Manuscript Sources of 17th Century Keyboard Music.* Studies in Musicology 18. Ann Arbor, MI: UMI Research Press, 1980.

Vogel, Emil. *Bibliothek der Gedruckten Weltlichen Vokalmusik Italiens aus den Jahren 1500–1700.* Berlin: A. Haack, 1892.

Vogel, Emil, Françoise Lesure, and Claudio Sartori. *Bibliografia della Musica Vocale Profana Pubblicata dal 1500 al 1700.* New ed. 3 vols. Pomezia: Staderni-Minkoff, 1977. ("Il Nuovo Vogel")

Walker, Diane Parr, and Paul Walker. *German Sacred Polyphonic Vocal Music Between Schütz and Bach: Sources and Critical Editions.* Detroit Studies in Music Bibliography 67. Warren, MI: Harmonie Park Press, 1992.

MUSIC PRINTING AND PUBLISHING

A glance at a printed music score makes it obvious that the science and skill required to produce such a document are more complicated than those required to print a book composed entirely of words. Music notation itself is composed of a variety of shapes carefully placed on lines and spaces; in the case of a vocal work, the text must be placed underneath specific notes. Added to this mix are dynamics, ornaments, and other expressive markings that must be placed exactly where the composer intended.

As pointed out by Krummel, Sadie, and many others, looking at a chronology of music printing should not imply that one technique succeeded another. Even though the technique of engraving offered many advantages over printing from type, music publishers would at times use these same techniques simultaneously. For example, in the eighteenth century, the Breitkopf and Härtel firm published an extensive thematic catalog of its offerings; while the examples in catalog itself were printed from type, an order for music would be fulfilled through a manuscript copied by hand (Figure 8–4).

Essential Sources of Information

(See also bibliography on pp. 195–197.)

King, A. Hyatt. *Four Hundred Years of Music Printing.* 2nd ed. London: British Museum, 1968.

Krummel, Donald W., and Sadie Stanley, eds. *Music Printing and Publishing.* Norton/Grove Handbooks in Music. New York: W. W. Norton, 1990.

British bibliographer and musicologist Alexander (Alec) Hyatt King (1911–94) was associated with the British Library's Music Department from 1934 until his retirement in 1971. He published widely on various aspects of bibliography, book collecting, Mozart, and Handel. His slim, 48-page book *Four Hundred Years of Music Printing* is a classic narrative history of music printing with lavish full-page illustrations.

Krummel and Sadie's *Music Printing and Publishing* is based on the articles on music printing and publishing in the 1980 edition of *New Grove* and the 1986 *New Grove Dictionary of American Music,* with updates and revisions. The chapters on music printing and music publishing are followed by a Dictionary of Music Printers and Publishers, a Glossary of Terms (by Stanley Boorman), and an extensive Bibliography (by Donald Krummel). This handbook is an essential reference tool on music printing and publishing.

Printing was first developed in Asia. There are examples of books printed from woodblocks as far back as the eighth century. The "modern" era of printing began in Europe in the latter half of the fifteenth century, when the German inventor Johannes Gutenberg (1399?–1468) printed a 42-line Latin Bible from moveable type, ca. 1455.[5] The type was made from cast metal: each letter of the alphabet appeared on its own block. Gutenberg may have produced between 150 and 180 copies of his Bible; some 48 are still in existence and preserved in library collections.[6]

Printing from type spread to northern and central Italy during the 1460s and was adopted throughout Europe after 1473. The period from 1450 to 1500 is known as the *Incunabula* period (derived from the Latin *incunabulum* = "cradle").

Although music was printed from woodblocks in liturgical books prior to the sixteenth century, the 1501 publication *Harmonice musices Odhecaton A* ("One Hundred Songs of Polyphonic Music") by the Venetian printer Ottavanio Petrucci (1466?–1539) is considered to be the first example of music printing, the equivalent of the Gutenberg Bible for music. It was printed from movable type using three impressions (one for staves, one for notes, one for text) and included three- and four-part chansons and motets by composers such as Agricola, Busnois, Compère, Hayne, Isaac, Japart, Josquin, Obrecht, Ockeghem, de Orto, Stockem, Tinctoris, and others: some 96 works in total, short of the 100 referenced in its title.

FIGURE 8–4   Page from *Breitkopf Thematic Catalog*. Edited and with Introduction and Indexes by Barry S. Brook. New York: Dover Publications, Inc., 1966

Source: *Breitkopf Thematic Catalog.* Edited and with Introduction and Indexes by Barry S. Brook. New York: Dover Publications, Inc., 1966. Pg. 24

Petrucci's *Odhecaton* and other publications were magnificent exemplars of printing technology, but his use of triple-impression printing was certainly not economical from a business perspective, as each page went through the press three times. In 1527–28, the French printer Pierre Attaingnant issued *Chansons nouvelles en musique á quatre parties: naguere imprimees á Paris,* one of the first examples of music printed from movable type using one impression. While single-impression printing was certainly more economical for printers, the result was less elegant than that produced by triple impressions, as notes on separate pieces of type were awkward to align on the staff (Figure 8–5).

Most sixteenth-century and seventeenth-century music publications were *anthologies* (*Recueils,* in French), or collections of works by different composers (see anthology, p. 206). These anthologies contained chansons, motets, madrigals, keyboard intabulations, and other genres popular at the time. Among the tools that document these publications are Eitner, RISM B/I, Howard Mayer Brown's bibliography, and other sources listed on pp. 184–185.

FIGURE 8–5 Example of Single Impression Movable Type.

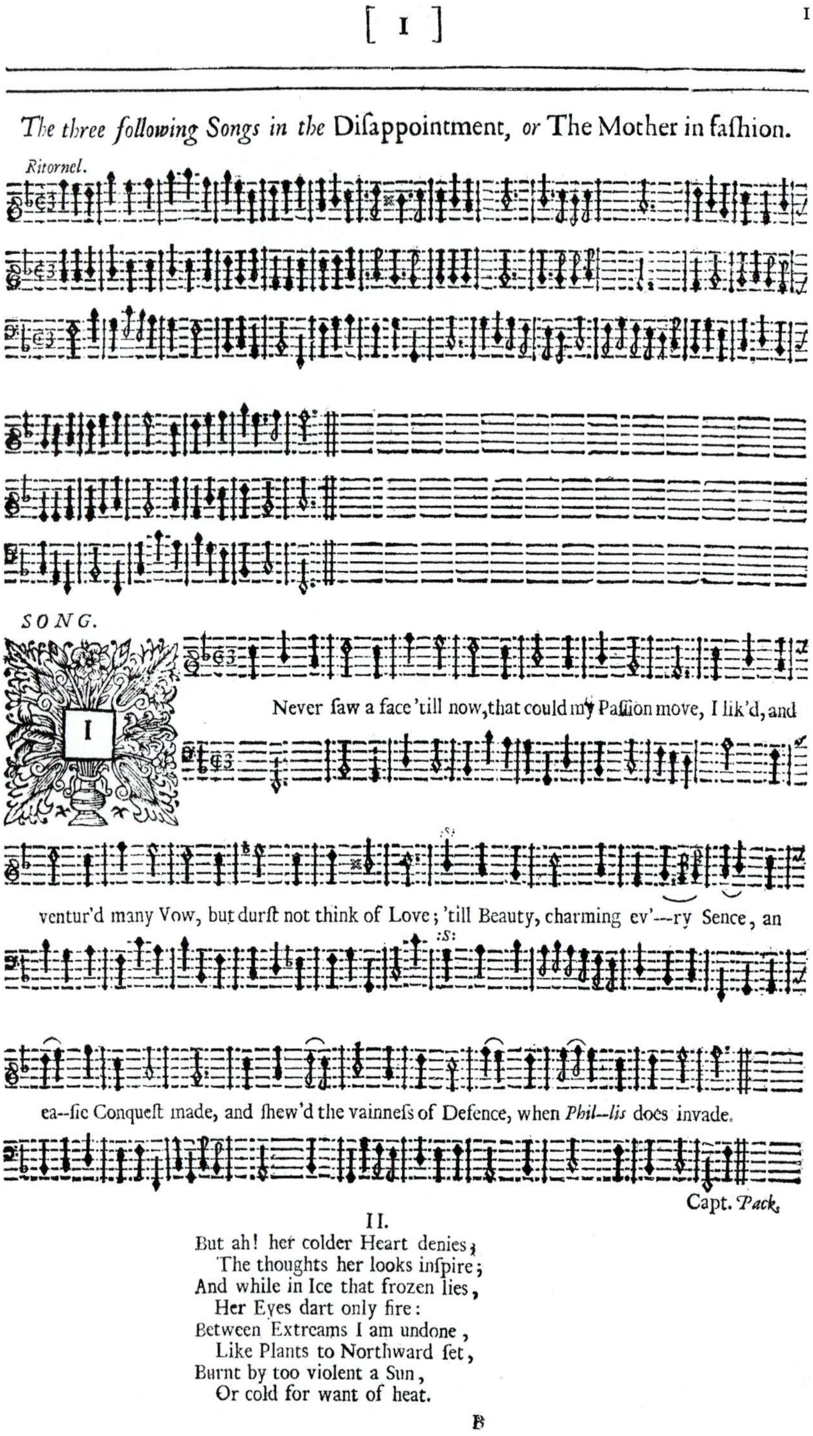

The three following Songs in the Diſappointment, *or* The Mother in faſhion.

Ritornel.

SONG.

Never ſaw a face 'till now, that could my Paſſion move, I lik'd, and

ventur'd many Vow, but durſt not think of Love; 'till Beauty, charming ev'---ry Sence, an

ea--ſie Conqueſt made, and ſhew'd the vainneſs of Defence, when *Phil--lis* does invade.

Capt. *Pack*,

II.
But ah! her colder Heart denies;
The thoughts her looks inſpire;
And while in Ice that frozen lies,
Her Eyes dart only fire:
Between Extreams I am undone,
Like Plants to Northward ſet,
Burnt by too violent a Sun,
Or cold for want of heat.

B

From the Robert Spencer Collection; reproduced by permission of the Royal Academy of Music.

While the fine-art typesetting done by Petrucci and the somewhat sloppy-looking movable type done by his followers could portray these shorter genres sufficiently, neither method was adequate or cost effective for the trio sonata or complex solo keyboard works that evolved in the Baroque era.

The technique that proved more suitable for these and later genres is engraving, a backwards version of manuscript copying. In the engraving process (also called *intaglio),* punches and other instruments are used to write notes backwards (right to left) on copper plates, so the text will appear in correct order after going through the press.

A colleague has suggested that Ginger Rogers provided the best way for us to compare the work of an engraver (who must create the text right to left) to that of the manuscript copyist (who creates the text left to right in normal fashion) when she said: "I can do everything Fred Astaire does, but backwards and in heels."

Although there are examples of engraved maps, playing cards, and book illustrations from the mid-fifteenth century, the first music produced from engraved plates was a 1536 collection titled *Intabolatura da leuto del divino Francesco de Milano.*[7] *Parthenia or the Maydenhead of the First Musiche that Ever was Printed for the Virginalls: Composed by Three Famous Masters: Wm. Byrd, Dr. John Bull and Orlando Gibbons* (RISM 1613), whose title page is frequently reprinted, is the first example of engraved music in England (Figure 8–6).

In their 1990 book *Music Printing and Publishing,* D. W. Krummel and Stanley Sadie refer to four distinct periods of music publishing: the Age of Letterpress 1501–1700; the Age of Engraving 1700–1860; the Age of Offset Printing 1860–1975; and Music Publishing Today."[8] Again, as noted earlier, this breakdown does not imply that one publishing technique overtook another. In all of these periods, publishers utilized different techniques (including manuscript copying) simultaneously, assessing market demand and in-house resources in order to make their businesses profitable.

That said, the predominance of engraving technique during the eighteenth and nineteenth centuries has important implications for scholarly study. Most of these publications were not dated, and bibliographers have had to use a variety of methods to determine printing dates and sequencing; guidance is provided by D. W. Krummel and James Fuld in their publications:

Krummel, Donald W., [and] International Association of Music Libraries, Commission for Bibliographical Research. *Guide for Dating Early Published Music.* Hackensack, NJ: J. Boonin, 1974.

Fuld, James. "Determining When, and by Whom, a Musical Work Was First Published; Determining the Date of a Particular Copy." In *The Book of World-Famous Music: Classical, Popular, and Folk,* 3–16. 5th ed. Rev. and enl. New York: Dover Publications, 2000.

Perhaps most significant for edition study is the fact that a publisher could make a correction in an engraved edition by reversing the punch mark on the copper plate but then reuse the same plate, creating some ambiguity in the copies printed from this plate. In other words, different copies of the same work in presumably the same edition may have different texts. Master bibliographer Donald

FIGURE 8–6 *Parthenia or the Maydenhead of the First Musiche that Ever was Printed for the Virginalls: Composed by Three Famous Masters: Wm. Byrd, Dr. John Bull and Orlando Gibbons* (RISM 1613)

PARTHENIA

or

THE MAYDENHEAD
of the first musicke that
euer was printed for the VIRGINALLS.

COMPOSED
By three famous Masters: William Byrd, D: John Bull, & Orlando Gibbons,
Gentilmen of his Ma:ties most Illustrious Chappell.

Ingrauen
by William Hole.

Lond: print: for M:ris Dor: Euans. Cum priuilegio. Are to be sould by G:
Lowe print' in Loathberry

Parthenia or Maydenhead. New York: Performers' Facsimiles, 1985. Reproduced by arrangement with Performers' Editions/Broude Brothers Limited.

Krummel presents important definitions for edition study on pp. 30–32 of his book *Guide for Dating Early Published Music,* as follows:

Edition: Copies printed from the same printing surfaces, sometimes with indication of first edition, new revised edition, or similar terms.

Issue: Subset of edition, with all copies printed from same printing surface and having identical title pages.

State (or variant): Term used when printing surface has been modified in some way, but title page remains unchanged.

These variant sources are most confounding to performers and editors, as changes can be uncovered only when comparing the text to other copies of the same edition/issue.[9] Imagine the frustration of having what appears to be the same score as your neighbor but finding out that there are differences inside.[10] While such differences may not be so critical in reading books with words, in music they can lead to very different performances of the same work.

Publishers typically organized the copper or pewter plates used in the engraving process by putting a unique *plate number (Plattennummer)* on the bottom center of the page of music (Figure 8–7). Plate numbers are useful guides for bibliographers and scholars seeking to determine differences between editions. Also important for music score identification purposes is the *publisher number (Verlagsnummer),* a unique number that the publisher uses to distinguish a particular edition. For additional information on these concepts see Krummel and Sadie, pp. 526–27 and 532–34. In the early 1990s, music publishers adopted use of the ISMN or International Standard Music Number, established to provide unique identifier numbers to music scores, similar to ISBNs for books and ISSNs for serial publications.[11]

Most manuscript and printed music prior to the nineteenth century was produced in oblong (landscape) format, rather than in the upright (portrait) format more common today. An excellent example of the change in formats may be seen in the five-volume Tecla facsimile/reprint publication of first editions of Beethoven Piano Sonatas, reproduced in the same format as the originals (the first four volumes, covering sonatas op. 2, 13, 14, 22, 26, 27, 28, 31, 49, 53, 54, 57, 78, 79, 81a, 90, 101, and 109 are in oblong format; volume 5 which includes sonatas op. 106, 110, 111 is in upright format).[12]

As well, most music publications prior to the mid-nineteenth century were "practical" editions, designed for performers and issued in separate parts. The rise of musicology as a discipline in the mid-nineteenth century and interest in the scholarly study of music encouraged publication of full scores and study scores. Albert Payne was one of the first publishers to specialize in miniature scores, or small-size study scores. In 1892, he sold his stock to Eulenburg, the publisher of the yellow-covered miniature scores familiar to most Western classical musicians.[13]

Study of editions, issues, and states falls into the category of descriptive or analytical bibliography (see pp. 40–41).

FIGURE 8–7 Example of music printed from engraved plates; plate number is visible at bottom center.

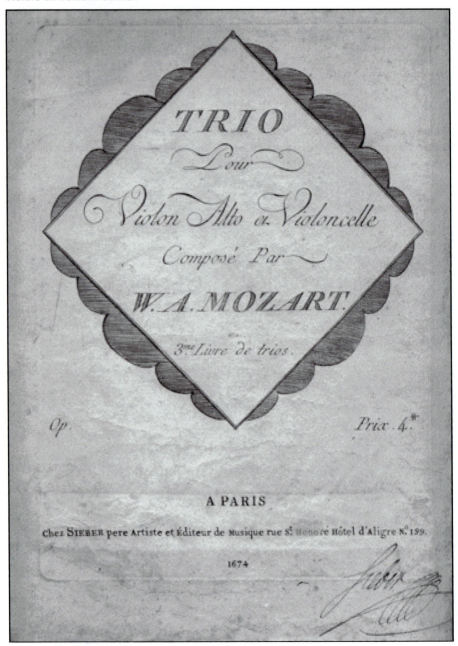

Credit: Gabriel Boyers, Schubertiade Antiquarian Music & Manuscripts.

As evident from the description of its process, engraving was labor intensive and time consuming. *Lithography,* the next printing innovation, was developed in 1796 by Alois Senefelder (1771–1834), a Bavarian actor and playwright who sought an inexpensive way to print his plays. Its principle is similar to that of engraving, but rather than using punches to etch on metal, the text is written on stone with greasy ink and washed with water and other substances to create the image.

In 1803, Senefelder established his *Chemische Druckerey,* or chemical printing firm in Vienna to distribute his lithographed publications; this company would later become part of the Haslinger firm. Among his music publications was an early (pirated) edition of Mozart's *Oeuvres Completes.*[14]

The music publishing industry experienced enormous growth during the nineteenth century, fueled in part by the growth of the middle class and the rise of amateur music makers. Although exact statistics of music publishing growth are impossible to ascertain, Krummel and Sadie present their educated guess as follows:

> The evidence is very incomplete, although the overall historical record is obvious. Up to 1700, annual world-wide production of music editions probably never exceeded a hundred titles. Based on data suggested above, it seems fair to fix the total at no more than five titles per year before about 1525 (i.e., from the beginnings to the age of Petrucci); 30 titles per year from 1525 to 1550 (during Attaingnant's major activity); 80 titles per year from 1550 to 1660 (when the four major centers were particularly active); and 60 titles per year during the 17th century. The vast increase during the 18th century reflects the rise of engraved sheet music and the proliferation of songsheets. While any estimates are frustrated by the practice of not dating music, the first half-century, with London as its main centre, probably produced about 150 titles per year; the next three decades probably saw around 300 new titles each year, as Parisian publishers entered the picture; while the last two decades saw a further proliferation, with the growth of Viennese and German publishers, so that the total swelled to about a thousand a year by 1800. The trend continued, stimulated by the commercial presses during the 19th century, with annual outputs reaching perhaps 2000 by 1835, 10,000 by 1850, 20,000 by 1870, and 50,000 by 1910, perhaps the apogee, just before the extensive distribution of commercial sound recordings.[15]

Another record of the growth in the music publishing industry may be seen in the publication statistics of the Leipzig publisher Friedrich Hofmeister's monthly sale catalog, *Monatsberichte,* which was published from 1829 until 1900. The number of publications listed by the Monatsberichte "at first comprised about 2,000 records per year, but by 1900 the annual total had risen to over 13,000, yielding a total of some 400,000 records over the period 1829–1900."[16]

Hofmeister's catalogs are considered to be one the most important tools for documentation of nineteenth-century music publications. The "Hofmeister XIX" project was established in 1989 in order to make the information in these catalogs more accessible to scholars and performers worldwide through a searchable database.[17]

Before the development of sound recording at the end of the nineteenth century, individuals could experience music only by attending a concert or playing from a score at home. Hard as it may be to imagine in the iPod age, if you attended an opera and enjoyed the music, the only way to re-create that music again would be to purchase printed music of an arrangement for piano or other instruments and play it at home. Thus we find numerous arrangements of various types listed in Hofmeister (Figure 8–8).

Another significant development in the latter half of the nineteenth century was the move from rag-based paper to wood pulp paper. The latter is much more susceptible to fading and disintegration, as is clear to anyone who saves newspapers for more than a week. It was not until the 1990s that music publishers followed the example of book publishers in committing themselves to the use of acid-free paper.

Figure 8–8   Hofmeister XIX http://www.hofmeister.rhul.ac.uk, April 1829, p. 27.

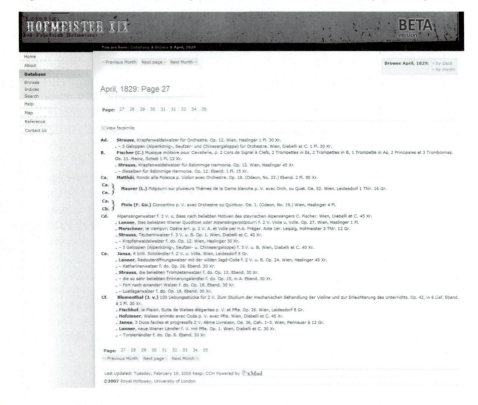

The invention of photography and development of off-set printing techniques in the latter part of the nineteenth century enabled publishers to expand their offerings further. Of special importance for the study of primary sources was the appearance of the first major music manuscript facsimile publications in 1868, Handel's *Messiah* and Schubert's *Erlkönig,* both produced through photolithographic process.[18]

By the latter half of the twentieth century, most scores were printed by computer processes. One of the earliest innovators to use technology to print music was Armando Dal Molin, who began experimenting with his "music typewriter" in the 1940s. Music encoding langauges, which convert musical notation to formats read by computers, were developed in the early 1960s. Among these were Barry Brook's "Plaine and easie code" and Stefan Bauer-Mengelberg's Digital Alternate Representation of Music Scores (DARMS). By the 1980s, composers and publishers could choose from a wide menu of computerized music printing programs, such as Finale, Sibelius, and SCORE.[19]

The Internet now makes it possible for individuals to study primary source materials firsthand, as seen in the references to the ever-growing collection of digital library sites described in Chapter 1. Scholars have also used the Internet to create specialized tools for music analysis and comparative study. ISMIR (International Conferences on Music Information Retrieval); http://ismir2002.ircam.fr/ is one of several organizations through which musicians and scholars may share ideas and develop collaborations.

It is fitting that today the names Gutenberg and Petrucci are connected with digital projects: Project Gutenberg for electronic books, www.gutenberg.org and the Petrucci Project for digital scores, http://www.soundpost.org/petrucci.html. One hopes that as innovators themselves, both men would be excited to witness what came of their inventions.

MUSIC PRINTING AND PUBLISHING: A SELECTED BIBLIOGRAPHY

Antolini, Bianca Maria. *Dizionario degli Editori Musicali Italiani 1750–1930.* Pisa: Edizioni ETS, 2000.

Bernstein, Jane A. *Print Culture and Music in Sixteenth Century Venice.* New York: Oxford University Press, 2001.

Boorman, Stanley. *Studies in the Printing, Publishing, and Performance of Music in the 16th Century.* Variorum Collected Study Series 815. Aldershot, England: Ashgate, 2005.

Carter, Tim. *Music, Patronage, and Printing in Late Renaissance Florence.* Aldershot, England: Ashgate, 2000.

Deutsch, Otto Erich. *Musikverlags Nummern: eine Auswahl von 40 datierten Listen, 1710–1900.* 2nd ed. Berlin: Verlag Merseburger, 1961.

Devriès, Anik, and Françoise Lesure. *Dictionnaire des editeurs de musique français.* 2 vols. Genève: Minkoff, 1979–88.

Duggan, Mary K. *Italian Music Incunabula: Printers and Type.* Berkeley: University of California Press, 1992.

Fenlon, Iain. *Music, Print, and Culture in Early Sixteenth Century Italy.* Oxford: Oxford University Press, 2002.

Gamble, William. *Music Engraving and Printing: Historical and Technical Treatise.* London: Sir Isaac Pitman & Sons, Ltd., 1923. Reprint, New York: Da Capo Press, 1971.

Hewlett, Walter B., and Eleanor Selfridge-Field. *The Virtual Score: Representation, Retrieval, Restoration.* Computing in Musicology 12. Cambridge, MA: MIT Press, 2001. See also other publications available from the Center for Computer Assisted Research in the Humanities: http://www.ccarh.org/.

Hopkinson, Cecil. *A Dictionary of Parisian Music Publishers, 1700–1950.* London: C. Hopkinson, 1954. Reprint, New York: Da Capo Press, 1979.

Hunter, David. *Music Publishing & Collecting: Essays in Honor of Donald W. Krummel.* Urbana: Graduate School of Library and Information Science, University of Illinois at Urbana-Champaign, 1994.

King, A. Hyatt. *Four Hundred Years of Music Printing.* 2nd ed. London: British Museum, 1968.

Krummel, Donald W. *English Music Printing 1553–1700.* London: Bibliographical Society, 1975.

_____, [and] International Association of Music Libraries, Commission on Bibliographical Research. *Guide for Dating Early Published Music: A Manual of Bibliographical Practices.* Hackensack, NJ: J. Boonin, 1974.

_____. *The Literature of Music Bibliography: An Account of the Writings on the History of Music Printing & Publishing.* Fallen Leaf Reference Books in Music 21. Berkeley, CA: Fallen Leaf Press, 1992.

Krummel, Donald W., and Sadie Stanley, eds. *Music Printing and Publishing.* Norton/Grove Handbooks in Music. New York: W. W. Norton, 1990.

Lenneberg, Hans. *On the Publishing and Dissemination of Music, 1500–1850.* Hillsdale, NY: Pendragon Press, 2003.

_____. "Revising the History of the Miniature Score." *Notes* 45, no. 2 (Dec. 1988): 258–61.

Lenneberg, Hans, ed. *The Dissemination of Music: Studies in the History of Music Publishing.* Musicology 14. Lausanne, Switzerland: Gordon and Breach, 1994.

Powell, Steven. *Music Engraving Today: The Art and Practice of Digital Notesetting.* New York: Brichtmark Music, 2002.

Selfridge-Field, Eleanor, ed. *Beyond MIDI: The Handbook of Musical Codes.* Cambridge, MA: MIT Press, 1997.

Twyman, Michael. *Early Lithographed Music: A Study Based on the H. Baron Collection.* London: Farrand, 1996.

Van Orden, Kate, ed. *Music and the Cultures of Print.* Garland Reference Library of the Humanities 2027; Critical and Cultural Musicology 1. New York: Garland Publishing, 2000.

Wolfe, Richard J. *Early American Music Engraving and Printing: A History of Music Publishing in America from 1787 to 1825 with Commentary on Earlier and Later Practices.* Urbana: Published in cooperation with the Bibliographical Society of America by the University of Illinois Press, 1980.

MUSIC PRINTING AND PUBLISHING: SELECTED STUDIES OF SPECIFIC PRINTERS/PUBLISHERS

ATTAINGNANT, PIERRE

Heartz, Daniel. *Pierre Attaingnant, Royal Printer of Music: A Historical Study and Bibliographical Catalogue.* Berkeley: University of California Press, 1969.

EAST, THOMAS

Smith, Jeremy L. *Thomas East and Music Publishing in Renaissance England.* New York: Oxford University Press, 2003.

GARDANO, ANTONIO

Lewis, Mary S. *Antonio Gardano, Venetian Music Printer 1538–1569: A Descriptive Bibliography and Historical Study.* 3 vols. New York: Routledge, 1988–2005.

NOVELLO

Cooper, Victoria L. *The House of Novello: Practice and Policy of a Victorian Music Publisher, 1829–1866.* Aldershot, England: Ashgate Publishing, 2003.

PETRUCCI, OTTAVIANO

Boorman, Stanley. *Ottaviano Petrucci: A Catalogue Raisonné.* Oxford: Oxford University Press, 2006.

PETERS

Lawford-Hinrichsen, Irene. *Music Publishing and Patronage: C.F. Peters: 1800 to the Holocaust.* Kenton: Edition Press, 2000.

SCOTTO PRESS

Bernstein, Jane A. *Music Printing in Renaissance Venice: The Scotto Press (1539–1572).* New York: Oxford University Press, 1998.

SUSATO

Polk, Keith, ed. *Tielman Susato and the Music of His Time: Print Culture, Compositional Technique and Instrumental Music in the Renaissance.* Bucina: The Historic Brass Society Series 5. Hillsdale, NY: Pendragon Press, 2005.

CHRONOLOGY OF PRINTING, PUBLISHING, AND COPYRIGHT: LANDMARKS

1403 First movable type produced in Korea.
1409 First book produced by movable type in Korea.
1450– First European book printed from movable type:
55 *Gutenberg Bible.* Digital copy in British Library: http://www.bl.uk/onlinegallery/themes/landmarks/gutenberg.html.
This form of printing spread to northern and central Italy during the 1460s and was adopted throughout Europe after 1473.
1473? *Constance Gradual:* Liturgical book, considered by scholars to be the first evidence of printed music, produced from woodblocks.

The only surviving copy of this book is found in the British Library. The period from 1450 to 1500 is known as the *Incunabula* period (derived from the Latin *incunabulum* = "cradle").

1500–1700: AGE OF LETTERPRESS (KRUMMEL AND SADIE)

1501 Petrucci. *Harmonice musices Odhecaton A* (RISM 1501) printed from movable type using three impressions (one for staves, one for notes, one for text); equivalent of the Gutenberg Bible for music. Petrucci's publications are important sources for both bibliographers and scholars of Renaissance music. Facsimile editions and transcriptions include

> *Harmonice musices Odhecaton A.* Edited by Stanley Boorman and Ellen S. Beebe. Introduction by Stanley Boorman. Critical Facsimiles 7. New York: The Broude Trust, 2001.
> *Harmonice musices Odhecation A.* Edited by Helen Hewitt. Edition of the Literary Texts by Isabel Pope. Da Capo Press Music Reprint Series. New York: Da Capo Press, 1978. (transcription)
> *Canti B numero cinquanata, Venice, 1502.* Edited by Helen Hewitt, with an introduction by Edward E. Lowinsky. Texts edited and annotated by Morton W. Briggs. Translated by Norman B. Spector. Monuments of Renaissance Music 2. Chicago: University of Chicago Press, 1967.
> *Canti C numero cento cinquanata.* 1504. Reprint, New York: Broude, 1978.

1527– 28 Pierre Attaingnant issues *Chansons nouvelles en musique á quatre parties: naguere imprimees á Paris,* the first example of music printed from moveable type using one impression.

1536? *Intabolatura da leuto del divino Francesco de Milano,* the first music printed from engraved plates, although this process was used for other materials around 100 years earlier.

1613 *Parthenia or the Maydenhead of the First Musiche that Ever was Printed for the Virginalls: Composed by Three Famous Masters: Wm. Byrd, Dr. John Bull and Orlando Gibbons.* (RISM 1613), the first example of engraved music in England.

1640 Bay Psalm Book: Full title: *The Whole Book of Psalms Faithfully Translated into English Metre.* First book of music printed in the Americas by the Massachusetts Bay Puritans, to be used for their worship services.

1700–1860: AGE OF ENGRAVING (KRUMMEL AND SADIE)

1709 Statute of Anne, world's first copyright act, passed by the British Parliament.

1790 First U.S. federal copyright law, which protected works for life of the creator plus 14 years, with one renewal for an additional 14 years.

1796 Process of lithography invented by Alois Senefelder (1771–1834), a Bavarian actor and playwright seeking inexpensive ways to print his plays.

1800–1975: AGE OF OFFSET PRINTING (KRUMMEL AND SADIE)

1803   Senefelder establishes his *Chemische Druckerey,* or chemical printing firm in Vienna to distribute his lithographed publications.

1826–   Invention of photography by Nicephore Niépce and Louis
39   Daguerre.

1850–   Transition from rag-based paper to paper manufactured from
70   wood pulp.

1852   Invention of photolithography.

1868   First major manuscript facsimile editions produced: Handel's *Messiah* and Schubert's *Erlkönig.*

1909   U.S. copyright law revision, extended protection of copyright for life of the creator plus 28 years, with one renewal of 28 years.

1914   Establishment of ASCAP (American Society of Composers, Authors, and Publishers), the oldest of the three performing rights societies in the United States. See www.ascap.com.

1930   Establishment of SESAC (Original name, Society of European Stage Authors and Composers). See www.sesac.com.

1940   Establishment of BMI (Broadcast Music Inc.). See www.bmi.com.

1960–   Music encoding languages, "Plaine and easie code" and DARMS
63   (Digital Alternate Representation of Music Scores) developed by Barry S. Brook and Stefan Bauer-Mengelberg, respectively. These systems (and their numerous successors) convert musical notation to formats read by computers, enabling such musicological tools as the musical incipit indexes in RISM (Series A/II and selected Series B volumes), as well as the standard music notation systems used by composers and publishers almost universally today.

1976   Major copyright law revision (took effect January 1, 1978): extended copyright protection to life of the creator plus 50 years, with possible renewal of 50 years. (See also Copyright, pp. 213–217.)

1977   Invention of Musicomp (music typewriter) by Armando Dal Molin. Dal Molin had been working with automated music typography programs since the 1940s.

1986   Invention of Sibelius music publishing software.

1987   Invention of Finale music publishing software.

1996   URAA (Uruguay Round Table Agreements Act of 1994), implemented the General Agreement on Tariffs and Trades Treaty (GATT) treaty and restored copyright protection to certain foreign works published after 1920 that lacked protection in the United States, specifically those from the former Soviet Union. Copyright protection for these works was restored on January 1, 1996.

1998   Sonny Bono Copyright Term Extension Act (CTEA), passed October 27, 1998. Extends copyright protection from life of the author plus 50 years to life of the author plus 70 years. See Lolly Gasaway "When Works Pass Into the Public Domain" http://www.unc.edu/~unclng/public-d.htm.

1999 Digital Millennium Copyright Act (DCMA), a major revision of the 1976 copyright law. (See Copyright, pp. 213–217.)

TYPES OF EDITIONS AND THE PROCESS OF EDITING

With the exception of manuscript facsimiles, all printed music has gone through some type of editing process. If one naively assumes that the composer best expressed his or her true intentions in an autograph score, how does an editor prepare an edition of Mozart's Piano Concerto no. 26, K. 537 ("Coronation") when Mozart omitted the left hand part in many sections of the autograph score? Or an edition of Beethoven's Piano Sonata no. 29, op. 106 ("Hammerklavier"), for which there is no surviving autograph? Or an edition of Verdi's *La Traviata,* when, as is the case for many nineteenth-century operas, there are differences between the autograph score and the copyist manuscripts prepared for specific performances? These are just a few of the many examples that demonstrate the complexity of editing works of Western classical music.

The first step in understanding this process requires an overview of the different types of editions that are used by musicians and scholars:

TYPES OF EDITIONS

Definitions

I. Critical (text/critical) = Scholarly Edition

Editions compiled by scholars who seek to present an "authentic" musical text— one that represents the creator's intentions as closely as possible. To do so, scholars examine all available primary and secondary source materials for the work (autograph, first edition, important copyist manuscripts, original correspondence that may reveal composer's thoughts) and develop a *stemma,* or family tree of sources from which they may re-create its compositional and editorial history.

Further, we expect critical editions to clearly distinguish editors' markings from those of the composer. Composer complete editions or *Gesamtausgaben* usually do this through publication of separate volumes of critical commentary, or *Kritische Bericht.*

It is important to note that these critical editions are not Urtext editions: the term *Urtext,* or original text, is completely misleading; it has been overused and misunderstood by performers and students for many decades, not to mention by publishers who have freely stamped their editions Urtext to imply some sort of divine quality and to increase sales. As Walter Emery firmly states in his book *Editions and Musicians,* "There is no such thing as an 'original text' of any piece of old music, unless there is only one source, or all of the sources give identical readings."[20] The most fundamental aspect of an edition is that it has been edited by someone. Thus, Bärenreiter's *Neue Bach Ausgabe* or *Neue Mozart Ausgabe* scores are critical editions, not Urtext editions.

Critical editions can be further subdivided into the following categories:

- Collected Editions = Gesamtausgaben = Oeuvres Complètes = Sämtliche Werke = Opere Complete = Tutte le Opera = Opera Omnia, all of which refer to complete, critical editions of works of individual composers.

- Historical Series, including *Denkmäler* (Monuments) = multivolume sets containing works of similar genres or styles, or representative of a national group or country. Examples include *Das Chorwerk, Drammaturgia musicale veneta, The English Madrigal School, Denkmäler Der Tonkunst In Bayern* (DTB), or *Musica Britannica: A National Collection of Music.*

As they are multivolume sets with more than one work in each volume, these critical editions require special indexing tools to help users locate specific works within them (see pp. 203–208).

II. Performing or Practical Editions

(referred to as "Interpretative Editions" by James Grier)[21] are designed for practical use by performers—in other words, editions to be placed on a music stand or carried around in an instrument case. While practical/performing editions may be based on a critical/historical edition (as is the case with Bärenreiter editions based on composer critical editions, which often have indications resembling "seals of approval" that state "Based on the text of the *Neue Bach Ausgabe*"), their format and design (not to mention significantly lower price) demonstrate their intended audience of performers.

Some performing editions are edited by renowned performers and include his/her interpretative marks in the text. For example, Beethoven piano sonatas have been edited by dozens of performers, among them Claudio Arrau, Hans von Bülow, Moritz Moskowski, and Arthur Schnabel. Some of these editions, particularly the older ones, are problematic in that the text does not clearly distinguish the editor's marks from those of the composer.

Again, consumers should be cautioned not to trust that an indication of Urtext on the cover of a performing edition guarantees its scholarship. Good-quality performing editions will be those that clearly distinguish editor's markings from those of the composer and provide at least some brief commentary on the editorial process.

III. Facsimile Editions = Photographic Copies of the Original

Facsimiles of manuscript scores enable the study of these unique sources beyond those who are able to travel to the owning library to view the originals. For a detailed survey of facsimile editions and techniques of their production, see Steven Immel's article "Facsimile" in *Grove Music Online*.

In addition to facsimiles of manuscripts, scholarly publishers have produced facsimiles or copies of early printed editions. Examples include the five-volume Tecla publication of first editions of Beethoven Piano Sonatas, Broude Brothers "Performer Facsimile" series, or the Garland series *The London Pianoforte School* and *Piano Music of Parisian Virtuosos*.[22] These publications allow modern performers to have the direct experience of performing from an edition produced closer to the composer's own time.

Historical Background on Composer Critical Editions (Old and New)

Numerous important complete/critical editions of works of major composers were launched in the latter half of the nineteenth century, coinciding with the development of musicology as a discipline and its corollary interest in scholarly editing. The Bach Gesellschaft began in 1851, Handel edition in 1858, Palestrina and Beethoven editions in 1862, Mendelssohn in 1874, Mozart in 1877, Chopin in 1878, Schumann in 1880, Schubert in 1884, Schutz in 1885, Lassus in 1894, Berlioz in 1899, Haydn in 1907, and Brahms in 1926.[23]

Many of these editions were published by Breitkopf & Härtel in Leipzig and are no longer protected by copyright. Dover, Kalmus, and Masters Music reprint editions (along with their digital counterparts) are frequently reprints of these nineteenth-century critical editions.

After World War II, scholars saw the need for new critical editions of works for many major composers. Approaches to scholarly editing had advanced considerably since the nineteenth century, and the availability of microfilming and photocopying techniques allowed broader dissemination of unique source materials. Thus, after 1950, new editions (or Neue Ausgaben) for many major composers appeared: the *Neue Bach Ausgabe* was established in 1954, *Neue Mozart Ausgabe* in 1955, *Beethoven Werke* in 1961, *Neue Schubert Ausgabe* in 1964, and Berlioz *New Edition of the Complete Works* in 1967. New Brahms, Debussy, Schumann, Rossini, and Verdi editions were established in the 1980s and 1990s. As well, critical editions of twentieth-century composers' works were established in the latter half of the twentieth century, among them those for Arnold Schoenberg (1966–), Alban Berg (1984–), and Kurt Weill (1996–).

These new editions are broader in scope and coverage than their predecessors and usually come with more detailed critical commentary volumes. Some editions also include the composer thematic catalog volume as part of the series (the case for Berlioz, Corelli, and Robert Schumann) or iconographical and documentary studies, for example, the four-volume *Bach-Dokumente,* issued as a supplement to the *Neue Bach Ausgabe.*[24]

The most recent development in production of scholarly composer editions is the use of digitization: in 2006, the Internationale Stiftung Mozarteum announced the availability of the entire *Neue Mozart Ausgabe* in digital format.[25]

Study of the musical text presented in composer critical editions is essential for performers and scholars: the editors of these critical editions have examined sources for a musical work in a more detailed and comprehensive manner than could be done by most individuals. That said, it is naïve to assume that any edited text will be the final word for interpretative purposes, or that new editions are always superior to their predecessors. In some cases, editors have even issued a revised edition of a work already published in the series. An example of this is the *Neue Bach Ausgabe* edition of Bach's "Easter Oratorio" (*Himmelfahrts-Oratorium,* BWV 11 [NBA II, 8, published 1978]), for which the editors published a revised edition of the same volume (NBA II 8b, published 1983), reflecting changes brought about by a recent discovery of the performance parts for the work.

As of this writing, few of the *Neue Ausgaben* have been completed.[26] Subscribers to these series (libraries or individuals) receive new volumes as they are published, and it is rare that volumes are published in consecutive order. Thus, the library may have Series I, vols. 1 and 3 of the new Beethoven Edition on its shelf, but not Series I, vol 2.

Locating Individual Works within Critical Edition Series: Numbering and Organization

The contents of these critical editions are not usually analyzed individually in library catalogs, and all volumes in the series have similar-looking bindings. The problem of locating individual works in these larger sets and series is one that has perplexed music library users for generations.

The numbering and organization of volumes in the composer complete editions may also seem peculiar. Typically, a roman numeral indicates the main series in which the work is found, that is, orchestral works or stage works. For the Beethoven edition referenced earlier, Series I covers orchestral works. In the case of Mozart, Series I includes "Masses, Mass Movements, Requiem"; his operas are found in Series II, and symphonies in Series IV. It should be noted that the same series order is used for the composer's *Grove Music Online* works list.

There are further subdivisions within the roman numeral series, for example, Mozart's opera *Lo Sposo Deluso* is numbered II, 5, 14:

Series II = Bühnwerke (Stage Works)
Werkegruppe 5 = Opern und Singspiele
Bd. 14 = *Lo Sposo Deluso,* the specific work

Most of the older *Gesamtausgaben* used different series numbering systems; for example, Mozart's operas are in Series V in the older edition, the *Mozart Werke.*

To complicate matters further, the Kalmus reprint editions of some of the older Gesamtausgaben, such as the *Beethoven Werke,* use their own numbering system.[27] Sometimes the title pages of these reprint editions provide a concordance of work locations.

Chapter 10: Composer Thematic Catalogs, provides information on the old and new critical editions for specific composers.

Real Life Scenario

A student is told to look for the "critical" edition of J. S. Bach's Toccata and fugue in D Minor, BWV 538 (the "Dorian"). The librarian directs him to the composer complete edition section of the library, where he finds several shelves of the *Neue Bach Ausgabe* brown-bound volumes. It's a bit difficult to see the gold lettering on the spines of the volumes, but he finally gets to the ones that say "Orgelwerke." Okay, but how to find BWV 538? Open each volume and glance at the title page? This will take time and his coaching begins in 15 minutes.

Answer: *Grove Music Online* work lists indicate location of an individual work in both the old and new composer complete works edition. BWV 538 is located in Series IV, vol. 5, p. 76 of the *Neue Bach Ausgabe* (see Fig. 8–9).

Historical Series *(Denkmäler)*

While composer critical editions present works of a single composer edited with scholarly scrutiny, the broad category of historical series refers to multivolume series of works by more than one composer edited by scholars and brought together as representative of a country, style, or historical period. Within this category are *Denkmäler*, German for "monument," the first of which was established by German musicologists in the latter half of the nineteenth century, representing both scholarly excellence and nationalistic spirit.

Examples include *Denkmäler der Tonkunst In Bayern (DTB)*, or monuments of music in Bavaria and *Denkmäler der Tonkunst in Österreich (DTO)*, monuments of music in Austria. The nationalistic focus of this type of series is not limited to Germany. *Musica Britannica: A National Collection of Music* is the *Denkmäler* of music in the British Isles; *Monumenti Musici Italiani*, the *Denkmäler* for Italy.

Numbering protocols in the *Denkmäler* series are even more complicated than those of composer complete editions, as many of the series have both volume and *Jahrgang* (German for annual set) numbers. To further complicate matters, some composer complete editions are published as part of larger historical series. This is the case for the Frescobaldi *Opera Omnia*, which is part of *Monumenti Musici Italiani*.

Among the historical series launched in the twentieth century are A-R Edition exemplary Recent Researches series *(Recent Researches in the Music of the Renaissance, Recent Researches in the Music of the Baroque*, and *Recent Researches in the Music of the Classical Period)*.[28] These editions serve as both critical and performing editions: they have extensive introductions and usually include sets of parts for ensemble works. The publisher also provides a generous "copyright-sharing policy," which allows the patrons of a subscribing library to photocopy scores and parts.

Lists of historical series are found in the "Editions, historical" article in *Grove Music Online* and the "Editions, historical" article in the *New Harvard Dictionary of Music*.

As noted earlier, because these series include works by more than one composer, and most library catalogs will not provide access to the contents of the series, it is therefore necessary to use one of the following *indexes* in order to locate a particular work:

Charles, Sydney Robinson. *A Handbook of Music and Music Literature in Sets and Series.* New York: Free Press, 1972.

Heyer, Anna Harriett. *Historical Sets, Collected Editions, and Monuments of Music: A Guide to their Contents.* 3rd ed. 2 vols. Chicago: American Library Association, 1980.

Hill, George R., and Norris L. Stephens. *Collected Editions, Historical Series and Sets, and Monuments of Music: A Bibliography.* Fallen Leaf Press Books in Music 14. Berkeley, CA: Fallen Leaf Press, 1997. Available online as *Index to Printed Music.*

Lists vs. Indexes

As explained in Chapter 6: Periodicals, Periodical Indexes, and Databases, there are important differences between a list of sources and an index: the former is simply a list of titles, while the latter is a tool that provides access to the contents of each title.

Organ

Independent of chorales

BWV	BC	Title	Remarks	BG	NBA
131a	J 62	Fugue, g	arr. from 131	xxxviii, 217	—
525–30	J 1–6	6 sonatas (E♭, c, d, e, C, G)	c1730; no.3: cf 1044; no.4 arr. from 76	xv, 3–66	IV/vii, 2–76
531	J 9	Prelude and fugue, C	? before 1705	xv, 81	IV/v, 3
†532	J 13, 54, 70	Prelude and fugue, D	? before 1710	xv, 88	IV/v, 58; IV/vi, 95
†533	J 18, 72	Prelude and fugue, e	? before 1705	xv, 100	IV/v, 90; IV/vi, 106
534	J 20	Prelude and fugue, f	? before 1710	xv, 104	IV/v, 130
†535	J 23	Prelude and fugue, g	? before 1705; rev. ?1708–17	xv, 112	IV/v, 157; IV/vi, 109
536	J 24	Prelude and fugue, A	?1708–17	xv, 120	IV/v, 180; IV/vi, 114
537	J 40	Fantasia and fugue, c	? after 1723	xv, 129	IV/v, 47
538	J 38	Toccata and fugue, 'Dorian', d	?1712–17	xv, 136	IV/v, 76
†539	J 15, 71	Prelude and fugue, d	? after 1720; fugue adapted from vn sonata, 1001	xv, 148	IV/v, 70
†540	J 39, 55, 73	Toccata and fugue, F	toccata ? after 1712; fugue before 1731	xv, 154	IV/v, 112
†541	J 22	Prelude and fugue, G	? after 1712; rev. c1724–5	xv, 169	IV/v, 146
†542	J 42, 57, 67	Fantasia and fugue, g	fugue: before 1725; fantasia: c1720	xv, 177	IV/v, 167
†543	J 26	Prelude and fugue, a	after 1715; fugue: cf 944	xv, 189	IV/v, 186; IV/vi, 121
544	J 27	Prelude and fugue, b	1727–31	xv, 199	IV/v, 198
†545	J 10, 51	Prelude and fugue, C	? before 1708; rev. ?1712–17	xv, 212	IV/v, 10; IV/vi, 77
†546	J 12, 53, 69	Prelude and fugue, c	?1723–9	xv, 218	IV/v, 35
547	J 11	Prelude and fugue, C	? by 1725	xv, 228	IV/v, 20
548	J 19	Prelude and fugue, e	rev. 1727–31	xv, 236	IV/v, 95
†549	J 14	Prelude and fugue, c/d	before 1705; rev. ? after 1723	xxxviii, 3	IV/v, 30; IV/vi, 101
550	J 21	Prelude and fugue, G	? before 1710	xxxviii, 9	IV/v, 138
551	J 25	Prelude and fugue, a	? before 1707	xxxviii, 17	IV/vi, 63
552	J 16	Prelude and fugue, 'St Anne', E♭	in Clavier-Übung, iii, (Leipzig, 1739), see 669–89	iii, 173, 254	IV/vi, 2, 105

Source: *Grove Music Online.*

Hill and Stephens's book and its online version are updates and expansions of Heyer's path-breaking 1980 source. As of this writing, the online version is not yet complete, and users will still need to use the 1980 edition of Heyer to locate individual works within some series.

These tools also provide access to publisher series, which fall into the category of Performing Editions, as described on p. 201.

- Publishers Series = compositions by different composers, brought together by a publisher in a numbered series that is uniform in style. Examples include the Bärenreiter series *Nagels Musik-Archiv, Hortus Musicus,* or Sikorski's *Exempla Nova.*

Real Life Scenario

Arnold Schoenberg's Cello Concerto was based on Georg Matthias Monn's *Concerto per Claviercembalo,* composed in 1746. A cellist is looking for the score of the Monn work but does not find it listed in the library catalog. Heyer's *Historical Sets, Collected Editions, and Monuments of Music* (which has not yet been completely replaced by the online *Index to Printed Music*), reveals that Monn's works may be found in DTO (Denkmäler der Tonkunst in Österreich), vol. 31, jhr. XV/2 and DTO vol. 39, jhr. XIX/2. The *Concerto for Claviercembalo* is found in the latter volume.

Real Life Scenario

Your chamber music group has been engaged to produce a series of concerts featuring works by women composers from all historic periods. You'd like to perform Ruth Crawford Seeger's Suite no. 2 for Four Strings and Piano but do not see the work listed in your library's catalog. Is it possibly published within a historical series? *IPM Online* reveals that the work is published within the series *Recent Researches in American Music,* vol. 19.

As is evident from these examples, historical series may contain repertoire that is otherwise unavailable.

While Charles, Heyer, and IPM also provide access to contents of individual composer complete editions, it is usually simpler to use *Grove Music Online* works lists to locate individual works within the composer complete edition series.

Anthologies

The term *anthology* is used in two ways when referring to editions of music.[29]

1. *Collections of works by different composers.* Petrucci's landmark *Odhecaton* is such a collection, as are the works listed in Eitner's *Sammelwerke* volumes, and

RISM Series B/I and B/II. Examples that may be more familiar to contemporary performers include Alessandro Parisotti's *Anthology of Italian Songs of the Seventeenth and Eighteenth Century,* or *The Broadway Belter's Songbook,* the former including songs and arias by Carissimi, Cacini, Marcello and others; the latter with songs by Irving Berlin, John Kander, Cole Porter, Richard Rodgers, and other musical theatre composers. As these collections are typically cataloged under title or editor, libraries should include full contents notes for each collection in the catalog; otherwise, users need indexing tools such as Sears, DeCharms, *SongCite,* or one of the other vocal music indexes listed in Chapter 9, pp. 238–240.

2. *Collections of* excerpts *of historical repertoire used to illustrate particular styles or genres.* It is common for music history textbooks to have accompanying score anthologies to help students examine music of the past. All of the editions of the standard music history textbooks (Burkholder; Stolba, Bonds, et al.) come with accompanying score (and recording) anthologies.

The following tools provide access to excerpt-based anthologies:

Hilton, Ruth B. *An Index to Early Music in Selected Anthologies.* Music Indexes and Bibliographies 13. Clifton, NJ: European American Music Corp., 1978.
Murray, Sterling E. *Anthologies of Music: An Annotated Index.* 2nd ed. Detroit Studies in Music Bibliography 68. Warren, MI: Harmonie Park Press, 1992.
Perone, James E. *Musical Anthologies for Analytical Study: A Bibliography.* Music Reference Collection 48. Westport, CT: Greenwood Press, 1995.

SUMMARY

Musicians and scholars use three different types of editions:

I. Critical editions
    A. Composer complete editions (published as a series)
    B. Historical series (including *Denkmäler*)

II. Performing editions
    • Publisher series

III. Facsimile editions (photographic reproductions)
    • Facsimiles of manuscripts
    • Facsmiles (reprints) of published editions

Series (composer complete editions, historical series, and publisher series) require specialized tools to access individual works within each volume: Charles, Heyer, and the online *Index to Printed Music* (IPM) provide access to works within all of these series.

For composer complete editions, it is usually easier to locate an individual work by using the composer works list in *Grove Music Online.*

THE PROCESS OF EDITING

James Grier's article on "Editing" in *Grove Music Online* and his 1996 book *The Critical Editing of Music: History, Method, and Practice* provide detailed overviews of editorial processes and historical perspectives on the art of scholarly editing.[30] Additional resources are listed on the select bibliography on pp. 210–211. Guidelines and models for editing particular repertoire may also be found in the editorial commentary sections published as part of critical editions. See, for example, the editorial commentary in volumes in any of A-R's *Recent Researches* series, in *Musica Britannica,* or in the *Neue Brahms Ausgabe, Oeuvres complètes de Claude Debussy, The Works of Giuseppe Verdi,* or other composer complete editions and historical series.[31]

When editors develop a *stemma,* or family tree of sources for a musical work, they must examine all extant materials to determine primary and secondary sources and then sketch out the relationship among these sources. (This process is also referred to as *filiation,* again expressing analogy to a family tree.) Editors must also determine which sources are *derivative* sources, and which are *variant* sources. The former refers to a source based directly on a primary source, such as a copyist manuscript based on the composer's autograph, while the latter refers to sources that may present differences from the primary source but are not necessarily based on it.

Pertinent evidence on a manuscript source is not limited to study of the handwriting on the page. In some cases, the *foliation,* or physical arrangement of folio leaves in the manuscript may be quite significant. Walter Emery provides just one example of important evidence found in foliation in his description of stemma for J. S. Bach's Organ Sonatas, BWV 525–530. There are two sources for this work: the autograph score (housed in Berlin's Deutscher Staatsbibliothek and available in facsimile edition) and a copyist's manuscript, half of which is in the hand of Wilhelm Friedemann Bach (W. F.), and half in the hand of Anna Magdalena Bach (A. M.). Close study of the physical construction of the copyist manuscript and its foliation revealed that A. M.'s portion of the manuscript was written first; of even greater significance is the fact that it had more ornaments than the part copied by W. F. Bach, leading scholars to conclude that the A. M. manuscript was based on the autograph, with ornaments written in by the composer himself.[32]

Other evidence may be garnered from study of the paper itself, especially through its *watermarks,* which help scholars estimate the date of a manuscript based on when the composer may have used a particular batch of paper. The *Neue Bach Ausgabe* includes two volumes devoted to watermarks for the works of J. S. Bach, demonstrating their significance for conjectural dating of Bach's works (Figure 8–10).[33]

Physical examination may also include *rastrology,* or the study of the staff-ruling on the paper. Before commercial music paper with preprinted staff lines became common at the end of the nineteenth century, composers and copyists would draw their own staff lines on manuscript paper with a special writing instrument called a *rastrum*. Scholars have used rastrological evidence to aid in dating and provenance of manuscripts by Bach, Beethoven, and other composers.[34] The use of rastrum did not disappear in the twentieth century; Igor Stravinsky developed his own instrument for notating his compositions.

Few composers of the past left crystal clear evidence of their compositional intentions to aid editors in creating "ideal" editions of their works: Brahms tended to discard his manuscripts once the work was sent to his publisher. Thus, the *Stichvorlagen,* or engraver's proof copies of his scores take on special significance, especially when they include corrections by the composer. For copyright reasons, Chopin had his works copied by different copyists for publication in different cities (London, Paris, and Leipzig), resulting in numerous discrepancies among editions.[35] Beethoven manuscripts were notoriously sloppy: one sympathizes with the copyists and editors who had to make sense of his scribbles and then suffer the composer's wrath for their misreadings. The scholarly literature is filled with commentary on editor misinterpretations of sources and errors that are replicated over and over again in editions based on other editions (see also prior discussion of new and old complete works editions, pp. 202–203).[36]

Finally, editors must also have a thorough understanding of the historical context in which the work was composed. As Grier explains:

> Individual sources preserve musical texts that are faithful to the circumstances in which they were created and used: they are historical documents. Their unique variants represent the way the work was performed, or might have been performed when the source was used. Consequently, for many works, each source is a viable record of one form of the work, and so can be treated as a possible "best text." All sources, however, have the potential to contain errors, readings that are impossible within the stylistic conventions of the repertory, as understood by the editor. These can only be identified and mended through the editor's intimate knowledge of style, processes of transmission, and the work's history. Therefore no theory provides a fully self-contained method for editing, but, within the historical approach, each contributes some valuable processes and procedures.[37]

Or, as Philip Gossett, the general editor of the new Rossini and Verdi editions, describes editing texts of nineteenth-century Italian opera in his book *Divas and Scholars: Performing Italian Opera:*

> You cannot publish critical editions of nineteenth-century Italian opera without studying the performing traditions of the period and their subsequent transformations. And in studying the traditions you begin to

FIGURE 8–10 **Watermark from paper used by J. S. Bach.**

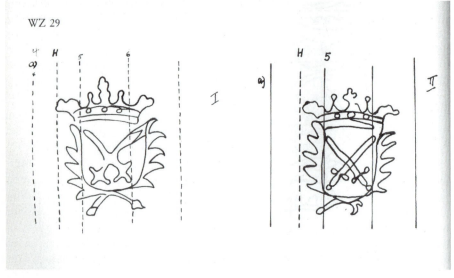

Source: *Johann Sebastian Bach Neue Ausgabe Samticher Werke.* Series IX, Volume 1. Kassel: Bären-reiter, 1985. Pg. 28. (WZ29, BWV4). Reproduced by permission.

understand the relationship between history and practice. Without know-ing something about the instruments for which Rossini and Verdi were writing, you cannot understand why their scores look the way they do. . . . Without grasping nineteenth-century stagecraft, you will inevitably be puzzled by the structure of a nineteenth-century libretto. And without comprehending the social milieu for which these operas were written, you cannot draw lessons from the history of their transmission.[38]

The importance of editorial decisions in Western classical music cannot be underestimated, as they shape how we perform and hear musical works.

EDITING AND EDITIONS: A SELECTED BIBLIOGRAPHY (*SEE ALSO* BIBLIOGRAPHY IN GRIER)

Badura-Skoda, Eva, and Piero Weiss. "Textual Problems in Masterpieces of the 18th and 19th Centuries." *The Musical Quarterly* 51, no. 2 (April 1965): 301–17.

Bent, Margaret. "Editing Early Music: The Dilemma of Translation." *Early Music* 22, no. 3 (August 1994): 373–92.

Bente, Martin, ed. *Musik Edition Interpretation: Gedenkschrift Gunter Henle.* München: Henle, 1980.

Bilson, Malcolm. "Do We Really *Know* How to Read Urtext Editions? or, The Case of the Missing Dot." *Piano & Keyboard* 175 (August 1995): 24–30.

_____. *Knowing the Score: Do We Really Know How to Read Urtext Editons and How Can This Lead to Expressive and Passionate Performance?* DVD. Ithaca, NY: Cornell University Press, 2005.

Brett, Philip. "Text, Context, and the Early Music Editor." In *Authenticity and Early Music: A Symposium,* ed. Nicholas Kenyon, 83–114. Oxford: Oxford University Press, 1988.

Caldwell, John. *Editing Early Music.* 2nd ed. Oxford: Clarendon Press, 1995.

Dart, Thurston, Walter Emery, and Christopher Morris. *Editing Early Music: Notes on the Preparation of Printer's Copy.* London: Novello, 1963.

Eisen, Cliff. "The Old and New Mozart Editions" *Early Music* 19, no. 4 (November 1991): 513–32.

Emery, Walter. *Editions and Musicians.* London: Novello, 1957.

Feder, Georg. *Musikphilologie: Eine Einführung in die Musikalische Textkritik, Hermeneutik und Editionstechnik.* Darmstadt: Wissenschaftliche Buchgesellschaft, 1987.

Gossett, Philip. *Divas and Scholars: Performing Italian Opera.* Chicago: University of Chicago Press, 2006.

Grier, James. *The Critical Editing of Music: History, Method, and Practice.* Cambridge: Cambridge University Press, 1996.

_____. "Editing." *Grove Music Online.* Edited by L. Macy. http://www.grovemusic .com.

Mendel, Arthur. "The Purposes and Desirable Characteristics of Text-Critical Editions." In *Modern Musical Scholarship,* ed. Edward Olleson, 14–27. Oxford International Symposia. Stocksfield, England: Oriel Press, 1980.

Mosser, Daniel W., Michael Saffle, and Ernest W. Sullivan, eds. *Puzzles in Paper: Concepts in Historical Watermarks.* Essays from the International Conference on the History, Function, and Study of Watermarks, Roanoke, Virginia. New Castle, DE: Oak Knoll Press; London: The British Library, 2000.

STUDY OF MANUSCRIPTS VIA SURROGATES: FACSIMILES, MICROFILM, AND DIGITAL COPIES

A manuscript is, by its nature, a unique source: no two manuscripts will be exactly the same. Unlike printed editions, copies of which may be held by several library collections, a manuscript can only be physically held in one location. Therefore manuscript study has been facilitated by dissemination of surrogates: facsimiles, microfilms, and digital copies.

As Steven Immel details in his *Grove Music Online* article on "Facsimile" (*Grove Music Online* or *New Grove,* 2nd edition, was the first edition of the dictionary to include a separate article about this subject), the invention of photography in the mid-nineteenth century fostered the publication of the first music facsimile editions. Handel's *Messiah* and Schubert's *Erlkönig,* both published in 1868, were among the first complete works of Western classical music to be produced in facsimile. Since that time, students and scholars worldwide have been able to study autographs of major works through facsimiles. Many facsimile publications are themselves quite lavish in style (and expensive in price) as they seek to mimic the original as much as possible. Facsimile editions that come with extensive introductions about the manuscript by noted scholars can be especially helpful to students as they work to understand complex manuscript sources. See, for example, Martha Frohlich's facsimile edition of Beethoven's Piano Sonata no. 15, op. 28, which includes a facsimile of the autograph, the sketches, and the first edition, along with commentary by Professor Frohlich.[39]

Microfilming techniques were also developed in the nineteenth century, again as an outgrowth of the invention of photography. Microfilming, as its name implies, produces greatly reduced images of a document. However, while filming serves to preserve volumes of text, the resulting media (either microfilm reels or microfiche cards) are awkward to use: scholars must either pore through the film on a special microfilm/fiche reader or print out pages from the film.

In spite of its awkwardness, microfilming remains an important preservation measure for libraries and archives. When requesting a copy of an original source from a library, it is still quite common to receive a microfilm. As standards for preservation of digital images evolve, there are many who believe that microfilming remains the best preservation measure.

Finally, digital photography has proved to be a wonderful mechanism for access to original sources. The abundance of digital music materials on the Internet (see Chapter 1, pp. 11–22) provides scholars, performers, and audience members the opportunity to study manuscript sources firsthand.

Just as predictions of the demise of the printed book have proven to be premature, it is also likely that facsimile editions will continue to be studied and valued, for there is no substitute for holding a volume that closely replicates an original source.

LISTS OF FACSIMILE EDITIONS

Abravanel, Claude. "A Checklist of Music Manuscripts in Facsimile Edition." *Notes* 34, no. 3 (March 1978): 557–70.

Coover, James. "Music Manuscripts in Facsimile Edition: Supplement." *Notes* 37, no. 3 (March 1981): 533–56.

_____. "Composite Music Manuscripts in Facsimile." *Notes* 38, no. 2 (Dec. 1981): 275–95.

Dedel, Peter. *Johannes Brahms: A Guide to His Autograph in Facsimile.* MLA Index and Bibliography Series 18. Ann Arbor, MI: Music Library Association, 1978.

Drabkin, William, and Scott G. Burham, "Beethoven, Ludwig van: Bibliography, i. Editions of Autographs and Sketchbooks, (i) Facsimiles of Major Autographs, (ii) Sketchbooks in Facsimile, or in Complete or Substantial Transcription." *Grove Music Online.* Edited by L. Macy. www.grovemusic.com.

See also catalogs produced by OMI: Old Manuscripts and Incunabula: www .omifacsimiles.com.

ABOUT FACSIMILES

Broude, Ronald. "Facsimiles and Historical Performance: Promises and Pitfalls." *Historical Performance* 3, no. 1 (Spring 1990): 19–22.

Immel, Steven. "Facsimile." *Grove Music Online.* Edited by L. Macy. www.grovemusic .com.

Kramer, Richard. "Review: Beethoven Facsimiles." *Nineteenth Century Music* 6, no. 1 (1982–83): 76–81.

Kramer expresses the value of studying manuscript facsimiles as follows: "An autograph is like a snapshot, catching its subject in a private moment, in the midst of an act, spontaneous or posed. The facsimile of an autograph makes this moment public and guarantees its longevity. These private moments are not equally revealing"[40]

Silbiger, Alexander. "In Defense of Facsimiles." *Historical Performance* 7, no. 2
(Fall 1994): 101–4.

Temperley, Nicholas. "On Editing Facsimiles for Performance." *Notes* 41, no. 4
(June 1985): 683–88.

COPYRIGHT

Copyright, or government-authorized protection of creator rights, is an important factor in determining availability of materials in music libraries. Copyright laws are particularly complex in relationship to music, as they extend to printed music, to live performances of music, and to recorded performances.

Copyright laws were established in most European countries in the eighteenth century. The first U. S. copyright law of 1790 was based on the British Statute of Anne of 1709: the 1790 U.S. law protected works for 14 years, with one renewal of another 14 years. As defined in the U.S. Constitution (Article II, Section 8), the purpose of copyright is "to promote the progress of science and useful arts, by securing for limited times to authors and inventors the exclusive right to their respective writings and discoveries." The phrase "limited times" has evolved over the years: under the terms of the current law, works are protected for the life of the creator plus 70 years.

Most copyright laws require registration of copyright with a government agency, along with deposit of a copy of the work, usually in the national library.[41] This system of copyright deposit helped create the huge music collections found in national libraries such as the Bibliothèque Nationale, the British Library, and the Library of Congress (see Chapter 1: Types of Libraries, pp. 10–22).

Background

Most of what we do in the United States is governed by the 1976 copyright law, which went into effect on January 1, 1978. The 1976 law was a major revision of the previous (1909) U.S. copyright law; most important, it extended the term of copyright protection from 28 years (with one renewal of another 28 years) to life of the author plus 50 years.

Copyright protection is available to both published and unpublished works, Section 106 of the 1976 Copyright Act generally gives the owner of copyright the exclusive right to do and to authorize others to do the following:

- To reproduce the work in copies or phonorecords;
- To prepare derivative works based upon the work;
- To distribute copies or phonorecords of the work to the public by sale or other transfer of ownership, or by rental, lease, or lending;
- To perform the work publicly, in the case of literary, musical, dramatic, and choreographic works, pantomimes, and motion pictures and other audiovisual works;
- To display the work publicly, in the case of literary, musical, dramatic, and choreographic works, pantomimes, and pictorial, graphic, or sculptural

works, including the individual images of a motion picture or other audio-visual work; and

- In the case of sound recordings, to perform the work publicly by means of a digital audio transmission.[42]

These rights are not boundless, however. Section 107 of the law outlines "fair use" limitations on the copyright holder's exclusive rights, for purposes of teaching, scholarship, and research:

107. Limitations on exclusive rights: Fair use
Notwithstanding the provisions of sections 106 and 106A, the fair use of a copyrighted work, including such use by reproduction in copies or phonorecords or by any other means specified by that section, for purposes such as criticism, comment, news reporting, teaching (including multiple copies for classroom use), scholarship, or research, is not an infringement of copyright. In determining whether the use made of a work in any particular case is a fair use the factors to be considered shall include—

1. the purpose and character of the use, including whether such use is of a commercial nature or is for nonprofit educational purposes;
2. the nature of the copyrighted work;
3. the amount and substantiality of the portion used in relation to the copyrighted work as a whole; and
4. the effect of the use upon the potential market for or value of the copyrighted work.[43]

To aid in interpretation of fair use, many libraries follow the Music Publishers Association's "Guidelines for Educational Uses of Music," which outline permissible and prohibited use of copyrighted material, as follows:

PERMISSIBLE

1. Make a copy of a lost part in an emergency, if it is replaced with a purchased part in due course.
2. Make one copy per student of up to 10 percent of a musical work for class study as long as that 10 percent does not constitute a performable unit.
3. Make a single recording of a student performance for study and for the school's archive.
4. Make a single recording of aural exercises or tests using copyrighted material.
5. Make up to three copies to replace a copy that is damaged, deteriorating, lost, or stolen from a public library or archive (or if the existing format has become obsolete, and if, after reasonable effort by the library/archive, an unused replacement cannot be obtained at a fair price).
6. Make one copy of a short verbal or a graphic work for teacher's use in preparation for or during a class.

The following, however, are expressly prohibited:

1. Copying to avoid purchase.
2. Copying music for any kind of performance (but note the emergency exception above).
3. Copying without including a copyright notice.
4. Copying to create anthologies or compilations.
5. Reproducing materials designed to be consumable (such as workbooks, standardized tests, and answer sheets).
6. Charging students beyond the actual cost involved in making copies as permitted above.[44]

In cooperation with other library organizations, the Music Library Association has developed somewhat more liberal guidelines for educational uses of copyrighted material, particularly as they relate to use of material in the electronic age. These are available on the Music Library Association Copyright Web site, "Copyright for Music Librarians": http://www.lib.jmu.edu/org/mla/.

We must caution that none of these referenced guidelines are in fact the law. Rather, these are policy statements developed by organizations representing libraries and library users, and organizations representing copyright holders. Courts reviewing copyright cases will not necessarily make a ruling based on one of these guidelines.

Recent Legislation

New legislation passed since 1996 has further complicated the copyright agenda in the United States and mostly made things more restrictive for libraries, and by extension, for their users. Among these are implementation of the General Agreement on Tariffs and Trades Treaty (GATT), which restored copyright protection to certain foreign works published after 1920 that lacked protection in the United States, specifically those from the former Soviet Union. Copyright protection for these works was restored on January 1, 1996.[45]

GATT has had a major impact on music libraries, as well as on those who purchase printed music for study and performance. The Kalmus and Dover reprint editions of the works of Prokofiev, Shostakovich, Rachmaninoff, Stravinsky, and other former Soviet composers have been withdrawn, and other publishers, such as Boosey & Hawkes and Sikorski, are offering new editions of these works, usually at much higher prices.

The next major legislation of significance to music libraries was the Sonny Bono Copyright Extension Act (CTEA), which was passed on October 27, 1998. (The late Sonny Bono, congressman from California who died in 1998 and the primary sponsor of this bill, was perhaps better known as the Sonny of Sonny & Cher, the 1960s pop duo.) This bill put the duration of U.S. copyright protection in conformance with that of the European Union, which in 1995 extended the term of copyright protection from life of the author plus 50 years to life plus 70. This applies to all works created after 1978, with some complicated retroactive protection for works published from 1923 to 1978. (Works published prior to 1923 are in the public domain.) Professor Laura Gasaway's Web site "When Works Pass into the Public

Domain" and its update by Peter Hirtle (http://www.unc.edu/~unclng/public -d.htm; http://www.copyright.cornell.edu/training/Hirtle_Public_Domain.htm) provide excellent guidance for determining when works may be out of copyright. CTEA also outlined duration of copyright protection for unpublished works and works of corporate authorship.

The Digital Millennium Copyright Act (DMCA), which was passed October 28, 1999, is a major revision of the 1976 act. An outgrowth of the U.S. adoption of the WIPO (World Intellectual Property Organization) treaty by the Diplomatic Conference in Geneva on December 20, 1996, it presented modifications of copyright law with respect to emerging digital technologies.[46] Among these modifications (many of which are rather technical in detail) is a limitation of liability for online service providers (OSPs) for copyright infringement on the part of users. (Thus, AOL is not necessarily liable for infringements on the part of its account holders; similar provisions apply to protect educational institutions from infringements on the part of faculty and students.) Overall, the modifications in DCMA reflect intensive lobbying efforts on the part of rights holders, particularly those in the entertainment business, as they seek to guard their rights at a time when it is all-too-easy to transmit information over the Internet.[47]

Public Domain and Orphan Works

As noted earlier, works published prior to 1923 are in the public domain. That said, anyone wishing to create a new arrangement of a presumed public domain work should thoroughly check its legal status, in the event that a copyright was renewed or a familiar arrangement is still under copyright protection. Perhaps the most notorious example of a familiar song protected by copyright is that of "Happy Birthday to You." As discussed by James Fuld in his *Book of World Famous Music: Classical, Popular, and Folk,* "Happy Birthday," by Mildred J. Hill and Patty S. Hill, was originally published in 1893 with the title "Good Morning to All."[48] While the melody of "Good Morning" and "Happy Birthday" is almost exactly the same, in a rather complicated scenario, the former is now in the public domain, while the latter is still protected by the 1935 copyright registered (and renewed) by the Summy-Birchard Company.[49]

Copyright information on particular works may be located via the databases of the performing rights societies (see pp. 217–218), through searches in the Library of Congress Copyright Office and library catalogs and databases, and through use of specialized tools such as the Public Domain Report: http://www.pubdomain.com.

Perhaps the best way to ensure against illegal use of copyrighted material is to contact the copyright holder for permission. This is especially helpful to musicians who seek printed scores of works that are no longer available for purchase but are still protected by copyright. In some cases, the publisher of the original edition no longer exists, and it is difficult to locate the appropriate rights holder. Such works are referred to as "orphan works"; the U.S. Congress has recently taken up legislation to address limitations on liability for use of orphan works.[50]

It is important to remember that copyright protects the rights of creators, allowing composers, authors, and arrangers and the publishers or agencies that represent them to benefit from use of their creations. At the same time, fair use enables others to use certain portions of protected works under special conditions for teaching, scholarship, and research. Copyright laws will always struggle to balance the fundamentally divergent views of rights holders and those who seek to use copyrighted material.

Current technologies allowing immediate transmission of text, sound, and images complicate matters further, as all that is possible is not necessarily legal.

Lawrence Lessig established Creative Commons (www.creativecommons .org) in 2001 as a grass-roots effort to allow creators to take advantage of current technologies and make their work more freely available via the Internet. This philosophy has fostered projects such as Wikipedia (www.wikipedia.org) and MIT's Open Course software (http://ocw.mit.edu/index.html) and encouraged many recording artists to release digital downloads of their works for free.

Note: Information in this section is a general overview of copyright; more detailed information may be found in the resources in the select bibliography: For real advice, contact an attorney!

COPYRIGHT: A SELECTED BIBLIOGRAPHY
On the History of Music Copyright Laws

Fuld, James J. "Copyright Laws." In *The Book of World Famous Music: Classical, Popular, and Folk,* 5th ed., 16–24. Revised and enlarged. New York: Dover Publications, 2000.
Kallberg, Jeffrey. "Chopin in the Marketplace." In *Chopin at the Boundaries: Sex, History, and Musical Genre,* 161–214. Cambridge: Harvard University Press, 1996.
Lenneberg, Hans. "Copyright History." In *On the Publishing and Dissemination of Music, 1500–1850,* 116–26. Hillsdale, NY: Pendragon Press, 2003.

On Current Laws and Practice

American Library Association. "Copyright." http://www.ala.org/ala/washoff/woissues/ copyrightb/copyright.cfm.
Davidson, Mary Wallace. "Copyright." In *Music Librarianship at the Turn of the Century,* edited by Richard Griscom and Amanda Maple, 36–42. Music Library Association Technical Reports 27. Lanham, MD: Scarecrow Press, 2000.
Gasaway, Laura N. "When Works Pass into the Public Domain." http://www.unc.edu/ ~unclng/public-d.htm. Updated by Peter Hirtle, Cornell University: http://www .copyright.cornell.edu/training/Hirtle_Public_Domain.htm.
Library of Congress. U.S. Copyright Office. http://www.copyright.gov/.
Music Library Association. "Copyright for Music Librarians." http://www.lib.jmu.edu/ org/mla/.

PERFORMING RIGHTS SOCIETIES

The right to perform a work publicly can be quite lucrative for copyright holders of musical works. As explained by attorney Mark Halloran is his book *The Musician's Business and Legal Guide,* "The concept 'performance' includes live performances and the rendering of previous performances that are fixed in records, videotapes, or film. When a radio station broadcasts a song it is being publicly performed, even though the recording artist is not performing it live. Thus, the radio station must be licensed by the copyright owner to play the song."[51] That Madonna is among the richest women in the world, with a reported wealth of $72 million,[52] is largely because performances of her songs generate millions of dollars in royalties. These royalties are collected on her behalf by ASCAP, of which she is a member.

ASCAP, the oldest of the three performing rights societies in the United States, was established in 1914 by Victor Herbert and other composers who sought to ensure that they would receive financial compensation from performances of their works. Among the other notable members from its early years were Irving Berlin, Jerome Kern, and John Philip Sousa.[53] It currently boasts of more than 300,000 members who represent all styles of music. In addition to Madonna, ASCAP members include Bruce Springsteen, Wynton Marsalis, Richard Rodgers, and Stephen Sondheim.[54] Works licensed by ASCAP are listed in its searchable database, ACE: http://www.ascap.com/ace/.

BMI (Broadcast Music Inc: www.bmi.com), which operates similarly to ASCAP, was established in 1940. It too has a searchable database of titles (http://repertoire.bmi.com), in which one may find works by BMI members such as Milton Babbitt, Miles Davis, Keith Jarrett, B. B. King, and Christina Aguilera.

SESAC (originally named Society of European Stage Authors and Composers: www.sesac.com), the smallest of the three societies, was established in 1930. Its catalog (http://www.sesac.com/repertory/sRepertorySQL.asp) includes works by the Indigo Girls, Guns and Roses, and the Rolling Stones.

Distinct from performance rights are mechanical rights, which cover sound recordings in physical or digital format. The Harry Fox Agency (www.harryfox.com) manages mechanical licenses for many U.S. publishers.

A succinct and detailed overview of the complex world of music licensing is provided by Diane Rapaport in her article "Music Licensing: A Primer."[55]

For additional resources on performing rights societies and other aspects of the music business, see Chapter 12: Resources for Careers in Music and Other Miscellaneous Tools.

Note again: Information in this section is a general overview of performing rights societies; more detailed information may be found in the resources on the select bibliography in Chapter 12: For real advice, contact an attorney!

NOTES

1. For further information about RISM, see Rita Benton, "Répertoire International des Sources Musicale," *Grove Music Online*, ed. Laura Macy. www.grovemusic.com and RISM Web site: http://rism.stub.uni-frankfurt.de/index_f.htm.

2. Benton, "Répertoire International des Sources Musicale."

3. See John Howard, "*Plaine and Easie Code: A Code for Music Bibliography*" in *Beyond Midi: The Handbook of Musical Codes*, ed. Eleanor Selfridge-Field (Cambridge, MA: MIT Press, 1997), 362–71.

4. Howard Mayer Brown, *Instrumental Music Printed Before 1600: A Bibliography* (Cambridge: Harvard University Press, 1965),

1. See pp. 184–185 for complete bibliographic information on his references to Robert Eitner, Emil Vogel, Claudio Sartori, and RISM.

5. For more information on Gutenberg and his work, see Martin Davies, *The Gutenberg Bible* (San Francisco: Pomegranate Artbook, in association with the British Library, n.d.) and *The British Library Treasures in Full: Gutenberg Bible.* http://www.bl.uk/treasures/gutenberg/homepage.html. The latter also has a digital copy of the British Library's Gutenberg Bible.

6. http://www.bl.uk/treasures/gutenberg/howmany.html

7. Donald W. Krummel and Stanley Sadie, *Music Printing and Publishing.* The Norton/Grove Handbooks in Music (New York: W. W. Norton, 1990), 40–41.

8. Ibid., v. This same breakdown is used in the *Grove Music Online* article "Printing and Publishing of Music."

9. Donald W. Krummel, *Guide for Dating Early Published Music: A Manual of Bibliographical Practices* (Hackensack, NJ: J. Boonin, 1974), 30–32.

10. A wonderful example of an ambiguous engraving correction in Beethoven's famous "Waldstein" Sonata is recounted by Susan T. Sommer in her article "Jacob Lateiner, Bibliophile and Collector" in *Pianist, Scholar, Connoisseur: Essays in Honor of Jacob Lateiner,* eds. Bruce Brubaker and Jane Gottlieb. Festschrift Series 15. (Stuyvesant, NY: Pendragon Press, 2000), 238–40.

11. For additional information see Web site of the International Standard Music Number Agency: http://www.ismn-international.org/whatis.html.

12. Ludwig van Beethoven, *The 32 Piano Sonatas: In Reprints of the First and Early Editions, Principally from the Anthony van Hoboken Collection of the Austrian National Library.* With prefaces by Dr. Brian Jeffery (London: Tecla Editions, 1989).

13. For further information see Hans Lenneberg, "Revising the History of the Miniature Score." *Notes* 45, no. 2 (Dec. 1988): 258–61.

14. This was a pirated edition of the Breitkopf & Härtel *Oeuvres Completes,* 1804–1812. See Ludwig van Kochel, *Chronologish-thematisches Verzeichnis sämtliche Tonwerke*

Wolfgang Amadé Mozarts, 6th ed. (Wiesbaden: Breitkopf & Härtel, 1964), 919.

15. Krummel and Sadie, *Music Printing and Publishing,* 129.

16. http://www.hofmeister.rhul.ac.uk/cocoon/hofmeister/content/about/project.html.

17. Hofmeister XIX is a joint project of the International Association of Music Libraries, the British Library, Österreichische Nationalbibliothek, Centre for Computing in the Humanities (King's College, London) and Royal Holloway, University of London. See http://www.hofmeister.rhul.ac.uk/cocoon/hofmeister/content/about/project.html for additional information.

18. See Steven Immel, "Facsimile," *Grove Music Online,* ed. L. Macy. http://www.grovemusic.com.

19. For further information on music notation programs, see Eleanor Selfridge-Field, *Beyond Midi: The Handbook of Musical Codes* (Cambridge, MA: MIT Press, 1997).

20. Walter Emery, *Editions and Musicians* (London: Novello, 1957), 9.

21. James Grier, "Editing," *Grove Music Online,* ed. L. Macy. www.grovemusic.com.

22. Beethoven, *The 32 Piano Sonatas;* Nicholas Temperley, ed., *London Pianoforte School, 1766–1860.* 20 vols. (New York: Garland Publishing, 1985–87;) Jeffrey Kallberg, ed., *Piano Music of Parisian Virtuosos, 1810–1860: A Ten-Volume Anthology.* 10 vols. (New York: Garland Publishing, 1993).

23. Sydney Robinson Charles, et al. "Editions, historical" *Grove Music Online,* ed. L. Macy. www.grovemusic.com.

24. D. Kern Holoman, *Catalogue of the Works of Hector Berlioz.* New Edition of the Complete Works: Hector Berlioz 25 (Kassel: Bärenreiter, 1987); Hans Joachim Marx, *Die Überlieferung der Werke Arcangelo Corellis: catalogue raisonné.* Issued as a supplementary volume to Historisch-kritische Gesamtausgabe der musikalischen Werke (Köln: A. Volk, 1980); Margit L. McCorkle, *Robert Schumann Neue Ausgabe sämtlicher Werke: thematisch-bibliographisches Werkverzeichnis. Robert Schumann Neue Ausgabe sämtlicher Werke.* Series VIII, Supplement, Bd. 6 (Mainz: Schott, 2003); *Bach Dokumente,* ed. Bach-Archiv, Leipzig. 4 vols. (Kassel: Barenreiter, 1963–79). Supplement to Johann Sebastian Bach. Neue Ausgabe Sämtlicher Werke.

25. Internationale Stiftung Mozarteum and Packard Humanities Institute. *NMA Online:* http://dme.mozarteum.at/mambo/index.php.

26. The editors of the *Neue Mozart Ausgabe* announced completion of publication of music volumes on February 6, 1991: see Wolfgang Rehm "Ideal and Reality: Aspects of the *Neue Mozart Ausgabe.*" *Notes* 48, no. 1 (Sept. 1991): 11–19; the editors of the *Neue Bach Ausgabe* announced its completion on June 13, 2007, with publication of the 100th volume of music. In both cases, additional volumes of commentary or revisions will continue to be published.

27. *Ludwig van Beethoven: Complete Edition of All His Works* (Leipzig: Breitkopf & Härtel, 1864–90; Reprint, Huntington Station, NY: Edwin F. Kalmus, 1967).

28. See www.areditions.com for complete listing.

29. The *Grove Music Online* article on "Anthologies" is a discussion of the first definition, while its discussion and listing of anthologies in the "Editions, historical" article centers primarily on the latter definition.

30. James Grier, "Editing," *Grove Music Online,* ed. Laura Macy. www.grovemusic.com; *The Critical Editing of Music: History, Method, and Practice* (Cambridge, MA: Harvard University Press, 1996).

31. A-R series include *Recent Researches in American Music* (Madison, WI: A-R Editions, 1977–); *Recent Researches in the Music of the Baroque Era* (Madison, WI: A-R Editions, 1964–); complete list is available on Web site: www.areditions.com; *Musica Britannica* (London: Stainer & Bell, 1951–); *Neue Brahms Ausgabe* (München: G. Henle Verlag, 1966–); *Oeuvres complètes de Claude Debussy* (Paris: Durand-Costallat, 1985–); and *The Works of Giuseppe Verdi* (Chicago: University of Chicago Press; Milano: Ricordi, 1983–).

32. Emery, *Editions and Musicians,* 24–26.

33. Wisso Weiss and Yoshitake Kobayashi, eds. *Katalog der Wasserzeichen in Bach's Handschriften. Neue Bach Ausgabe,* IX, Bds, 1a, 1b (Kassel: Barenreiter, 1985).

34. See Stanley Boorman, "Rastrology," *Grove Music Online,* ed. L. Macy. www.grovemusic.com; Jean K. and Eugene

35. K. Wolf, "Rastrology and Its Use in Eighteenth-Century Manuscript Studies." In *Studies in Musical Sources and Style: Essays in Honor of Jan LaRue,* eds. Eugene K. Wolf and Edward H. Roesner (Madison, WI: A-R Editions, 1990), 237–91.

35. See Jeffrey Kallberg, "Chopin in the Marketplace, Part I: France and England." *Notes* 39, no. 3 (March 1983): 535–69. This essay is also published in Kallberg's book *Chopin at the Boundaries: Sex, History, and Musical Genre* (Cambridge, MA: Harvard University Press, 1996), 161–214.

36. See Eva Badura-Skoda and Piero Weiss, "Textual Problems in Masterpieces of the 18th and 19th Centuries," *The Musical Quarterly* 51, no. 2 (April 1965): 301–17.

37. Grier, *The Critical Editing of Music,* 109.

38. Philip Gossett, *Divas and Scholars: Performing Italian Opera* (Chicago: University of Chicago Press, 2006), xiv.

39. Ludwig van Beethoven, *Piano Sonata, op. 28: Facsimile of the Autograph, the Sketches, and the First Edition With Transcription and Commentary by Martha Frohlich.* Veröffentlichungen des Beethoven-Hauses in Bonn. Neue Folge. Reihe 3 ; Bd. 10 (Bonn: Beethoven-Haus, 1996).

40. Richard Kramer, "Review: Beethoven Facsimiles." *19th Century Music* 6, no. 1 (1982–83): 76.

41. It should be noted that under the terms of the current U.S. law, copyright registration is recommended but not required. See http://www.copyright.gov/help/faq/faq-general.html#register.

42. Library of Congress. Copyright Office. "What is Copyright?" http://www.copyright.gov/circs/circ1.html#wci.

43. Library of Congress. Copyright Office. Copyright Law of the United States of America. http://www.copyright.gov/title17/92chap1.html#107.

44. National Association for Music Education (MENC), Music Publishers Association of the United States, Music Teachers National Association, National Association of Schools of Music, National Music Publishers Association, "The United States Copyright Law: A Guide for Music Educators" (revised 2003): http://menc.org/resources/view/united-states-copyright-law-a-guide-for-music-educators.

45. Works with restored copyrights may be searched on the LC Web site: "Notices of

Restored Copyrights": http://www
.copyright.gov/gatt.html.

46. The full text of the WIPO treaty is available
     on the U.S. Copyright Office Web site: http://
     www.copyright.gov/wipo/treaty1.html. For
     the complete copyright law, see http://www
     .copyright.gov/title17/.

47. UCLA Online Institute for Cyberspace
     Law and Policy. "The Digital Millennium
     Copyright Act": http://www.gseis.ucla.edu/
     iclp/dmca1.htm.

48. James J. Fuld, *The Book of World Famous
     Music: Classical, Popular, and Folk,* 5th ed.
     (New York: Dover, 2000), 266–67.

49. Summy-Birchard is now part of
     Warner-Chappell Music.

50. See the American Library Association Web
     site: http://www.ala.org/ala/washoff/
     woissues/copyrightb/orphanworks/
     orphanworks.cfm#rptjan06.

51. Mark Halloran and Diane Rapaport,
     "Performing Rights Organizations: An
     Overview," in *The Musician's Business and

Legal Guide, ed. Mark Halloran, 4th ed.
     (Upper Saddle River, NJ: Prentice Hall,
     2008), 126. See also "Performing Rights
     Organizations" in M. William Krasilovsky
     and Sidney Shemel, *This Business of Music:
     The Definitive Guide to the Music Industry,*
     9th ed. (New York: Billboard Books, 2003),
     133–52.

52. See "Forbes: The Celebrity 100": http://
     www.forbes.com/lists/2007/53/07celebrities
     _Madonna_KMJ4_print.html; others on the
     Forbes list of multimillionaire musicians are
     the Rolling Stones, Elton John, Bon Jovi,
     Celine Dion, U2, Justin Timberlake, and
     Tim McGraw.

53. "The Era of the Player Piano (The Early
     1900s)," *ASCAP History:* http://www
     .ascap.com/about/history/1900s.html.

54. "About ASCAP." http://www.ascap.com/
     about/.

55. Diane Rapaport, "Music Licensing: A
     Primer," in *The Musician's Business and
     Legal Guide,* 135–38.

C H A P T E R

Bibliographies of Music

INTRODUCTION

Tools for locating music for performance and study are numerous and complex and go way beyond a "music-in-print" source. Even if a comprehensive music-in-print tool existed (and it does not), users would still need to locate music that has never been printed or published. Indeed, the most comprehensive sources for locating music are library catalogs (see Chapter 1 for more information), as they document materials in a variety of formats.

Users are frequently surprised to learn that besides the large library databases such as WorldCat (www.worldcat.org), we do not have a computerized database listing all music. In a dream scenario, this database would be searchable by composer, medium of performance, nationality of composer, date of composition, duration, and other factors. Further, once the music was identified, it would print out the score on demand and download a recording. This database would quickly answer requests such as "I need the score of Duke Ellington's "Zonky Blues" arranged for string quartet, and I'd like to know what other scores of Ellington's works are available," "I'd like the sheet music for Mariah Carey's hit "Don't Forget About Us," and "Help me find new works for piano trio (piano, violin, violoncello) written in the last 50 years."

This chapter is divided into four sections:

I. **Bibliographies of Music and Indexes:** sources that provide access to performance scores and include information on publisher or manuscript source. These bibliographies may list music either alphabetically or in a classified form, similarly to bibliographies of music literature described in Chapter 2.

Indexes are tools to locate individual compositions within a volume, similar to locating articles in periodicals. Many vocal compositions are published in multicomposer volumes, for example, *French Art Song of the 19th Century: 39 Works from Berlioz to Debussy,* or *The Big Book of '50s and '60s Swinging Songs.* Users need tools such as published indexes (or library catalogs that index complete contents of these collections) to locate titles such as Vincent D'Indy's song "Lied Maritime" (found in the former volume) or "Can't Take My Eyes Off of You," popularized by singers from Rudi Valli to the Pet Shop Boys, which is found in the latter volume.

II. *Musical Settings of Poets and Writers:* sources that list musical compositions based on a poet or author whose works have been set to music by composers. These tools allow performers to search for repertoire by text, rather than by composer. Not all of these sources include publisher information.

III. *Regional bibliographies and other specialized tools.*

IV. *Resources for locating music publishers.*

Repertoire may also be found in the bibliographies of early music discussed in the last chapter.

REAL QUESTION NO. 1:
"My string quartet has been asked to play some works by Duke Ellington at my cousin's wedding, specifically, his 'Zonky Blues.' Is this available in an arrangement for string quartet, and what other Ellington published scores are available?"

REAL ANSWER NO. 1:
One of the most efficient ways to determine if a score is available is to search WorldCat: www.worldcat.org. This will tell us if a published score is available in a library collection. Use "Advanced Search" with author name: Duke Ellington (note that it's not in inverted form "Ellington, Duke," as we find in most library catalogs.) Put "Zonky" in key word and limit by format "Musical Score." This brings up several Ellington scores, which presumably have this work within their contents.

REAL QUESTION NO. 2:
'I'd like the sheet music to Mariah Carey's hit "Don't Forget About Us."

REAL ANSWER NO. 2:
Again, we would begin with WorldCat, as it's the largest database for scores, books, and recordings found in library collections. The search here is a bit more straightforward: we find the sheet music to the individual song, as well as collections of her works that include this particular song.

REAL QUESTION NO. 3:
"Help me find new works for piano trio written in the last 50 years."

REAL ANSWER NO. 3:
A bit more involved, but also, dare we say, a bit more fun. Here we want to find a broad selection of works for this instrumentation, from which the ensemble may develop some programs:
Yes, begin with WorldCat.   (continued on following page)

> *REAL ANSWER NO. 3:* continued
> You also want to use some of the printed bibliographies found in the this chapter, for example:
> Drucker. *American Piano Trios.*
> Hinson. *The Piano in Chamber Ensemble,* 2nd ed. This source has a classified arrangement and brief description of each work. See under "Music for Three Instruments: Trios for Piano, Violin, Cello."
> And, your group wants to present diverse programming, including works by underrepresented composers (African Americans and Women). See
> Horne. *Keyboard Music of Black Composers.* Use index under Three Instruments: Piano Trio.
> Walker-Hill. *Piano Music by Black Women Composers: A Catalog of Solo and Ensemble Works.* See Appendix: Ensemble Instrumentation.
> Other relevant tools for this search include
> >*International Directory of Contemporary Music: Instrumentation*
> >Catalogs of music information centers (see: www.iamic.net)
> >Some of the regional bibliographies, such as *The Boston Composers Project: A Bibliography of Contemporary Music.*

BIBLIOGRAPHIES OF MUSIC AND INDEXES

African American Music/Black Music

A number of the bibliographies listed here focus specifically on music of African American and black composers. See titles by Aaron Horne under BRASS MUSIC, PIANO MUSIC, STRING MUSIC, and WIND MUSIC; by Helen Walker-Hill under PIANO MUSIC; by Patricia Johnson Trice and Evelyn Davidson White under CHORAL MUSIC; by Irene V. Jackson under GOSPEL MUSIC; and by Kathleen Abromeit under VOCAL MUSIC. *Basic Music Library,* 3rd ed., includes an appendix with references to works by black composers documented in the book. See also DIGITAL SHEET MUSIC COLLECTIONS (pp. 240–242): Brown University Library, *African-American Sheet Music, 1850–1920: From the Collections of Brown University Library.*

AMERICAN MUSIC (SEE ALSO OPERA/MUSIC THEATRE, ORCHESTRAL MUSIC)

Drucker, Arno P. *American Piano Trios: A Resource Guide.* Lanham, MD: Scarecrow Press, 1999.
Heintze, James R. *American Music Before 1865 in Print and on Records: A Biblio-Discography.* Rev. ed. Brooklyn: Institute for Studies in American Music, Conservatory of Music, Brooklyn College of the City University of New York, 1990.

BASSOON

Beebe, Jon P. *Music for Unaccompanied Solo Bassoon: An Annotated Bibliography.* Jefferson, NC: McFarland, 1990.
Bulling, Burchard. *Fagott Bibliographie.* Wilhelmshaven: F. Noetzel, 1989.
Fletcher, Kristine Klopfenstein. *The Paris Conservatoire and the Contest Solos for Bassoon.* Bloomington: Indiana University Press, 1988.

Jansen, Will. *The Bassoon: Its History, Construction, Makers, Players, and Music.* 5 vols. Buren, The Netherlands: F. Knuf, 1978.

Koenigsbeck, Bodo. *Bassoon Bibliography.* Monteux, France: Musica Rara, 1994.

Wilkins, Wayne. *The Index of Bassoon Music Including the Index of Baroque Trio Sonatas.* Magnolia, AR: Music Register, 1976; supplements: 1976–77, 1978.

BRASS MUSIC (SEE ALSO NAMES OF INDIVIDUAL INSTRUMENTS.)

Anderson, Paul G. *Brass Ensemble Music Guide.* Evanston, IL: Instrumentalist Co., 1976.

_____. *Brass Solo and Study Material Music Guide.* Evanston, IL: Instrumentalist Co., 1976.

Horne, Aaron. *Brass Music of Black Composers: A Bibliography.* Westport, CT: Greenwood Press, 1996.

Thompson, J. Mark, and Jeffrey Jon Lemke. *French Music for Low Brass Instruments: An Annotated Bibliography.* Bloomington: Indiana University Press, 1994.

CHAMBER MUSIC

Altmann, Wilhelm. *Kammermusik-Katalog: ein Verziechnis von seit 1841 veröffentlichen Kammermusikwerken.* 1910. Reprint, Hofheim am Taunus: Hofmeister, 1967. (Succeeded by Richter.)

Drucker, Arno P. *American Piano Trios: A Resource Guide.* Lanham, MD: Scarecrow Press, 1999.

Everett, William A. *British Piano Trios, Quartets, and Quintets, 1850–1950: A Checklist.* Warren, MI: Harmonie Park Press, 2000.

Hinson, Maurice. *The Piano in Chamber Ensemble: An Annotated Guide.* 2nd ed. Bloomington: Indiana University Press, 2006.

Lawrence, Ian. *The Twentieth-Century String Quartet: A Historical Introduction and Catalogue.* Lanham, MD: Scarecrow Press, 2001.

Rangel-Ribeiro, Victor, and Robert Markel. *Chamber Music: An International Guide to Works and Their Instrumentation.* Computer program designed and developed by Glenn H. Babakian. New York: Facts on File, 1993.

Richter, Johannes Friedrich. *Kammermusik-Katalog: Verzeichnis der von 1944 bis 1958 veröffentlichen Werke für Kammermusik und für Klavier vier-und sechshändig sowie für zwei und mehr Klaviere.* Leipzig: F. Hofmeister, 1960. (Update of Altmann.)

Scott, William. *A Conductor's Repertory of Chamber Music: Compositions for Nine to Fifteen Solo Instruments.* Westport, CT: Greenwood Press, 1993.

(See also Music in Print series; Cohn, Arthur. *The Literature of Chamber Music.* 4 vols. Chapel Hill, NC: Hinshaw Press, 1997 (listed in Chapter 3: Dictionaries and Encyclopedias: Special Subjects, p. 80).

CHORAL MUSIC (SEE ALSO MEMORIAL MUSIC; MUSIC IN PRINT; VOCAL MUSIC: SACRED.)

Chase, Robert. *Dies Irae: A Guide to Requiem Music.* Lanham, MD: Scarecrow Press, 2003.

DeVenney, David P. *American Choral Music Since 1920: An Annotated Guide.* Fallen Leaf Reference Books in Music 27. Berkeley, CA: Fallen Leaf Press, 1993.

_____. *American Masses and Requiems: A Descriptive Guide.* Fallen Leaf Reference Books in Music 15. Berkeley, CA: Fallen Leaf Press, 1990.

_____. *Early American Choral Music: An Annotated Guide.* Fallen Leaf Reference Books in Music 10. Berkeley, CA: Fallen Leaf Press, 1988.

_____. *Nineteenth-Century American Choral Music: An Annotated Guide.* Fallen Leaf Reference Books in Music 8. Berkeley, CA: Fallen Leaf Press, 1987.

DeVenney, David P., and Craig R. Johnson. *The Chorus in Opera: A Guide to the Repertory.* Metuchen, NJ: Scarecrow Press, 1993.

Green, Jonathan D. *A Conductor's Guide to Choral-Orchestral Works.* Metuchen, NJ: Scarecrow Press, 1994.

_____. *A Conductor's Guide to Choral-Orchestral Works: The Twentieth Century, Part II: The Music of Rachmaninov through Penderecki.* Lanham, MD: Scarecrow Press, 1998.

_____. *A Conductor's Guide to Choral-Orchestral Works of J. S. Bach.* Lanham, MD: Scarecrow Press, 2000.

_____. *A Conductor's Guide to Choral-Orchestral Works: Classical Period, Vol. 1: Haydn and Mozart.* Lanham, MD: Scarecrow Press, 2002.

_____. *A Conductor's Guide to Nineteenth-Century Choral-Orchestra Works.* Lanham, MD: Scarecrow Press, 2008.

Laster, James. *Catalogue of Choral Music Arranged in Biblical Order.* 2nd ed. Lanham, MD: Scarecrow Press, 1996.

Rice, Paul F. *The Solo Cantata in Eighteenth-Century Britain: A Thematic Catalog.* Warren, MI: Harmonie Park Press, 2003.

Rosewall, Michael. *Directory of Choral-Orchestral Music.* New York: Routledge, 2007.

Tiemstra, Suzanne Spicer. *The Choral Music of Latin America: A Guide to Compositions and Research.* New York: Greenwood Press, 1992.

Trice, Patricia Johnson. *Choral Arrangements of the African-American Spirituals: Historical Overview and Annotated Listings.* Westport, CT: Greenwood Press, 1998.

Wachsmuth, Karen. *A Bibliography of Twentieth-Century Hungarian Choral Music.* Lawton, OK: American Choral Directors Association, 2002.

White, Evelyn Davidson. *Choral Music by African American Composers: A Selected, Annotated Bibliography.* 2nd ed. Lanham, MD: Scarecrow Press, 1996.

CLARINET

Gee, Harry R. *Clarinet Solos de Concours, 1897–1980: An Annotated Bibliography.* Bloomington: Indiana University Press, 1981.

Gillespie, James E. *Solos for Unaccompanied Clarinet: An Annotated Bibliography of Published Works.* Detroit: Information Coordinators, 1973.

Opperman, Kalmen. *Repertory of the Clarinet.* New York: Ricordi, 1960.

University of Maryland Libraries. *International Clarinet Association Research Center.* http://www.lib.umd.edu/PAL/SCPA/icarinfo.html.

Wilkins, Wayne. *The Index of Clarinet Music.* Magnolia, AR: Music Register, 1975; supplements: 1976–77, 1978.

CORNETT

Collver, Michael, and Bruce Dickey. *A Catalog of Music for the Cornett.* Bloomington: Indiana University Press, 1996.

DANCE MUSIC

Emerson, Isabelle Putnam. *Twentieth-Century American Music for the Dance: A Bibliography.* Westport, CT: Greenwood Press, 1996. (Lists works created specifically for concert dance by American composers [p. viii]).

DOUBLE BASS

Grodner, Murray. *Comprehensive Catalog of Available Literature for the Double Bass.* 3rd ed. Bloomington, IN: Lemur Musical Research, 1974.
Planyavsky, Alfred. *Geschichte des Kontrabasses.* Zweite wesentlich Auflage, unter Mitarbeit von Herbert Seifert. Tutzing: H. Schneider, 1984.

ELECTRONIC MUSIC

Davies, Hugh. *Répertoire International des Musiques Electroacoustiques = International Electronic Music Catalog.* Cambridge, MA: Distributed by M.I.T. Press, 1968. Expanded online as Hein, Folkmar. *International Documentation of Electroacoustic Music:* http://www.kgw.tu-berlin.de/EMDoku/Vorwort-E.html.
Edwards, J. Michele. *Literature for Voices in Combination with Electronic and Tape Music: An Annotated Bibliography.* MLA Index and Bibliography Series 17. Ann Arbor, MI: Music Library Association, 1977.
Melby, Carol. *Computer Music Compositions of the United States, 1976.* 2nd ed. Urbana: University Library, University of Illinois, 1976.
(See also International Computer Music Association: http://www.notam02.no/icma/.)

EUPHONIUM

Guide to the Euphonium Repertoire: The Euphonium Source Book. Compiled and edited by Lloyd E. Bone Jr. and Eric Paull under the supervision of R. Winston Morris. Bloomington: Indiana University Press, 2007.

FILM MUSIC

Those who are interested in studying and analyzing film music may be surprised to know that it is quite difficult to locate published scores; the extant copies of full scores used for movies are rarely published in sale editions. These scores may sometimes be available on a rental basis from publishers, but more commonly they remain the possession of the composer or the studio that commissioned the work.

The sources below are primarily listings of films and their composers; some also include references to recordings. H. Stephen Wright's *Film Music Collections in the United States* lists the studio and library collections that house these scores; Wright's *Film Music at the Piano* lists published piano reductions of the scores, as these are, in most cases, the only published representation of the work.[1] Stubblebine's books similarly list vocal scores to film music scores.

The Film Music Society (formerly the Society for the Preservation of Film Music), established in 1974, "promotes the preservation of film and television music in all of its manifestations, including published and unpublished scores, orchestrations, recordings and all related materials."[2] Further information is available on its Web site: http://www.filmmusicsociety.org/. The organization's quarterly journal *Cue Sheet* publishes scholarly articles about film music composers and resources.

Anderson, Gillian B. *Music for Silent Films, 1894–1929: A Guide.* Washington, DC: Library of Congress, 1988.

Benjamin, Ruth, and Arthur Rosenblatt. *Movie Song Catalog: Performers and Supporting Crew for the Songs Sung in 1460 Musical and Nonmusical Films, 1928–1988.* Jefferson, NC: McFarland, 1993.

Burlingame, Jon. *Sound and Vision: Sixty Years of Motion Picture Soundtracks.* New York: Billboard Books, 2000.

Internet Movie Database. www.imdb.com (Provides detailed information [including composer] on movies and TV shows).

Limbacher, James L. *Film Music; From Violins to Video.* Metuchen, NJ: Scarecrow Press, 1974.

_____. *Keeping Score: Film Music, 1972–1979.* Metuchen, NJ: Scarecrow Press, 1981.

Limbacher, James L., and H. Stephen Wright. *Keeping Score: Film and Television Music, 1980–1988: With Additional Coverage of 1921–1979.* Metuchen, NJ: Scarecrow Press, 1991.

Marill, Alvin H. *Keeping Score: Film and Television Music, 1988–1997.* Lanham, MD: Scarecrow Press, 1998.

McCarty, Clifford. *Film Composers in America; A Filmography, 1911–1970.* 2nd ed. New York: Oxford University Press, 2000.

Stubblebine, Donald J. *British Cinema Sheet Music: A Comprehensive Listing of Film Music Published in the United Kingdom, Canada, and Australia, 1916 through 1994.* Jefferson, NC: McFarland, 1997.

_____. *Cinema Sheet Music: A Comprehensive Listing of Published Film Music from "Squaw Man" (1914) to "Batman" (1989).* Jefferson, NC: McFarland, 1991.

Wright, H. Stephen. *Film Music at the Piano: An Index to Piano Arrangements of Instrumental Film and Television Music in Anthologies and Collections.* Lanham, MD: Scarecrow Press, 2003.

Wright, H. Stephen, and Stephen M. Fry, eds. *Film Music Collections in the United States: A Guide.* Hollywood, CA: Society for the Preservation of Film Music, 1996.

FLUTE

Boenke, Heidi M. *Flute Music by Women Composers: An Annotated Catalog.* New York: Greenwood Press, 1988.

Baker, Serena, Spencer Hunter, and Steve Jones. *National Flute Association Catalog.* 6th ed. Tuscon: University of Arizona Library, 1992. (Catalog of National Flute Association collection housed in University of Arizona Library; updated in *Flutist Quarterly* and available online: http://www.nfaonline.org/resLibrary.asp.)

Busch-Salmen, Gabriele, und Adelheid Krause-Pichler. *Handbuch Querflöte: Instrumente, Lehrwerke, Aufführungspraxis, Musik, Ausbildung, Beruf.* Kassel: Bärenreiter, 1999.

Howell, Thomas. *The Avant-Garde Flute: A Handbook for Composers and Flutists.* Berkeley: University of California Press, 1974.

Munster, Peter Van. *Repertoire Catalogue: Piccolo, Alto Flute, Bass Flute, including ca. 900 Works for Flute Choir or Flute Orchestra.* Rome: Riverberi Sonori, 2004. (Updated online: http://petervanmunster.googlepages.com/supplement.)

Pellerite, James J. *A Handbook of Literature for the Flute: Compilation of Graded Method Materials, Solos, and Ensemble Music for Flutes.* Bloomington, IN: Zalo Publications, 1978.

Pierreúse, Bernard. *Flute Literature: General Catalog of Published and Unpublished Works by Instrumental Category.* Paris: Société des Editions Jobert, 1982.

Potter, Christine. *Alto and Bass Flute Resource Book.* Nashua, NH: Falls House Press, 2005.

Toff, Nancy. *The Flute Book: A Complete Guide for Students and Performers.* 2nd ed. New York: Oxford University Press, 1996.

Vester, Franz. *Flute Music of the 18th Century: An Annotated Bibliography.* Monteux, France: Musica Rara, 1985.

_____. *Flute Repertoire Catalog: 10,000 Titles.* London: Musica Rara, 1967.

Wilkins, Wayne. *The Index of Flute Music Including the Index of Baroque Trio Sonatas.* Magnolia, AR: Music Register, 1974; supplements: 1975, 1976–77.

GOSPEL MUSIC

Jackson, Irene V. *Afro-American Religious Music: A Bibliography and a Catalogue of Gospel Music.* Westport, CT: Greenwood Press, 1979. (Bibliography of resources on Afro-American religious music, and catalog of the Library of Congress's holdings of black gospel music copyrighted between 1938 and 1965.)

GREGORIAN CHANT (SEE ALSO HYMNS, HYMN TUNES AND HYMNALS.)

Bryden, John R., and David G. Hughes. *An Index to Gregorian Chant.* 2 vols. Cambridge, MA: Harvard University Press, 1969. (Vol. I: Alphabetical Index; Vol. II: Thematic Index)

GUITAR (SEE ALSO MUSIC IN PRINT.)

Gilmore, George, and Mark Pereira. *Guitar Music Index: A Cross-Indexed and Graded Listing of Music in Print for Classical Guitar and Lute.* Honolulu: Galliard Press, 1976.

Helleu, Laurence. *La Guitare en Concert: Catalogue des oeuvres avec guitare (duos, trios, musique de chambre, orchestre, concertos) du XX° siecle.* Paris: Éditions musicales Transatlantiques, [1983?].

Maroney, James F. *Music for Voice and Classical Guitar, 1945–1996: An Annotated Catalog.* Jefferson, NC: McFarland, 1997.

Rezits, Joseph. *The Guitarist's Resource Guide: Guitar Music in Print and Books on the Art of Guitar.* San Diego, CA: Pallma Music Co., 1983.

Smith, Dorman, and Laurie Eagleson. *Guitar and Lute Music in Periodicals: An Index.* Fallen Leaf Reference Books in Music 13. Berkeley, CA: Fallen Leaf Press, 1990.

HARP

Brigham Young University. Music Library. International Harp Archives. http://music.lib .byu.edu/IHA/ahsll.html. (Includes IHA lending library of audio and video recordings, as well as extensive archival collections of renowned harpists.)

Michel, Catherine, and Françoise Lesure. *Répertoire de la Musique Pour Harpe Publiée du XVIIe au Début XIXe Siècle: Bibliographie.* Paris: Aux Amateurs de Livres International, 1990.

Palkovic, Mark. *Harp Music Bibliography: Compositions for Solo Harp and Harp Ensemble.* Bloomington: Indiana University Press, 1995.

_____. *Harp Music Bibliography Supplement: Compositions for Solo Harp and Harp Ensemble.* Lanham, MD: Scarecrow Press, 2002.

_____. *Harp Music Bibliography: Chamber Music and Concertos.* Lanham, MD: Scarecrow Press, 2002.

Zingel, Hans Joachim. *Harfenmusik Verzeichnis der Gedruckten und zur Zeit greifbaren Literatur für Pedalharfe.* Hofheim am Taunus: Hofmesiter, 1965.

_____. *Harp Music in the Nineteenth Century.* Translated and edited by Mark Palkovic. Bloomington: Indiana University Press, 1992.

HORN

Bruchle, Bernhard. *Horn Bibliographie.* 3 vols. Wilhelmshaven: Heinrichshofen, 1970–83.

Wilkins, Wayne. *The Index of French Horn Music.* Magnolia, AR: Music Register, 1978.

HYMNS, HYMN TUNES, AND HYMNALS

Graham, Fred Kimball. *"With One Heart and One Voice": A Core Repertory of Hymn Tunes Published for Use in the Methodist Episcopal Church in the United States, 1808–1878.* Drew University Studies in Liturgy 12. Lanham, MD: Scarecrow Press, 2004.

Kroeger, Karl, and Marie Kroeger. *An Index to Anglo-American Psalmody in Modern Critical Editions.* Recent Researches in American Music 40. Madison, WI: A-R Editions, 2000.

Leaver, Robin A. "Hymnals, Hymnal Collections and Collection Development." *Notes* 47, no. 2 (March 2003): 664–67.

Hoon, Jos de, Simeon Boden, and Peter Becker. *Bibliography of Hymns and Gregorian Chants from the Sixteenth Century to 1991.* Utrecht: Hogeschool voor de Kunsten Utrecht, 1996.

Temperley, Nicholas, Charles G. Manns, and Joseph Herl. *The Hymn Tune Index: A Census of English-Language Hymn Tunes in Printed Sources from 1535 to 1820.* 4 vols. New York: Oxford University Press, 1998. Online version: http://hymntune.music .uiuc.edu/default.asp.

Wasson, D. Dewitt. *Hymntune Index and Related Hymn Materials.* 3 vols. Lanham, MD: Scarecrow Press, 1998.

Wenk, Arthur. *Musical Resources for the Revised Common Lectionary.* Metuchen, NJ: Scarecrow Press, 1994.

JAZZ SCORES

Meadows, Eddie. "Chapter IX: Pedagogy Materials" and "Chapter X: Transcriptions." In *Jazz Scholarship and Pedagogy: A Research and Information Guide,* 443–574. 3rd ed. Routledge Music Bibliographies. New York: Routledge, 2006.

Voigt, John. *Jazz Music in Print and Jazz Books in Print.* 3rd ed. Boston: Hornpipe Music Publishing Co., 1982.

MEMORIAL MUSIC

Chase, Robert. *Memento Mori: A Guide to Contemporary Memorial Music.* Lanham, MD: Scarecrow Press, 2007.

Fling, R. Michael. *Musical Memorials for Musicians: A Guide to Selected Compositions.* MLA Index and Bibliography Series 29. Lanham, MD: Scarecrow Press: Music Library Association, 2001.

MISCELLANEOUS

A Basic Music Library: Essential Scores and Sound Recordings. Compiled by the Music Library Association: Elizabeth Davis, coordinating editor; Pamela Bristah and Jane Gottlieb, scores editors; Kent Underwood and William E. Anderson, sound recording editors. 3rd ed. Chicago: American Library Association, 1997. (A specialized tool with selected lists of published scores and sound recordings, designed to assist libraries in developing music collections.)

Fuld, James J. *Book of World-Famous Music: Classical, Popular and Folk.* 5th ed. Revised and enlarged. New York: Dover Publications, 2000.

A fascinating compendium of information on hundreds of—as the title implies— "famous" compositions: classical, popular, and folk—everything from "Chopsticks" to Schubert's *Erklönig.* Each entry includes a brief musical incipit; background on the work and its composer; and, most prominently, its publishing history. A renowned collector and bibliographer (and an attorney by profession), Fuld was passionate about locating the first editions, first issues of all of these works. Upon announcing its acquisition of Mr. Fuld's collection in 1995, the Pierpont Morgan Library mounted a major exhibit titled "Auld Acquaintances. Famous Music from the James Fuld Collection."[3]

In addition to its copious information on each work, Fuld's book includes an important set of essays on "Determining When, and by Whom, a Musical Work Was First Published," "Determining Date of a Particular Copy," and "Copyright Laws." These essays provide a roadmap for researchers, bibliographers, and collectors who seek to navigate the complex world of first and early editions. See also p. 189.

MUSIC AND WAR

Arnold, Ben. *Music and War: A Research and Information Guide.* New York: Garland Publishing, 1993.

MUSIC IN PRINT

International Database for Printed Music and Music Products (IDNV). Hrsg., Deutscher Musik-Verleger Verbad e,V., Gesamtverband Deutscher Musikfachgeschäfte e.V., 2002– . (available on CD-ROM)

Music in Print Series. (See also Farish, *String Music in Print,* which was originally published outside of the series.)

Available online as E-MusicQuest. *Music-in-Print Series:* www.emusicquest.com.

Choral Music in Print: Master Index 1991. Philadelphia: Musicdata, Inc., 1991.

Classical Guitar Music in Print. Philadelphia: Musicdata, Inc., 1989; supplement: 1998.

Classical Vocal Music in Print. Philadelphia: Musicdata, Inc., 1976; supplements: 1985, 1995. *Master Index,* 1995.

Music in Print: Annual Supplement. Philadelphia: Musicdata, Inc. (last issue: 1986).
Music in Print: Master Composer Index 1999. 2 vols. Philadelphia: Musicdata, Inc., 1999.
Music in Print: Master Title Index 1999. Philadelphia: Musicdata, Inc., 1999.
Orchestral Music in Print. Philadelphia: Musicdata, Inc., 1979; supplements: 1983, 1994, 1999. *Master Index,* 1994, 1999.
Organ Music in Print. 2nd ed. Philadelphia: Musicdata, Inc., 1984; supplements: 1990, 1997. *Master Index,* 1997.
Sacred Choral Music in Print. 2nd ed. Philadelphia: Musicdata, Inc., 1985; supplements: 1988, 1992, 1996.
  Arranger Index, 1987
  Master Index, 1992, 1996
Secular Choral Music in Print. 2 vols. 2nd ed. Philadelphia: Musicdata, Inc., 1987; supplements: 1991, 1993, 1996.
  Arranger Index, 1987
  Master Index, 1993, 1996
Woodwind Music in Print. Philadelphia: Musicdata, Inc., 1997.
(See also Voigt, John. *Jazz Music in Print.* 1978, supp., 1979.)

MUSIC IN PRINT: PERFORMING RIGHTS SOCIETIES

The three major performing rights organizations, ASCAP, BMI, and SESAC, have online listings of works by their member-composers:

ASCAP ACE Title Search: www.ascap.com/ace
BMI: www.bmi.com
SESAC: http://www.sesac.com/repertory/repertory_main.asp

OBOE/ENGLISH HORN

Gifford, Virginia Snodgrass. *Music for Oboe, Oboe d'Amore and English Horn: A Bibliography of Materials at the Library of Congress.* Westport, CT: Greenwood Press, 1983.
Haynes, Bruce. *Music for Oboe, 1650–1800: A Bibliography.* 2nd ed. rev.; Fallen Leaf Reference Books in Music 16. Berkeley, CA: Fallen Leaf Press, 1992.
Hošek, Miroslav. *Oboen Bibliographie I.* Wilhelmshaven: Heinrichshofen, 1975.
McMullen, William. *Soloistic English Horn Literature from 1736–1984.* Juilliard Performance Guides 4. Stuyvesant, NY: Pendragon Press, 1994.
Wilkins, Wayne. *The Index of Oboe Music Including the Index of Baroque Trio Sonatas.* Magnolia, AR: Music Register, 1976; supplements: 1976–77, 1978.

OPERA/MUSIC THEATRE (SEE ALSO VOCAL MUSIC.)

Boldrey, Richard. *Guide to Operatic Roles and Arias.* Dallas: Pst, 1994.
_____. *Guide to Operatic Duets.* Dallas: Pst, 1994.
Borroff, Edith. *American Operas: A Checklist.* Warren, MI: Harmonie Park Press, 1992.
Central Opera Service. "Directory of Operas and Publishers." *Central Opera Service Bulletin* 18, nos. 2 & 3 (1976). (Central Opera Service is now part of Opera America.)
Eaton, Quaintance. *Opera Production: A Handbook.* Minneapolis: University of Minnesota Press, 1961.

_____, and Randolph Mickelson. *Opera Production II: A Handbook, with Production Problems in Handel's Operas.* Minneapolis: University of Minnesota Press, 1974.

Kornick, Rebecca H. *Recent American Opera: A Production Guide.* New York: Columbia University Press, 1991.

Lucha-Burns, Carol. *Musical Notes: A Practical Guide to Setting and Staging Standards of the American Musical Theatre.* New York: Greenwood Press, 1986.

Opera America. "New Works Directory": http://www.operaamerica.org/artists/newworks/index.html.

Stubblebine, Donald J. *Broadway Sheet Music: A Comprehensive List of Published Music from Broadway and Other Stage Shows, 1918–1993.* Jefferson, NC: McFarland, 1996.

_____. *Early Broadway Sheet Music: A Comprehensive Listing of Published Music from Broadway and Other Stage Shows, 1843–1918.* Jefferson, NC: McFarland, 2002.

Summers, W. Franklin. *Operas in One Act: A Production Guide.* Lanham, MD: Scarecrow Press, 1997.

ORCHESTRAL EXCERPTS

Rabson, Carolyn. *Orchestral Excerpts: A Comprehensive Index.* Fallen Leaf Reference Books in Music 25. Berkeley, CA: Fallen Leaf Press, 1993.

ORCHESTRAL MUSIC (SEE ALSO CHORAL MUSIC; MUSIC IN PRINT.)

Aronowsky, Solomon. *Performing Times of Orchestral Works.* London: E. Benn, 1959.

ASCAP Symphonic Catalog. 3rd ed. New York: R. R. Bowker, 1977.

BMI Symphonic Catalog: Supplement number one. New York: Broadcast Music, 1971; supplement: 1978.

Bonner Katalog: Verzeichnis reversgebundener musikalischer Aufführungsmateriale. Herausgegeben vom Deutsches Musikarchiv, Deutsche Bibliothek und Deutscher Musikverleger-Verband. 4th ed. 2 vols. Munich: K.G. Saur, 2000. (also on CD-ROM; lists rental scores)

Daniels, David. *Orchestral Music: A Handbook.* 4th ed. Lanham, MD: Scarecrow Press, 2005. Updated on www.orchestralmusic.com. Also available online through OPAS (Orchestra Planning and Administration System): http://www.fineartssoftware.com/OPAS/index.htm.

The Edwin A. Fleisher Collection of Orchestral Music in the Free Library of Philadelphia: A Cumulative Catalog, 1929–1977. Boston: G. K. Hall, 1979. http://www.library.phila.gov/libserv/fleisher.htm.

(Lending library of orchestral music.)

Koshgarian, Richard. *American Orchestral Music: A Performance Catalog.* Metuchen, NJ: Scarecrow Press, 1992.

Saltonstall, Cecilia D., and Henry Saltonstall. *A New Catalog of Music for Small Orchestra.* Clifton, NJ: European American Music Corp., 1978.

Yaklich, Richard Eldon. *An Orchestra Conductor's Guide to Repertoire and Programming.* Lewiston, NY: E. Mellen Press, 2003.

ORGAN (SEE ALSO MUSIC IN PRINT; PIANO/HARPSICHORD.)

Arnold, Corliss Richard. *Organ Literature: A Comprehensive Survey.* 3rd ed. 2 vols. Metuchen, NJ: Scarecrow Press, 1995.

Hardwick, Peter. *British Organ Music of the Twentieth Century: The Composers, Their Music, and Their Musical Style.* Lanham, MD: Scarecrow Press, 2003.

Laster, James. *Catalogue of Music for Organ and Instruments.* Lanham, MD: Scarecrow Press, 2005.

Lukas, Viktor. *A Guide to Organ Music.* Translated by Anne Wyburd from the 5th edition. Portland, OR: Amadeus Press, 1989.

Spelman, Leslie P. *Organ Plus: A Catalogue of Ensemble Music for Organ with Other Instruments.* 4th ed. New York: American Guild of Organists, 1992.

PERCUSSION

Carroll, Raynor. *Symphonic Repertoire Guide for Timpani and Percussion.* Pasadena, CA: Batterie Music, 2005.

Holland, James. "List of Works." In *Practical Percussion: A Guide to the Instruments and Their Sources.* Rev. ed. Lanham, MD: Scarecrow Press, 2005.

Larrick, Geary. *An Annotated Bibliography of Percussion Music Publications.* Lewiston, NY: E. Mellen Press, 2005. (Annotated bibliography of percussion music published by Per-Mus Publications in Ohio.)

Percussive Arts Society. *Solo and Ensemble Literature for Percussion.* Terre Haute, IN: Percussive Arts Society, 1978.

Siwe, Thomas, ed. *Percussion Ensemble and Solo Literature.* Champaign, IL: Media Press, 1993.

_____, ed. *Percussion Solo Literature.* Champaign, IL: Media Press, 1995.

_____, ed. *Percussion Ensemble Literature.* Champaign, IL: Media Press, 1998.

PIANO/HARPSICHORD MUSIC (INCL. INDEXES) (SEE ALSO CHAMBER MUSIC.)

Altmann, Wilhelm. *Verzeichnis von Werken für Klavier vier-und sechshändig sowie für zwei und mehr Klaviere.* Leipzig: F. Hofmeister, 1943.

Axford, Elizabeth C. *Traditional World Music Influences in Contemporary Solo Piano Literature: A Selected Bibliographic Survey and Review.* Lanham, MD: Scarecrow Press, 1997.

Barnard, Trevor, and Elizabeth Gutierrez. *A Practical Guide to Solo Piano Music.* Galesville, MD: Meredith Music Publications, 2006.

Bedford, Frances. *Harpsichord and Clavichord Music of the Twentieth Century.* Fallen Leaf Reference Books in Music 22. Berkeley, CA: Fallen Leaf Press, 1993.

Chang, Frederic Ming, and Albert Faurot. *Concert Piano Repertoire: A Manual of Solo Literature for Artists and Performers.* Metuchen, NJ: Scarecrow Press, 1976.

_____. *Team Piano Repertoire: A Manual of Music for Multiple Players at One or More Pianos.* Metuchen, NJ: Scarecrow Press, 1976.

Dees, Pamela Youngdahl. *A Guide to Piano Music by Women Composers.* 2 vols. Westport, CT: Greenwood Press, 2002–04.

Edel, Theodore. *Piano Music for One Hand.* Bloomington: Indiana University Press, 1994.

Friskin, James, and Irwin Freundlich. *Music for the Piano: A Handbook of Concert and Teaching Material from 1580 to 1952.* New York: Rinehart, 1954. Reprint, New York: Dover, 1973.

Fuszek, Rita M. *Piano Music in Collections: An Index*. Detroit, MI: Information Coordinators, 1982.

Gillespie, John, and Anna Gillespie. *A Bibliography of Nineteenth-Century American Piano Music with Location Sources and Composer Biography-Index*. Westport, CT: Greenwood Press, 1984.

Heinrich, Adel. *Organ and Harpsichord Music by Women Composers: An Annotated Catalog*. New York: Greenwood Press, 1991.

Hinson, Maurice. *Guide to the Pianist's Repertoire*. 3rd ed. Bloomington: Indiana University Press, 2000.

_____. *Music for More than One Piano: An Annotated Guide*. Bloomington: Indiana University Press, 2001.

_____. *Music for Piano and Orchestra: An Annotated Guide*. Bloomington: Indiana University Press, 1981. Enl. ed., 1993.

_____. *The Pianist's Guide to Transcriptions, Arrangements, and Paraphrases*. Bloomington: Indiana University Press, 1990.

Hinson, Maurice, and Wesley Roberts. *The Piano in Chamber Ensemble: An Annotated Guide*. 2nd ed. Bloomington: Indiana University Press, 2006.

Horne, Aaron. *Keyboard Music of Black Composers: A Bibliography*. Westport, CT: Greenwood Press, 1992.

Jestremski, Margret, and Insa Bernds. *Europaische Klaviermusik um 1900: Catalogue raisonné*. Munich: G. Henle, 2001.

Lubin, Ernest. *The Piano Duet: A Guide for Pianists*. 1970. Reprint, New York: Da Capo Press, 1976.

McGraw, Cameron. *Piano Duet Repertoire: Music Originally Written for One Piano, Four Hands*. Bloomington: Indiana University Press, 1981. Rev. ed., 2001.

Magrath, D. Jane. *The Pianist's Guide to Standard Teaching and Performance Literature*. Van Nuys, CA: Alfred Publishing Co., 1995.

Maxwell, Grant L. *Music for Three or More Pianists: A Historical Survey*. Metuchen, NJ: Scarecrow Press, 1993.

Patterson, Donald L. *One Handed: A Guide to Piano Music for One Hand*. Westport, CT: Greenwood Press, 1999.

Phemister, William. *American Piano Concertos: A Bibliography*. Detroit, MI: Information Coordinators, published for the College Music Society, 1985.

Rezits, Joseph. *The Pianist's Resource Guide: Piano Music in Print and Literature on the Pianistic Art*. Park Ridge, IL: Pallma Music Co.; San Diego, CA: Distributed by Kjos West, 1978.

Sitsky, Larry. *Australian Piano Music of the Twentieth Century*. Westport, CT: Praeger Publishers, 2005.

Sloane, Sally Jo. *Music for Two or More Players at the Clavichord, Harpsichord, Organ: An Annotated Bibliography*. New York: Greenwood Press, 1991.

Walker-Hill, Helen. *Piano Music by Black Women Composers: A Catalog of Solo and Ensemble Works*. New York: Greenwood Press, 1992.

SAXOPHONE

Gee, Harry R. *Saxophone Soloists and Their Music, 1844–1985: An Annotated Bibliography*. Bloomington: Indiana University Press, 1986.

Londeix, Jean-Marie. *A Comprehensive Guide to the Saxophone Repertoire, 1844–2003*. Cherry Hill, NJ: Roncorp, 2003.

Wilkins, Wayne. *The Index of Saxophone Music*. Magnolia, AR: Music Register, 1979.

STRING MUSIC: GENERAL (SEE ALSO CHAMBER MUSIC.)

Farish, Margaret. *String Music in Print.* 2nd ed. Philadelphia: Musicdata, Inc., 1980. Supplement, 1984. Supplement, 1998, edited by Robert W. Cho, Donald T. Reese, and Frank James Staneck.

Horne, Aaron. *String Music of Black Composers: A Bibliography.* New York: Greenwood Press, 1991.

Iotti, Oscar R. *Violin and Violoncello in Duet Without Accompaniment.* Detroit, MI: Information Coordinators, 1972.

Klugherz, Laura. *A Bibliographical Guide to Spanish Music for the Violin and Viola, 1900–1997.* Westport, CT: Greenwood Press, 1998.

TROMBONE MUSIC (SEE ALSO BRASS MUSIC.)

Arling, Harry J. *Trombone Chamber Music: An Annotated Bibliography.* 2nd ed., rev. and enl. Nashville: Brass Press, 1983.

Everett, Thomas G. *Annotated Guide to Bass Trombone Literature.* 3rd ed., rev. and enl. Nashville: Brass Press, 1985.

Gregory, Robin. *The Trombone: The Instrument and Its Music.* New York: Praeger, 1973.

Kagarice, Vern. *Solos for the Student Trombonist: An Annotated Bibliography.* Nashville: Brass Press, 1979.

TRUMPET (SEE ALSO BRASS MUSIC.)

Hiller, Albert. *Music for Trumpets from Three Centuries (c.1600–after 1900): Compositions for 1–24 (natural) Trumpets With and Without Timpani.* Köln: W. G. Haas, 1993.

TUBA

Bird, Gary. *Program Notes for the Solo Tuba.* Bloomington: Indiana University Press, 1994.

Morris, R. Winston, and Daniel Perantoni, eds. *Guide to the Tuba Repertoire: The New Tuba Source Book.* Indiana Repertoire Guides. Bloomington: Indiana University Press, 2006.

TWENTIETH/TWENTY-FIRST CENTURY MUSIC

As noted in the introduction, there is no single comprehensive source that documents twentieth- and twenty-first-century music, but a number of the bibliographies on this list focus on music from this period, and especially on music from the latter part of the twentieth century (1950–). See, for example, titles by Ian Lawrence under CHAMBER MUSIC; by David DeVenney, Jonathan Green, and Karen Wachsmuth under CHORAL MUSIC; by Harry R. Gee under CLARINET MUSIC; by Isabelle Emerson under DANCE MUSIC; by Laurence Helleu and James F. Maroney under GUITAR MUSIC; by Peter Hardwick under ORGAN MUSIC; by Elizabeth Axford, Frances Bedford, and Larry Sitsky under PIANO/HARPSICHORD MUSIC; by Harry R. Gee, and Jean-Marie Londeix under SAXOPHONE MUSIC; by Laura Klugherz under STRING MUSIC; by Michael Alan Weaver under VIOLA MUSIC; by Donald Homuth under VIOLONCELLO MUSIC; and by JoAnn Padley Hunt, Kenneth S. Klaus, and Patricia Lust under VOCAL MUSIC.

International Directory of Contemporary Music 2000–2001: Composers; Instrumentation. 2 vols. New York: CMIIS, 2000.

Regrettably, the 2000–2001 edition was the last of this title to be published. It included 22,250 scores by 3,472 composers worldwide. The two-volume sets documented both published and unpublished works by contemporary composers deposited in the Bibliothèque International de Musique Contemporaine in Paris. The composer volume listed works by composer; the instrumentation volume listed works by instrumentation according to numbered categories (categories were delineated in the back of the book). When a composer had deposited more than five scores in the library, his/her listing also included brief biographical information. The scores documented in these volumes have been donated to the Paris Conservatoire (Médiathèque Hector Berlioz, Le Conservatoire de Paris). Also of note is a related gateway of contemporary music resources in France, a joint project of six institutions: the Conservatoire de Paris, the Centre de documentation de la musique contemporaine (CDMC: http://www.cdmc .asso.fr/), the Cité de la Musique, the Ensemble Intercontemporain, Ircam, and the Médiathèque musicale Mahler: http://www.musiquecontemporaine.fr

Musicians seeking recent music should also consult the resources provided by the Music Information Centers (see pp. 22–23), many of which have online databases.

VIOLA MUSIC (SEE ALSO STRING MUSIC.)

Jappe, Michael. *Viola Bibliographie: Das Repertoire für die historische Bratsche von 1649 bis nach 1800.* Winterthur: Amadeus, 1999.

Letz, Hans. *Music for the Violin and Viola.* New York: Rinehart, 1948. (Lists works for each instrument, not violin and viola duets.)

Weaver, Michael Alan. *Works for the Viola by Pulitzer Prize Winning Composers: An Annotated Bibliography.* Lewiston, NY: E. Mellen, 2006.

Wilkins, Wayne. *The Index of Viola Music.* Magnolia, AR: Music Register, 1976; supplements: 1976–77, 1978.

Williams, Michael D. *Music for Viola.* Detroit: Information Coordinators, 1979.

Zeyringer, Franz. *Literatur für Viola: Verzeichnis der Werke für Viola-Solo, Duos mit Viola, Trios mit Viola, Viola-Solo mit Begleitung, Blockflöte mit Viola, Gesang mit Viola und der Schul- und Studienwerke für Viola.* Neue, erw. Ausg. Hartberg: J. Schönwetter, 1985. Updated on Web site of William Primrose Viola Archive at Brigham Young University, Provo, Utah: http://music.lib.byu.edu/piva/ZeyringerNP2.htm.

VIOLA DA GAMBA MUSIC

Hoffmann, Bettina. *Catalogo della musica solistica e cameristica per viola da gamba.* Lucca, Italy: Antiqua, 2001.

VIOLIN MUSIC (SEE ALSO STRING MUSIC; VIOLA MUSIC.)

Johnson, Rose-Marie. *Violin Music by Women Composers: A Bio-Bibliographical Guide.* New York: Greenwood Press, 1989.

Wilkins, Wayne. *The Index of Violin Music.* Magnolia, AR: Music Register, [1973?].

———. *The Index of Violin Music: Winds, Including the Index of Baroque Trio Sonatas.* Magnolia, AR: Music Register, [1973].

———. Supplement to *The Index of Violin Music.* Magnolia, AR: Music Register, 1973–77.

Violoncello Music (See also String Music.)

Cowling, Elizabeth. *The Cello.* 2nd ed., rev. New York: Charles Scribner's Sons, 1983. (Includes extensive discussion of cello repertoire.)

Homuth, Donald. *Cello Music Since 1960: A Bibliography of Solo, Chamber, and Orchestral Works for the Solo Cellist.* Fallen Leaf Reference Books in Music 26. Berkeley, CA: Fallen Leaf Press, 1994.

Kenneson, Claude. *Bibliography of Cello Ensemble Music.* Detroit: Information Coordinators, 1974.

Lambooij, Henk, and Michael Feves. *A Cellist's Companion: A Comprehensive Catalogue of Cello Music.* Amsterdam: Stichting The Cellist's Companion, 1999, 2007. http://www.cellocompanion.com.

Markevitch, Dmitry. *The Solo Cello: A Bibliography of Unaccompanied Violoncello Literature.* Fallen Leaf Reference Books in Music 12. Berkeley, CA: Fallen Leaf Press, 1989.

Sensbach, Stephen. *French Cello Sonatas 1871–1939.* Dublin: Lilliput Press, 2001.

Wilkins, Wayne. *The Index of Cello Music, Including the Index of Baroque Trio Sonatas.* Magnolia, AR: Music Register, 1979.

Vocal Music: General (incl. Indexes) (See also Opera; Music in Print; Music Theater.)

Abromeit, Kathleen A. *An Index to African-American Spirituals for the Solo Voice.* Westport, CT: Greenwood Press, 1999.

Carman, Judith E., William K. Gaeddert, Rita M. Resch, and Gordon Myers. *Art-Song in the United States 1801–1987: An Annotated Bibliography.* 3rd ed. Lanham, MD: Scarecrow Press, 2001.

Boytim, Joan Frey. *Solo Vocal Repertoire for Young Singers: An Annotated Bibliography.* [n.p.]: National Association of Teachers of Singing, 1982.

Brusse, Corre Berry. *Vocal Chamber Duets: An Annotated Bibliography.* [n.p.]: National Association of Teachers of Singing, 1981.

Clark, Mark Ross. *Guide to the Aria Repertoire.* Bloomington: Indiana University Press, 2007.

Coffin, Berton. *The Singer's Repertoire.* 5 vols. New York: Scarecrow Press, 1960. Selected volumes published in new editions: Lanham, MD: Scarecrow Press, 2005.

De Charms, Desiree, and Paul F. Breed. *Songs in Collections, an Index.* Detroit: Information Service, 1966.

DeVenney, David P. *The Broadway Song Companion: An Annotated Guide to Musical Theatre Literature by Voice Type and Song Style.* Lanham, MD: Scarecrow Press, 1998.

Doscher, Barbara. *From Studio to Stage: Repertoire for the Voice.* Edited and annotated by John Nix. Lanham, MD: Scarecrow Press, 2002.

Dunlap, Kay, and Barbara Winchester. *Vocal Chamber Music: A Performer's Guide.* 2nd ed. New York: Routledge, 2008.

Emmons, Shirley, and Stanley Sonntag. *The Art of the Song Recital.* Prospect Heights, IL: Waveland Press, 2002.

Goleeke, Tom. *Literature for Voice: An Index of Songs in Collections and Source Book for Teachers of Singing.* Metuchen, NJ: Scarecrow Press, 2002.

Goodfellow, William D. *SongCite: An Index to Popular Songs.* New York: Garland Publishing, 1995.

———. *SongCite: An Index to Popular Songs, Supplement I.* New York: Garland Publishing, 1999.

Green, Jeff. *The Green Book of Songs by Subject: The Thematic Guide to Popular Music.* 5th ed. Nashville: Professional Desk References, 2002.

Havlice, Patricia Pate. *Popular Song Index.* Metuchen, NJ: Scarecrow Press, 1975. First supp., 1978; second supp., 1984; fourth supp., 1988–2002, 2005.

Hopkin, J. Arden. *Songs for Young Singers: An Annotated List for Developing Voices.* Lanham, MD: Scarecrow Press, 2002.

Hovland, Michael. *Musical Settings of American Poetry: A Bibliography.* Westport, CT: Greenwood Press, 1986.

Hunt, JoAnn Padley. "Analyses of Music for Solo Voice and Percussion, 1950–1990: An Annotated Catalogue of Representative Repertoire." Ed. D., Columbia University, 1992.

Kagen, Sergius. *Music for the Voice, A Descriptive List of Concert and Teaching Material.* Rev. ed. Bloomington: Indiana University Press, 1968.

Kimball, Carol. *Song: A Guide to Art Song Style and Literature.* 2nd ed. Milwaukee: Hal Leonard, 2005.

Kivivirta, Nina. *Suomalaisen yksinlauluohjelmiston luettelo = Catalog of Finnish Art Songs.* Helsinki: Suomalaisen laulumusiikin akatemia, 2003.

Klaus, Kenneth S. *Chamber Music for Solo Voice and Instruments 1960–1989: An Annotated Guide.* Berkeley, CA: Fallen Leaf Press, 1994.

Lax, Roger, and Frederick Smith. *The Great Song Thesaurus.* 2nd ed. New York: Oxford University Press, 1989.

Lewine, Richard, and Alfred Simon. *Songs of the Theater.* New York: H. W. Wilson, 1984.

Luchinsky, Ellen. *The Song Index of the Enoch Pratt Free Library.* 2 vols. New York: Garland Publishing, 1998.

Lust, Patricia. *American Vocal Chamber Music, 1945–1980: An Annotated Bibliography.* Westport, CT: Greenwood Press, 1985.

Manning, Jane. *New Vocal Repertory.* 2 vols. Oxford: Clarendon Press; Oxford and New York: Oxford University Press, 1994, 1998.

Maroney, James F. *Music for the Voice and Classical Guitar, 1945–1996: An Annotated Catalog.* Jefferson, NC: McFarland, 1997.

Newman, Marilyn Stephanie Mercedes. *The Comprehensive Catalogue of Duet Literature for Female Voices: Vocal Chamber Duets with Keyboard Accompaniment Composed Between 1820–1995.* Lanham, MD: Scarecrow Press, 1999.

Ord, Alan J. *Songs for Bass Voice: An Annotated Guide to Works for Bass Voice.* Metuchen, NJ: Scarecrow Press, 1994.

_____. *Songs for Beginning Bass Voice.* Lanham, MD: Scarecrow Press, 2002.

Parker, Bernard S. *World War I Sheet Music: 9,670 Patriotic Songs Published in the United States, 1914–1920, With More Than 600 Covers Illustrated.* 2 vols. Jefferson, NC: McFarland, 2007.

Pollock, Bruce. *The Rock Song Index: The 7500 Most Important Songs of the Rock and Roll Era, 1944–2000.* 2nd ed. New York: Routledge, 2005.

Sears, Minnie E. *Song Index: An Index to More Than 12,000 Songs in 177 Song Collections.* New York: H. W. Wilson, 1926.

_____. *Supplement: An Index to More Than 7,000 Songs in 104 Collections.* New York: H. W. Wilson, 1934.

Shapiro, Nat, and Bruce Pollock, eds. *Popular Music, 1920–1979: A Revised Cumulation.* 3 vols. Detroit, MI: Gale Research Co., 1985.

Stecheson, Anthony, and Anne Stecheson. *The Stecheson Classified Song Directory.* Hollywood, CA: Music Industries Press, 1961. Supplement, 1978.

Swanekamp, Joan. *English Ayres: A Selectively Annotated Bibliography and Discography.* Westport, CT: Greenwood Press, 1984.

Villamil, Victoria. *A Singer's Guide to the American Art Song 1870–1980.* Metuchen, NJ: Scarecrow Press, 1993.

DIGITAL SHEET MUSIC COLLECTIONS: A SELECTED LIST (SEE ALSO LISTS OF LIBRARY DIGITAL COLLECTIONS IN CHAPTER 1.)

What Is Sheet Music?

To some, the term *sheet music* refers to any music printed on paper. Web sites and vendors such as SheetMusicPlus.com (www.sheetmusicplus .com) and Virtual Sheet Music (www.virtualsheetmusic.com) sell scores of both classical and popular music. To music librarians, the term *sheet music* refers more specifically to the physical format of the score, specifically, single or double folios (a folio being one sheet folded in half or quarters), usually having eight to ten pages.[4] Since many popular songs were published in this format, the term has also been closely associated with popular music. These sheet music editions of popular songs often had pictorial title pages, which themselves offer many opportunities for study and analysis (Figure 9–1).

Although it may be hard for today's iPod users to imagine, throughout the eighteenth, nineteenth, and most of the twentieth century, individuals purchased and collected music in order to sing and play their favorite songs. Prior to the development of recording in 1877 (see Chapter 7), music could be only disseminated on paper. The level of musical literacy was much higher: homes typically had pianos, and children were encouraged to learn to read scores. The music publishing industry boomed as popular songs, along with instrumental arrangements of arias from favorite operas or symphonies, were published for purchase by music lovers.

Libraries amassed significant collections of sheet music of popular songs, both through donation and purchase. Many of these collections have recently been digitized; selections are listed here.

Brown University Library Digital Collection. *African-American Sheet Music, 1850–1920: From the Collections of Brown University:* http://dl.lib.brown.edu/sheetmusic/afam/index.html; also available through the Library of Congress *American Memory* project: http://memory.loc.gov/ammem/collections/sheetmusic/brown/.

Duke University. Rare Book, Manuscript, and Special Collections Library. *Historic American Sheet Music, 1850–1920:* http://scriptorium.lib.duke.edu/sheetmusic/; also available through the Library of Congress *American Memory* project: http://memory.loc.gov/ammem/award97/ncdhtml/hasmhome.html.

Indiana University. Lilly Library. *Sheet Music Collections:* http://www.indiana.edu/~liblilly/collections-sheetmusic.shtml.

Johns Hopkins University. Milton S. Eisenhower Library. Special Collections. *The Lester S. Levy Collection of Sheet Music:* http://levysheetmusic.mse.jhu.edu/.

FIGURE 9–1   "Hi! Yi! Yer off now!" by Ittalie N. Guitarr (Baltimore, MD: Otto Sutro & Co., c1895). From Brown University African American Sheet Music, 1850–1920.

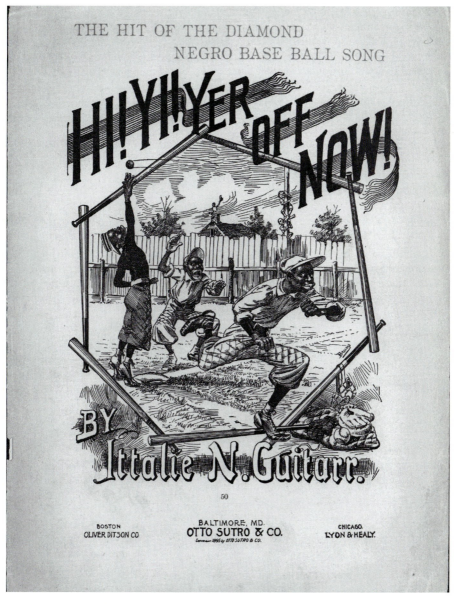

Source: Brown University Library.

Library of Congress. Rare Book and Special Collections Division. *"We'll Sing to Abe Our Song!": Sheet Music about Lincoln, Emancipation, and the Civil War from the Alfred Whital Stern Collection of Lincolniana:* http://memory.loc.gov/ammem/scsmhtml/scsmhome.html.

Library of Congress. *America Singing: 19th Century Song Sheets:* http://memory.loc.gov/ammem/amsshtml/amsshome.html.

Library of Congress. Music Division. *Music for the Nation: American Sheet Music: 1820–1860; 1870–1885:* http://memory.loc.gov/ammem/mussmhtml/mussmhome.html.

National Library of Australia. *Digitised Sheet Music:* http://www.nla.gov.au/digicoll/music.html.

UCLA Music Library. Digital Archive. *Popular American Music: American Popular Songs in the Form in Which They Were Originally Published:* http://digital.library.ucla.edu/apam/.

See also Lois Schultz, "Sheet Music Collections" *Duke University Music Library and Music Media Center* Web site for an extensive listing of sheet music collections: http://library.duke.edu/music/sheetmusic/collections.html.

VOCAL MUSIC: SACRED

Brusse, Corre Berry. *Sacred Vocal Duets: An Annotated Bibliography.* n.p.: National Association of Teachers of Singing, 1987.

Dox, Thurston. *American Oratorios and Cantatas: A Catalog of Works Written in the United States from Colonial Times to 1985.* 2 vols. Metuchen, NJ: Scarecrow Press, 1986.

Espina, Noni. *Vocal Solos for Christian Churches.* 3rd ed. Metuchen, NJ: Scarecrow Press, 1984.

Laster, James, and Diana Reed Strommen. *Catalogue of Vocal Solos and Duets Arranged in Biblical Order.* 2nd ed. Lanham, MD: Scarecrow Press, 2003.

WEDDING MUSIC

Goodfellow, William D. *Wedding Music: An Index to Collections.* Metuchen, NJ: Scarecrow Press, 1992.

WIND MUSIC

Gillaspie, Jon A., Marshall Stoneham, and David Lindsey Clark. *The Wind Ensemble Catalog.* Westport, CT: Greenwood Press, 1998.

———. *The Wind Ensemble Sourcebook and Biographical Guide.* Westport, CT: Greenwood Press, 1997.

Gillespie, James E. *The Reed Trio: An Annotated Bibliography of Original Published Works.* Detroit, MI: Information Coordinators, 1971.

Helm, Sanford M. *Catalog of Chamber Music for Wind Instruments.* Rev. ed. New York: Da Capo Press, 1969.

Horne, Aaron. *Woodwind Music of Black Composers.* New York: Greenwood Press, 1990.

Hošek, Miroslav. *Das Bläserquintett = The Woodwind Quintet.* Grünwald: B. Brüchle, 1979.

Houser, Roy. *Catalogue of Chamber Music for Woodwind Instruments.* New York: Da Capo Press, 1973.

Peters, Harry B. *The Literature of the Woodwind Quintet.* Metuchen, NJ: Scarecrow Press, 1971.

Secrist-Schmedes, Barbera. *Wind Chamber Music: Winds With Piano and Woodwind Quintets: An Annotated Guide.* Lanham, MD: Scarecrow Press, 1996.
_____. *Wind Chamber Music: For Two to Sixteen Winds: An Annotated Guide.* Lanham, MD: Scarecrow Press, 2002.
Voxman, Himie, and Lyle Merriman. *Woodwind Music Guide: Ensemble Music in Print.* Evanston, IL: The Instrumentalist Co., 1982.
(See also Music-in-Print series, Chamber Music, String Music, Wind Music.)

WOMEN COMPOSERS

Mayer, Clara, ed. *KOM: Komponistinnen im Musikverlag.* Kassel: Furore, 1996.
See also titles by Heidi Boenke under FLUTE; by Pamela Dees Younghal, Adele Heinrich, and Helen Walker-Hill under PIANO MUSIC; and by Rose-Marie Johnson under VIOLIN MUSIC. Aaron Cohen's 2-volume *International Encyclopedia of Women Composers* (New York: Books & Music USA, 1987) includes an appendix listing works by "women composers by instrument and music form" (pp. 872–988). *Basic Music Library,* 3rd ed., includes an appendix with references to works by women composers documented in the book. Supplement, 1995.

MUSICAL SETTINGS OF POETS AND WRITERS

GENERAL

Bradley, Carol. *Index to Poetry in Music: A Guide to the Poetry Set as Solo Songs by 125 Major Composers.* New York: Routledge, 2003.
Hovland, Michael. *Musical Settings of American Poetry: A Bibliography.* Music Reference Collection 8. Westport, CT: Greenwood Press, 1986.
Snyder, Lawrence D. *German Poetry in Song: An Index of Lieder.* Fallen Leaf Reference Books in Music 30. Berkeley, CA: Fallen Leaf Press, 1995. Supplement, 1995.

SPECIFIC WRITERS

(Note: To search for musical settings of particular writers, use subject heading with writer's name followed by subdivision—Musical Settings (Example: Joyce, James—Musical Settings)

BLAKE, WILLIAM

Fitch, Donald. *Blake Set to Music: A Bibliography of Musical Settings of the Poems and Prose of William Blake.* University of California Publications. Catalogs and Bibliographies 5. Berkeley: University of California Press, 1989.

BROWNING, ROBERT

Keith, Sally, ed. *Browning Music: A Descriptive Catalog of the Music Related to Robert Browning and Elizabeth Barrett Browning in the Armstrong Browning Library: 1972.* Waco, TX: Armstrong Browning Library, 1973.

DICKINSON, EMILY

Lowenberg, Carlton. *Musicians Wrestle Everywhere: Emily Dickinson and Music.* Fallen Leaf Reference Books in Music 19. Berkeley, CA: Fallen Leaf Press, 1992.

HEINE, HEINRICH

Metzner, Günther. *Heine in der Musik: Bibliographie der Heine-Vertonungen.* 12 vols. Tutzing: Hans Schneider, 1989–94.

JOYCE, JAMES

Bauerle, Ruth, ed. *The James Joyce Songbook.* Garland Reference Library of the Humanities 316. New York: Garland Publishing, 1982.

Bowen, Zach. *Bloom's Old Sweet Song: Essays on Joyce and Music.* Florida James Joyce Series. Gainsville: University Press of Florida, 1995.

_____. *Musical Illusions in the Works of James Joyce: Early Poetry through Ulysses.* Albany: State University of New York Press, 1974.

Russel, Myra. "Myra Russel Collection of Musical Settings of James Joyce, 1909–1993." "The Myra Russel Collection of Musical Settings of James Joyce consists of music scores for songs set to the words of the writer by a variety of contemporary composers, which were amassed by Myra Teicher Russel, a professor and authority on the works of James Joyce." New York Public Library. Music Division: http://www.nypl.org/research/manuscripts/music/musrusse.xml.

SHAKESPEARE, WILLIAM

Dean, Winton, Dorothy Moore, and Phyllis Hartnoll. "Catalog of Musical Works Based on the Plays and Poetry of Shakespeare." In *Shakespeare in Music: Essays by John Stevens, Charles Cudworth, Winton Dean, Roger Fiske, with A Catalogue of Musical Works,* edited by Phyllis Hartnoll, 243–321. London: Macmillan; New York: St. Martin's Press, 1966.

Gooch, Bryan N.S., and David Thatcher. *A Shakespeare Music Catalog.* 5 vols. Oxford: Clarendon Press, 1991.

Hotaling, Edward R. *Shakespeare and the Musical Stage: A Guide to Sources, Studies, and First Performances.* Boston: G. K. Hall, 1990.

SHELLEY, PERCY BYSSHE

Pollin, Burton R. *Music for Shelley's Poetry: An Annotated Bibliography of Musical Settings of Shelley's Poetry.* New York: Da Capo Press, 1974.

REGIONAL BIBLIOGRAPHIES AND OTHER SPECIALIZED TOOLS (See also Library Catalogs, Chapter 1.)

American Music Center. Catalog of the American Music Center Library. 4 vols. New York: American Music Center, 1975–82.

Vol. 1: Finell, Judith Greenberg, ed. *Catalog of Choral and Vocal Works.* 1975.

Vol. 2. Famera, Karen, ed. *Chamber Music.* 1978.

Vol. 3. _____, ed. *Music for Orchestra, Band, and Large Ensemble.* 1982.

Vol. 4. Richmond, Eero, ed. *Opera and Music Theatre Works.* 1983.

(The American Music Center is the United States Music Information Center. Its library holdings were transferred to the New York Public Library for the Performing Arts in 2001.)

Bloch, Henry. *Directory of Conductors' Archives in American Institutions.* Lanham, MD: Scarecrow Press, 2006.

Bradley, Carol. *Music Collections in American Libraries: A Chronology.* Detroit Studies in Music Bibliography 46. Detroit, MI: Information Coordinators, 1981.

Boston Area Music Libraries. *The Boston Composers Project: A Bibliography of Contemporary Music.* Cambridge, MA: MIT Press, 1983.

British Broadcasting Corporation. Central Music Library. *BBC Music Library Catalogues.* 13 vols. London: British Broadcasting Corporation, 1965–82.

Charteris, Richard. *An Annotated Catalogue of the Music Manuscripts in the Folger Shakespeare Library, Washington, D.C.* Annotated Reference Tools in Music 6. Hillsdale, NY: Pendragon Press, 2005.

Krummel, Donald William, et al. *Resources of American Music History: A Directory of Source Materials from Colonial Times to World War II.* Urbana: University of Illinois Press, 1981.

Matsushita, Hitoshi. *A Checklist of Published Instrumental Music by Japanese Composers.* Tokyo: Academia Music, 1989.

Schneider, Tina M. *Hymnal Collections of North America.* Studies in Liturgical Musicology 10. Lanham, MD: Scarecrow Press, 2003.

SIBMAS International Directory of Performing Arts Collections. Haslemere: Emmett, 1996. Available online: http://www.sibmas.org/idpac/index.html.

Tischler, Alice. *A Descriptive Bibliography of Art Music by Israeli Composers.* Detroit Studies in Music Bibliography 62. Warren, MI: Harmonie Park Press, 1988.

———. *Fifteen Black American Composers: A Bibliography of Their Works.* Detroit Studies in Music Bibliography 45. Detroit, MI: Information Coordinators, 1981.

RESOURCES FOR LOCATING MUSIC PUBLISHERS

International ISMN Agency. *Music Publishers' International ISMN Directory.* 2nd ed. München: K. G. Saur, 1998.

Music Publishers Association: www.mpa.org.

NOTES

1. See also H. Stephen Wright's review of film music Web sites, *Notes* 59, no. 1 (Sep. 2002): 128–30, and Ben Winters, "Catching Dreams: Editing Film Scores for Publication." *Journal of the Royal Music Association* 132, no. 1 (2007): 115–40.

2. "About the Film Music Society: History": http://www.filmmusicsociety.org/about/about.html.

3. For published catalog of this exhibit, see J. Rigbie Turner, *Auld Acquaintances: Famous Music from the James Fuld Collection.* Preface by Charles E. Pierce Jr.,

foreword by James Fuld (New York: The Pierpont Morgan Library, 1995).

4. Music librarians and specialists: For further information see Lois Schultz and Sarah Shaw, eds. *Cataloging Sheet Music: Guidelines for Use with AACR2 and the MARC Format.* Music Library Association Technical Reports 28 (Lanham, MD: Scarecrow Press, 2003); see also Schultz, "About Sheet Music" *Historic American Sheet Music, 1850–1920*: http://scriptorium.lib.duke.edu/sheetmusic/about.html.

CHAPTER

10

Composer
Thematic Catalogs

INTRODUCTION

Bibliographic Source

Brook, Barry S., and Richard J. Vinao. *Thematic Catalogues in Music: An Annotated Bibliography*. 2nd ed. RILM Retrospective Series 4. Stuyvesant, NY: Pendragon Press, 1997.

Just as James Coover was the master bibliographer/historian of music dictionaries and encyclopedias, the late Barry S. Brook (1918–97) was the master researcher for music thematic catalogs. This connection in no way diminishes his central role in other path-breaking twentieth-century musicological research, notably the development of cooperative international projects such as RILM and RIdIM.[1] Brook's publication *Thematic Catalogues in Music: An Annotated Bibliography* (first published in 1972; revised second edition published with Richard Vinao in 1997) is our most extensive resource on thematic catalogs of all types. Brook authored the articles on thematic catalogs in both the 1980 and 2001 editions of *New Grove*, and he prepared numerous other resources relating to thematic catalogs, such as his reference volume for *The Symphony 1720–1840*, a historical series featuring works by primarily eighteenth-and early-nineteenth-century composers.[2] His development of the "plaine and easie code for musik,"[3] which uses computer technology to encode musical incipits using normal type for relatively smooth output of musical notation, has led to the development of valuable resources such as the inclusion of music incipits in the database of RISM A/II: *Music Manuscripts Since 1600* (see pp. 176–177).

Themes vs. Incipits

As Brook points out in his *New Grove* articles and in the introduction to his book (titled "An Essay on the Definitions, History, Functions, Historiography, and Future of the Thematic Catalogue"), most composer thematic catalogs are really "incipit" catalogs, rather than theme catalogs, the former being the opening notes of a work, while the latter is the true theme. Among the few examples of true theme catalogs are Barlow and Morgenstern's *A Dictionary of Musical Themes* (1948) and

Dictionary of Vocal Themes (1950).[4] (Both of these sources are listed in Chapter 3: Dictionaries and Encyclopedias.)

Brook explains the development and use of thematic catalogs through examination of their history and function in nine broad categories: "Mneumonic Aid; Table of Contents; Guide to a Composer's Output; Inventory of Library Holdings; Copying Firm Advertisement; Publishing Firm Advertisement; Legal Documents; Index of Themes; and Musicological Documentation."[5] It should be noted that Brook examines thematic catalogs quite broadly, going way beyond our familiar Köchel, Schmieder, Hoboken, and Deutsch catalogs. His essay and accompanying bibliography cover various types of non-composer thematic catalogs (both published and unpublished), such as multicomposer catalogs produced by publishers or copying houses to advertise their holdings. Although Brook's essay is essential reading for all students, this chapter refers specifically to four of Brook's categories that are most relevant to an understanding of the present state of composer thematic catalogs: Guide to a Composer's Own Output, Publishing Firm Advertisement, Legal Documents, and Musicological Documentation.

Guide to a Composer's Own Output refers to any method used by composers to document their compositions, usually for personal or business reasons. Perhaps the most famous example of such a catalog is Mozart's *Verzeichnüss aller meiner Werke vom Monath Febraio 1784 bis [15 Nov1791].*[6] Another notable example is Haydn's '*Entwurf Katalog', c1765–c1805* (or sketch catalog, recording his works from 1765 to 1805),[7] which is used as an "authentication tool" to document what the composer actually wrote.

Legal Documents, including musical incipits, provide similar documentation for composers or their heirs. Perhaps the most famous example in this category is C. P. E. Bach's *Verzeichniss des musicalischen Nachlasses des vestorbenen Capellmeisters C.P.E. Bach* (1790), or estate catalog.[8]

Publishing Firm Advertisement refers to catalogs produced by publishers to document and advertise the works of one or several composers through presentation of musical incipits. Such catalogs of the works of Brahms (by Simrock), Mendelssohn (by Breitkopf and Härtel), Liszt (by Breitkopf and Härtel), and Robert Schumann (by J. Schuberth) were the only thematic catalogs to exist before publication of true thematic catalogs with rich musicological documentation, as described later.

Musicological Documentation refers to the scholarly catalogs we rely upon for identification of primary source materials for musical works. Interest in this type of rigorous scholarly tool coincided with the development of musicology as a discipline in the middle of the nineteenth century. As presented by Brook (relying upon earlier work by Alexander Hyatt King in his article "The Past, Present, and Future of the Thematic Catalogue," *Monthly Musical Record,* lxxxiv (1954): 10–13, 39–46), essential features for such catalogs are:[9]

1. "title, opus or other identification numbers, references to standard and complete editions, author or other source of text, date and place of composition;

2. incipits of each movement, noting the number of bars in each movement where applicable and indicating variants among sources;
3. full description, location, and shelf-mark of autographs;
4. description of significant copies, their shelf-marks, dates, and important differences or special markings;
5. bibliographical description of first editions, including date, imprint, price and plate number, and of all subsequent editions or arrangements published in the composer's lifetime or reflecting changes made or sanctioned by him;
6. references to contemporary diaries, memoirs and newspapers, thematic and non-thematic catalogues; and
7. references to significant citations in scholarly studies."

The first catalog to include these musicological features was Ludwig Ritter von Köchel's *Chronologisch-thematisches Verzeichnis sämtlicher Tonwerke Wolfgang Amadé Mozarts: nebst Angabe der verloren gegangenen, angefangenen, übertragenen, zweifelhaften und unterschobenen Kompositionen desselben* (Leipzig: Breitkopf and Härtel, 1862). Köchel's work served as the model for the "alphabet soup" of thematic catalog compilers who, following his lead, lent their initials to the works of major composers: Hoboken for Haydn (1957), Schmieder for Bach (1950), and Deutsch for Schubert (1951, rev. 1978). While the compilers of thematic catalogs for composers who systematically used opus numbers, such as Beethoven (Kinsky), Brahms (McCorkle), and Schumann (McCorkle) will not have their initials indelibly attached to the composers' names, their achievements are no less significant for scholars and performers. For composers who used opus numbers, those of their works that lacked opus numbers are inevitably subject to identification by Mr./Ms. WoO, or Werke ohne Opuszahl.

Thematic catalogs are usually arranged in either a chronological or classified manner. The latter, found for example in the Schmieder catalog of J. S. Bach, is often used when it is difficult or impossible to date a composer's works accurately and thus develop a meaningful chronology. In a chronological arrangement, such as in the Köchel catalog of Mozart's works, a higher number generally means that the work was written later in the composer's life. Chronological arrangements become confusing, however, when new sources are discovered and must be inserted in between already numbered sources, as is evident in the numerous revisions to Köchel's catalog. Overall, however, the arrangement of a thematic catalog provides a key to the composer's musical output and the approaches used by scholars to organize this output.

Many recently published or updated thematic catalogs take advantage of online dissemination, which enables more elegant updating of information as new sources are discovered.

The selected list of composer thematic catalogs presented in this section is arranged as follows: thematic catalogs are listed in order of publication, with the most recently published catalog listed first, immediately below the composer's name. Brief annotations indicating basic principles of arrangement or other pertinent information are provided for selected entries. The catalog listing is followed by references to the critical/complete editions of the composer's works, both new and old, with references to arrangement/abbreviations in the *Grove Music Online* work lists. Finally, entries include selected references to related sources of information that deal primarily with compositional or editorial issues. Users should also consult the composer resource manuals and other bibliographic tools listed in Chapter 4. Excluded from the lists of selected references are citations for collected editions of the composer's correspondence, which may be found in library catalogs and *Grove Music Online*.

It is hoped that this information will be helpful to students and performers who are intimidated by the German-language text of most of the major composer thematic catalogs; a select glossary of German terms is found on pp. 325–329.

COMPOSER THEMATIC CATALOGS

ALBENIZ, ISAAC

Torres, Jacinto. *Catálogo Sistemático Descriptivo de las Obras Musicales de Isaac Albéniz.* Madrid: Instituto de Bibliografía Musical, 2001.

Baytelman, Pola. *Isaac Albeniz: Chronological List and Thematic Catalog of His Piano Works.* Warren, MI: Harmonie Park Press, 1993.

BACH, CARL PHILIPP EMANUEL

Helm, E. Eugene. *Thematic Catalogue of the Works of Carl Philipp Emanuel Bach.* New Haven, CT: Yale University Press, 1989. Abbreviated in *Grove Music Online* as [H].

In his "new" thematic catalog of C. P. Bach's works, with text entirely in English, Eugene Helm lists "all of Emanuel Bach's known works chronologically within categories, with incipits of all movements, and with information about manuscripts, early prints, authenticity, relations among works, and whatever else scholars and prospective editors might find useful."[10]

See the review of Helm's catalog by Leta F. Miller in *Notes* 47, no. 3 (March 1991): 743–47. Miller also provides a summary of the previous catalogs of C. P. E. Bach's works. Of particular importance to later catalogers of C. P. E. Bach's works was his estate catalog, or *Nachlass Verzeichnis.* This source is referenced in *Grove Music Online* works list as NV.

Wotquenne, Alfred. *Thematisches Verzeichnis der Werke von Carl Philipp Emanuel Bach.* 1905. Reprint, Weisbaden: Breitkopf & Härtel, 1964. Abbreviated in *Grove Music Online* as [W]

COMPLETE WORKS EDITIONS

Corneilson, Paul, et al. *Carl Philipp Emanuel Bach: The Complete Works.* Los Altos, CA: Packard Humanities Institute, 2001–. www.cpebach.org.

Wade, Rachel, and E. Eugene Helm. *Carl Philipp Emanuel Bach Edition.* Oxford: Oxford University Press, 1989–95.

Oxford University Press published a new edition of C. P. E. Bach's works under the general editorship of Rachel Wade and Eugene Helm. Four volumes of this edition were published between 1989 and 1995, when it ceased publication. The current edition of C. P. E. Bach's works is the Packard Humanities Institute's *Carl Philipp Emanuel Bach: The Collected Works* (2001–). (It should be noted that the PHI edition refers to works by Wq [Wotquenne] numbers, rather than H [Helm] numbers; the latter is used when works are not in Wotquenne.[11]) The Packard Institute's collaborators are the Bach-Archiv in Leipzig, Harvard University, and the Saxon Academy of Sciences; the editorial board is chaired by Christopher Hogwood. A unique component of this edition is its incorporation of online dissemination, with delivery of text and music in electronic formats, and the possibility for online updates and advanced searching. See Paul Corneilson, "The C. P. E. Bach Edition and the Future of Scholarly Editions," *Music Reference Services Quarterly* 8, no. 1 (2001), 27–36.

The *Grove Music Online* works list includes references to works by Helm [H] number and Wotequenne [W] catalog numbers.

Also of note is a facsimile edition of C. P. E. Bach's keyboard works:

Bach, Carl Philipp Emanuel. *The Collected Works for Solo Keyboard: In Six Volumes.* Edited with introductions by Darrell Berg. New York: Garland Publishing, 1985. This edition includes reproductions of manuscripts and early printed editions, with introduction and critical notes by Berg. It is referenced throughout the keyboard section of Helm's catalog.

Research on Johann Sebastian Bach, C. P. E. Bach, and other eighteenth- and ninteenth-century composers has been greatly aided by a major discovery in Kiev of sources from the Berlin Sing-Akademie. In a significant post–World War II diplomatic move, these materials were returned in 1991 to the Staatsbibliothek zu Berlin, their original home. See

Kulukundis, Elias N. "C. P. E. Bach in the Library of the Singakademie zu Berlin." In *C. P. E. Bach Studies,* edited by Stephen L. Clark, 159–76. Oxford: Clarendon Press, 1988. Includes a list of the C. P. E. Bach sources found in the Sing-Akademie collection.

Wolff, Christoph. "Recovered in Kiev: Bach et al. A Preliminary Report on the Berlin Sing-Akademie." *Notes* 58, no. 2 (Dec. 2001): 259–71.

Catalog of Bach sources in this collection

Ensslin, Wolfram, ed. *Die Bach-Quellen der Sing-Akademie zu Berlin.* 2 vols. Leipziger Beiträge zur Bach-Forschung, Bd. 8, 1–2. Hildesheim: Olms, 2006.

A microfiche set of the manuscripts in the Sing-Akademie has been published by K. G. Saur: *Musikhandschriften aus der Staatsbibliothek zu Berlin—Preussicher Kulturbesitz:* Pt. 6: *Die Sammlung der Sing-Akademie zu Berlin* (2004–).[12]

BACH, JOHANN CHRISTIAN

Warburton, Ernest, ed. *Johann Christian Bach: Thematic Catalogue.* 3 vols. Supplement to *The Collected Works of Johann Christian Bach.* Edited by Ernest Warburton. New York: Routledge, 1999.

Vol. 1: *Thematic Catalogue.* Classified arrangement.

Entries include musical incipits, location of manuscript sources, information on first and early editions, as well as modern editions and arrangements. Library catalogs generally use W. numbers.

Vol. 2: *Sources and Documents.*
Detailed description of manuscript sources and early editions, arranged according to RISM siglia. Also includes sections on librettos (manuscript and printed), letters, and other documents. Concordances to Terry catalog as well as to work lists in resources by Stephen Roe and Fritz Tutenberg:

Roe, Stephen. *The Keyboard Music of J. C. Bach: Source Problems and Stylistic Development in the Solo and Ensemble Works.* Outstanding Dissertations in Music from British Universities. New York: Garland Publishing, 1989.

Tutenberg, Fritz. *Die Sinfonik Johann Christian Bachs: ein Beitrag zue Entwicklungsgeschichte der Sinfonie von 1750–80.* Wolfenbüttel-Berlin: Kallmeyer, 1928.

Vol. 3: *Music Supplement* (supplemental volume to complete works edition).

Terry, Charles Sanford. *Johann Christian Bach.* 2nd ed. 1967. Reprint, Westport, CT: Greenwood Press, 1980. (Thematic Catalogue of Vocal and Instrumental Works begins on p. 193.)

COMPLETE WORKS EDITION

Warbuton, Ernest, ed. *The Collected Works of Johann Christian Bach.* 43 vols. New York: Garland Publishing 1984–93. Abbreviated in *Grove Music Online* as [CW].

BACH, JOHANN SEBASTIAN

Schulze, Hans-Joachim, and Christoph Wolff. *Bach Compendium: Analytisch-bibliographisches Repertorium der Werke Johann Sebastian Bach.* 4 vols. Frankfurt: C. F. Peters, 1985–89.

A new thematic catalog of Bach's works? Will BC numbers replace BWV numbers, ensuring library workers both steady employment and the need for sedatives? The compilers of the *Bach Compendium,* foremost Bach scholars, say their aim is not to replace BWV numbers, but rather to create a new catalog that provides more detailed bibliographical and analytical information on Bach's oeuvre.[13] The project began in the late 1970s and was projected for publication in 1985, the tercentenary of Bach's birth. Four volumes of Part I were published between 1985 and 1989. According to editor Christoph Wolff, in 2007 the project work was transferred to the Bach-Archiv Leipzig, which will assume responsibility for BWV and use information from the *Compendium* as part of a supplemental database. The bibliographic references in BC (under "Literatur") focus on literature published since 1950.

BC divides Bach's output into the following workgroups:

A Cantatas for the Sundays and feasts days of the liturgical year
B Sacred works for special occasions
C Motets
D Passions and oratorios
E Latin church music
F Chorals and sacred songs
G Secular cantatas for court, nobility, and bourgeoisie
H Vocal chamber music

I   Free organ works
K   Chorale-based organ works
L   Keyboard music
M   Chamber music for one instrument
N   Chamber music for duo or trio ensembles
O   Chamber music for larger ensembles
P   Canons
R   Sketches and drafts
S   Original collections
T   Dubious vocal works
U   Dubious instrumental works
V   Spurious vocal works
W   Spurious instrumental works
X   Copies (and essentially straightforward arrangements) of vocal works
     by other composers
Y   Copies (and essentially straightforward arrangements) of instrumental
     works by other composers
Z   Contemporary collections[14]

In addition to its inclusion of incipits, BC provides musical examples "representing each movement's structural demarcations and its ending."[15] This is done in keeping with the project's goal "to provide reliable information, both bibliographical and analytical, on Bach's entire output."[16]

Volume I of BC has a concordance of BC numbers and BWV numbers. Example: BWV 4 *(Christ lag in Todes Banden)* = BC54a

Other features of BC not found in Schmieder are its detailed inclusion of information on copyists (scribes); the editors indicate that "a corresponding catalog of scribes is currently in progress."[17]

Schmieder, Wolfgang. *Thematisch-Systematisches Verzeichnis der Musikalischen Werke von Johann Sebastian Bach: Bach-Werke-Verzeichnis.* 2nd rev. and enl. ed. Weisbaden: Breitkopf & Härtel, 1990.

Wolfgang Schmieder's catalog, first published in 1950 (the same year that the *Neue Bach Ausgabe* began) was conceived as a guide to the old Bach Gesellschaft (nineteenth-century complete works edition). It is arranged in a classified manner, by genre:

Kantaten
Motetten
Messen, Magnificat
Passionen und Oratorien
Vierstimmige Chorale
Lieder, Arien und Quodlibet
Werke für Orgel
Werke für Klavier
Werke für Lauteninstrumente
Kammermusik

Konzerte
Overtüren, Sinfonien
Kanons
Musikalisches Opfer, Kunst der Fuge

Schmieder (S.) numbers and BWV (Bach Werke Verzeichnis) numbers are the same. Some older library catalogs still have S. numbers, but most now use BWV numbers. The second edition of Schmieder corrected errors in the 1950 edition, relocated some works in the catalog, and added works numbered BWV 1081–1120. (These works on listed on pages 803–804 of the catalog, with references to their inserted placement within the main classified listings.)

The introduction to the second edition of Schmieder is available in an English translation within the volume. The second edition of Schmieder also uses a numerical system to identify manuscript sources, providing more detailed perspective on dates of composition and hierarchy of sources than was available in the first edition:

1. Handschriften überwiegend von der Hand J. S. Bachs (Autographe)
2. Handschriften bzw. Abschriften ays der 1. Hälfte des 18. Jahrhunderts, zum Teil noch unter Mitwirkung J. S. Bachs
3. Handschriften bzw. Abschriften aus der 2. Hälfte des 18. Jahrhunderts
4. Handschriften bzw. Abschriften aus der 1. Hälfte des 19. Jahrhunderts
5. Handschriften, die vom Verfasser nicht eingesehen werden konntensdv
6. Verschollene Handschriften

See Christoph Wolff's review of Schmieder, 2nd ed., in *Notes* 49, no. 2 (Dec. 1992): 543–44. A detailed description of Bach's thematic catalogs is found in Daniel R. Melamed and Michael Marissen, *Introduction to Bach Studies* (New York: Oxford University Press, 1998), 3–7.

Dürr, Alfred, Yoshitake Kobayashi, and Kirsten Beiswenger, eds. *Bach-Werke-Verzeichnis: Kleine Ausgabe* (BWV^{2a}). Weisbaden: Breitkopf & Härtel, 1998. Abbreviated in *Grove Music Online* as BWV; A = Anhang.

Nicknamed "Kleine Schmeider" (or "little Schmieder"), BWV^{2a} was designed as a condensed and relatively brief update to the second edition of Schmieder. Of most significance for users is its relocation of works deemed to be of dubious authenticity from the main section of the catalog to the *Anhang* or Appendix (which is usually where dubious works are located in thematic catalogs), and its inclusion of citations for literature published from 1950 to 1997.

It is necessary to use both the second edition of Schmieder and *Kleine Schmieder,* as well as BC, to get a complete listing of bibliographic references (to 1997) for particular works. For more recent information, these listings should then be supplemented via a search through Yo Tomita's "Bach Bibliography": http://www.music.qub.ac.uk/~tomita/bachbib/index.html.

The *Grove Music Online* works list (example follows) provides BC and BWV numbers for each work, as well as locations of works in old Bach edition (Bach Gesellschaft, abbreviated as BG) and *Neue Bach Ausgabe* (abbreviated as NBA).

COMPLETE WORKS EDITIONS

Neue Ausgabe sämtliche Werke, herausgeben vom Johann-Sebastian-Bach-Institut, Göttingen und vom Bach-Archiv-Leipzig. Kassel: Bärenreiter, 1954–2007. Abbreviated in *Grove Music Online* as [NBA].
Werke, herausgegeben von der Bach-Gesellschaft. Leipzig: Breitkopf & Härtel, 1851–99. Abbreviated in *Grove Music Online* as [BG]. (See Figure 10–1.)

RELATED SOURCES (SEE ALSO LIST OF BACH CANTATA SOURCES IN CHAPTER 11: TEXTS AND TRANSLATIONS).

Bach-Archiv Leipzig. http://www.bach-leipzig.de/.
Beisswenger, Kirsten. *Johann Sebastian Bach's Notenbibliothek.* Catalogus Musicus 13. Kassel: Bärenreiter, 1992.
Herz, Gerhard. *Bach-Quellen in Amerika (Bach Sources in America).* Kassel: Bärenreiter; Ann Arbor, MI: UMI Research Press, 1984.
Internationale Bachakademie Stuttgart: http://www.bachakademie.de/de/nav/9.htm.
Göttinger Bach-Katalog: Die Quellen der Bach-Werke. (searchable database of Bach sources to 1850: http://www.bach.gwdg.de/bach_engl.html.)
Kast, Paul. *Die Bach-Handschriften der Berliner Staatsbibliothek.* Trossingen: Hohner-Verlag, 1958.
Lehmann, Karen. *Die Anfänge einer Bach-Gesamtausgabe: Editionen der Klavierwerke durch Hoffmeister und Kühnel (Bureau de Musique) und C.F. Peters in Leipzig 1801–1865; ein Beitrage zur Wirkungsgeschichte J.S. Bachs.* Leipziger Beiträge zur Bach-Forschung 6. Hildesheim: G. Olms, 2004.
Die Neue Bach-Ausgabe, 1954–2007: Eine Dokumentation. Herausgegeben von Johann-Sebastian-Bach-Institut Göttingen. Kassel: Bärenreiter, 2007.
Papillon, André. *Index des mélodies de chorals dans l'œuvre de Bach.* Saint-Nicolas (Québec), Canada: Les Presses de L'Université Laval, 2006. (with thematic incipits)
Prinz, Ulrich, ed. *Johann Sebastian Bachs Instrumentarium: Originalquellen, Besetzing, Verwendung.* Schriftenreihe der Internationale Bachakademie Stuttgart 10. Kassel: Bärenreiter, 2005.
Whaples, Marian. *Bach Aria Index.* Music Library Association Index Series 11. Ann Arbor, MI: Music Library Association, 1971.

BACH, WILHELM FRIEDEMANN

Wollny, Peter. *Thematisch-systematisches Verzeichnis der Werke Wilhelm Friedemann Bachs. Bach-Repertorium,* ii. Stuttgart: Carus (in preparation). Abbreviated in *Grove Music Online* as [BR].
_____. "Studies in the Music of Wilhelm Friedemann Bach: Sources and Style." PhD Diss, Harvard University, 1993.
Falck, Martin. *Wilhelm Friedemann Bach: Sein Leben und seine Werke, mit thematischem Verzeichnis seiner Kompositionen und zwei Bildern.* 1913. Reprint, Hildesheim: G. Olms, 1977, 2003. Abbreviated in *Grove Music Online* as [Fk]; also, Fk† = addn from Wollny, 1993 (see earlier).

FIGURE 10–1 *Grove Music Online,* J. S. Bach works list.

Oxford **Music** Online

ALL CONTENT | BIOGRAPHIES | SUBJECT ENTRIES | LEARNING RESOURCES

[ ] SEARCH

Advanced Search

Grove Music Online

Results list | Next result »

Bach, §III: (7) Johann Sebastian Bach

Article | **Works** | Multimedia | Related Content

🖶 Print ✉ Email 📋 Cite

Works

Bach did not always define instruments unambiguously; 'corno' could mean the normal horn of his time, the need for a brass player but not necessarily a trumpeter, or possibly the most suitable brass instrument (horn, cornett, slide-trumpet [tromba da tirarsi] etc.); parts for 'three oboes' at Leipzig may indicate any combination of oboes, oboes d'amore, tailles (tenor oboes in F, with no solo material) or oboes da caccia (a specific local tenor type, designed for obbligato work); four trombones indicate SATB and three ATB (usually below a cornett)

Dates of later copies or performances are given only if modifications are involved

Editions:

J.S. Bach: Werke, ed. Bach-Gesellschaft. i–xlvii (Leipzig, 1851–99/R) [BG]

J.S. Bach: Neue Ausgabe sämtlicher Werke (Neue Bach-Ausgabe), ed. Johann-Sebastian-Bach-Institut, Göttingen, and Bach-Archiv, Leipzig, ser. I–VIII (Kassel and Basle, 1954–) [vols. in square brackets are in preparation] [NBA; CC = Critical Commentary]

Catalogues:

W. Schmieder: Thematisch-systematisches Verzeichnis der musikalischen Werke Johann Sebastian Bachs: Bach-Werke-Verzeichnis (Leipzig, 1950, enlarged 2/1990, rev. and abridged 1998 by A. Dürr, Y. Kobayashi and K. Beisswenger as Bach-Werke-Verzeichnis) [BWV; A = Anhang]

H.-J. Schulze and C. Wolff: Bach Compendium: analytisch-bibliographisches Repertorium der Werke Johann Sebastian Bachs(Leipzig and Frankfurt, 1985–) [BC]

†-variant versions exist; see bwv and BC

Church cantatas

Advent I = 1st Sunday in Advent; Trinity/Easter I = 1st Sunday after Trinity/Easter, etc.; most texts are compilations including at least one chorale; only single text sources given; where the text is entirely or mainly based on that of a chorale, its author's name is given in parentheses

BWV	BC	Title (text/librettist)	Occasion; 1st perf.	Scoring	BG	NBA
1	A 173	Wie schön leuchtet der Morgenstern, chorale (P. Nicolai)	Annunciation; 25 March 1725	S, T, B, 4w, 2 hn, 2 ob da caccia, str, bc	i, 1	I/xxviii.2, 3
2	A 98	Ach Gott, vom Himmel sieh darein, chorale (M. Luther)	Trinity II; 18 June 1724	A, T, B, 4w, 4 trbn, 2 ob, str, bc	i, 55	I/xvi, 83
3	A 33	Ach Gott, wie manches Herzeleid, chorale (M. Möller)	Epiphany II; 14 Jan 1725	S, A, T, B, 4w, hn, trbn, 2 ob d'amore, str, bc	i, 75	I/v, 191
†4	A 54	Christ lag in Todes Banden, chorale (Luther)	Easter; probably by 1708	S, A, T, B, 4w, cornett, str, bc [3 trbn added 1725]	i, 97	I/ix, 1
5	A 145	Wo soll ich fliehen hin, chorale (J. Heermann)	Trinity XIX; 15 Oct 1724	S, A, T, B, 4w, tpt da tirarsi, 2 ob, str, bc	i, 127	I/xxiv, 135

Source: *Grove Music Online.*

BADINGS, HENK

Klemme, Paul. *Henk Badings, 1907–87: Catalog of Works.* Detroit Studies in Music Bibliography 71. Warren, MI: Harmonie Park Press, 1993.

BARBER, SAMUEL

Heyman, Barbara. *A Comprehensive Thematic Catalog of the Complete Works of American Composer Samuel Barber.* (forthcoming)

BARTÓK, BÉLA

Antokoletz, Elliott. "Catalogue of Compositions." In *Béla Bartók: A Guide to Research.* 2nd ed. 5–48. New York: Garland Publishing, 1997.

Somfai, Laszlo. "List of Works and Primary Sources." In *Béla Bartók: Composition, Concepts, and Autograph Sources,* 297–320. Berkeley: University of California Press, 1996. Abbreviated in *Grove Music Online* as [BB]. This is the numbering system that will be used in Somfai's forthcoming Bartók thematic catalog. *Grove Music Online* works list has BB numbers and opus numbers.

Dille, Denijs. *Thematisches Verzeichnis der Jugendwerke Béla Bartóks, 1890–1904.* 2nd ed. Kassel: Bärenreiter, 1976. Abbreviated in *Grove Music Online* as [DD].

Szöllösy, András. "Bibliographie des oeuvres musicales et écrits musicologiques de Béla Bartók." *Bartók, sa vie et son oeuvres,* edited by Bence Szabolcsi, 299–345. Budapest: Corvina, 1956. Abbreviated in Antokoletz and other sources as [Sz].[18]

COMPLETE WORKS EDITIONS

No complete, critical edition. *Grove Music Online* works list and Antokoletz catalog list publishers of individual works.

BEETHOVEN, LUDWIG VAN

Kinsky, Georg. *Das Werke Beethovens; thematisch-bibliographisches Verzeichnis seiner Sämtlichen vollendenten Komponistionen.* Munchen: G. Henle Verlag, 1955.

Georg Kinsky's thematic catalog of Beethoven's works is arranged in three sections: works with opus numbers (op. 1 through op. 138 — Leonore Overture no. 1); works without opus numbers (Werke ohne Opuszahl) or WoOs; and *Anhang,* for works of doubtful authenticity. Entries include incipit, location of manuscript, information on first edition, and related details typically found in a composer thematic catalog. It also includes references to the location of the work in *Ludwig van Beethoven Werke* (the "old" Gesamtausgaben, which began publication in 1862); this is abbreviated in both Kinsky and *Grove Music Online* as GA.

Beethoven regularly assigned opus numbers to his major works, thus making the task of his thematic catalog compiler somewhat easier.

Dorfmüller, Kurt. *Beiträge zur Beethoven-Bibliographie: Studien und Materialien zum Werkverzeichnis von Kinsky-Halm.* Munchen: Henle, 1979.

Includes essays by various Beethoven scholars as well as the "Supplement zum Thematisch-bibliographischen Verzeichnis von Kinsky-Halm Zusammengetellt von Kurt Dorfmüller," which provides corrections and additions to Kinsky-Halm. Use

Kinsky-Halm and the Dorfmüller supplement together for complete information about particular works.

Hess, Willy. *Verzeichnis der nicht Gesamtausgabe veröffenlichte Werke Ludwig van Beethovens. Zusammengestellt für die Ergänzung der Beethoven-Gesamtausgabe.* Weisbaden: Breitkopf & Härtel, 1957.

Green, James F., ed. *The New Hess Catalog of Beethoven's Works: Edited, Updated and Translated from the Original German with a New Foreword by James F. Green, and a New Introduction by Sieghard Brandenburg.* West Newbury, VT: Vance Brook Publishing, 2003.

The Swiss musicologist Willy Hess (1906–97) published numerous works of Beethoven not included in the old complete works edition. His 1957 publication (recently translated by James F. Green) is an index to these works. The works themselves were published in his *Supplemente zur Gesamtausgabe* (1959–71), which is indicated in the Beethoven *Grove Music Online* works list as HS.

Nottebohm, Gustav. *Ludwig van Beethoven: Thematisches Verzeichnis nebst der Biblioteca Beethoviana. Versuch einer Beethoven-Bibliographie von Emerich Kastner, ergänzt von Theodor Frimmel.* Leipzig: Breitkopf & Härtel, 1925; Reprint, Vaduz: Sändig Reprint, 1995.

REAL LIFE SCENARIO

An oboist, you are seeking the score of Beethoven's arrangement on the theme "La ci darem la mano" from *Don Giovanni* for two oboes and bassoon. Your library does not appear to have a separately published edition of this work. The librarian checks the *Grove Music Online* Beethoven works list, which indicates that this work is number (WoO28—Werke ohne opuszahl 28) and is published in the Hess supplement of the Beethoven Gesamtausgaben [HS vii].

Finally, a new edition of Kinsky is in process. Edited by Norbert Gertsch and Kurt Dorfmüller, the new Kinsky will incorporate important findings in Beethoven scholarship of the past 50 years and will provide additional details on both historical and bibliographical details for each work. It may also include links to sources on the Internet, such as the Beethoven Haus's project to digitize all of Beethoven's manuscripts. See Norbert Gertsch and Kurt Dorfmüller, "The Revision of the Beethoven Catalogue of Works," *Fontes Artis Musicae* 50, n.s. 2–4 (April–Dec. 2003): 130–39.

COMPLETE WORKS EDITIONS

The new edition of Beethoven's works (neue Ausgabe) began publication in 1961:

Werke. Herausgegeben vom Beethoven-Archiv, Bonn, unter Leitung von Joseph Schmidt-Görg. München: Henle, 1961– . Abbreviated in *Grove Music Online* works list as [NA].

Werke: Vollständige kritisch durchgesehene überall berechtigte Ausgabe. Leipzig: Breitkopf & Härtel, 1862–88. Reprint, Huntington Station, NY: Kalmus, 1967. Abbreviated in *Grove Music Online,* as [GA].
Supplemente zur Gesamtausgabe. Hrsg. Von Willy Hess. Wiesbaden: Breitkopf & Härtel, 1959–71. Supplement to the old complete works edition; abbreviated in *Grove Music Online* as [HS]

For a fuller discussion of Beethoven bibliographies, thematic catalogs, and complete editions, see Nicholas Marston, "Editions of the Music" and "Bibliographies, Catalogues, and Indexes" in Cooper, Barry, ed. *The Beethoven Compendium: A Guide to Beethoven's Life and Music* (London: Thames and Hudson, 1991), 313–17, 324–26.

REPRINT EDITIONS

As noted in Chapter 8, most of the older complete works editions produced in the ninteenth century are no longer protected by copyright. Reprint editions produced by Dover, Kalmus, and Masters are often reprints of works from the old Gesamtausgaben. While Dover editions usually provide this information on the verso of the title page of the edition, Kalmus and Masters do not. See also, "Locating individual works in complete editions," pp. 203–206.

BELLINI, VINCENZO
COMPLETE WORKS EDITION

Uvietta, Marco, gen. ed. *Edizione critica delle opere di Vincenzo Bellini.* Milano: Ricordi, 2003– .

BERG, ALBAN

Hilmar, Rosemary. *Katalog der Musikhandschriften, Schriften und Studien Alban Bergs im Fond Alban Berg und der weiteren handschriftlichen Quellen im Besitz der Österreichischen Nationalbibliothek.* Vienna: Universal Edition, 1980.

_____. *Katalog der Schriftstücke von der Hand Alban Bergs, der fremdschriftlichen und gedruckten Dokumente zur Lebensgeschichte und zu seinem Werk.* Wien: Universal Edition, 1985. (Catalogs of Berg's manuscripts and letters in the Austrian National Library.)
See also:
Newsom, Jon, and Alfred Mann, eds. *The Rosaleen Moldenhauer Memorial: Music History from Primary Sources: A Guide to the Moldenhauer Archives.* Washington, DC: Library of Congress, 2000. Includes a summary of Berg holdings in the Bayerische Staatsbibliothek.

COMPLETE WORKS EDITION

Berg, Alban. *Sämtliche Werke.* Editionsleitung, Rudolf Stephan, Regina Busch; herausgegeben von der Alban Berg Stiftung. Wien: Universal, 1984– .

BERLIOZ, HECTOR

Holoman, D. Kern. *Catalogue of the Works of Hector Berlioz. New Edition of the Complete Works.* Vol. 25. Kassel: Bärenreiter, 1987.
A user-friendly catalog with text entirely in English, Holoman's catalog arranges Berlioz's works chronologically by terminal date of composition. He assigns catalog "index numbers" to Berlioz's 143 works (which, as the author points out in his foreword, is a deceptively small number, because "many of these entries embrace multiple versions of the same piece or several compositions at once."[19]) Holoman's index numbers are different from the opus numbers assigned by Berlioz: Appendix I (p. 491) is a listing of the opus (or oeuvre) numbers; *Grove Music Online* works list has columns for both opus numbers (when they exist) and Holoman numbers.

Holoman includes copious information on all of the composer's musical compositions and prose works, including autograph sources, printed editions, and all known performances in the composer's lifetime.[20]

For printed editions, Holoman includes a transcription of the title page, in an effort to convey the "look" of the title page of first editions without including full reproductions, as is found in Hofmann's title pages catalogs of Brahms and Schumann (pp. 262, 299), and Haberkamp's title page catalog of Mozart (p. 285). (See Figure 10–2B.)

Holoman's foreword provides a succinct description of the problems relating to cataloging Berlioz's works. See also a review of Holoman by Donald W. Krummel, *Journal of the American Musicological Society* 43, no. 2 (summer 1990): 367–75.

Hopkinson, Cecil. *A Bibliography of the Musical and Literary Works of Hector Berlioz, 1803–1869: With Histories of the French Music Publishers Concerned.* Edinburgh: Edinburgh Bibliographical Society, 1951. Rev. 2nd ed., incorporating the author's additions and corrections by R. Macnutt, 1980.

COMPLETE WORKS EDITIONS

New Edition of the Complete Works. Kassel: Bärenreiter, 1969– . New Berlioz edition, abbreviated in *Grove Music Online* works list as [NBE].
Werke. Herausgegeben von Ch. Malherbe und F. Weingartner. 20 vols. Leipzig: Breitkopf & Härtel, 1900–1907. Old Berlioz edition, abbreviated in *Grove Music Online* works list as [B & H]. (See Figure 10–2A.)

BOCCHERINI, LUIGI

Gerard, Yves. *Thematic, Bibliographical and Critical Catalogue of the Works of Luigi Boccherini.* London: Oxford University Press, 1969.

COMPLETE WORKS EDITION

Speck, Christian, ed. *Opera omnia.* Bologna: Ut Orpheus Edizione, 2005– . http://www.luigiboccherini.com/home.php?l=ing. (will include new thematic catalog)
Pais, Aldo, ed. *L'edizione critica delle opera Luigi Boccherini.* Padua: Zanibon, 1977–96. Abbreviated in *Grove Music Online* as [P]. *Grove Music Online* Boccherini works list also includes other editions of Boccherini works that were devoted to particular genres (quintets, symphonies, etc.).

FIGURE 10–2 (a) *Grove Music Online,* H. Berlioz Works list;

Oxford Music Online
ALL CONTENT | BIOGRAPHIES | SUBJECT ENTRIES | LEARNING RESOURCES

| berlioz | **SEARCH** |

Advanced Search

Grove Music Online

Results list | Next result »

Berlioz, Hector

| Article | **Works** | Multimedia | Related Content |

🖨 Print   📧 Email   💬 Cite

Works

Editions:

H. Berlioz: Werke, ed. C. Malherbe and F. Weingarten (Leipzig, 1900–10) [B&H]

New Berlioz Edition, general ed. H. Macdonald (Kassel, 1967–) [NBE]

Catalogue:

Catalogue of the works of Hector Berlioz, ed. D.K. Holoman (Kassel, 1987) [H]

Operas

op.	Title	Genre, acts	Libretto	Composed	First performance	Sources	B&H NBE	H	Remarks
	Estelle et Némorin	op	H.-C. Gerono, after Florian	1823				17	lost
	Les francs-juges	drame lyrique, 3	H. Ferrand	1825–6	unperf.	frags., *F-Pn**, lib. *Pc*, ov. (Paris, 1836)	ov., iv, 4	23	rev. 1829; portions adopted for 1833 as *Le cri de guerre du Brisgau* (1, T. Gounet); 5 complete movts extant
23	Benvenuto Cellini	opéra semi-seria, 2	L. de Wailly, A. Barbier and A. de Vigny	1836–8	Paris, Opéra, 10 Sept 1838	*Pc**, excerpts (Paris, 1839), vs (Brunswick, 1856)	ov., v, 1a–d	76	rev. version, in 3 acts, Weimar, 17 Nov 1852

RELATED SOURCE

Speck, Christian. "Reports: Christian Speck Discusses the Aims of the New Critical Edition of the Complete Works of Luigi Boccherini." *Eighteenth Century Music* 3, no. 1 (2006): 171–72.

BRAHMS, JOHANNES

McCorkle, Margit L. *Johannes Brahms: thematisch-bibliographisches Werkverzeichnis.* Munchen: G. Henle, 1984.

    McCorkle's thematic catalogs of the works of Brahms (1984) and Schumann (2003) provide essential documentation on the works of both composers. They are also

FIGURE 10–2 (b) D. Kern Holoman, *Catalogue of the Works of Hector Berlioz* (Kassel: Bärenreiter, 1987), 294.

294   **111** La Damnation de Faust

the completion begun in pencil), Méphistophélès (id.; a fair, complete copy of the previous part). Set C is on various kinds of paper. Except where noted below, prepared by Rocquemont. Both French and German text. 4 parts: Faust (oblong green, 10 staves; German text added in red; one fasc. of oblong white, 8 staves; German text only for *Invocation à la nature*), Méphistophélès (oblong white, 8 staves; German copyist, French filled in; some pp. by Rocquemont), Brander (oblong green, 10 staves; German text added in red), Marguerite (id.). Set D is a single part for Brander, oblong white, 10 staves. French text only. Possibly post 1869.

F–Pc L 17227. Solo part for Méphistophélès. Oblong green, 8 staves. Copied by Rocquemont, with aut. TP. Also one part for Ophicléides. Upright green, 12 staves. Copied by Rocquemont and a German copyist. Both ex Société des Concerts.

Manuscript Chorus Parts: F–Pc D 16471. Upright white octavo, 12 hand-made staves. German copyist and German text. 3 parts: Tén. (*Chor der Trinker aus Faust*), Sopr. I (*Le Ciel*), Sopr. II (id.).

F–Pc L 17228 (A–F). Oblong green, 12 staves. Copied by Rocquemont and his staff for the first performance. 62 parts: Sopr. I (10), Sopr. II (10), Tén. I (10), Tén. II (10), Basses I (9), Basses II (9); Petit chœur: Sopr. I (2), Sopr. II (2).

Printed Score: *à Franz* LISZT. / LA / DAMNATION DE FAUST / *Légende Dramatique* / EN QUATRE PARTIES / *Musique de* / HECTOR BERLIOZ / Œuv: 24. / GRANDE PARTITION / *avec texte Français et Allemand.* / *Quelques morceaux du Livret sont empruntés a la traduction* / *Française du Faust de Goëthe par Mr Gérard de Nerval; une* / *partie des Scènes 1, 4, 6, et 7 est de Mr Gandonnière; tout le reste des* / *paroles est de Mr H. Berlioz.* / *Traduction Allemande par Mr Minslaff.* / *Prix: 60^f net.* / *Parties séparées d'Orchestre. net. 60^f Parties séparées de Chœurs. net. 3^f* / *Partition in 8° Chant et Piano. net. 20^f* / *Paris,* S. RICHAULT, *Editeur, Boulevard Poissonnière 26 au 1er* / [L.:] *Londres, Cramer et Beale* [R.:] *Leipsick, Fr. Hofmeister.* / 11,605. à 7.R. In a decorative border listing the composer's works. Paris: Richault, [1854] (London: Cramer & Beale; Leipzig: Hofmeister). Pl. no. 11605.R. (11605. à 7.R. on TP and [i]). TP, TP^v blank, [i] *Personnages* and *Table*, [ii] blank, 1–4 = *Avant-Propos* in French and German; [5]–32 = text in French and German, 1–410. Foot of p. 32 (preliminaries): IMPRIMERIE CENTRALE DES CHEMINS DE FER DE NAPOLÉON CHAIX ET Cie, RUE BERGÈRE, 20. Foot of p. 1 (music): *Imp^{ie}. Langlet rue Cadet 18.* The earliest copies have a frontispiece portrait of Berlioz by C. Baugniet (Londres, 1851), followed by a lithograph of Faust descending into Hell by F. Sorrieu (facs. in Boschot, *Faust*, 168). Later issues have many different arrangements for the lithographs, including the familiar Prinzhofer portrait. Advertised in *FM*, 2–IV–54. *Dépôt légal*, 6–IX–54. Contract with Richault, 30–III–53, allowed the composer 10 copies of the full score and a set of the orchestral parts. Hopkinson 54A. Copies: F–Pc A 559; F–Pn Vm^2 663 (dep. 1854); F–Po A 705 a; A–Wgm III 24660 (H 27831); B–Bc H 1051; B–Lc 320–NK–IX; D–brd–DT Mus. n 1430 (loose pp.); D–ddr–Bds Kb 492/1 (no frontispiece); GB–En H. B. 1/54; GB–TWmacnutt; US–NYj C 46 B456d; US–Wc M3.3.B5 op. 24.

Variant A: lacking *Personnages* and *Table*. Hopkinson 54A(*a*). Copies: F–Pn Vm^2 1052 (with lithograph of Faust at end; ex coll. Thierry-Poux); F–G V 4478; D–brd–Mbs 2° Mus. pr. 10884; GB–Ob Mus. 1 c 309(5); US–Cn Thomas 27.

Variant B: lacking *Personnages* leaf and frontispieces. Hopkinson 54A(*b*). Copies: F–CSA (lacks all preliminaries); GB–Lbl Hirsch IV 693 (with prices erased); GB–Lcm I K 13.

Variant C: with a monogram, *JB*, on TP and an advertisement for the chorus parts. See Hopkinson, 215. Copy: GB–TWmacnutt.

Printed Score (Excerpts): Paris, Richault, [c. 1862–66]. Hopkinson 54A(*f*). *Marche hongroise*. Copy: GB–Lcm I K 29. *Ballet des sylphes*. Copy: GB–En H. B. 2/43 (1). *Le Roi de Thulé*. Copy: GB–Ob Mus. 1 c 309(23). *Menuet des follets*. Copy: GB–Lbl Hirsch M 776. *Forêts et cavernes*. Copy: GB–Ob Mus. 1 c 309(26).

Printed Orchestral Parts: Paris: Richault [1854]. Pl. no. 11606.R. Vns I has the TP of the full score and, at foot of p. 2: *Imp: LANGLET rue Cadet 18.* Advertised in *FM*, 2–IV–54, at 60^f Dépôt légal, 25–IX–54. Hopkinson 54B. 24 parts: Fl. I–II (P. fl. I–II), Fl. III (P. fl.), Hb. I–II (C. a. I–II), Cl., Cl. b., Bns I–II, Bns III–IV, Cors I–II, Cors III–IV, Tromp., C. à p., Tromb. I, Tromb. II, Tromb. III, Oph. & Tuba, Tamb. & Tri., G. c. & Cymb., Tam-tam & Cloches, Harpe I, Harpe II, Vns I, Vns II, Altos, Vlles & Cb. Copies: F–Pc D 16473 (lacks all parts between Fl. III and Tromb. I as well as Harpe II); ex Société des Concerts); F–Psoc; B–Lc 68–NN–III (with 75 ms. chorus parts); D–brd–DT Mus. n 1430.

Printed Chorus Parts: pl. no. 11607.R. Octavo. Advertised in *FM*, 2–IV–54, at 3^f Hopkinson 54C.

---

user-friendly: the texts are in German, but each has translated the introductory matter into English. In the case of Brahms, the introduction includes valuable essays on "The Previous Catalogues of Brahms's Works," "The Publication History of Brahms's Works," and "The History of Brahms's Music Manuscripts." Of significance in the discussion of the latter is the fact that the composer destroyed many (but not all, as McCorkle points out) of his working manuscripts, intentionally leaving few signs of his compositional process. These essays are followed by "A Descriptive Guide to the Catalog," including a "Conflated Paradigm of the Catalogue Entries," which, again, being in English, provides useful guidance to those uneasy about using German-language texts.

The catalog itself is arranged similarly to the Kinsky catalog: works with opus numbers (1–122) followed by works without opus numbers. The latter is subdivided into sections for instrumental works (WoO 1–15), vocal works (WoO 16–30), and folksong arrangements (WoO 31–38). Appendices include

Works of other composers, arranged by Brahms
Lost works and arrangements
Varia, fragments, and sketches
Unauthenticated and misattributed works
Holograph collections and copies
Works of other composers, edited by Brahms

Indices include

List of Brahms's Works by Genre
List of Text Titles and Incipits
List of Literary Text Sources
Chronology by Date of Composition (very useful!)
List of Arrangers
List of Dedicatees
List of Publishers
List of Copyists
List of Manuscript Repositories
General Register

See reviews of McCorkle by Michael Musgrave in *Music & Letters* 71, no. 1 (Feb. 1990): 115–20; and David Brodbeck in *Journal of the American Musicological Society* 42, no. 2 (Summer 1989): 418–31.

The 1982 edition of Thomas Quigley's *Johannes Brahms: An Annotated Guide to the Literature* (for full citation see p. 101) was compiled in conjunction with McCorkle's catalog (Quigley worked as McCorkle's research assistant at the University of British Columbia; she also wrote the foreword to his bibliography)

Hofmann, Kurt. *Die Erstdrucke der Werke von Johannes Brahms: Bibliographie mit Wiedergabe von 209 Titelblättern.* Tutzing: Schneider, 1975. Documents first editions of Brahms's works through reproductions of their title pages.

COMPLETE WORKS EDITIONS

Neue Ausgabe sämtlicher Werke, herausgegeben von der Johannes Brahms Gesamtausgabe e.V., Editionsleitung Kiel, in Verbindung mit der Gesellschaft der Musikfreunde in Wien. München: G. Henle Verlag, 1996– . Abbreviated in *Grove Music Online* as [NA].

Sämtliche Werke Ausgabe der Gesellschaft der Musikfreunde in Wien. 16 vols. Edited by Hans Gál and Eusebius Mandyczewski. Leipzig, 1926–27. Reprint, Wiesbaden: Breitkopf & Härtel, 1926–27. Old complete works edition, abbreviated in *Grove Music Online* as [BW].

The old Brahms's complete works edition was known to be problematic, for a variety of reasons. See section on "Issues in Editing Brahms's Music" (items 32–38) in Heather Platt's *Johannes Brahms: A Guide to Research* (New York: Routledge, 2003) for discussions of this issue.

Johannes Brahms Gesamtausgabe Forschungsstelle Kiel. http://www.brahmsausgabe.
uni-kiel.de/
    Includes information on status of new complete works edition.

RELATED SOURCES

Dedel, Peter. *Johannes Brahms: A Guide to His Autograph in Facsimile.* MLA Index and
    Bibliography Series 18. Ann Arbor, MI: Music Library Association, 1978.
Krummacher, Friedhelm, Michael Struck, Constantin Floros, and Peter Peterson, eds.
    *Johannes Brahms: Quellen, Text, Rezeption, Interpretation: Internationaler Brahms-
    Kongress, Hamburg 1997.* München: G. Henle Verlag, 1999.
Pascall, Robert. "The Editor's Brahms." In *The Cambridge Companion to Brahms,*
    edited by Michael Musgrave, 250–67. Cambridge: Cambridge University Press, 1999.

BRIDGE, FRANK

Hindmarsh, Paul. *Frank Bridge: A Thematic Catalogue, 1900–1941.* London: Faber Music
    in association with Faber and Faber, 1983.
No complete works edition. Further information on the composer's life and works may
    be found on the Web site of the Frank Bridge Bequest: http://www.impulse-music.co.uk/
    frankbridge.htm.

BRITTEN, BENJAMIN

Britten-Pears Library and University of East Anglia. "Benjamin Britten Thematic Cata-
    logue." http://www.brittenpears.org/?page=projects/ahrc/index.html (Forthcoming in
    electronic and print form.)

RELATED SOURCES

The Britten-Pears Foundation (http://www.brittenpears.org/) is the most comprehensive
    resource for information on the composer and his works. See also bibliographic sources
    cited in Chapter 4.
Choa, Sharon. "Rejuvenating Britten: The First Report on the Production of a Web-
    Based Thematic Catalogue of Britten's Works." *Brio* 44, no. 1 (Spring-Summer 2007):
    25–33.

BRUCKNER, ANTON

Grasberger, Renate. *Werkverzeichnis Anton Bruckner:* (WAB). Instituts für Öesterre-
    ichische Musikdokumentation, Publikationen 7. Tutzing: Schneider, 1977.

COMPLETE WORKS EDITIONS

*Sämtliche Werke, herausgegeben von der Generaldirektion der Österreichischen National-
    bibliothek und der Internationalen Bruckner-Gesellschaft; unter Leitung von Leopold
    Nowak.* Vienna: Musikwissenschaftlicher Verlag der International Bruckner-
    Gesellschaft, 1951– . Abbreviated in *Grove Music Online* as [B].
Sämtliche Werke: Kritische Gesamtausabe. Edited by Robert Haas. 15 vols. (incomplete).
    Vienna: Musikwissenschaftlicher Verlag, 1930–53. Vols. i–ii, iv–viii, xiv–xv, (Augsburg,

1930–53); vol. iii, ed. F. Oeser (Wiesbaden, 1950); vols. ix, xi, ed. A. Orel (Vienna, 1934); vol. xiii, ed. R. Haas and L. Nowak (Leipzig, 1940); vols. x, xii, not published. Abbreviated in *Grove Music Online* as [A].

There are numerous problems relating to the critical editions of Bruckner's works, in part as a result of his working methods and the works' publication history, as well as the preparation of the first critical edition under the direction of Robert Haas and its connection to the Nazi regime. For further information and related studies, see the following sources:

Anton Bruckner: ein Handbuch. Edited by Uwe Harten, Renate Grasberger, and Anton-Bruckner-Institut Linz. Salzberg: Residenz, 1996.
Hawkshaw, Paul. "Anton Bruckner," 6 "Publication and Reception History." *Grove Music Online.* Edited by L. Macy. www.grovemusic.com.
_____. "The Bruckner Problem Revisited," *19th Century Music* 21, no. 1 (Summer 1997): 96–107.
_____. "The Manuscript Sources for Anton Bruckner's Linz Works: A Study of His Working Methods from 1856 to 1868." Ph.D. diss., Columbia University, 1984.
Horton, Julian. *Bruckner's Symphonies: Analysis, Reception, and Cultural Politics.* Cambridge: Cambridge University Press, 2004.
_____. "Recent Developments in Bruckner Scholarship." *Music & Letters* 85, no. 1 (2004): 83–94.
Kortvedt, Benjamin Marcus. "Return to the 'Pure' Sources: The Ideology and Text-Critical Legacy of the First Bruckner *Gesamtausgaben.*" In *Bruckner Studies,* edited by Timothy L. Jackson and Paul Hawkshaw, 91–109. Cambridge: Cambridge University Press, 1997.
Notley, Margaret. "Bruckner Problems, in Perpetuity." *19th Century Music* 30, no. 1 (Summer 2006): 81–93.
Solvik, Morten. "The International Bruckner Society and the N.S.D.A.P.: A Case Study of Robert Haas and the Critical Edition." *Musical Quarterly* 82, no. 2 (Summer 1998): 362–82.
Other relevant references are found in the *Grove Music Online* Bruckner bibliography.

BUSONI, FERRUCCIO

Kindermann, Jurgen. *Thematisch-chronologisches Verzeichnis der Musikalischen von Ferruccio B. Busoni.* Regensburg: Bosse, 1980.

BUXTEHUDE, DIETRICH

Karstadt, Georg. *Thematisch-Systematisches Verzeichnis der Musikalischen Werke von Dietrich Buxtehude: Buxtehude-Werke-Verzeichnis (BuxWV).* 2nd en. and rev. ed. Wiesbaden: Breitkopf & Härtel, 1985. (Classified arrangement.)

COMPLETE WORKS EDITIONS

Dietrich Buxtehude: The Collected Works. Edited by Kerala J. Snyder et al. New York: Broude Bros., 1987– . Abbreviated in *Grove Music Online* as [CW].

Dietrich Buxtehudes Werke. Edited by W. Gurlitt et al. Hamburg: Ungrino, 1925–37. (incomplete; continued as previous edition)

BYRD, WILLIAM
NON-THEMATIC WORKS CATALOG IN

Turbet, Richard. *William Byrd: A Guide to Research.* 2nd ed. Routledge Music Bibliographies. New York: Routledge, 2006. Works arranged by "T" numbers.

COMPLETE WORKS EDITIONS

The Byrd Edition. Edited by Philip Brett. London: Stainer & Bell, 1971–2004. Abbreviated in *Grove Music Online* as [B].
The Collected Works of William Byrd. Edited by Edmund H. Fellowes and revised under general editorship of Thurton Dart. London: Stainer & Bell, 1937–50; rev. ed., 1962–70. Abbreviated in *Grove Music Online* as [F]; rev. ed. abbreviated in *Grove Music Online* as [D].
Other editions listed at head of *Grove Music Online* works list; also in Turbet, pp. 2–9.

CHAMBONNIÈRES, JACQUES CAMPION DE

Gustafson, Bruce. *Thematic Catalogue of the Works of Jacques Champion de Chambonnières.* JSCM Instrumenta 1. Urbana 5 IL: Society of Seventeenth Century Music, 2007. http://sscm-jscm.press.uiuc.edu/instrumenta01.html.

CHOPIN, FREDERIC

Chominski, Józef Michal, and Teresa Dalila Turlo. *Katalog dziel Fryderyka Chopina.* Kraków: Polskie Wydawnictwo Muzyczne, 1990. Abbreviated in *Grove Music Online* as CT.
   Provides information on manuscript sources, first editions, and significant later editions. Arranged alphabetically by title of work. Although the text is in Polish, the introduction and headings are available in English translation.
Kobylanska, Krystyna. *Frédéric Chopin: thematisch-bibliographisches Werkverzeichnis.* München: G. Henle, 1979. Abbreviated in *Grove Music Online* as KK. Originally published in Polish: *Rękopisy utworów Chopina: Katalog.* 2 vols. Kraków: Polskie Wydawnictwo Muzyczne, 1977.
   The original Polish edition was primarily a catalog of Chopin's manuscripts. Comparisons of the Polish and German editions as well as valuable information on some of the many problems of cataloging Chopin's works are provided in reviews by Jeffrey Kallberg in *Journal of the American Musicological Society* 34, no. 2 (Summer 1981): 357–65, and Michael Griffel in *Notes* 37, no. 4 (June 1981): 847–49.
Brown, Maurice J. E. *Chopin: An Index of His Works in Chronological Order.* 2nd rev. ed. New York: Da Capo Press, 1972. Abbreviated in *Grove Music Online* as [B].
   Arranges works in chronological order, with classified index and index of works with and without opus numbers.
Smialek, William. "Catalogs." In *Frederic Chopin: A Guide to Research,* 14–16. Composer Resource Manuals 50. New York: Garland Publishing, 2000.

COMPLETE WORKS EDITIONS

Wydarie Narodowe Dziel Frederyka Chopin (Polish national edition). Edited by Jan Ekier. Warsaw and Kraków: Polskie Wydawn. Muzyczne, 1967–2005. The only edition referenced in *Grove Music Online* works list.

Works. Edited by Ewald Zimmermann. München: G. Henle, 1963– .

Fryderyk Chopin: Complete Works, According to the Autographs and Original Editions, With a Critical Commentary. Edited by Ignacy J. Paderewski et al. 21 vols. Warsaw: Fryderyk Chopin Institute, 1949–62.

Friedrich Chopin's Werke. Edited by Woldemar Bargiel et al. 16 vols. Leipzig: Breitkopf & Härtel, 1878–1902.

Note: The *Grove Music Online* works list for Chopin does not provide locations of works in complete editions.

Approaches to cataloging Chopin's works and creating critical or authentic editions are beset with problems, in part because of the manner in which the composer dealt with his manuscripts and with his publishers. A brief overview of these complex issues is presented in the section on "Sources and Editions" in the *Grove Music Online* Chopin article. See also the list of resources on this subject in the *Grove Music Online* Chopin article bibliography under "Section O: editorial questions, interpretation,"as well as the chapter titled "Works of the Composer" in William Smialek's *Frederic Chopin: A Guide to Research* (New York: Garland Publishing, 1982), 59–118. Jeffery Kallberg and John Rink have written extensively on this subject. See the references to their articles in *Grove Music Online*, as well as Kallberg's dissertation "The Chopin Sources: Variants and Versions in Later manuscripts and Printed Editions" (Ph.D. diss. University of Chicago, 1982). Finally, Chopin researchers have taken advantage of new technologies to deal with editorial and source issues and created several sites with digital copies of Chopin manuscripts and first editions (see following).

RELATED SOURCES

Chopin, Frédéric. *Oeuvres pour piano: fac-similé de l'exemplaire de Jane W. Stirling avec annotations et corrections de l'auteur (ancienne collection Edouard Ganche).* Introduction by Jean-Jacques Eigeldinger; preface by Jean-Michel Nectoux. Paris: Bibliothèque nationale, 1982.
> Reproduces scores with manuscript annotations from Chopin student Jane Stirling's collection, which was later owned by Edouard Ganche and is now preserved in the Bibliothèque nationale.

Platzman, George. *A Descriptive Catalogue of Early Editions of the Works of Frédéric Chopin in the University of Chicago Library.* 2nd ed., rev. and enl. Chicago: University of Chicago Library. Distributed by the University of Chicago Press, 2003.
> Catalog of some of the more than 400 first and early editions of Chopin's works in the University of Chicago Special Collections Library. These editions are also available in digital form on the University of Chicago Web site: http://chopin .lib.uchicago.edu/.

DIGITAL PROJECTS

Online Chopin Variorum Edition (OCVE): project under the direction of John Rink to digitize Chopin sources and allow editorial analysis and comparisons online: http://www.ocve.org.uk/.
   Also incorporates *Chopin's First Editions Online* (CFEO): http://www.cfeo.org.uk/, with digital copies of Chopin first editions; for descriptions of these sources, see Christophe Grabowski and John Rink, *Annotated Catalogue of Chopin's First Editions* (Cambridge: Cambridge University Press, 2007).

Naradowy Instytut Fryderyka Chopina (Fryderyk Chopin Institute) http://www.nifc.pl/chopin/composition/listing
   The institute has embarked on a project to publish all of Chopin's manuscripts in facsimile editon: http://en.chopin.nifc.pl/institute/publications/facsimile

CLEMENTI, MUZIO

Tyson, Alan. *Thematic Catalogue of the Works of Muzio Clementi.* Tutzing: Hans Schneider, 1967.

COMPLETE WORKS EDITIONS

Muzio Clementi Opera Omnia. Bologna: UT Orpheus Edizioni, 2000–
Oeuvres complettes. Leipzig: Breitkopf & Härtel, 1803–19. Reprint, New York: Da Capo, 1973. (incomplete)

CORELLI, ARCANGELO

Marx, Hans Joachim. *Die Überlieferung der Werke Arcangelo Corellis: catalogue raisonné.* Historisch-kritische Gesamtausgabe der musikalischen Werke 6. Köln: A. Volk, 1980.

COMPLETE WORKS EDITIONS

Arcangelo Corelli: Historisch-kritische Gesamtausgabe der musikalischen Werke, Herausgegeben im Musikwissenschaftlichen Institut der Universität Basel von Hans Oesch. Laaber: Laaber-Verlag, 1976–2006. Abbreviated in *Grove Music Online* as [M], reflecting the original editorship of Hans Joachim Marx.
Les oeuvres de Arcangelo Corelli. 5 vols. Edited by J. Joachim and F. Chrysander. London: Augener, 1888–91. Abbreviated in *Grove Music Online* as [JC].

COUPERIN, FRANÇOIS

Cauchie, Maurice. *Thematic Index of the Works of François Couperin.* Monaco: Lyrebird Press, 1949.

COMPLETE WORKS EDITIONS

Oeuvres complètes de François Couperin. Edited by Maurice Cauchie et al. 12 vols. Paris: Oiseau-Lyre, 1932–3. Abbreviated in *Grove Music Online* as [C]; Revised by Kenneth

Gilbert and Davitt Moroney, ser. I–V and suppl. Monaco: Oiseau-Lyre, 1980– . Abbreviated in *Grove Music Online* as [GM].

DAVIES, SIR PETER MAXWELL

Bayliss, Colin. *The Music of Sir Peter Maxwell Davies: An Annotated Catalogue.* Beverley, MA: Highgate Press, 1991.

DEBUSSY, CLAUDE

Lesure, Francois. *Claude Debussy: biographie critique: suivie du catalogue de l'œuvre.* Paris: Fayard, 2003.

COMPLETE WORKS EDITION

Oeuvres complètes de Claude Debussy. Edited by François Lesure. Paris: Durand-Costallat, 1985– .

DELIUS, FREDERICK

Threlfall, Robert. *A Catalogue of the Compositions of Frederick Delius: Sources and References.* London: Delius Trust, 1977.
_____. *Frederick Delius: A Supplementary Catalogue.* London: Delius Trust, 1986.
Non-thematic catalogs (term used for catalogs that lack musical incipits)

COMPLETE WORKS EDITION

Frederick Delius: Complete Works. Edited by Thomas Beecham and Robert Threlfall. London: Boosey and Hawkes, 1951– . Not specifically referenced in *Grove Music Online* works list.

RELATED SOURCES

Lowe, Rachel. *Frederick Delius, 1862–1934: Catalogue of the Music Archive of the Delius Trust.* London: Delius Trust, 1974.
Delius Trust: http://www.delius.org.uk/.

DONIZETTI, GAETANO

Inzaghi, Luigi. "Catalogo generale delle opere." In *Gaetano Donizetti,* edited by Giampiero Tintori and Luigi Inzaghi, 133–278. Milan: Nuove Edizioni, 1983. Non-thematic catalog.
Cassaro, James P. "Catalogs." In *Gaetano Donizetti: A Guide to Research,* 21–25. Composer Resource Manuals 51. New York: Garland Publishing, 2000.

COMPLETE WORKS EDITION

Edizione critica delle opere di Gaetano Donizetti. Milan: Ricordi, 1991– .

DVOŘÁK, ANTONÍN

Burghauser, Jarmil, and John Clapham. *Antonín Dvořák: thematicky katalog; bibliografie; prehled zivota a dila* [Thematic Catalogue; Bibliography; Survey of Life and Works]. 2nd ed. Praha: Bärenreiter Editio Supraphon, 1996.

The introduction to the first edition of Burghauser's catalog (Prague: 1960) includes detailed information on the many problems involved with organizing a thematic catalog of Dvořák's works. (As with the updated second edition, all of the introductory matter is published in Czech, German, and English.) Chief among these is the inconsistency in numbers assigned by the composer and by Simrock, his primary publisher: for example, Dvořák's famous New World Symphony — Symphony no. 9 in E minor, B. 178 — was first published as Symphony no. 5. Otakar Sourek was the first to approach cataloging Dvořák's works, and his S numbers are listed alongside B numbers and opus numbers in the *Grove Music Online* works list. Burghauser revised Sourek's listing, and his catalog presents all of Dvořák's works in chronological order.

Library catalogs include a combination of both B numbers and opus numbers (the latter when they were assigned by the composer). "See" references (as described in Chapter 1) direct the user to the correct heading under which the work is found.

The first edition of Burghauser's catalog also included a discography. This is omitted in the second edition, because of the publication of John H. Yoell's *Antonín Dvořák on Records* (New York: Greenwood Press, 1991).

COMPLETE WORKS EDITION

Souborné vydání děl Antonína Dvořáka = Gesamtausgabe der Werke Antonín Dvořáks = Complete edition of Antonín Dvořák's works = Edition complete des oeuvres d'Antonín Dvořák. Edited by O. Sourek et al. Prague, Czechoslovakia: Artia, 1955– . Abbreviated in *Grove Music Online* as [AD].

ELGAR, SIR EDWARD

NON-THEMATIC CATALOGS

Craggs, Stewart. "Catalogue raisonné." In *Edward Elgar: A Source Book,* 35–106. Aldershot, England: Scolar Press, 1995.

Kent, Christopher. "Elgar's Compositions 1866–1933." In *Edward Elgar: A Guide to Research,* 1–368. Composer Resource Manuals 37. New York: Garland Publishing 1993.

COMPLETE WORKS EDITION

The Elgar Complete Edition. London: Novello 1981–93; continued as *Elgar Society Edition.* London: Elgar Society, 2002– . Abbreviated in *Grove Music Online* as [E]. For a brief history of the edition and its current status see http://www.elgar.org/9welcome .htm.

RELATED SOURCES

Anderson, Robert. *Elgar in Manuscript.* Portland, OR: Amadeus Press, 1990.

Kent, Christopher. "Edward Elgar, a Composer at Work: A Study of His Creative Processes as Seen Through His Sketches and Proof Corrections." Ph.D. diss., University of London, 1978.

Edward Elgar Society and The Elgar Foundation. http://www.elgar.org/welcome.htm.

FAURÉ, GABRIEL

"Gabriel Fauré Catalog of Works" projected for 2009.

Oeuvres Complètes. Kassel: Bärenreiter, 2009– .

NON-THEMATIC WORKS LISTS

Nectoux, Jean-Michel. *Gabriel Fauré: Les voix du clair-obscur.* Paris: Flammarion, 1990.

_____. *Gabriel Fauré: A Musical Life.* Translated by Roger Nichols. Cambridge: Cambridge University Press, 1991.

Phillips, Edward R. "Works." In *Gabriel Fauré: A Guide to Research,* 7–53. Composer Resource Manuals 49. New York: Garland Publishing, 2000.

FIELD, JOHN

Hopkinson, Cecil. *A Bibliographical Thematic Catalogue of the Works of John Field, 1782–1837.* London: Author, 1961.

FROBERGER, JOHANN JACOB

COMPLETE WORKS EDITION

Neue Ausgabe sämtlicher Clavier- und Orgelwerke (New edition of the complete keyboard and organ works). Edited by Siegbert Rampe. Kassel: Bärenreiter, 1993– .

GABRIELI, ANDREA

COMPLETE WORKS EDITION

Edizione nazionale delle opere di Andrea Gabrieli [1533]–1585. Edited by Denis Arnold and David Bryant. Milan: Ricordi, 1988– . Abbreviated in *Grove Music Online* as [AG].

GABRIELI, GIOVANNI

Charteris, Richard. *Giovanni Gabrieli (ca. 1557–1612): A Thematic Catalogue of His Music with a Guide to the Source Materials and Translations of His Vocal Texts.* Thematic Catalogues 20. Stuyvesant, NY: Pendragon Press, 1996.

Kenton, Egon. *Life and Works of Giovanni Gabrieli.* Musicological Studies and Documents 16. [n.p.]: American Institute of Musicology, 1967. (Includes thematic catalog, pp. 223–51. Charteris has concordance with Kenton catalog, p. 439.)

COMPLETE WORKS EDITION

Opera Omnia. Corpus Mensurabilis Musicae 12. Edited by Denis Arnold (vols. 1–6) and Richard Charteris (vols. 7–12). Rome: American Institute of Musicology, 1956– . Abbreviated in *Grove Music Online* as [A].

GESUALDO, CARLO (PRINCIPE DE VENOSA)

COMPLETE WORKS EDITION

Sämtliche Werke. Edited by Wilhelm Weismann and Glenn E. Watkins. Hamburg: Ugrino Verlag, 1957–67. Abbreviated in *Grove Music Online* as [W].

GLUCK, CHRISTOPH WILLIBALD RITTER VON

Hopkinson, Cecil. *A Bibliography of the Printed Works of C. W. von Gluck, 1714–1787.* 2nd rev. and augmented ed. New York: Broude Bros., 1967.

Wotquenne, Alfred. *Thematisches Verzeichnis der Werke von Chr. W. v. Gluck (1714–1787).* Leipzig, 1904. Reprinted as *Catalogue thématique des œuvres de Chr. W. v. Gluck.* Hildesheim, Germany: Georg Olms Verlag, 1967.

COMPLETE WORKS EDITION

Sämtliche Werke. Rudolf Gerber, gen. ed. Kassel: Bärenreiter, 1951– . Abbreviated in *Grove Music Online* as [G].

GRIEG, EDVARD

Grinde, Kristi, and Øyvind Norheim. *Edvard Grieg Werkverzeichnis.* Frankfurt: Edition Peters, 2007.

Fog, Dan. *Grieg-Katalog: en fortegnelse over Edvard Griegs trykte kompositioner: Verzeichnis der im Druck erschienenen Kompositionen von Edvard Grieg.* Københan: D. Fog, 1980.

Norheim, Øyvind. "The New Thematic Catalogue of Edvard Grieg's Works, and Its Predecessors." *Fontes Artis Musicae* 51, no. 2 (April-June 2004): 257–61.

COMPLETE WORKS EDITION

Samlede verker = Gesamtausgabe = Complete works. Frankfurt: C. F. Peters, 1977–95. Abbreviated in *Grove Music Online* as [GGA].

RELATED SOURCES

Benestad, Finn, and Dag Schjelderup-Ebbe. *Edvard Grieg: The Man and the Artist.* Translated by William H. Halverson and Leland B. Sateren. Lincoln: University of Nebraska Press, 1988.

Grieg Archives, Bergen Public Library, Bergen, Norway. http://www.bergen.folkebibl.no/grieg-samlingen/engelsk/grieg_grieg_eng.html.

Includes all of the composer's autograph manuscripts, letters, and other documents. Grieg and his wife Nina bequeathed their archives to the Bergen Public Library with the intent that they be preserved and accessible to the public. See Steen, Siren. "The Grieg Archives at Bergen Public Library." *Fontes Artis Musicae* 51, no. 2 (April-June 2004): 250–56.

HANDEL, GEORGE FRIDERIC

Eisen, Walter, and Margret Eisen, eds. *Handel-Handbuch.* 4 vols. Kassel: Bärenreiter, 1978–86.

Bd. I. *Lebens-und Schaffendaten* [biographical and creative chronology] Compiled by Siegfried Flesch; *Thematisch-systematisches Verzeichnis Bühnenwerke* [thematic index to stage works] Compiled by Bernd Baselt. Kassel: Bärenreiter, 1979.

Bd. II. *Thematisch-systematisches Verzeichnis: Oratorische Werke, Vocale Kammermusik, Kirchenmusik* [thematic index to oratorios, vocal chamber music and church music] Compiled by Bernd Baselt. Kassel: Bärenreiter, 1984.

Bd. III. *Thematisch-systematisches Verzeichnis: Instrumentalmusik; Pasticci und Fragmente.* Compiled by Bernd Baselt. Kassel: Bärenreiter, 1986.

Bd. IV. *Dokumente zu Leben und Schaften: Auf der Grundlage von Otto Erich Deutsch Handel: A Documentary Biography.* Kassel: Bärenreiter, 1985.

Bell, A. Craig. *Handel: Chronological Thematic Catalog.* Darley: Grian-Aig Press, 1972.
Smith, William C. *Handel: A Descriptive Catalogue of the Early Editions.* 2nd ed. Oxford: Blackwell, 1970. (non-thematic)

RELATED SOURCES

Best, Terence. *Handel Collections and Their History.* New York: Oxford University Press, 1993.
Burrows, Donald, and Martha J. Ronish. *A Catalogue of Handel's Musical Autographs.* New York: Oxford University Press, 1994.
Roberts, John H., ed. *Handel Sources: Materials for the Study of Handel's Borrowing.* 9 vols. New York: Garland Publishing, 1986.

COMPLETE WORKS EDITIONS

Hallische Händel-Ausgabe. Edited by M. Schneider, R. Steglich et al. Kassel: Bärenreiter, 1955– . Abbreviated in *Grove Music Online* as [HHA]. http://www.haendelgesellschaft .haendelhaus.de/
George Friedrich Händels Werke: Ausgabe der Deutschen Händelgesellschaft. Edited by Friedrich Chrysander. Leipzig: Breitkopf & Härtel, 1858–1902. Reprint, Ridgewood, NJ: Gregg Press, 1965. Abbreviated in *Grove Music Online* as [HG]. Available online: http://freebooksource.info/?p=6644
(See Figure 10–3.)

Handel's popularity as a composer may be assessed in part by the number of attempts at publishing complete editions of his works, the first of which was Samuel Arnold's eighteenth-century incomplete edition, published between 1787 and 1797.

FIGURE 10–3   *Grove Music Online,* G. F. Handel Works list

Trio sonatas

HWV	Op.	Key	Scoring	Remarks	HG	HHA
386[b]	2 no.1	b	fl/vn, vn, bc	HG, op.2 no.1*b*; most MSS have transposed version in c, not indentical with ?orig. version in c (see HWV386[a] below)	xxvii, 92	iv/10/1/, 3
387	2 no.2	g	2 vn, bc	in *GB-Mp* copy: 'Compos'd at the Age of 14'	xxvii, 105	iv/10/1, 15
388	2 no.3	B♭	2 vn, bc	HG, op.2 no.4; related to ov. to Esther and org conc. op.4 no.2	xxvii, 115	iv/10/1, 23
389	2 no.4	F	fl/rec/vn, vn, bc	HG, op.2 no.5; related to ovs. to Chandos anthems O sing unto the Lord, O come let us sing, and ov. to Parnasso in festa	xxvii, 122	iv/10/1, 35
390[a]	2 no.5	g	2 vn, bc	HG, op.2 no.6; related to org conc. op.4 no.3; arr. with org continuo (HWV 390[b]; HG xlviii, 118) unlikely to be Handel's	xxvii, 128	iv/10/1, 45
391	2 no.6	g	2 vn, bc	HG, op.2 no.7	xxvii, 136	iv/10/1, 61
396	5 no.1	A	2 vn, bc	movts from ov. to Chandos anthem I will magnify and Arianna ballets, with 2 new movts	xxvii, 156	iv/10/2, 3
397	5 no.2	D	2 vn, bc	movts from ov. to Chandos anthem O be joyful and Ariodante ballets; for movts 6–7 see Marches in 'Music for wind ensembles'	xxvii, 156	iv/10/2, 11
398	5 no.3	e	2 vn, bc	movts from ov. to Chandos anthem As pants the hart, Terpsicore/Il pastor fido and Ariodante ballets, and Ezio, with new movt	xxvii, 166	iv/10/2, 19
399	5 no.4	G	2 vn, bc	movts from ovs. to Athalia and Parnasso in festa, Il pastor fido, 1734, and Alcina ballets	xxvii, 172	iv/10/2, 29
400	5 no.5	g	2 vn, bc	movts from Terpsicore, and new movts arr. from Tamerlano, Athalia and 2 kbd fugues (see 'Keyboard', 83, 163); movt 6 ? not new	xxvii, 182	iv/10/2, 49
401	5 no.6	F	2 vn, bc	2 movts based on no.15; pubd version has orig. finale replaced by minuet	xxvii, 188	iv/10/2, 63
402	5 no.7	B♭	2 vn, bc	movts from ovs. to Chandos anthems Let God arise and O sing unto the Lord, Oreste ballets and Terpsicore	xxvii, 195	iv/10/2, 75
386[a]	—	c	rec/fl, vn, bc	HG, op.2 no.1*a*; ?orig. version of op.2 no.1	xxvii, 99	iv/10/1, 113
392	—	F	2 vn, bc	*c*1707–9; HG, op.2 no.3; *D-Dl*; see op.5 no.6	xxvii, 109	iv/10/1, 73
393	—	g	2 vn, bc	HG, op.2 no.8; *Dl*; authenticity uncertain	xxvii, 142	iv/10/1, 85
394	—	E	2 vn, bc	HG, op.2 no.9; *Dl*; authenticity doubtful	xxvii, 148	iv/10/1, 99
395	—	e	2 fl, bc	ed. F. Nagel (Mainz, 1971); authenticity uncertain	—	iv/19, 68

(Arnold's edition also holds the distinction of being the first composer complete works edition.) The Handel Society of London produced another incomplete edition (16 volumes) between 1844 and 1858. The eminent German musicologist Friedrich Chrysander did succeed in producing a "complete" edition, issuing 94 volumes of the *George Friedrich Handels Werke* between 1858 and 1902. While admirable in its achievement, twentieth-century scholars saw the need to update Chrysander's edition and established the *Hallische Handel-Ausgabe* (named for Handel's birthplace in Halle) in 1955. The editorial policies of this edition have evolved over the years, and volumes issued since 1980 are considered to be more reliable. For further information, see

Hicks, Anthony. "George Frideric Handel: 24. Sources and Editions." In *Grove Music Online.* Edited by L. Macy. www.grovemusic.com.

Parker, Mary Ann. "Work-Lists, Collected Editions, and Catalogues." In *G.F. Handel: A Guide to Research,* 141–43. 2nd ed. Routledge Music Bibliogaphies. New York: Routledge, 2005.

HAYDN, JOSEPH

Hoboken, Anthony van. *Joseph Haydn: thematisch-bibliographisches Werkverzeichnis.* 3 vols. Mainz: B. Schott's Söhne [1957–78].

Bd. 1. Instrumentalwerke (1957)
Bd. 2. Vokalwerke (1971)
Bd. 3. Register, Addenda und Corrigenda (1978)

Hoboken's three-volume catalog of Haydn's works organizes the composer's vast and complex compositional output in a classified manner, with works arranged within 32 sections, or "Gruppen," identified by Roman numerals:

    I. Symphonies
   II. Divertimentos for four or more instruments
  III. String quartets
  IV. Divertimentos for three instruments
   V. String trios
  VI. Duos for various instruments
 VII. Concertos:
     VIIa. Violin
     VIIb. Cello
     VIIc. Double bass
     VIId. Horn
     VIIe. Trumpet
     VIIf. Flute
     VIIg. Oboe
VIII. Marches
  IX. Dances
   X. Works for various instruments with baryton
  XI. Trios for baryton, viola (or violin) and cello
 XII. Duos for baryton with or without bass

XIII. Concertos for baryton
XIV. Divertimentos for keyboard with three or more instruments
XV. Keyboard trios
XVI. Keyboard sonatas
XVII. Keyboard pieces
XVIII. Keyboard concertos
XIX. Pieces for flute clock
XX/1 Seven Last Words of Christ (instrumental version)
XX/2 Seven Last Words of Christ (vocal version)
XXI. Oratorios
XXII. Masses
XXIII. Small sacred works
XXIV. Cantatas
XXV. Multi-voice songs
XXVI. Songs with keyboard acc.
XXVII. Canons
XXVIII. Operas
XXIX. Marionette operas and German operas
XXX. Incidental music
XXXI. Arrangements of Scottish and Welsh folksongs
XXXII. Pasticcios

Note: the abbreviations used in Hoboken are found in a Supplement inserted in the pockets of Vols. 1 and 2 and printed within the text of Vol. 3, pp. 237–53.

WHO WAS HOBOKEN?

Anthony van Hoboken (1887–1983) was a Dutch collector and bibliographer. He amassed a collection of more than 5,000 first editions, including works by Bach, Beethoven, Brahms, Chopin, Gluck, Handel, Haydn, Liszt, Mendelssohn, Schubert, Schumann, and Weber. This collection is now at the Austrian National Library, documented in the 16-volume printed catalog set *Katalog der Sammlung Anthony van Hoboken in der Musiksammlung der Österreichischen Nationalbibliothek: musikalische Erst- und Frühdrucke* (Tutzing: H. Schneider, 1982–98; see p. 16). Hoboken's establishment of the *Photogrammarchiv* in 1927 at the Austrian National Library, with photocopies of major autograph manuscripts proved to be quite prescient, as many of the sources he preserved were lost or displaced during World War II.

Fuchs, Aloys. *Thematisches Verzeichnis der sämtlichen Kompositionen von Joseph Haydn.* Facsimile-reprint edited by Richard Schaal. Quellenkataloge zur Musikgeschichte 2. Wilhelmshaven: Heinrichshofen's Verlag, 1968.

Collector and musicologist Aloys Fuchs (1799–1853) was one of the earliest compilers of thematic catalogs, none of which were published. In addition to Haydn, he compiled catalogs of works of Beethoven, Corelli, Gluck, Handel, and Vivaldi. These sources have served as useful documentation for later musicologists.

COMPLETE WORKS EDITIONS

Werke. Edited by Jens Peter Larsen (1958–61), Georg Feder (1962–90), and others (1990–). 78 vols. Munich: Henle, 1958– . Abbreviated in *Grove Music Online* as [HW]. See Web site of Haydn Institut for information: http://www.haydn-institut.de/index .html.

Joseph Haydns Werke. Edited by Eusebius Mandyczewski et al. 10 vols. Leipzig: Breitkopf & Härtel, 1907–33. Abbreviated in *Grove Music Online* as [M]. In 1950, this edition was continued under the editorship of Jens Peter Larsen, 4 vols., with title *Joseph Haydn: Kritische Gesamtausgabe* (Boston, Leipzig, and Vienna: Breitkopf & Härtel, 1950–51). Abbreviated in *Grove Music Online* as [L].

Grove Music Online works list also lists location of works in the following series: *Kritische Ausgabe sämtlicher Symphonien*, i–xii. Edited by H. C. Robbins Landon. Philharmonia ser. Vienna: Universal Edition, 1965–68. Abbreviated in *Grove Music Online* as [P].

Diletto musicale. Edited by H. C. Robbins Landon. Vienna: Doblinger, 1959– . Abbreviated in *Grove Music Online* as [D].

AUTHENTICATION SYMBOLS

The authentication symbols used in the *Grove Music Online* work list refer to the sources used to verify or authenticate individual works. This is especially important in the case of Haydn given the many arrangements of his works and the confusion surrounding authorship in some cases. Haydn made the task simpler for his bibligraphers by his own careful accounting of his works in several thematic catalogs. See

Jens Peter Larsen. *Three Haydn catalogues = Drei Haydn Kataloge*. 2nd facsim. Edited and with a new survey of Haydn's oeuvre. New York: Pendragon Press, 1979.

Includes facsimile reproductions of the three catalogues compiled by Haydn or his associates to organize his output: *Entwurf Katalog* (or "draft" catalog; abbreviated in *Grove Music Online* as [EK]; *Kees-Katalog;* and *Haydn-Verzeichnis* (1805), abbreviated in *Grove Music Online* as [HV]. The latter was compiled by Johann Elssler, one of Haydn's copyists, under the composer's supervision. It includes works written by the composer from ages 18 to 73, "as far as he was able to remember them"[21]

Some of these catalogs are referenced in the *Grove Music Online* works list under "Authentication Symbols."

The entry on "Catalogues" in David Wyn Jones's *Haydn*. Oxford Composer Companions. (New York: Oxford University Press, 2002) (see p. 106) provides an excellent overview of the thematic and non-thematic catalogs of the composer's works. As Jones points out, Hoboken includes detailed information on Haydn first editions (including title page transcriptions) but does not provide information on library locations for those editions. Jones recommends using RISM A/I, vols. 4 and 12 (Addenda and Corrigenda) to locate the editions refrenced in the catalog.

LOCATING HAYDN WORKS

Performers typically refer to Haydn's string quartets by opus number rather than Hoboken number, which can make it difficult to locate specific works. For example, Haydn's String Quartet op. 76, no. 1 is Hoboken Group III, no. 75. Figure 10–4 is the library catalog entry for this work.

FIGURE 10–4 Bibliographic record for Haydn. String Quartet, op. 76, no. 1.

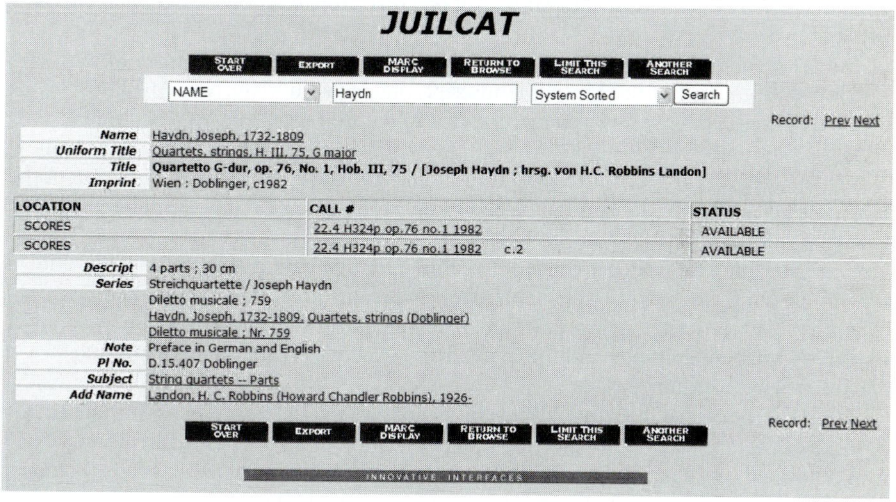

Source: The Juilliard School Library.

RELATED SOURCES

Bryant, Stephen C., and Gary M. Chapman. *Melodic Index to Haydn's Instrumental Music: A Thematic Locator for Anthony van Hoboken's Thematisch-bibliographisches Werkverzeichnis, volumes I & III.* New York: Pendragon Press, 1982.

Landon, H. C. Robbins. *Haydn: Chronicle and Works.* 5 vols. Bloomington: Indiana University Press, 1976–80.

HOLST, GUSTAV

Holst, Imogen. *A Thematic Catalogue of Gustav Holst's Music.* London: Faber Music Ltd., 1974.

HUMMEL, JOHANN NEPOMUK

Zimmerschied, Dieter. *Thematisches Verzeichnis der Werke von Johann Nepomuk Hummel.* Hofheim am Taunus: F. Hofmeister, 1971.

Sachs, Joel. "A Checklist of the Works of Johann Nepomuk Hummel." *Notes* 30, no. 4 (Sept. 1974): 732–54. Non-thematic composer catalog; see also Sachs's review of Zimmerschied in *Musical Times,* 114, no. 1567 (Sept. 1973): 898–99, and Sachs's article on Hummel in *Grove Music Online.*
No complete works edition. Piano works available in
The Complete Works for Piano: A Six-Volume Collection of Reprints and Facsimiles. Edited by Joel Sachs. New York: Garland Publishing, 1989–1990.

IVES, CHARLES

Sinclair, James B. *A Descriptive Catalogue of the Music of Charles Ives.* New Haven, CT: Yale University Press, 1999.
The predecessor for Sinclair's catalog was John Kirkpatrick's "Temporary Mimeographed Catalogue of the Music Manuscripts and Related Materials of Charles Edward Ives, 1874–1954: Given by Mrs. Ives to the Library of the Yale School of Music, September 1955" (1960). This catalog was based on Kirkpatrick's study of the Ives manuscripts at Yale University Library in New Haven, CT. At the initiation of the Charles Ives Society, the late Paul Echols undertook a new catalog, completed by James Sinclair after Echols's death in 1994.
Sinclair's catalog is arranged by genre and then alphabetically by work title within each genre category (as he explains in his introduction, it would be near impossible to attempt a chronological arrangement of Ives's works, given the composer's working methods and the manner in which his extant manuscripts and sketches were organized).
The works list in *Grove Music Online* follows the same format as Sinclair's catalog. Both sources include information on publication in the Ives critical edition, which is published by Peer Southern under the auspices of the Charles Ives Society. Volumes in this edition are published somewhat sporadically and take the form of "performing editions with brief critical commentary"; they tend to lack the extensive critical commentaries found in other critical editions.
An online edition of Sinclair's catalog (with updates) is available on the Web site of the Charles Ives Society: http://www.charlesives.org/.

JANÁČEK, LEOŠ

Simeone, Nigel, John Tyrrell, and Alena Němcová. *Janacek's Works: A Catalogue of the Music and Writings of Leoš Janáček.* New York: Oxford University Press, 1997. Abbreviated in *Grove Music Online* as [JW].

COMPLETE WORKS EDITION

Souborné kritické vydání děl Leoše Janáček = Kritische Gesamtausgabe der Werke von Leoš Janáček = Complete Critical Edition of the Works of Leoš Janáček. Praha: Supraphon, 1978– . Abbreviated in *Grove Music Online* as [SKV].
See also http://www.leos-janacek.org.

JOSQUIN DES PREZ

Metzger, Heinz-Klaus, and Rainer Riehn. *Josquin des Prez: Werkverzeichnis.* München: Edition Text + Kritik, 1982.

Sherr, Richard, ed. *The Josquin Companion.* New York: Oxford University Press, 2000. Abbreviated in *Grove Music Online* as [JC].
  Collection of essays by major Josquin scholars. It includes Sherr's "Chronology of Josquin's Life and Career"; Appendices with List of Works and Discography, both by Peter Urquart; as well as other essays that inform on Josquin's musical compositions.

COMPLETE WORKS EDITIONS

New Josquin Edition. Utrecht: Vereniging voor Nederlandse Muziekgeschiedenis, 1987– . Abbreviated in *Grove Music Online* as [NJE].

Werken van Josquin des Près. Edited by Albert Smijers et al. Amsterdam: G. Alsbach, 1921–69. See additional notes at head of *Grove Music Online* works list.

LALANDE, MICHEL-RICHARD DE

Sawkins, Lionel. *A Thematic Catalogue of the Works of Michel-Richard de Lalande (1657–1726).* New York: Oxford University Press, 2005. Abbreviated in *Grove Music Online* as [S].

LASSO, ORLANDO DI

COMPLETE WORKS EDITIONS

Sämtliche Werke. Zweite, nachden Quellen revidierte Auflage. Edited by Horst Leuchtmann. Wiesbaden: Breitkopf & Härtel, 1968– . Abbreviated in *Grove Music Online* as [L].

Sämtliche Werke. Neue Reihe. Edited by Siegfried Hermelink et al. Kassel: Bärenreiter, 1956–96. Abbreviated in *Grove Music Online* as [H].

Sämtliche Werke. Herausgegeben von Franz Xavier Haberl & Adolf Sandberger. 21 vols. Leipzig: Breitkopf & Härtel, 1894–1927. Abbreviated in *Grove Music Online* as [S].

The Complete Motets. Edited by Peter Berquist. 21 vols. and supplement. Recent Researches in the Music of the Renaissance, 102, 103, 105, 109–12, 114, 115, 117, 118, 120, 124, 128, 130–33, 141, 147, 148, 148S. Madison, WI: A-R Editions, 1995–2006.

RELATED SOURCES

Leuchtmann, Hans, and Bernhold Schmid. *Orlando di Lasso: seine Werke in zeitgenössischen Drucken, 1555–1687. Orlando di Lasso: Sämtliche Werke: Supplement.* Kassel: Bärenreiter, 2001.

Berquist, Peter, ed. *Orlando di Lasso Studies.* New York: Cambridge University Press, 1999.

Erb, James. "Works of Orlando di Lasso." In *Orlando di Lasso: A Guide to Research,* 33–152. Composer Resource Manuals 25. New York: Garland Publishing, 1990. (Includes discussion and listing of these various editions, along with a title index.)

LEHÁR, FRANZ

Franz Lehár: thematischer Index. London: Glocken Verlag, 1985.
Compiled by Glocken Verlag, Lehár's primary publisher, in honor of their 50th anniversary. Classified arrangement of Lehár's works; includes alphabetical notation index and title index.

LISZT, FRANZ

Charnin Mueller, Rena, and Maria Eckhardt. *Thematisches Verzeichnis der Werke Franz Liszts.* (Munich, in preparation). Abbreviated in *Grove Music Online* as [LW]. The *Grove Music Online* Liszt works list uses the arrangement of works in the forthcoming thematic catalog; each category has a letter designation, with individual works arranged chronologically within those categories. While the 1980 edition of *New Grove* Liszt works list by Humphrey Searle (revised by Sharon Winkelhofer) included Liszt's many arrangements of other composers' works in separate categories, LW includes these works alongside Liszt's original works for piano solo.

Howard, Leslie, and Michael Short. *Franz Liszt (1811–1886): A Thematic Catalog of His Works.* Edited by Michael Saffle. 2 vols. Franz Liszt Study Series 12. Hillsdale, NY: Pendragon Press, 2007.

Chiappari, Luciano. *Liszt: 'Excelsior', op.1400: Catalogo delle composizioni cronologico, tematico, alfabetico.* Pisa: Pacini, 1996. Abbreviated in *Grove Music Online* as [C].

Raabe, Peter. *Franz Liszt: Leben und Schaffen.* 2 vols. Stuttgart: Cotta, 1931. 2nd ed., rev., F. Raabe. Tutzing: Schneider, 1968. Abbreviated in *Grove Music Online* as [R]; non-thematic composer catalog.

Searle, Humphrey. *The Music of Liszt.* London: William & Norgate, 1954. Reprint, New York: Dover, 1966.

_____. "Liszt, Franz." *In New Grove Dictionary of Music and Musicians.* Edited by Stanley Sadie. 6th ed. London: Macmillan Publishers, 1980; Revised by Sharon Winkelhofer in *The New Grove Early Romantic Masters 1: Chopin, Schumann, Liszt* (New York: W. W. Norton, 1985.) Abbreviated in *Grove Music Online* as [S]; non-thematic composer catalog.

Thematisches Verzeichnis der Werke, bearbeitungen und transcriptionen von F. Liszt. Leipzig: Breitkopf & Härtel, 1877.

Cataloging of Liszt's works is enormously complicated, due in part to the composer's habit of continuous revision, as well as to the issues surrounding publication of his works. The new thematic catalogs endeavor to create new order and enhanced bibliographical control of his compositional output. For futher information, see

Saffle, Michael. "Musical Catalogs and Related Studies." In *Franz Liszt: A Guide to Research*, 45–52. 2nd ed. Routledge Music Bibliograpahies. New York: Routledge, 2004.

Short, Michael, and Michael Saffle. "Compiling Lis(z)ts: Cataloging the Composer's Works and the *New Grove 2* Works List." *Journal of Musicological Research* 21, no. 3 (July–Sept. 2002): 233–62.

RELATED SOURCES

Auman, Elizabeth A., and Raymond A. White, comps. *The Music Manuscripts, First Editions, and Correspondence of Franz Liszt (1811–1886) in the Collections of the Music Division, Library of Congress.* Washington, DC: The Division, 1991.

Eckhardt, Maria. "A New Thematic Catalogue of Liszt's Compositions." *Journal of the American Liszt Society* 27 (1990): 53–57.

_____. *Franz Liszt's Music Manuscripts in the National Széchényi Library, Budapest.* Translated by Erzsébet Mészáros; revised by Rena Mueller. Budapest: Akadémiai Kiadó; Stuyvesant, NY: Pendragon Press, 1986.

Short, Michael, "A New Liszt Catalogue." In *Liszt and His World: Proceedings of the International Liszt Conference Held at Virginia Polytechic Institute and State University 20–23 May 1993,* edited by Michael Saffle, 75–100. Stuyvesant, NY: Pendragon Press, 1998. (See p. 76, chronological listing of Liszt catalogs.)

LULLY, JEAN-BAPTISTE

Schneider, Herbert. *Chronologisch-thematisches Verzeichnis sämtlicher Werke von Jean-Baptiste Lully.* Mainzer Studien zur Musikwissenschaft 14. Tutzing: Hans Schneider, 1991.

Gustafson, Bruce, and Matthew Leshinskie. *A Thematic Locator for the Works of Jean-Baptiste Lully Coordinated with Herbert Schneider's Chronologisch-thematisches Verzeichnis sämtlicher Werke von Jean-Baptiste Lully (LWV).* New York: Performers' Editions, 1989.

COMPLETE WORKS EDITIONS

Oeuvres complètes. Edited by Jérôme de la Gorce and Herbert Schneider. Musica Gallica. Hildesheim: G. Olms, 2001– .

Oeuvres complètes. Edited by Henry Prunières. Paris: Éditions de la Revue musicale, 1930–39. Abbreviated in *Grove Music Online* as [P]; other selected editions listed at head of *Grove Music Online* works list.

MAHLER, GUSTAV

Banks, Paul. *The Music of Gustav Mahler: A Catalogue of Manuscript and Printed Sources.* Available on-line: http://www.cph.rcm.ac.uk/MahlerCat/pages/index.htm

The most detailed non-thematic works lists are found in Henri-Louis de la Grange, *Gustav Mahler: Vol. 2: Vienna: The Years of Challenge, 1897–1904* (New York: Oxford University Press, 1995), 721–29, *Gustav Mahler: Vol. 3: Vienna: Triumph and Disillusion, 1904–1907* (New York: Oxford University Press, 1999), 799–807, and *Gustav Mahler: Vol. 4: A New Life Cut Short, 1907–1911* (New York: Oxford University Press, 2008), 1279–1574. These lists include location of autograph sources, as well as information on editions, and first performances.

Other catalogs are listed in the Filler, Namenwirth, and Vondenhoff bibliographies noted in Chapter 4 (p. 109).

COMPLETE WORKS EDITION

Sämtliche Werke: kritische Gesamtausgabe. Edited by the Internationale Gustav Mahler Gesellschaft. Vienna: Universal Edition, 1960– . Abbreviated in *Grove Music Online* as [MW].

RELATED SOURCES

Weiss, Günther. *Gustav Mahler: Briefe und Musikautographen aus den Moldenhauer-Archiven in der Bayerischen Staatsbibliothek.* Berlin: Kulturstiftung der Länder, 2003.

MARCELLO (BENEDETTO AND ALESSANDRO)

Selfridge-Field, Eleanor. *The Works of Benedetto and Alessandro Marcello: A Thematic Catalog with Commentary on Composers, Repertory, and Sources.* New York: Oxford University Press, 1990.

MARTINŮ, BOHUSLAV

Halbreich, Harry. *Bohuslav Martinů: Werkverzeichnis und Biographie.* 2nd ed. Mainz: Schott, 2005. Abbreviated in *Grove Music Online* as [H].
Online works catalog: http://www.martinů.cz/katalog/.
Cervinková, Blanka, et al. *Bohuslav Martinů, 8.12.1890–28.8.1959: Bibliograficky Katalog = Bibliographical Catalogue.* Praha: Panton, 1990.
Bohuslav Martinů Complete Edition. Prague: Bohuslav Martinů; Institution, 2009– . http://www.martinů.cz/english/novinky.php.

MENDELSSOHN-BARTHOLDY, FELIX

Wehner, Ralf. *Felix Mendelssohn Bartholdy, Thematisch-systematisches Verzeichnis der musikalischen Werke (MWV), Studien-Ausgabe.* Leipziger Ausgabe der Werke von Felix Mendelssohn Bartholdy (Leipzig Edition of the Works of Felix Mendelssohn Bartholdy), Series XIII, Vol. 1A. Wiesbaden: Breitkopf & Härtel, 2009 (forthcoming)
Cooper, John Michael. "Mendelssohn's Works: Prolegomenon to a Comprehensive Inventory." In *The Mendelssohn Companion*, edited by Douglass Seaton, 701–85. Westport, CT: Greenwood Press, 2001.
  As Cooper points out in the introduction to his list (pg. 701), the lack of a modern thematic catalog of Mendelssohn's works has made it much more difficult for scholars and performers to research manuscript sources and publication history for individual works. See also
    Cooper, John Michael. "Principal Editions, Facsimiles, and Publications of Mendelssohn's Works." In *Felix Mendelssohn Bartholdy: A Guide to Research*, 223–77. Composer Resource Manuals 54. New York: Routledge, 2001.
Thematischer Verzeichnis der im Druck erschienenen Compositionen von Felix Mendelssohn. 3rd ed. Leipzig: Breitkopf & Härtel, 1882. Reprint, Leipzig: Martin Sändig, 1973.

COMPLETE WORKS EDITIONS

Leipziger Ausgabe der Werke von Felix Mendelssohn Bartholdy. Herausgegeben von der Sächsische Akademie der Wissenschaften zu Leipzig: Breitkopf & Härtel, 1997– . Abbreviated in *Grove Music Online* as [L2]. https://www.breitkopf.com/downloads/kataloge/pdf_en/29_MendelssohnGA.pdf.

Leipziger Ausgabe der Werke Feliz Mendelssohn Bartholdys. Herausgegeben von der Internationale Felix-Mendelssohn-Gesellschaft. Leipzig: Deutscher Verlag für Musik, 1960–77. Abbreviated in *Grove Music Online* as [L1].

Felix Mendelssohn Bartholdy's Werke: kritisch durchgesehene Ausgabe. Edited by Julius Rietz. Leipzig: Breitkopf & Härtel, 1874–77. Abbreviated in *Grove Music Online* as [R].

RELATED SOURCES

Klein, Hans-Günther. "Verzeichnis de rim Autograph überlieferten Werke Felix Mendelssohn Bartholdy im Besitz der Staatsbibliothek zu Berlin." *Mendelssohn Studien* 10 (1997): 181–215.

MESSIAEN, OLIVIER

Simeone, Nigel. *Olivier Messiaen: A Bibliographical Catalogue of Messiaen's Works: First Editions and First Performances, with Illustrations of the Title Pages, Programmes and Documents.* Musikbibliographische Arbeiten 14. Tutzing: H. Schneider, 1998. (Non-thematic composer catalog.)

MOZART, WOLFGANG AMADEUS

Köchel, Ludwig Ritter von. *Chronologisch-thematisches Verzeichnis sämtlicher Tonwerke Wolfgang Amadé Mozarts.* 6th ed. Wiesbaden: Breitkopf & Härtel, 1964.

First published in 1862, Ludwig Ritter von Köchel's thematic catalog of Mozart's works is considered to be the first "modern" thematic catalog, with its inclusion of features that all other scholarly catalogs have emulated to one degree or another (see introduction to this chapter). As its title indicates, Köchel arranged Mozart's works in chronological order, from K. 1, Andante für Klavier, composed in 1761 when Mozart was five years old, to K. 626, his unfinished Requiem.

Neal Zaslaw's essay on "A Brief History of the Köchel Catalog" explains each of the subsequent revisions to Köchel and the resulting confusion involving numbering; confusion, it is hoped, that will be cleared up by the long–awaited publication of Zaslaw's *Der neue Köchel,* his completely revised new edition.

As Zaslaw explains, the inherent problems in adopting a chronological arrangement arose when scholars after Köchel sought to insert newly discovered works, omit works found to be spurious, or even change positions of works to reflect revised chronology. Significant changes were inserted into the third edition (revised by Alfred Einstein in 1936) and the sixth edition, revised by Franz Giegling, Alexander Weinmann, and Gerd Sievers and published in 1964. The latter (which was reprinted as the seventh edition) is the edition found on most library shelves today.

Zaslaw, Neal. "A Brief History of the Köchel Catalogue" In *Mozart's Symphonies: Context, Performance Practice, Reception,* 558–61. New York: Oxford University Press, 1989.

_____. "Der neue Köchel." *Mozart Society of America Newsletter* 1, no. 1 (Jan. 27, 1997): 4–5; reprinted in Boerner, Steve. *The Mozart Project.* www.mozartproject.org/ essays/zaslaw.html.

Mozart, Wolfgang Amadeus. *Mozart's Thematic Catalogue: A Facsimile, British Library, Stefan Zweig MS 63.* Introduction and transcription by Albi Rosenthal and Alan Tyson. Ithaca, NY: Cornell University Press, 1990. Digital copy from British Library, with sound files: http://www.bl.uk/onlinegallery/themes/music/mozartlge.html.

Mozart began his own thematic catalog in February 1784. He documented incipits of works from his Piano Concerto, K. 449 to his last Cantata, K. 623. The latter was entered on November 15, 1791, just three weeks prior to his death. This beautiful facsimile edition cited above was published for the Mozart bicentennial celebrations in 1991. It reproduces the blank pages at the end of the notebook, in a touching representation of what was lost with the composer's death at the age of 35. The volume also includes essays by Albi Rosenthal on "The History of Mozart's Thematic Catalogue" and by Alan Tyson on "Description of the Manuscript" and "Transcription of Mozart's Entries." (See Figure 10–5.)

FIGURE 10–5 Cover of W. A. Mozart, *Verzeichnüss aller meiner Werke.*

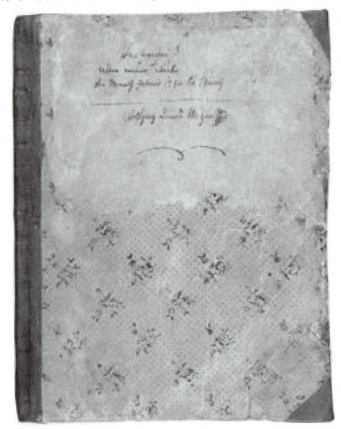

Source: *Mozart's Thematic Catalogue,* The British Library. Used by permission.

Mueller von Asow, E. H., ed. *Verzeichnis aller meiner Werke; und Leopold Mozart, Verzeichnis der Jugendwerke W.A. Mozarts.* Wien: L. Doblinger, 1956.

RELATED SOURCES

Hill, George R., and Murray Gould. *Thematic Locator for Mozart's Works, as Listed in Koechel's Chronologisch-thematisches Verzeichnis.* 6th ed. Hackensack, NJ: J. Boonin, 1970.

    Similar to Bryant and Chapman locator guide for Haydn's works (see p. 277), Hill and Gould provide two separate indexes to Mozart's works: themes arranged by intervallic size and themes arranged alphabetically (after transposition to C).

Haberkamp, Gertraut. *Die Erstdrucke der Werke von Wolfgang Amadeus Mozart: Bibliographie.* 2 vols. Tutzing: Hans Schneider, 1986. (Reproductions of title pages of first editions.)

Konrad, Ulrich. *Mozart: Catalog of His Works.* Translated by J. Bradford Robinson. Kassel: Bärenreiter, 2006.

    Non-thematic catalog. It provides a "systematic overview" of his works with references to locations in new and old complete works editions. Also includes Mozart's "Arrangements of Works by Other Composers; Fragments; Sketches, Studies, Drafts, Varia; and, Manuscript Copies of Works by other Composers." Includes indexes of works by K numbers, K. deest; K. Anhang; K. Anghang A; K. Anhang B; K. Anhang C; Fragments; and, Sketches. The latter are quite helpful for locating works in these categories. The term *K* deest refers to works not found in Köchel.

Zaslaw, Neal, and Fiona Morgan Fein. *The Mozart Repertory: A Guide for Musicians, Programmers, and Researchers.* Ithaca, NY: Cornell University Press, 1991.

    Derived from the database used for the Mozart Bicentennial at Lincoln Center, this handy guide provides quick access to Mozart's works by K. number and by genre. The latter section includes location of work in new and old complete works editions, date and place of composition, and durations.

Zaslaw, Neal, and William Cowdery. *The Compleat Mozart: A Guide to the Musical Works of Wolfgang Amadeus Mozart.* New York: Mozart Bicentennial at Lincoln Center; W. W. Norton, 1990.

    Also prepared in conjunction with the Mozart Bicentennial, *Compleat Mozart* includes program notes (primarily reproduced from other sources) for all of Mozart's works.

ABOUT KÖCHEL

Konrad, Thomas Edmund. *K for Köchel: The Life and Works of Ludwig Ritter von Köchel, Cataloguer of Mozart.* Lanham, MD: Scarecrow Press, 2001.

COMPLETE WORKS EDITIONS

Neue Ausgabe sämtlicher Werke. Edited by the Internationale Stiftung Mozarteum Salzburg. Kassel: Bärenreiter, 1955–2007. Abbreviated in *Grove Music Online* as [NMA].

Available online: *Neue Mozart-Ausgabe/Digital Mozart Edition*.
http://dme.mozarteum.at/DME/nma/start.php?l=2.
Wolfgang Amadeus Mozarts Werke. Edited by Johannes Brahms et al. Leipzig: Breitkopf
& Härtel, 1877–1905; Reprint, New York: Kalmus, 1968. Abbreviated in *Grove Music
Online* as [MW].

ABOUT THE EDITIONS

Berke, Dietrich, and Wolfgang Rehm. *Die Neue Mozart Ausgabe: Texte — Bilder —
Chronik, 1955–2007*. Kassel: Bärenreiter, 2007.
Rehm, Wolfgang. "Collected Editions." In *The Mozart Compendium: A Guide to Mozart's
Life and Music*, edited by H. C. Robbins Landon, 422–28. New York: Schirmer Books,
1990.

MUSSORGSKY, MODEST

No separate thematic catalog.
Reilly, Edward R. *The Music of Mussorgsky: A Guide to the Editions*. New York: The
Musical Newsletter, 1980.

COMPLETE WORKS EDITIONS

Polnoye akademicheskoye sobraniye sochineniy M.P. Musorgskogo [Complete Academic
Collection of Works]. Moscow: Muzyka, 1996– . Abbreviated in *Grove Music Online* as
[ASM].
M.P. Musorgskiy: polnoye sobraniye sochineniy [Complete Collection of Works]. Edited
by P. Lamm with B. Asaf'yev. Moscow: State Music Publishers, 1928–39. Reprint, New
York: Kalmus, 1969. Abbreviated in *Grove Music Online* as [L].

NIELSEN, CARL

Carl-Nielsen-Verzeichnis. (forthcoming).

COMPLETE/CRITICAL EDITION

Vaerker [Works]. Udgivet af Carl Nielsen Udgaven, Det Kongelige Bibliotek. Copenhagen: W. Hansen, 1998– . http://www.ewh.dk/sites/cnu/cnu_en.htm.

RELATED SOURCES

Carl Nielsen Studies. Copenhagen: Royal Library, 2003– . http://www.kb.dk/en/kb/nb/mta/
cnu/studies.html.
Kraabe, Niels. "A Survey of the Written Reception of Carl Nielsen, 1931–2006." *Notes* 64,
no. 1 (Sept. 2007): 43–59.

OBRECHT, JACOB

No separate composer thematic catalog. Works list and commentary in Martin Picker,
Johannes Ockeghem and Jacob Obrecht: A Guide to Research (New York: Garland Publishing, 1988).

COMPLETE WORKS EDITIONS

New Obrecht Edition. Edited by Chris Maas et al. Utrecht: Vereiging voor Nederlandse Muziekgescgiednis, 1983–99. Abbreviated in *Grove Music Online* as [M].
Werken van Jacob Obrecht. Edited by Johannes Wolf. Amsterdam and Leipzig: Alsbach, 1908–1921; Reprint, Farnborough, England: Gregg Press, 1968. Abbreviated in *Grove Music Online* as [W].
Opera Omnia. Edited by Albert Smijers and Marcus van Crevel. Amsterdam: Alsbach, 1953–64. Discountinued (not referenced in *Grove Music Online*). For complete discussion of these editions, see Picker, pp. 54–55.

OCKEGHEM, JOHANNES

No separate composer thematic catalog. Works list and commentary in Martin Picker, *Johannes Ockeghem and Jacob Obrecht: A Guide to Research* (New York: Garland Publishing, 1988).

COMPLETE WORKS EDITIONS

Masses and Mass Sections. Edited by Jaap van Benthem. Utrecht: KoninklijkeVereniging voor Nederlandse Muziekgeschiedenis, 1994– . Abbreviated in *Grove Music Online* as [B].
Johannes Ockeghem: Sämtliche Werke (Messen I–VIII). Edited by Dragan Plamenac. *Publikationen älterer Musik,* Jg.i/2. Leipzig: Breitkopf & Härtel, 1927; various revisions by Plamenac and others; for complete listing see Picker, *Johannes Ockeghem and Jacob Obrecht: A Guide to Research* (New York: Garland Publishing, 1988), 16–17. Abbreviated in *Grove Music Online* as [P].

OFFENBACH, JACQUES

Almeida, Antonio de. "Jacques Offenbach: A Thematic Catalogue of Works." Unpublished.

COMPLETE WORKS EDITION

Keck, Jean-Christophe, ed. *Offenbach Edition Keck.* Berlin: Boosey & Hawkes; Bote & Bock, 1999– .

RELATED SOURCE

Yon, Jean-Claude. *Jacques Offenbach.* Paris: Gallimard, 2000. See review by Andrew Lamb in *Music & Letters* 82, no. 4 (Nov. 2001): 642–44.

PACHELBEL, JOHANN

Perreault, Jean M. *Thematic Catalog of the Musical Works of Johann Pachelbel.* Lanham, MD: Scarecrow Press, 2004.

COMPLETE EDITION

Johann Pachelbel Sämtliche Vokalwerke = The Complete Vocal Works. Kassel: Bärenreiter, 2008– .

PAGANINI, NICCOLO

Moretti, Maria Rosa, and Anna Sorrento. *Catalogo tematico delle musice di Niccolo Paganini.* Genova: Comune di Genova, 1982.

COMPLETE WORKS EDITION

Edizione Nazionale delle Opere di Niccolo Paganini. Rome: Instituto Italiano per la Storia Della Musica, 1976– .

PAISIELLO, GIOVANNI

Robinson, Michael, and Ulrike Hoffman. *Giovanni Paisiello, a Thematic Catalogue of His Music.* 2 vols. Thematic Catalogues 15. Stuyvesant, NY: Pendragon Press, 1991–94.

PALESTRINA, GIOVANNI PIERLUIGI DA

No separate thematic catalog. For discussion of sources and editions, see
Marvin, Clara, "Modern Editions of Palestrina's Music I: Comprehensive Editions." In *Giovanni Pierluigi da Palestrina: A Guide to Research,* 135–188. Composer Resource Manuals 56. New York: Routledge, 2002.
Lockwood, Lewis, Noel O'Regan and Jessie Ann Owens, "Giovanni Pierluigi da Palestrina, 11. Posthumous Reputation." *Grove Music Online.* Edited by L. Macy www .grovemusic.com.

COMPLETE WORKS EDITIONS

Edizione Anastatica delle Fonti Palestriniane. Edited by Lino Bianchi. Rome: Fondazione Giovanni Pierluigi da Palestrina, 1975– .
Le opere complete. Edited by Raffaele Casimiri, Knud Jeppesen, and Lino Bianchi. Rome: Fratelli Scalera, 1939–99. Abbreviated in *Grove Music Online* as [C].
Opera Omnia. Edited by F. X. Haberl et al. Leipzig: Breitkopf & Härtel, 1862–1907. Abbreviated in *Grove Music Online* as [H].

PARTCH, HARRY

McGeary, Thomas. *The Music of Harry Partch: A Descriptive Catalog.* I.S.A.M. Monographs 31. Brooklyn, NY: Institute for Studies in American Music, 1991.

PERGOLESI, GIOVANNI BATTISTA

Paymer, Marvin E. *Giovanni Battista Pergolesi, 1710–1736: A Thematic Catalog of the Opera Omnia with an Appendix Listing Omitted Compositions.* Thematic Catalogues 1. New York: Pendragon Press, 1977.

COMPLETE WORKS EDITION

Giovanni Battista Pergolesi: The Complete Works. Edited by Barry S. Brook et al. New York: Pendragon Press, 1985– .

Pleyel, Ignace

Benton, Rita. *Ignace Pleyel: A Thematic Catalogue of his Compositions.* New York: Pendragon Press, 1977.

Ponchielli, Amilcare

Sirch, Licia. *Catalogo Tematico delle Musiche di Amilcare Ponchielli.* Cremona: Fondazione Claudio Monteverdi, 1989.

Poulenc, Francis

Schmidt, Carl B. *The Music of Francis Poulenc (1899–1963): A Catalogue.* Oxford: Clarendon Press, 1995. Non-thematic catalog.

Prokofiev, Sergei

No separate composer thematic catalog.

COMPLETE WORKS EDITION

Collected Works of Sergei Prokofiev. Melville, NY: Belwin Mills 1979. (Reprint of the edition published by the State Music Publishers, Moscow, 1955–78.) *Grove Music Online* works list does not reference location of works in complete edition.

RELATED SOURCES

The Serge Prokofiev Archive at Goldsmiths College, University of London: http://www
.goldsmiths.ac.uk/departments/music/prokofiev-archive/index.php.
The Serge Prokofiev Foundation: http://www.sprkfv.net/indexin.html.

Puccini, Giacomo

Schickling, Dieter. *Giacomo Puccini: Catalogue of the Works.* Co-author and English translation, Michael Kaye. Kassel: Bärenreiter, 2003.
　　Chronological, non-thematic catalog, with details of manuscripts and editions within each entry; includes concordance of Schickling numbers and Hopkinson numbers.
Hopkinson, Cecil. *A Bibliography of the Works of Giacomo Puccini, 1858–1924.* New York: Broude Brothers, 1968. Focuses primarily on detailed descriptions of editions; manuscript sources and locations listed in Appendix A.
No complete/critical works edition.

RELATED SOURCES

Centro Studi Giacomo Puccini: http://www.puccini.it/.

Purcell, Henry

Zimmerman, Franklin B. *Henry Purcell, 1659–1695: An Analytical Catalogue of His Music.* New York: St. Martin's Press, 1963.

COMPLETE WORKS EDITION

The Works of Henry Purcell. Purcell Society. London: Novello, Ewer & Co., 1878–1965; rev. ed., 1961– . Abbreviated in *Grove Music Online* as [PS].

RELATED SOURCE

Shay, Robert, and Robert Thompson. *Purcell Manuscripts: The Principal Musical Sources.* New York: Cambridge University Press, 2000.

QUANTZ, JOHANN JOACHIM

Augsbach, Horst. *Johann Joachim Quantz, thematisches Verzeichnis der musikalischen Werke: Werkgruppen QV2 und QV3.* Dresden: Sächsisches Landesbibliothek, 1984.

RACHMANINOFF, SERGEI

Threlfall, Robert, and Geoffrey Norris. *A Catalogue of the Compositions of S. Rachmaninoff.* London: Scolar Press, 1982.
  Non-thematic composer catalog. Provides details of autograph score, publication, first performance information, and other notes.

COMPLETE WORKS EDITION

Critical Edition of the Complete Works. Moscow: Russian Music Publishing, 2005– . Information on earlier Rachmaninoff editions is provided in Threlfall under "Rachmaninoff's Publishers," pp. 19–24.

RAMEAU, JEAN-PHILIPPE

Bouissou, Sylvie, and Denis Herlin. *Jean-Philippe Rameau, catalogue thématique des oeuvres musicales.* Tome 1: Musique instrumentale. Musique vocale religieuse et profane. Tome 2: Livrets. Paris: CNRS Editions: Bibliothèque nationale de France, 2003. Collection Sciences de la musique. Série Références. Opera omnia de Rameau; OOR VI.1/2.

COMPLETE WORKS EDITIONS

Opera omnia. Edited by Sylvie Bouissou et al. Paris: Billaudot, 1996– . Abbreviated in *Grove Music Online* as [OOR].
Oeuvres complètes. Edited by Camille Saint-Saëns et al. Paris: Durand et fils, 1895–1924. (Incomplete) Abbreviated in *Grove Music Online* as [OC].
Grove Music Online also references the following editions:
Pièces de clavecin. 4th ed. Edited by Erwin R. Jacobi. Kassel: Bärenreiter, 1972. Abbreviated in *Grove Music Online* as [Jc].
Pièces de clavecin. Edited by Kenneth Gilbert. Paris: Heugel, 1979– . Abbreviated in *Grove Music Online* as [G].
The Complete Theoretical Writings of Jean-Philippe Rameau. Edited by Erwin R. Jacobi, American Institute of Musicology. Miscellanea, 3. [n.p]: American Institute of Musicology, 1967–72. Abbreviated in *Grove Music Online* as [Jw].

RAVEL, MAURICE

Catalogue de l'oeuvre de Maurice Ravel. Paris: Fondation Maurice Ravel, 1954.
Marnat, Marcel. *Maurice Ravel.* Paris: Fayard, 1986.
Orenstein, Arbie. *Ravel: Man and Musician.* New York: Columbia University Press, 1975.
  Reprint, New York: Dover Publications, 1991.
Non-thematic composer catalogs; see descriptions of each source in
Zank, Stephen. *Maurice Ravel: A Guide to Research.* Routledge Music Bibliographies.
  New York: Routledge, 2005.

REGER, MAX

Stein, Fritz. *Thematisches Verzeichnis der im Druck erschienenen Werke von Max Reger.*
  Leipzig: Breitkopf & Härtel, 1934, 1953.

COMPLETE WORKS EDITION

Sämtliche Werke. Edited by Max-Reger-Institut. Wiesbaden: Breitkopf & Härtel, 1954–68.
  Abbreviated in *Grove Music Online* as [R].

REICHA, ANTON

Sotolova, Olga. *Antonín Rejcha: A Biography and Thematic Catalog.* Praha: Supraphon,
  1990.

RIMSKY-KORSAKOV, NICOLAY

No separate thematic catalog.

COMPLETE WORKS EDITION

N. Rimsky-Korsakov: Polnoye sobraniye sochineniy [Collected works]. Edited by A. Rimsky-
  Korsakov et al. (Moscow: Gosudarstvennoe Muzykal'noe Izdalel'stvo, 1946–70); Reprint,
  New York: Belwin Mills, 1981–82. Abbreviated in *Grove Music Online* as [RK].

Also important for the study of Rimsky-Korsakov are editions of his collected correspondence and literary works. See listings in *Grove Music Online* bibliography and Gerald R. Seaman, *Nikolai Andreevich Rimsky-Korsakov: A Guide
to Research* (New York: Garland Publishing, 1988).

ROSETTI, ANTONIO (ANTON RÖSLER)

Murray, Sterling E. *Antonio Rosetti (Anton Rösler) ca. 1750–1972: A Thematic Catalog.*
  Warren, MI: Harmonie Park Press, 1996.

ROSSINI, GIOACCHINO

Gossett, Philip. "Catalogo delle opera." In *Gioacchino Rossini,* edited by Luigi Rognoni,
  440–503. Rev. ed. Turin: Einaudi, 1977. Non-thematic catalog.

_____ "The Rossini Thematic Catalog: When Does Bibliographical Access Become Bibliographical Excess?" *Music Reference Services Quarterly* 2, nos. 3–4 (1993): 271–80.

COMPLETE WORKS EDITIONS

Edizione critica delle opere di Gioacchino Rossini. Edited by Bruno Cagli, Philip Gossett, and Alberto Zedda. Pesaro: Fondazione Rossini, 1979–2005; continued by Kassel: Bärenreiter, 2007– . Abbreviated in *Grove Music Online* as [EC].
Quaderni rossiniani. Edited by Fondazione Rossini. Pesaro: Fondazione Rossini, 1954–76. Abbreviated in *Grove Music Online* as [QR].

RELATED SOURCES

Web site of Foundazione Rossini: http://www.fondazionerossini.org/index.htm.
Lettere e documenti. Edited by Bruno Cagli and Sergio Ragni. Pesaro: Fondazione Rossini Pesaro, 1992– .
Tutti I libretti di Rossini. Edited by Marco Beghelli and Nicola Gallino. Milan: Garzanti, 1991.

ROUSSEL, ALBERT

Labelle, Nicole. *Catalogue Raisonné de L'Oeuvre d'Albert Roussel.* Louvain-la-Neuve: Département d'archéologie et d'histoire de l'art, Collège Érasme, 1992.

SAINT-SAËNS, CAMILLE

Ratner, Sabina Teller. *Camille Saint-Saëns, 1835–1921: A Thematic Catalogue of His Complete Works. Vol. I: The Instrumental Works.* Oxford: Oxford University Press, 2002– .

SALIERI, ANTONIO

Parodi, Elena Biggi. *Catalogo Thematico delle Composizioni Teatrali di Antonio Salieri: Gli Autografi.* Lucca: Liberia Musicale Italiana, 2005.

SAMMARTINI, GIOVANNI BATTISTA

Jenkins, Newell, and Bathia Churgin. *Thematic Catalog of the Works of Giovanni Battista Sammartini: Orchestral and Vocal Music.* Cambridge, MA: Published for the American Musicological Society by Harvard University Press, 1976.

SCARLATTI, DOMENICO

Goldberg, Laurette, and Patrice Mathews. *Domenico Scarlatti: Thematic Index of the Keyboard Sonatas According to the Kirkpatrick Catalogue.* Berkeley, CA: MusicSources Publications, 1999.

Includes concordances of numbering systems by Kirkpatrick, Longo, and Fadini numbers, as well as concordance of works by key.

Kirkpatrick, Ralph. *Domenico Scarlatti.* Bd. II, *Anhang, Dokumente und Werkverzeichnis.* München: Ellermann, 1972. English-language edition: Princeton, NJ: Princeton University Press, 1953.

(Lacks full thematic index found in German edition but includes "Catalogue of Scarlatti Sonatas and Table of Principal Sources in Approximately Chronological Order," pp. 442–59.) Abbreviated in *Grove Music Online* as [K].

Longo, Alesandro. *Indice Tematico della Sonate per Clavicembalo* [Thematic Index of the Harpsichord Sonatas]. Milan: G. Ricordi, 1952. Abbreviated in *Grove Music Online* as [L].

Pestelli, G. *Le Sonate di Domenico Scarlatti: Proposta di un Ordinamento Cronologico.* Torino: G. Giappichelli, 1967. Abbreviated in *Grove Music Online* as [P].

EDITIONS OF THE KEYBOARD WORKS

Opere complete per Clavicembalo. Edited by Alesandro Longo. Milan: Ricordi, 1906–10. Abbreviated in *Grove Music Online* as [L; S = supplement].

Sixty Sonatas, Edited in Chronological Order from the Manuscripts and Earliest Printed Sources with a Preface by Ralph Kirkpatrick. 2 vols. New York: G. Schirmer, 1953. Abbreviated in *Grove Music Online* as [‡].

Complete Keyboard Works in Facsimile from the Manuscript and Printed Sources. Edited by Ralph Kirkpatrick. New York: Johnson Reprint Corp., 1972. Abbreviated in *Grove Music Online* as [K].

Sonates. Edited by Kenneth Gilbert. *Le Pupitre,* L.P. 31–41. Paris: Heugel, 1971–84. Based on Kirkpatrick's numbering system.

Sonate per Claviercembalo. Edited by Emilia Fadini. Milano: G. Ricordi, 1978– . Abbreviated in *Grove Music Online* as [F].

The *Grove Music Online* work list provides numbering of sonatas in K (Kirkpatrick), F (Fadini), and L (Longo) editions. (See Figure 10–6.)

There are numerous problems relating to cataloging Domenico Scarlatti's works, in part because all of the available sources are copyists' manuscripts; there are no extant autographs, and compilers of editions from Ralph Kirkpatrick to Emilia Fadini have used various approaches in organizing these sources. For further discussion of these issues, see

Boyd, Malcolm. *Domenico Scarlatti — Master of Music.* New York: Schirmer Books, 1986.

Choi, Seunghyun. "Newly Found Eighteenth-Century Manuscripts of Domenico Scarlatti's Sonatas and Their Relationship to Other Eighteenth- and Early Nineteenth-Century Sources." Ph.D. diss., University of Wisconsin, Madison, 1974.

Pagano, Robert. "Domenico Scarlatti: Reception." *Grove Music Online.* Edited by L. Macy. http://www.grovemusic.com.

Sheveloff, Joel. "Domenico Scarlatti: Tercentenary Frustrations." *Musical Quarterly* 71, no. 4 (1985): 399–436; Part II. *Musical Quarterly* 72, no. 1 (1986): 90–118. (Also includes listing of manuscripts titled "Scarlatti Source Control.")

_____. "The Keyboard Music of Domenico Scarlatti: A Re-evaluation of the Present State of Knowledge in the Light of the Sources." Ph.D. diss., Brandeis University, 1970.

FIGURE 10–6 *Grove Music Online,* D. Scarlatti Works list.

Solo keyboard

K	F	L	Description	Primary source (variant)
1		366	d, C, Allegro	E1
2		388	G, 3/8, Presto	E2
3		378	a, ⫣, Presto‡	E3
4		390	g, C, Allegro	E4
5		367	d, 3/8, Allegro	E5
6		479	F, 3/8, Allegro	E6
7		379	a, 3/8, Presto‡	E7
8		488	g, 3/4, Allegro	E8 (R1)
9		413	d, 6/8, Allegro	E9
10		370	d, 3/8, Presto	E10
11		352	c, C, –	E11
12		489	g, C, Presto	E12
13		486	G, 2/4, Presto	E13
14		387	G, 12/8, Presto	E14
15		374	e, 3/8, Allegro	E15
16		397	B♭, ⫣, Presto‡	E16
17		384	F, 3/8, Presto	E17
18		416	d, C, Presto‡	E18
19		383	f, 2/4, Allegro	E19
20		375	E, 2/4, Presto	E20
21		363	D, 3/8, Allegro	E21
22		360	c, 2/4, Allegro	E22
23		411	D, C, Allegro	E23
24		495	A, C, Presto	E24
25		481	f♯, 2/4, Allegro	E25
26		368	A, 3/8, Presto	E26
27		449	b, 3/4, Allegro	E27
28		373	E, 3/8, Presto‡	E28
29		461	D, C, Presto‡	E29
30		499	g, 6/8, Moderato	E30
31	53	231	g, 2/4, Allegro	R3
32		423	d, 3/8, Aria	R6
33	39	424	D, 3/8, Allegro	V xiv, 43 (R7)
34		S7	d, 3/4, Larghetto	R9
35		386	g, C, Allegro	R12
36	23	245	a, 3/8, Allegro	V xiv, 25
37	37	406	g, C, Allegro	V xiv, 41
38	25	478	F, 3/8, Allegro	V xiv, 27
39		391	A, C, Allegro	R28
40		357	c, 3/4, Minuetto	R30
41			d, C, Andante moderato	PA iii, 30 (R42)
42		S36	B♭, 3/4, Minuetto	R43

See also *Grove Music Online* bibliography and footnotes to Sheveloff's *Musical Quarterly* articles. While Sheveloff critiques all of the Scarlatti thematic cataloging systems, he states that "K. [Kirkpatrick] and F. [Fadini] number seem about equally usable, with all their faults; until further notice, I will stay with the K. system since I know it best, adding my Hoboken-like prefixes for pieces in various doubtful categories."[22]

SCHEIN, JOHANN HERMANN

COMPLETE WORKS EDITION

Neue Ausgabe sämtlicher Werke. Edited by Adam Adrio et al. Kassel: Bärenreiter, 1963– . Abbreviated in *Grove Music Online* as [A].
Sämtliche Werke. Edited by Arthur Prüfer. Leipzig: Breitkopf & Härtel, 1901–23. Abbreviated in *Grove Music Online* as [P].

SCHEIDT, SAMUEL

Samuel-Scheidt-Werke-Verzeichnis. Edited by Klaus-Peter Koch. Wiesbaden: Breitkopf & Härtel, 2000. Abbreviated in *Grove Music Online* as [SSWV].

COMPLETE WORKS EDITION

Werke. Edited by Gottlieb Harms, Christhard Mahrenholz, and Christoph Wolff. Vols. 1–13, Hamburg: Ugrino/Abteilung Verlag, 1923–65; vols. 14–17, Leipzig: Deutscher Verlag für Musik, 1971–. Abbreviated in *Grove Music Online* as [S].

SCHOENBERG, ARNOLD

Rufer, Joseph. *The Works of Arnold Schoenberg: A Catalogue of His Compositions, Writings, and Paintings.* Translated by Dika Newlin. New York: Free Press of Glencoe, 1963. Non-thematic composer catalog, with the following chapters:[23]

Music

I. Published Works (subdivided into works with opus numbers, works without opus numbers)

II. Unpublished Works (subdivided into completed, unfinished, and miscellaneous)

III. Sketchbooks

Writings

I. Theoretical Works

II. Poems, Lectures, Essays, Notes

Oil Paintings, Water-Colors, Drawings
Recordings
Microfilms of original manuscripts
Complete List of Works

Chronological List of Works
Dates of World Premieres
Appendix

The book also includes 25 facsimiles of manuscripts (listed on p. 13), and several reproductions of Schoenberg's paintings.

COMPLETE WORKS EDITION

Sämtliche Werke. Herausgegeben von Josef Rufer, in Zusammenarbeit mit Richard Hoffmann et al., unter dem Patronat der Akademie der Künste, Berlin. Mainz: B. Schott's Söhne; Wien: Universal Edition, 1966–.
Information on the status of this edition and numerous other resources on Schoenberg are found on the Web site of the Arnold Schoenberg Center in Austria, Vienna: http://www.schoenberg.at/7_research/gesamtausgabe_e.htm. The center also publishes the *Kritische Gesamtausgabe der Schriften Arnold Schönbergs* [Complete Critical Edition of the Composer's Writings].

OTHER RELATED SOURCES

Christensen, Jean, and Jesper Christensen. *From Arnold Schoenberg's Literary Legacy: A Catalog of Neglected Items.* Detroit Studies in Music Bibliography 59. Warren, MI: Harmonie Park Press, 1988.
The Arnold Schoenberg-Hans Nachod Collection. Compiled by John A. Kimmey. Detroit, MI: Information Coordinators, 1979. (Catalog of collection at North Texas State University.)
Arnold Schoenberg: Catalogue Raisonné. Edited by Christian Meyer and Therese Muxeneder. 2 vols. Wien: Arnold Schoenberg Center, 2005. (Illustrated catalog of the composer's art works.)
Nono-Schoenberg, Nuria. *Arnold Schoenberg, 1874–1951: Lebengeschicte in Begegnungen.* Klagenfurt, Austria: Ritter Klagenfurt, 1998.

SCHUBERT, FRANZ

Deutsch, Otto Erich. *Franz Schubert: thematisches Verzeichnis seiner Werke in chronologischer Folge.* Neue Schubert Ausgabe Ser. 8: Supplement, Bd. 4. Kassel: Bärenreiter, 1978.
First published in London in 1951 with the title *Schubert: A Thematic Catalogue of His Works,* a revised edition of Otto Erich Deutsch's thematic catalog of Schubert's works was published in 1978 as part of the *Neue Schubert Ausgabe.* It is arranged chronologically (facilitated by the fact that Schubert dated most of his manuscripts)[24] with dated works numbered D1–965B and undated works numbered D966–D998. A concordance of opus numbers is provided (opus numbers are not included in the *Grove Music Online* works list). Appendices include spurious and doubtful works, Schubert's arrangements of other composer's works, and Schubert's copies of other composer's works. In addition to the concordance of opus numbers, there are lists of Schubert's posthumous songs; first editions by J. P. Gotthard, Wien, and C. F. Peters, Leipzig; and lists of works in the old Schubert edition (AGA) and Neue Schubert Ausgabe (NSA). Other indices include a general index, owners of manuscripts, publishers of first editions, authors of texts, titles and first lines of vocal music, and instrumental music.

Features of each entry are provided by Deutsch in his preface, p. xiii. The catalog entries include only single-stave incipits, a compromise that Deutsch attributes to the fact that the first edition was compiled during a time of "Wartime austerity."[25]

Grove Music Online works list includes NSA series numbers for each genre at the head of that part of the works list. The songs are listed in order of D no.; the list is followed by an index to the songs.[26] (See Figure 10–7.) As is also evident from glancing at the *Grove Music Online* Schubert works list, some of the composer's works were first published in the *Neue Schubert Ausgabe.*

Nottebohm, Gustav. *Thematisches Verzeichniss der im Druck erschienenen Werke von Franz Schubert.* Wien: F. Schreiber, 1874.

FIGURE 10–7 *Grove Music Online,* F. Schubert Works list.

RELATED SOURCE

Hilmar, Ernst. *Verzeichnis der Schubert-Handschriften in der Musiksammlung der Wiener Stadt- und Landesbibliothek.* Catalogus musicus 8. Kassel: Bärenreiter, 1978. Robert Winter reviews the 1978 edition of Deutsch and Hilmar's book in his important article "Cataloging Schubert," *19th Century Music*, 3, no. 2 (Nov. 1979): 154–62. This article includes corrections to selected entries in both sources, as does his earlier article, "Schubert's Undated Works: A New Chronology" in *The Musical Times*, 119, no. 1624 (June 1978): 498–500.

COMPLETE WORKS EDITIONS

Neue Ausgabe sämtlicher Werke. Hrsg. von der Internationalen Schubert-Gesellschaft. Kassel: Bärenreiter, 1964– . Abbreviated in *Grove Music Online* as [NSA, ser./vol.]. *Franz Schuberts Werke: kritisch durchgesehene Gesamtausgabe.* Edited by E. Mandyczewski, J. Brahms et al. Leipzig: Breitkopf & Härtel, 1884–97. Reprint, New York: Dover, 1965–69. 19 vols. Abbreviated in *Grove Music Online* as [SW].

RELATED SOURCES

http://www.schubert-online.at/activpage/index_en.htm.
Digital collection of Schubert autographs.

Schütz, Heinrich

Brieg, Werner. *Schütz-Werkeverzeichnis* (SWV). Kassel: Bärenreiter, forthcoming (to be published as Supplement to *Neue Ausgabe sämtlicher Werke*). Bittinger, Werner. *Schütz-Werke-Verzeichnis* (SWV). Kleine Ausgabe, im Auftrag der Neuen Schütz-Gesellschaft. Kassel: Bärenreiter, 1960. Non-thematic composer catalog. Miller, D. Douglas, and Anne L. Highsmith. *Heinrich Schütz: A Bibliography of the Collected Works and Performing Editions.* Music Reference Collection 9. Westport, CT: Greenwood Press, 1986. Non-thematic catalog, with references to locations in complete works editions.

COMPLETE WORKS EDITIONS

Stuttgarter Schütz-Ausgabe: sämtliche Werke nach dem Quellen neu hrsg. von Günter Graulich unter Mitarbeit von Paul Horn. Neuhausen-Stuttgart: Hänssler-Verlag, 1971– . Abbreviated in *Grove Music Online* as [S]. *Neue Ausgabe sämtlicher Werke.* Edited by Werner Bittinger et al. Kassel: Bärenreiter, 1955– . Abbreviated in *Grove Music Online* as [N]. *Sämtliche Werke.* Edited by Philip Spitta. 18 vols. Leipzig: Breitkopf & Härtel, 1885–1927. Reprint, Wiesbaden: Breitkopf & Härtel, 1968. Abbreviated in *Grove Music Online* as [G].

Schumann, Robert

McCorkle, Margit. *Robert Schumann: thematisch-bibliographisches Werkverzeichnis.* Robert Schumann neue Ausgabe samtlicher Werke. Serie VIII, Supplemente, Bd. 6. München: Henle, 2003.

Hofmann, Kurt. *Die Erstdrucke der Werke von Robert Schumann: Bibliographie mit Wiedergabe von 234 Titelblättern.* Tutzing: H. Schneider, 1979. Abbreviated in *Grove Music Online* as [woos]. (Reproduction of title pages of first editions.)

Hofmann, Kurt, and Siegmar Keil. *Robert Schumann: thematisches Verzeichnis sämtlicher im Druckerschienenen musikalischen Werke mit Angabe des Jahres ihres Entstehens und Erscheinens.* 5th enl. and rev. ed. Hamburg: Schuberth, 1982. Rev. and enl. ed. of *Thematisches Verzeichniss sämmtlicher im Druck erschienenen Werke Robert Schumann's mit Angabe des Jahres ihres Entstehens.* [189?–].

Similar in arrangement and presentation to McCorkle's Brahms catalog, her 2003 thematic catalog of Schumann's works (which was published in conjunction with the new Schumann complete works edition) finally makes it possible for scholars and performers to thoroughly research the compositional history of his works. The "old" thematic catalog was an enlarged reprint of the nineteenth-century catalog, which was originally published in 1860. McCorkle's introduction (with all components translated into English, as in the Brahms catalog) includes essays on "The Previous Catalogues of the Works," "The Reception History of the Works," "The Publication History of the Works," and "The History of the Music Manuscripts," as well as a "Descriptive Guide to the Catalogue" and "Paradigm of the Catalogue Entries."

In both the Brahms catalog and the Schumann catalog, references to literature about the work are included in the body of the entries rather than in a separate section marked "Literatur" (p. 80).

Clara Schumann was the general editor of the older Schumann *Gesamtausgabe.* She was assisted by Brahms and several other musicians of their circle (see McCorkle, p. 70). Although certainly done with care, the older complete works edition, as is true for many other nineteenth-century publications of this type, lacks critical apparatus and other features found in the *Neue Ausgaben.*

Dover performing editions of Schumann's works are primarily reprints from the old Schumann *Gesamtausgaben.*

Similar to his catalog of Brahms's first edition title pages, Kurt Hofmann's *Die Erstdrucke der Werke von Robert Schumann* (Tutzing: Hans Schnieder, 1979) reproduces the title pages of Schumann's first editions. Schumann's title pages are generally more interesting, however, since he worked closely with his publishers to commission artists who would create decorative title pages that were somehow connected to the music. See, for example, the artist Friedrich Krätzschmer's title page of *Carnaval,* op. 9, with the tiny commedia dell'arte figures on each letter. (Figure 10–8). Hoffman's bibliography is preceded by introductory essays on

FIGURE 10–8   Robert Schumann. Title page of *Carnaval,* op. 9 (Leipzig: Beritkopf & Härtel, 1837), with commedia dell'arte figures visible on each letter.

Source: Kurt Hofmann, *Die Erstdrucke der Werke von Robert Schumann.* (Tutzing: Hans Schneider, 1979), 23. Reprinted by permission of the publisher. All rights reserved.

"Robert Schumann und seine Verleger," "Schumanns Einflussnahme auf die Ausstattung seiner Werke," and " Die Gestalter der Titelblätter."

COMPLETE WORKS EDITIONS

Neue Ausgabe sämtlicher Werke. Hrsg. von der Robert-Schumann-Gesellschaft Düsseldorf durch Akio Mayeda und Klaus Wolfgang Niemöller in Verbindung mit dem Robert-Schumann-Haus Zwickau. Mainz: Schott, 1991– . Abbreviated in *Grove Music Online* as [NSA].

Robert Schumanns Werke. Hrsg. von Clara Schumann. Leipzig: Breitkopf & Härtel, 1881–93. Reprinted by Kalmus. Abbreviated in *Grove Music Online* as [SW].

RELATED SOURCES

Roesner, Linda Correll. "Studies in Schumann Manuscripts: With Particular Reference to Sources Transmitting Instrumental Works in the Larger Forms." Ph.D. diss., New York University, 1973.

Robert Schumann Research Institute: http://members.aol.com/schumannga/index.htm.

Schumann Portal: http://www.schumann-portal.de/.

SCRIABIN, ALEKSANDR NIKOLAYEVICH

Bosshard, Daniel. *Thematisch-chronologisches Verzeichnis der musikalischen Werke von Aleksander Skrjabin.* Ardez: Ediziun Trais Giats, 2003.

SHOSTAKOVICH, DMITRI

Hulme, Derek. *Dmitri Shostakovich: A Catalogue, Bibliography and Discography.* 3rd ed. Lanham, MD: Scarecrow Press, 2002.

  Non-thematic composer catalog. Classified arrangement, with works listed alphabetically within each category. Entries include date of composition, premiere, location of autograph, editions (including location in old complete works edition), duration, bibliographic references, and list of recordings.

COMPLETE WORKS EDITIONS

Novoe sobranie sochinenii = New Collected Works. Moscow: Izdatepstvp DSCH, 2002– .

Sobranie sochinenii = Collected Works. Edited by Dvukh Tomakh. 42 vols. Moscow: Izdatel'stvo Muzyka, 1979–87.

Note: The *Grove Music Online* works list does not reference location of works in either of these editions.

SIBELIUS, JEAN

Dahlström. Fabian. *Jean Sibelius: thematisch-bibliographisches Verzeichnis seiner Werke.* Wiesbaden: Breitkopf & Härtel, 2003.

Dahlström's catalog provides essential documentation for Sibelius's works. Sibelius's manuscripts were donated to the Helsinki University Library in 1982, which has aided cataloging and documentation of his works. They are described in Kilpeläinen, Kari. *The Jean Sibelius Musical Manuscripts at Helsinki University Library: A Complete Catalogue = Die Musikhandschriften von Jean Sibelius in der Universitätsbibliothek Helsinki: Ein vollständiges Verzeichnis.* Wiesbaden: Breitkopf & Härtel, 1991.

Dahlström's catalog includes introductory matter in Finnish, German, and English, with essays on "Transmission of the Manuscripts" "Jean Sibelius and Music Publishing," and "Jean Sibelius and Arrangements of His Works." The catalog itself is arranged in two parts: Works with Opus Numbers and Works Without Opus Numbers. The latter are numbered JS 1–225 and arranged in alphabetical order.

COMPLETE WORKS EDITION

Complete Works = Sämtliche Werke. Edited by Fabian Dahlström, Glenda Cross et al. Wiesbaden: Breitkopf & Härtel, 1999– . Abbreviated in *Grove Music Online* as [JSW]. The critical edition of Sibelius's works is published under the auspices of Helsinki University Library, the Sibelius Society of Finland, and Breitkopf and Härtel. The edition was established in 1996, and the first volumes appeared in 1999. Divided into 9 series, it is projected to include 52 volumes:

Series I: Orchestral Works
Series II: Works for Violin and Orchestra
Series III: Works for String Orchestra and Wind Orchestra
Series IV: Chamber Music
Series V: Piano Music
Series VI: Dramatic Works
Series VII: Choral Works
Series VIII: Works for Solo Voice
Series IX: Varia

Goss, Glenda Dawn. "Critical Edition for Jean Sibelius." *Fontes Artis Musicae.* 51, nos. 3–4 (July–Dec. 2004): 358–66.

SPOHR, LOUIS

Göthel, Folker. *Thematisch-bibliographisches Verzeichnis der Werke von Louis Spohr.* Tutzing: Schneider, 1981.
Two sections: works with opus numbers and works without opus numbers. Appendices include classified index of works and discography.

COMPLETE WORKS EDITIONS

Neue Auswahl der Werke. Edited by Folker Göthel and Herfried Homburg. Tutzing: Schneider, 1963– . Abbreviated in *Grove Music Online* as [X].
Selected Works of Louis Spohr, 1784–1859: A Ten-Volume Collection of Facsimiles, Reprints, and New Manuscript Sources. Edited by Clive Brown. New York: Garland Publishing, 1987–90. Abbreviated in *Grove Music Online* as [B i–x].

STRADELLA, ALESSANDRO

Gianturco, Carolyn, and Eleanor F. McCrickland. *Alessandro Stradella (1632–1682): A Thematic Catalog of His Compositions.* Thematic Catalogue Series 16. Stuyvesant, NY: Pendragon Press, 1990.

COMPLETE WORKS EDITIONS

Stradella, Alessandro. *Edizione nazionale dell'opera omnia di Alessandro Stradella.* Pisa: Edizione ETS, 2002– .

STRAUSS, JOHANN (1825–1899) ("STRAUSS SON"; "STRAUSS THE YOUNGER")

Wiener Institut für Strauss-Forschung. *Strauss-Elementar-Verzeichnis: (SEV) thematisch-bibliographischer Katalog der Werke von Johann Strauss (Sohn).* 7 vols. Schriftenreihe zur Musik. Tutzing: H. Schneider, 1990–97.
Weinmann, Alexander. *Verzeichnis sämtlicher Werke von Johann Strauss, Vater und Sohn.* Wien: Musikverlag L. Krenn, 1956.

COMPLETE WORKS EDITIONS

Neue Johann Strauss Gesamtausgabe = New Johann Strauss Complete Edition. Edited by Michael Rot. Wien: Strauss Edition Wien (Verlagsgruppe Hermann), 1999– .
Doblingers Johann Strauss Gesamtausgabe. Formerly edited by the Johann-Strauss-Gesellschaft, Wien under the direction of Fritz Racek, continued by Rudolf H. Führer, Johannes Martin Dürr, and Ernst Hilmar. Now edited in connection with the Wiener Institut für Strauss-Forschung under the direction of Norbert Rubey. Wien: Doblinger/Universal Edition, 1967– .[27] Abbreviated in *Grove Music Online* as [R] (for Racek).
For historical background and detailed information on differences between these two editions, see Andrew Lamb's review of selected volumes in the *Neue Johann Strauss Gesamtausgabe* in *Notes* 59, no. 2 (Dec. 2002): 431–34; also Aigner, Thomas. "The Vienna City Library's Johann Strauss II Collection." *Fontes Artis Musicae* 51, nos. 3–4 (July–Dec. 2004): 351–57.

RELATED SOURCE

Mailer, Franz, ed. *Leben und Werk in Briefen und Dokumenten: Johann Strauss (Sohn).* 10 vols. Tutzing: H. Schneider, 1983–2007. (second revised edition issued beginning with vol. 7 [2000].)

STRAUSS, RICHARD

Trenner, Franz, and E. H. Mueller von Asow. *Richard Strauss Verzeichnis (TrV).* 2nd ed. Wien: Verlag Dr. Richard Strauss, 1999. Abbreviated in *Grove Music Online* as [TrV].
Mueller von Asow, Erich Hermann. *Richard Strauss: Thematisches Verzeichnis.* 3 vols. Wien: L. Doblinger, 1955–74.

COMPLETE WORKS EDITIONS

Richard Strauss Edition. Wien: Verlag Dr. Richard Strauss, 1996–99. Vols. 1–18: Stage Works Vols. 19–30: Orchestral Work

Trenner, Franz, ed. *Richard Strauss Lieder = Gesamtausgabe = Complete Edition.* 4 vols. London: Boosey & Hawkes, 1964.

RELATED SOURCES

Trenner, Franz, and Florian Trenner. *Richard Strauss: Chronik zu Leben und Werk.* Wien: R. Strauss, 2003.

Richard Strauss Institut: http://www.richard-strauss-institut.de/.

STRAVINSKY, IGOR

Goubalt, Christian. *Igor Stravinsky.* Paris: Libr. H. Champion, 1991. Part I: La vie. Part II: Les oeuvres musicales (non-thematic composer catalog). Part III: Dictionnaire. Referenced in *Grove Music Online* works list as a source for "lost and fragmentary works."

Kirchmeyer, Helmut. *Kommentiertes Verzeichnis der Werke und Werkausgaben Igor Stravinsky bis 1971.* Leipzig: Verlag der Sächsischen Akademie der Wissenschaften zu Leipzig; Stuttgart: In Kommission bei S. Hirzel, 2002. Non-thematic composer catalog; continuation of White.

White, Eric Walter. *Stravinsky, the Composer and his Works.* 2nd ed. Berkeley: University of California Press, 1979. Part I: Biography; Part II: Register of works, which is detailed non-thematic composer catalog.

No complete works edition; *Grove Music Online* works list provides information on publishers of particular works. Stravinsky's autograph manuscripts and sketches are housed in the Paul Sacher Foundation, Basel, Switzerland. *See*

Jans, Hans Jörg, and Lukas Handschin, eds. *Igor Strawinsky: Musikmanuskripte.* Inventare der Paul Sacher Stiftung 5. Winterthur: Amadeus, 1989.

Strawinsky, sein Nachlass, sein Bild. Basel: Kunstmuseum, 1984.

SZYMANOWSKI, KAROL

Michałowski, Kornel. *Karol Szymanowski, 1882–1937: katalog tematyczny dzieł i bibliografia.* [Thematic catalogue of works and bibliography] Kraków: Polskie Wydawnictwo Muzyczne, 1967.

COMPLETE WORKS EDITION

Karol Szymanowski: Dzieła. Edited by Teresa Chylińska. Kraków: Polskie Wydawnictwo Muzyczne, 1973–. Abbreviated in *Grove Music Online* as [s].

TCHAIKOVSKY, PYOTR ILIYCH

Vajdman, Polina, Ljudmila Korabelnikova, and Valentina Rubcova, eds. *Tematiko-bibliograficheskii ukazatel sochinenii P.I. Chaikovskogo = Thematic and Bibliographical Catalogue of Tchaikovsky's (P.I. Čajkovskij's) Works.* Moscow: P.Jurgenson, 2006.

Classified arrangement, with works arranged chronologically within each genre; each work given $\check{C}$W number. Text in Russian and English.

Poznansky, Alexander, and Brett Langston. *The Tchaikovsky Handbook: A Guide to the Man and His Music*. Vol. 1: *Thematic Catalogue of Works, Catalogue of Photographs, Autobiography*. Vol. 2: *Catalogue of Letters, Genealogy, Bibliography*. Bloomington: Indiana University Press, 2002.

The first comprehensive sourcebook on Tchaikovsky's life and music, including thematic catalog of his works, with classified arrangement. Each work is given a distinctive number; list and concordance of opus numbers provided at end of Vol. 1 (e.g., *Eugene Onegin*, op. 24 is catalog number 5), along with chronological list of compositions, lists of titles and variant titles, and general index. Text entirely in English. The catalog of letters in Vol. 2 also includes an index of correspondents and locations of Tchaikovsky's autographs.

Systematisches Verzeichnis der Werke von Pjotr Iljitsch Tschaikowsky: ein Handbuch für die Musikpraxis. Hamburg: Musikverlag H. Sikorski, 1973.

Non-thematic composer catalog; classified arrangement.

Jurgenson, Boris Petrovich, ed. *Catalogue thématique des oeuvres de P. Tschaïkowsky*. Moscou: P. Jurgenson, 1897. Reprint, London, H. Baron, 1966.

Thematic catalog, with works arranged according to opus number. Jurgenson was Tchaikovsky's principal publisher. See Poznansky and Langston, pp. xvii–xxiv for detailed information on this and other early sources on the composer's works.

COMPLETE WORKS EDITIONS

Novoye polnoye sobraniye sochineniy. Moscow: Muzyka; Mainz: Schott, 1993– . Abbreviated in *Grove Music Online* as [NTE].

Polnoye sobraniye sochineniy. Edited by B.V. Asaf'yev et al. Moscow and Leningrad: State Music Publishers, 1940–71; supplement, 1990. Abbreviated in *Grove Music Online* as [T].

TELEMANN, GEORG PHILIPP

Ruhnke, Martin, ed. *Georg Philipp Telemann: Thematisch-systematisches Verzeichnis seiner Werke (TWV): Instrumentalwerke*. 3 vols. Kassel: Bärenreiter, 1984–99. Abbreviated in *Grove Music Online* as [TWV].

Menke, Werner. *Thematisches Verzeichnis der Vokalwerke von Georg Philipp Telemann*. 2nd ed. Vol. 1: *Church Cantatas*. Vol. 2: *Other Vocal Works*. Frankfurt am Main: V. Klostermann, 1988–95. Abbreviated in *Grove Music Online* as [TVWV].

Hoffmann, Adolf. *Die Orchestersuiten Georg Philipp Telemanns: TWV55*. Wolfenbüttel: Möseler, 1969.

Kross, Siegfried. *Das Instrumentalkonzert bei Georg Philip Telemann*. Tutzing: H. Schneider, 1969.

COMPLETE WORKS EDITIONS

Musikalische Werke. Herausgegeben im Auftrag der Gesellschaft für Musikforschung; Martin Ruhnke und Wolf Hobohm in Verbindung mit dem Zentrum für Telemann-Pflege und -Forschung, Magdeburg. Kassel: Bärenreiter, 1950– . Abbreviated in as *Grove Music Online* as [T]. http://www.baerenreiter.com/html/completeedi/telemann-ga.htm (selected edition)

Grove Music Online also lists other Telemann editions, as follows:
Orgelwerke. Hrsg. von Traugott Fedtke. Kassel: Bärenreiter, 1964. Abbreviated in *Grove Music Online* as [F].
Severinus Urtext Telemann Edition. Edited by Ian Payne. Sutton, St. Nicholas, Hereford, England: Thesaurus Harmonicus, 1995– . Abbreviated in *Grove Music Online* as [P].
Frankfurter Telemann-Ausgabe. Edited by Eric F. Fiedler and others. Frankfurt: Habsburger Verlag, 1996– . Abbreviated in *Grove Music Online* as [FTA].
Not listed in *Grove Music Online:*
Telemann-Archiv. Stuttgarter Ausgabe. Neuhausen-Stuttgart: Hänssler Verlag, 1977– .

The Center for Computer Assisted Research in the Humanities (CCARH) at Stanford University has used its "MusicDatas: encoding system" to prepare a full-text database for the works of Telemann, among other composers.[28] http://www.musedata.org/encodings/telemann/.

Telemann's large and complex output of more than 3,000 works has presented numerous challenges for performers, researchers, and library catalogers.

RELATED SOURCES

Swack, Jeanne. "Telemann Research Since 1975." *Acta Musicologica* 64, Fasc. 2. (July–Dec. 1992): 139–64.
Zohn, Steven. Review of *Georg Philipp Telemann: Thematisch-Systematisches Verzeichnis seiner Werke: Telemann-Werkverzeichnis (TWV): Instrumentakwerke. Vol. 3* by Martin Ruhnke. *Notes* 57, no. 1 (Sept. 2000): 110–12.

TUBIN, EDUARD

Rumessen, Vardo. *The Works of Eduard Tubin: Thematic and Bibliographic Catalogue of Works (ETW).* Stockholm: Gehrmans Musikförlag, 2003.

COMPLETE WORKS EDITION

The Works of Eduard Tubin. Stockholm: Gehrmans Musikförlag, 2003– .

RELATED SOURCES

Pärtlas, Margus. "Eduard Tubin: Current Research and Publishing Projects." *Fontes Artis Musicae* 51, nos. 3–4 (July–Dec. 2004): 332–38.
International Eduard Tubin Society: www.tubinsociety.com.

VAUGHAN WILLIAMS, RALPH

Kennedy, Michael. *A Catalogue of the Works of Ralph Vaughan Williams.* 2nd ed. New York: Oxford University Press, 1996.
The *Grove Music Online* works list refers to Kennedy for complete information on the composer's works.

VERDI, GIUSEPPE

Hopkinson, Cecil. *A Bibliography of the Works of Giuseppe Verdi, 1813–1901.* Vol. 1. *Vocal and Instrumental Works.* Vol. 2 *Operatic Works.* New York: Broude Bros., 1973–78. Non-thematic catalog, focusing on first editions.

Chusid, Martin. *A Catalog of Verdi's Operas.* Music Indexes and Bibliographies 5. Hackensack, NJ: J. Boonin, 1974. Non-thematic catalog, with information on location and details of manuscript sources.

COMPLETE WORKS EDITION

The Works of Giuseppe Verdi = Le opere di Giuseppe Verdi. Edited by Philip Gossett et al. Chicago: University of Chicago Press; Milano: Recordi, 1983– . Abbreviated in *Grove Music Online* as [V].

See also publications of the American Institute for Verdi Studies (Verdi Archive) at New York University: http://www.nyu.edu/projects/verdi/archive.html. Some of these are listed in the *Grove Music Online* Verdi bibliography under "catalogs."

VIVALDI, ANTONIO

Ryom, Peter. *Antonio Vivaldi: Thematisch-systematisches Verzeichnis seiner Werke (RV).* Wiesbaden: Breitkopf & Härtel, 2007.

———. *Repertoire des Oeuvres d'Antonio Vivaldi: Les Compositions Instrumentales.* Copenhague: Engstrøm & Sødring, 1986.

Fanna, Antonio. *Antonio Vivaldi (1678–1741): Catalogo Numerico-Tematico delle Opere Strumentali.* Milano: Ricordi, 1968.

———. *Opere Strumentali di Antonio Vivaldi. Catalogo Numerico-Tematico. Secondo la Catalogazione Fanna.* 2nd ed. rev. and enl. Milano: Ricordi, 1986.

COMPLETE WORKS EDITIONS

Nuova Edizione Critica delle opere di Antonio Vivaldi. Istituto Italiano Antonio Vivaldi. Milano: Ricordi, 1982–. Abbreviated in *Grove Music Online* as [N (unnumbered)].

Opere. Edited by G. F. Malipiero et al. Milano: Ricordi, 1947–72. Abbreviated in *Grove Music Online* as [M].

Opere incomplete, edizione critica. Edited by Instituto Italiano Antonio Vivaldi. Florence: Studio per edizioni Scelte, 2001– . Abbreviated in *Grove Music Online* as [I no.].

Vivaldi's works have been subjected to more cataloging and numbering systems than those of most other composers. This has created a maze (some would say nightmare) of confusion for modern librarians, performers, purchasers of recordings, and program note annotators. The modern thematic catalog of Vivaldi's works is Peter Ryom's catalog (2007), and RV numbers have largely replaced Pincherle, Rinaldi (opus numbers), and Fanna numbers. A concordance of the different numbering systems is found at the end of the 1986 edition of Ryom's catalog (pp. 710–18).

A separately published concordance (based on the Ricordi edition and covering works issued to 1965) was compiled by Lenore Coral and published as *A Concordance of the Thematic Indexes to the Instrumental Works of Antonio Vivaldi*, 2nd ed. (Ann Arbor, MI: Music Library Association), 1972. Michael Talbott also references several other concordances in his *Antonio Vivaldi: A Guide to Research* (New York: Garland Publishers, 1988), 109.

The *Grove Music Online* works list has columns for RV number, key, and location of work in Malipiero edition (abbreviated as [M]) and the new complete works edition (abbreviated as [N]). (See Figure 10–9.)

RELATED SOURCES

See also *Grove Music Online* Vivaldi article under "Reputation" and publications of the
Instituto Italiano Antonio Vivaldi:
> *Informazioni e studi Vivaldiani: Bollettino dell'Istituto Italiano Antonio Vivaldi,*
> *Venezia, Fondazione Giorgio Cini.* Milano: Ricordi, 1980–.

Talbott, Michael. *The Chamber Cantatas of Antonio Vivaldi.* Woodbridge, UK: Boydell
Press, 2006.

WAGNER, RICHARD

Deathridge, John, Martin Geck, and Egon Voss. *Wagner Werk-Verzeichnis (WWV): Verzeichnis der musikalischen Werke Richard Wagners und ihrer Quellen.* Mainz; New York:
Schott, 1986.

COMPLETE WORKS EDITIONS

Sämtliche Werke. Edited by Carl Dahlhaus et al. Mainz: Schott, 1970– . Abbreviated in
Grove Music Online as [SW].

Richard Wagners Werke. Edited by Michael Balling. Leipzig: Breitkopf & Härtel,
1912–29. Reprint, New York: Da Capo Press, 1971. Incomplete. Abbreviated in *Grove
Music Online* as [R].
> For further discussion of Wagner editions, see

Saffle, Michael. "The Documentary Legacy: Music Editions and Related Studies." In
Richard Wagner: A Guide to Research, 67–73. Routledge Music Bibliographies. New
York: Routledge, 2002. This chapter also includes a listing of published facsimile editions of Wagner manuscripts.

Also important for the study of Wagner are editions of his libretti, his prose works, and his correspondence. These are listed in *Grove Music Online* bibliography and described in Michael Saffle, *Richard Wagner: A Guide to Research* (New York: Routledge, 2002), 71–105.

WALTON, WILLIAM

Craggs, Stewart R. *William Walton: A Thematic Catalogue of His Works.* New York:
Oxford University Press, 1977.

FIGURE 10–9 *Grove Music Online,* A. Vivaldi Works list.

Oxford **Music** Online
ALL CONTENT | BIOGRAPHIES | SUBJECT ENTRIES | LEARNING RESOURCES

vivaldi   SEARCH
Advanced Search

Grove Music Online   « Previous result | Results list | Next result »
Vivaldi, Antonio

Article | Works | Related Content   🖶 Print   ✉ Email   🔊 Cite

Works

Catalogues:

P. Ryom: *Table de concordances des oeuvres (RV)* (Copenhagen, 1973); *Verzeichnis der Werke Antonio Vivaldis (RV): kleine Ausgabe* (Leipzig, 1974, 2/1979); *Répertoire des oeuvres d'Antonio Vivaldi: les compositions instrumentales* (Copenhagen, 1986) [RV]

A. Fanna: *Opere strumentali di Antonio Vivaldi (1678–1741): catalogo numerico-tematico secondo la catalogazione Fanna* (Milan, 1986) [F]

Editions:

Le opere di Antonio Vivaldi, ed. G.F. Malipiero and others (Milan, 1947–72) [M no.]

Nuova edizione critica delle opere di Antonio Vivaldi, ed. Istituto Italiano Antonio Vivaldi (Milan, 1982–) [N (unnumbered)]

Vivaldi: Opere incomplete, edizione critica, ed. Istituto Italiano Antonio Vivaldi (Florence, 2001–) [I no.]

Solo sonatas

with continuo; for violin unless otherwise stated

Sources:

Sonate, vn, hpd (Venice, 1709); as op.2 (Amsterdam, 1712)

VI sonate, vn/2 vn, bc, op.5 [continues numbering of op.2] (Amsterdam, 1716) [printed nos. given]

Il pastor fido, musette/vielle/fl/ob/vn, bc, 'op.13' (Paris, c1737) [pastiche by Nicolas Chédeville]

VI sonates, vc, bc (Paris, c1739)

RV	Key	F	M, N, I	Sources; remarks
1	C	XIII,34	399	op.2 no.6
2	C	XIII,11	369	*D-Dl*: facs. in Musik der Dresdener Hofkapelle (Leipzig, 1982); 2nd, 4th movts in RV4
3	C	XIII,8	366, N	*Dl, GB-Mp, I-CF*
4	C	—		*A-Gd,* inc.; 2nd, 4th movts in RV2
5	c	XIII,10	368	*D-Dl*
6	c	XIII,14	372, N	*Dl*; facs. in Musik der Dresdener Hofkapelle (Leipzig, 1982), *GB-Mp*
7	c	—		*A-Gd,* inc.
7a	c	XIII,61	N	*I-CF, UDa*; RV7 with different 3rd movt
8	c	XIII,35	400	op.2 no.7
9	D	XIII,39	404	op.2 no.11
10	D	XIII,6	364	*D-Dl*
11	D	—		*A-Gd,* inc.; also Breitkopf catalogue, see Brook
12	d	XIII,7	365, N	*D-Dl, GB-Mp*; 1st movt in RV582 (as 2nd movt)
13	d	XIII,50	—	*S-Skma,* spurious (? by J.H. Roman)
14	d	XIII,31	396	op.2 no.3
15	d	XIII,9	367	*D-Dl*

COMPLETE WORKS EDITION

William Walton Edition. Edited by David Lloyd-Jones et al. New York: Oxford University Press, 1998– .

WEBER, CARL MARIA VON

Jähns, Friedrich Wilhelm. *Carl Maria von Weber in seinen Werken. Chronologisch-thematisches Verzeichniss seiner sämmtlichen Compositionen nebst Angabe der unvollständigen, verloren gegangenen, zweifelhaften und untergeschobenen mit Beschreibung der Autographen, Angabe der Ausgaben und Arrangements, kritischen, kunsthistorischen und biographischen Anmerkungen, unter Benutzung von Weber's Briefen und Tagebüchern und einer Beigabe von Nachbildungen seiner Handschrift.* Berlin: Robert Lienau, 1967. (Unchanged reprint of the edition Berlin: Verlag der Schlesinger'schen Buch- und Musikhandlung, 1871).

COMPLETE WORKS EDITIONS

Sämtliche Werke = Complete Works. Edited by Gerhard Allroggen in association with the Gesellschaft zur Förderung der Carl-Maria-von-Weber-Gesamtausgabe. Mainz: Schott 1998– .
Musikalische Werke. Erste kritische Gesamtausgabe. Edited by Hans Joachim Moser. 3 vols. Augsburg: B. Filser, 1926–32. Incomplete. Reprint, New York: Broude Bros., 1977.

WEILL, KURT

The Kurt Weill Edition. Edited by David Drew et al. New York: Kurt Weill Foundation for Music; Valley Forge, PA: European American Music, 1996– .
Drew, David. *Kurt Weill: A Handbook.* Berkeley: University of California Press, 1987. Includes non-thematic catalog of works.

WOLF, HUGO

Hugo Wolf: Persönlichkeit und Werk: Eine Austellung zum 100. Geburstag. Edited by Franz Grasberger. Wien: Öesterreichiche National-bibliothek, 1960. Includes works list.
Wolf, Hugo. *Verzeichnis seiner Werke, mit einer Einführung von Paul Müller.* Leipzig: C. F. Peters, 1908.

COMPLETE WORKS EDITIONS

Sämtliche Werke. Edited by Hans Jancik et al. Wien: Musikwissenschaftlicher Verlag, 1960– . Abbreviated in *Grove Music Online* as [WW].
Nachgelassene Werke. Edited by Robert Haas and Helmut Schultz. Leipzig and Vienna: Musikwissenschaftlicher Verlag, 1936. Abbreviated in *Grove Music Online* as [NW].
Grove Music Online also lists
Hugo Wolf: Lieder aus der Jugendzeit. Edited by Ferdinand Foll. Leipzig: Lauterbach and Kuhn, 1903. Abbreviated in *Grove Music Online* as [LJ].
Detailed discussions of these editions are found in David Ossenkop, *Hugo Wolf: A Guide to Research.* (New York: Garland Publishers, 1988).

NOTES

1. For further information on Brook, see his biography on the Web site of the Barry S. Brook Center for Research and Documentation at the Graduate Center of the City University of New York: http://web.gc.cuny .edu/BrookCenter/bio.htm

2. Barry S. Brook, *The Symphony 1720–1840: Reference Volume: Contents of the Set and Collected Thematic Indexes* (New York: Garland Publishing, 1986).

3. Barry S. Brook and Murray Gould, *Notating Music with Ordinary Typewriter Characters: A Plaine and Easie Code System for Musicke.* (Flushing, NY: Queens College of the City University of New York, 1964); other writings on this subject by Brook and others are listed in the bibliography to the *Grove Music Online* "Thematic Catalogue" article.

4. Brook places these catalogs in his section on "Locator Catalogs." Also included in this section are other finding tools that utilize alphabetical indexes of various types to locate incipits of particular works. Such tools, which are listed as "related sources" in the main composer thematic catalog listing in this chapter, include Bryant and Chapman, *Melodic Index to Haydn's Instrumental Works* (1982), and Hill and Gould's *Thematic Locator for Mozart's Works* (1970).

5. Barry S. Brook and Richard J. Vinao, *Thematic Catalogues in Music: An Annotated Bibliography,* 2nd ed., Annotated Reference Tools in Music 5. (Stuyvesant, NY: Pendragon Press, 1992), ix–xviii; and Brook, "Thematic Catalogues," *Grove Music Online* ed. L. Macy. www.grovemusic.com.

6. First published by J. André in 1805 (Offenbach: J. Andres, 1805; pl. no. 1889) and in various facsimile editions, the most recent published in 1990 and edited by Albi Rosenthal and Alan Tyson. This edition, which was published for the bicentennial of Mozart's death, also reproduces the blank pages at the end of Mozart's book, a sad and touching document of all that was lost with the composer's early demise. The manuscript is also available in digital format on the British Library Web site: http://www.bl.uk/collections/treasures/ mozart/mozart_broadband.htm?top.

7. Published in facsimile in Jens Peter Larson, *Drei Haydn Katalog* (Stuyvesant, NY: Pendragon Press, 1979).

8. Carl Philip Emanuel Bach, *Verzeichnis des musikalischen Nachlasses des verstorbenen Capellmeisters C.P.E. Bach* (Hamburg, 1790); published in facsimile edition with preface by Rachel C. Wade, *The Catalog of Carl Philipp Emanuel Bach's Estate. A Facsimile of the Edition by Schniebes, Hamburg, 1790* (New York: Garland, Publishing 1981).

9. Brook, "Thematic Catalogues."

10. E. Eugene Helm, *Thematic Catalogue of the Works of Carl Philipp Emanuel Bach* (New Haven, CT: Yale University Press, 1989), xi.

11. "General Preface." *Carl Philipp Emanuel Bach: The Complete Works.* http://www .cpebach.org/cpeb/prefaces/general_preface. html; also included in each printed volume of the edition.

12. This collection is also referenced in Chapter 1 under "Berlin Staatsbibliothek," p. 12.

13. Hans-Joachim Schulze and Christoph Wolff, *Bach Compendium,* vol. 1 (Frankfurt: C. F. Peters, 1985), 10.

14. Ibid., 17.

15. Ibid., 19.

16. Ibid., 10.

17. Ibid., 20; see also abbreviations for scribes on pp. 26–27.

18. See Elliot Antokoletz, *Béla Bartók: A Guide to Research,* 2nd ed. (New York: Garland Publishing, 1997), 5 for more detailed information on Szöllösy and other catalogs of Bartók's compositions. See also Somfai, 297, for explanation of numbering scheme for new thematic catalog.

19. D. Kern Holoman, *Catalogue of the Works of Hector Berlioz. New Edition of the Complete Works* Vol. 25. (Kassel: Bärenreiter, 1987), vii.

20. Ibid., viii.

21. Jens-Peter Larsen, *Three Haydn Catalogues = Drei Haydn Katalog,* 2nd facsim. ed., with a new survey of Haydn's oeuvre (New York: Pendragon Press, 1979), ix.

22. Joel Sheveloff, "Domenico Scarlatti: Tercentenary Frustrations," *Musical Quarterly* 71, no. 4 (1985): 422.

23. Josef Rufer, *The Works of Arnold Schoen-berg,* trans. Dika Newlin (London: Faber & Faber, 1962), 11–13.

24. Otto Deutsch, *Franz Schubert thematisches Verzeichnis seiner Werke in chronologischer Folge* (Kassel: Bärenreiter, 1978), xii. Robert Winter questions this statement in his article "Cataloging Schubert," *19th Century Music* 3, no. 2 (Nov. 1979): 154–62.

25. Deutsch, *Franz Schubert,* xiii.

26. Among the other composers whose *Grove Music Online* work lists include indexes to their songs are Brahms, Schumann, and Wolf. Individual songs may be easily searched by title or thematic catalog number in *Grove Music Online.*

27. Description from Otto Harrassowitz "Composers' Collected Editions from Europe": http://www.harrassowitz.de/muscatalogs/cat2002/idx/colco31.html#STR%201061.

28. See Walter B. Hewlett, "Beyond MIDI: The Handbook of Musical Codes—The Muse-Data Representation of Musical Information." http://www.ccarh.org/publications/books/beyondmidi/online/musedata/.

CHAPTER

$$\boxed{11}$$

Text Translations
and Guides
to Pronunciation

INTRODUCTION

Most musicians, librarians, and concertgoers would agree that we can always use more easily accessible sources of text translations, particularly for individual songs and arias. While opera lovers have always had published librettos to consult, and now have the benefits of supertitles with translations projected during performances in many opera houses, singers and librarians are still surprised to find that translations of individual songs and arias are not as accessible as one might assume.

Song texts and translations are found in the following sources:

1. Separately published translation books devoted to one composer or groups of composers (such as the titles in this chapter)
2. Program notes
3. Liner notes for recordings
4. Within the score itself

Within these categories, it is useful to discuss these sources in terms of the types of translations or resources they provide. Standard translation guides, such as Philip Miller's *Ring of Words* or the *Fischer-Dieskau Book of Lieder* usually provide *poetic translations,* in which the translator endeavors to convey the poetic meaning of the text in the original language.

Word-by-word translations, found in sources such as Coffin's *Word-By-Word Translations of Songs and Arias,* provide the exact meaning of each word underneath the original; it is then up to the singer to create poetic meaning out of the text.

Phonetic readings are guides to pronunciation of the text, usually via the standard International Phonetic Alphabet (IPA), which uses symbols to convey sounds in any language.[1]

The translation sources listed on the following pages typically utilize one or more of these translation types or resources; sources such as *The Singer's Debussy, The Singer's Rachmaninoff,* and *The Singer's Schumann* include word-by-word and poetic translations, as well as IPA for each song.

Note: The list that follows includes primarily song and aria translation sources, with selected *collections* of opera libretti, such as Nico Castel's *French Opera Libretti* and *Italian Belcanto Opera Libretti.* It does not include single-composer or individual opera libretti.

SELECTED SOURCES

General (Czech, Finnish French, German, Italian, Latin, Spanish)

Bernac, Pierre. *The Interpretation of French Song.* New York: W.W Norton, 1978.

Castel, Nico. *French Opera Libretti: With International Phonetic Alphabet Transcriptions, Word for Word Translations, Including a Guide to the I.P.A. and Notes on the French Transcriptions by Nico Castel.* Foreword by Beverly Sills. 3 vols. Geneseo, NY: Leyerle, 1999–2005.

_____. *German Miscellaneous Opera Libretti: With International Phonetic Alphabet Transcriptions, Word for Word Translations, Including a Guide to the I.P.A. and Notes on the German Transcriptions.* Edited by Marcie Stapp. Foreword by Thomas Hampson. Geneseo, NY: Leyerle, 2005.

_____. *Italian Belcanto Opera Libretti. With International Phonetic Alphabet Transcriptions, Word for Word Translations, Including a Guide to the I.P.A. and Notes on the Italian Phonetics by Nico Castel.* Edited by Scott Jackson Wiley. Foreword by Dame Joan Sutherland. 3 vols. Geneseo, NY: Leyerle, 2000–2002.

_____. *Italian Verismo Opera Libretti: In Two Volumes With International Phonetic Alphabet Transcriptions, Word for Word Translations, Including a Guide to the I.P.A. and Notes on Italian Phonetics by Nico Castel.* Edited by Scott Jackson Wiley. Foreword by Plácido Domingo. Geneseo, NY: Leyerle, 2000– .

_____. *Libretti of Russian Operas.* Vol. 1: *Operas Based on the Poetry and Prose of Alexander Pushkin with International Phonetic Alphabet Transcriptions, Word for Word Translations, Including a Guide to the I.P.A. and Russian Lyric Diction by Anton Belov.* Edited by Ann Brash and Valeria Konstantinoskaya. Foreword by Nico Castel. Geneseo, NY: Leyerle, 2004.

_____. *The Nico Castel Ladino Song Book.* Arranged by Richard J. Neumann. Cedarhurst, NY: Tara Publications, 1981.

Cheek, Timothy. *Singing in Czech: A Guide to Czech Lyric Diction and Vocal Repertoire.* Lanham, MD: Scarecrow Press, 2001.

Coffin, Berton, et al. *Phonetic Readings of Songs and Arias.* 2nd ed., with revised German translations. Metuchen, NJ: Scarecrow Press, 1982.

Coffin, Berton, Werner Singer, and Pierre Delattre. *Word-by-Word Translations of Songs and Arias Part I—German and French.* New York: Scarecrow Press, 1966.

Schoep, Arthur, and Daniel Harris. *Word-by-Word Translations of Songs and Arias Part II—Italian.* Metuchen, NJ: Scarecrow Press, 1972.

Fischer-Dieskau, Dietrich. *The Fischer-Dieskau Book of Lieder: The Original Texts of over 750 Songs Chosen and Introduced by Dietrich Fischer-Dieskau, with English Translations by George Bird and Richard Stokes.* 1976. Reprint, New York: Limelight Editions, 1984.

Gerhart, Martha. *Italian Song Texts from the 17th through the 20th Centuries*. Vol I: *Italian Song Texts from the 17th Century*. Mt. Morris, NY: Leyerle Publications, 2002– .

Glass, Beaumont. *Selected Song Texts of Great German Lieder: 251 Selected Lieder Texts Including Many of the Most Famous Songs of Franz Schubert, Robert Schuman, Johannes Brahms, Hugo Wolf, and Richard Strauss; with International Phonetic alphabet Transcriptions, Word for Word Translations, and Commentary by Beaumont Glass*. Mt. Morris, NY: Leyerle, 2004.

Holman, Eugene. *Singing in Finnish: A Manual for Singers and Vocal Coaches: 75 Finnish Songs Phonetically Transcribed with Translations*. Publications of the Academy of Finnish Art Song 2. [Finland]: The Academy of Finnish Art Song, 2005.

Jeffers, Ron. *Translations and Annotations of Choral Repertoire*. Vol. I: *Sacred Latin Texts*. Corvallis, OR: Earthsongs, 1988.

_____. *Translations and Annotations of Choral Repertoire*. Vol. II: *German Texts*. Corvallis, OR: Earthsongs, 2000.

Johnson, Graham, and Richard Stokes. *A French Song Companion*. New York: Oxford University Press, 2000.

Lakeway, Ruth C., and Robert C. White Jr. *Italian Art Song*. Bloomington: Indiana University Press, 1989.

LeVan, Timothy. *Masters of the French Art Song: Translations of the Complete Songs of Chausson, Debussy, Duparc, Faure, and Ravel*. Metuchen, NJ: Scarecrow Press, 1991.

_____. *Masters of the Italian Art Song: Word-by-Word and Poetic Translations of the Complete Songs for Voice and Piano*. Metuchen, NJ: Scarecrow Press, 1990.

Miller, Philip L. *German Lieder*. The German Library 42. New York: Continuum, 1990.

_____. *The Ring of Words: An Anthology of Song Texts*. 1966. Reprint, New York: W. W. Norton, 1973.

Phillips, Lois. *Lieder Line by Line, and Word for Word*. Rev. ed. Oxford: Clarendon Press; New York: Oxford University Press, 1996.

Piatak, Jean, and Regina Avrashov. *Russian Songs and Arias: Phoentic Readings, Word-by-Word Translations, and a Concise Guide to Russian Diction*. Dallas: Pst, 1991.

Richardson, Dorothy, and Tina Ruta. *Arie antiche*. Orleans, MA: Paraclete Press, 1990.

Prawer, S. S. *The Penguin Book of Lieder*. Harmandsworth, Middlesex, England; New York: Penguin Books, 1984.

Singher, Martial. *An Interpretive Guide to Operatic Arias: A Handbook for Singers, Coaches, Teachers, and Students*. University Park: Pennsylvania State University Press, 1983.

Sobrer, Josep Miquel, and Edmon Colomer. *The Singer's Anthology of 20th Century Spanish Songs*. New York: Pelion Press, 1987.

The Spanish Song Companion. Devised and translated by Jacqueline Cockburn and Richard Stokes. Lanham, MD: Scarecrow Press, 2006.

Internet Resources

The Aria Database Index. www.aria-database.com.
   (Extensive listing of additional links to translation sites).
The Lied and Song Texts Page. www.recmusic.org/lieder/.
Alta Vista's *Babel Fish Translation*. http://babelfish.altavista.com/.

Some words of caution to users of Web-based translation sites: many of these sites rely on public domain or user-created translations; often the finest translation sources are still protected by copyright.

Pronunciation

Castel, Nico. *A Singer's Manual of Spanish Lyric Diction.* Foreword by Plácido Domingo. New York: Excalibur Publishing 1994.

Copeman, Harold. *Singing in Latin, or Pronunciation Explor'd.* Preface by Andrew Parrott. Oxford: H. Copeman, 1990.

De'Ath, Leslie. "Dictionaries of Pronunciation: A Bibliographic Guide for Musicians. Part I: English; Part II: Languages other than English." *Journal of Singing* 55, no. 3 (Jan.–Feb. 1999): 27–42; 55, no. 4 (March–April 1999): 5–16.

Fradkin, Robert A. *The Well-Tempered Announcer: A Pronunciation Guide to Classical Music.* Bloomington: Indiana University Press, 1996.

IPA Source: IPA Transcriptions and Literal Translations of Songs and Arias. http://www .ipasource.com/home. (subscription-based Web site)

Singing Early Music: The Pronunciation of European Languages in the Late Middle Ages and Renaissance. Edited by Timothy J. McGee with A. G. Rigg and David A. Klausner. Bloomington: Indiana University Press, 1996.

Individual Composers

BACH, JOHANN SEBASTIAN

Ambrose, Z. Philip. *J.S. Bach: The Vocal Texts in English Translation with Commentary.* [Philadelphia, PA?]: Xlibris Corp., 2005.

_____. *The Texts to Johann Sebastian Bach's Church Cantatas.* Neuhausen-Stuttgart: Hänssler-Verlag, 1984. http://www.uvm.edu/~classics/faculty/bach/.

Drinker, Henry S. *Texts of the Choral Works of Johann Sebastian Bach in English Translation.* 4 vols. New York: printed privately and distributed by the Association of American Colleges Arts Program, 1942–43.

Dürr, Alfred. *The Cantatas of J.S. Bach: With their Librettos in German-English Parallel Text.* Revised and translated by Richard D. P. Jones. New York: Oxford University Press, 2005.

Meyer, Ulrich. *Biblical Quotation and Allusion in the Cantata Libretti of Johann Sebastian Bach.* Lanham, MD: Scarecrow Press, 1997.

Reeder, Ray. *The Bach English-Title Index.* Berkeley, CA: Fallen Leaf Press, 1993.

Stokes, Richard. *The Complete Church and Secular Cantatas: J. S. Bach.* Lanham, MD: Scarecrow Press, 2000.

Unger, Melvin P. *Handbook to Bach's Sacred Cantata Texts: An Interlinear Translation with Reference Guide to Biblical Quotations and Allusions.* Lanham, MD: Scarecrow Press, 1996.

Young, W. Murray. *The Cantatas of J. S. Bach: An Analytical Guide.* Jefferson, NC: Mac-Farland, 1989.

_____. *The Sacred Dramas of J. S. Bach: A Reference and Textual Interpretation.* Jefferson: MacFarland, 1994.

BRAHMS, JOHANNES

Evans, Edwin. *Handbook to the Vocal Works of Johannes Brahms.* 1912. Reprint, New York: Burt Franklin, 1970.

Glass, Beaumont. *Brahms' Complete Song Texts in One Volume: Containing Solo Songs, Duets, Liebeslieder Waltzes (both sets), the Alto Rhapsody, Folk Song Arrangements, with*

International Phonetic Alphabet Transcriptions, Word for Word Translations, and Commentary by Beaumont Glass. Geneseo, NY: Leyerle, 1999.

Magner, Candace A. *Phonetic Readings of Brahms Lieder.* Metuchen, NJ: Scarecrow Press, 1987.

Sams, Eric. *The Songs of Johannes Brahms.* New Haven, CT: Yale University Press, 2000.

Stark, Lucien. *Brahms's Vocal Duets and Quartets with Piano: A Guide with Full Texts and Translations.* Bloomington: Indiana University Press, 1998.

_____. *A Guide to the Solo Songs of Johannes Brahms.* Bloomington: Indiana University Press, 1995.

DEBUSSY, CLAUDE

Cobb, Margaret G. *The Poetic Debussy: A Collection of his Song Texts and Selected Letters.* Translated by Richard Miller. Rev. 2nd ed. Rochester, NY: University of Rochester Press, 1994.

Rohinsky, Marie-Claire. *The Singer's Debussy.* New York: Pelion Press, 1987.

DVOŘÁK, ANTONÍN

Adams, David. *The Song and Duet Texts of Antonin Dvorak; Večerní písně of Bedřich Smetana: Original Texts, English Translations, Phonetic Transcriptions, Czech Pronunciation and Lyric Diction, Commentary by David Adams.* Geneseo, NY: Leyerle, 2003.

FAURÉ, GABRIEL

Gartside, Robert. *Interpreting the Songs of Gabriel Fauré.* Geneseo, NY: Leyerle, 1996.

HANDEL, GEORGE FRIDERIC

Castel, Nico. *Handel Opera Libretti: With International Phonetic Alphabet Transcriptions, Word for Word Translations, Notes on the Italian Transcriptions by Nico Castel.* 2 vols. Geneseo, NY: Leyerle, 2005– .

MONTEVERDI, CLAUDIO

Stevens, Denis. *Claudio Monteverdi, Songs and Madrigals.* Lanham, MD: Scarecrow Press, 1998.

MOZART, WOLFGANG AMADEUS

Castel, Nico. *The Libretti of Mozart's Completed Operas: In Two Volumes, with International Phonetic Alphabet Transcriptions, Word for Word Translations, Including a Guide to the I.P.A. and Notes on the Italian and German Transcriptions by Nico Castel.* Foreword by Julius Rudel. Geneseo, NY: Leyerle, 1997–1998.

MUSSORGSKY, MODEST

Richter, Laurence R. *Russian Texts of the Complete Songs of Modest Petrovich Mussorgsky with Phonetic Transcriptions, Literal and Idiomatic English Translations by Laurence R. Richter.* Geneseo, NY: Leyerle, 2002.

PUCCINI, GIACOMO

Castel, Nico. *The Complete Puccini Libretti: In Two Volumes: With International Phonetic Alphabet Transcriptions, Word for Word Translations, Including a Guide to the I.P.A. and Notes on the Italian Transcriptions by Nico Castel.* Foreword by Sherrill Milnes. 2 vols. Geneseo, NY: Leyerle, 1993–94.

RACHMANINOFF, SERGEI

Challis, Natalia. *The Singer's Rachmaninoff.* New York: Pelion Press, 1989.
Richter, Laurence R. *Russian Texts on the Complete Songs of Sergei Vasilyevich Rachmaninov, with Phonetic Transcriptions, Literal and Idiomatic English Translations by Laurence R. Richter.* Geneseo, NY: Leyerle, 2000.

RAVEL, MAURICE

Gartside, Robert. *Interpreting the Songs of Maurice Ravel.* Geneseo, NY: Leyerle, 1992.

RODRIGO, JOAQUÍN

Draayer, Suzanne. *A Singer's Guide to the Songs of Joaquín Rodrigo.* Lanham, MD: Scarecrow Press, 1999.

SCHUBERT, FRANZ

Glass, Beaumont. *Schubert's Complete Song Texts: Two Volumes: With International Phonetic Alphabet Transcriptions, Word for Word Translations, and Commentary by Beaumont Glass.* Geneseo, NY: Leyerle, 1996.
Magner, Candace A. *Phonetic Readings of Schubert Lieder.* Metuchen, NJ: Scarecrow Press, 1994.
Reed, John. *The Schubert Song Companion.* London: Faber and Faber, 1993.
Wigmore, Richard. *Schubert: Complete Song Texts.* New York: Schirmer Books, 1988.

SCHUMANN, ROBERT

Reinhard, Thilo. *The Singer's Schumann.* New York: Pelion Press, 1989.
Sams, Eric. *The Songs of Robert Schumann.* Rev. and enl. 3rd ed. Bloomington: Indiana University Press, 1993.

STRAUSS, RICHARD

Castel, Nico. *Four Strauss Opera Libretti. With International Phonetic Alphabet Transcriptions, Word for Word Translations, Including a Guide to the German I.P.A., and Notes on the German Transcriptions by Nico Castel.* Edited by Marcie Stapp. Foreword by Evelyn Lear. Geneseo, NY: Leyerle, 2002.

Glass, Beaumont. *Richard Strauss' Complete Song Texts.* Geneseo, NY: Leyerle, 2004.

TCHAIKOVSKY, PETER ILICH

Richter, Laurence R. *Tchaikovsky's Complete Song Texts: Russian Texts of the Complete Songs of Peter Ilyich Tchakovsky, with Phonetic Transcriptions, Literal and Idiomatic English Translations by Laurence R. Richter.* Geneseo, NY: Leyerle, 1999.

Sylvester, Richard D. *Tchaikovsky's Complete Songs: A Companion with Texts and Translations.* Bloomington: Indiana University Press, 2002.

VERDI, GIUSEPPE

Castel, Nico. *The Complete Verdi Libretti: In Four Volumes, with International Phonetic Alphabet Transcriptions, Word for Word Translations, Including a Guide to the I.P.A. and Notes on the Italian by Nico Castel.* Foreword by Sherrill Milnes. Geneseo, NY: Leyerle, 1994–96.

WAGNER, RICHARD

Castel, Nico. *Three Wagner Opera Libretti: With International Phonetic Alphabet Transcriptions, Word for Word Translations, Including a Guide to the German I.P.A., and Notes on the German Transcriptions by Nico Castel.* Edited by Marcie Stapp. Foreword by Thomas Stewart. Geneseo, NY: Leyerle, 2006.

WOLF, HUGO

Glass, Beaumont. *Hugo Wolf's Complete Song Texts in One Volume: Containing All Completed Solo Songs Including Those Not Published During the Composer's Lifetime, with International Phonetic Alphabet Transcriptions, Word for Word Translations, and Commentary by Beaumont Glass.* Geneseo, NY: Leyerle, 2000.

Sams, Eric. *The Songs of Hugo Wolf.* Bloomington: Indiana University Press, 1992. First published 1961 by Oxford University Press.

NOTES

1. For further information on IPA, see http://www.omniglot.com/writing/ipa.htm and http://www2.arts.gla.ac.uk/IPA/fullchart.html. The latter has a copy of the IPA chart.

CHAPTER

12

Resources for Careers in Music and Other Miscellaneous Tools

INTRODUCTION

Libraries house extensive resources that contain valuable information for those interested in careers in music. These include directories that provide current information on competitions, festivals, organizations, orchestras, and ensembles; specific tools about grants and other funding sources; and numerous guides to the music profession, from business- and legal-oriented books to those that assist with preparation of resumes and other practical information.

DIRECTORIES

Directory sources are used to locate current information on individuals or organizations. As we do with "yellow pages" (or "yellow books"), we expect directories to be kept up-to-date, with new editions issued annually. One of the directories most familiar to classical musicians is *Musical America's* annual *International Directory of the Performing Arts*, which provides information on competitions, festivals, orchestras, music schools, artist managers, performing arts series, and other resources in North America and abroad.

The listing that follows also includes several out-of-date directories, since they can sometimes be useful sources of historical information. For example, Christopher Pavlakis's *American Music Handbook* of 1974 was one of the few directory-style sources to include detailed information on chamber music ensembles, such as date of founding and lists of original personnel. It is often difficult to locate this information easily, without undertaking extensive research on the history of the ensemble.

Alink, Gustav A. *International Piano Competitions.* [The Hague]: G. A. Alink, 1990.

Vol. I: Gathering the Results
Vol. II: 15,000 Pianists
Vol. III: The Results

_____. *Piano Competitions Worldwide.* 4th ed. [The Hague]: G. A. Alink, 2003.

American Music Center. *Contemporary Music Ensembles: A Directory.* 4th ed. New York: American Music Center, 1991. Currently available online via subscription: www.amc.net.

_____. *Opera Companies and American Opera: A Directory.* 2nd ed. New York: American Music Center, 1992.

Billboard Directories. See http://www.orderbillboard.com/ShowGroups.aspx.

British and International Music Yearbook. London: Rhinegold Publishing Ltd., 1998– (annual). (also available on CD-ROM)

Career Guide for Singers. 6th ed. Washington, DC: Opera America, 2003. (See also lists of Opera America publications at http://www.operaamerica.org/.)

Chamber Music America. *A Directory of Festivals, Schools, and Workshops.* New York: Chamber Music America (annual).

_____. *Membership Directory.* (See Chamber Music America site: http://www.chambermusic.org/.)

College Music Society. *Directory of Music Faculties in Colleges and Universities, U.S. and Canada.* Binghamton, NY: College Music Society, 1971–92 (biennial); Missoula, MT: College Music Society, 1993– (annual). (also available online)

_____. *International Directory of Music Organizations.* 4th ed. Binghamton, NY: College Music Society, 1998. (also available online)

Other resources available from CMS include a *Music Vacancy List,* which lists music faculty job openings, and mailing labels for outreach to music faculty in specific areas. The *Music Vacancy List* is only available to CMS members. See http://www.music.org/cgi-bin/showpage.pl for complete information.

Concert Artist Guild's Guide to Competitions. New York: Concert Artist Guild, 1987– . (Also available online on a subscription basis: http://www.concertartists.org/.)

Cowden, Robert H., ed. *Opera Companies of the World: Selected Profiles.* New York: Greenwood Press, 1992.

Craven, Robert R., ed. *Symphony Orchestras of the United States: Selected Profiles.* New York: Greenwood Press, 1986.

Grey House Performing Arts Directory. Millerton, NY: Grey House Publishing, 2001– .

Handel's National Directory for the Performing Arts. 5th ed. 2 vols. Dallas: NDPA, 1988.

Music Industry Directory (formerly: *The Musician's Guide*). 7th ed. Chicago: Marquis Publications, 1983.

Music Teachers National Association (MTNA). Summer Programs Listing (annual): http://www.mtna.org/Publications/SummerProgramsListing2007/tabid/377/Default .aspx.

Musical America International Directory of the Performing Arts. Hightstown, NJ: K-III Directory Corp., 1968– (annual).

It should be noted that the indexes in *Musical America* refer to page numbers of advertisers, rather than to the listings themselves. For example, if one looks up the Boston Symphony Orchestra in the index, the page number references will be to the artist management companies that represent the orchestra, rather than to the orchestra's listing under "Orchestras: U.S. & Canada." *Musical America Online* at http:// www.musicalamerica.com/ available on a paid subscription basis.

Musical Instrument Auction Price Guide. San Anselmo, CA: String Letter Press, 1991– (annual).

Musik-Almanach. Kassel: Bärenreiter; Regensberg; G. Bosse, 1986– (biennial).

National Association of Schools of Music. *Directory.* 1950– (annual). (Available online through http://nasm.arts-accredit.org/index.jsp?page=index.)

Opitz, Helmut, ed. *International Music Directory, 2006/07: Orchestras, Music Theatres, Prizes, Festivals, Agencies, Radio and Television, Associations and Foundations, Teaching and Instruction, Documentation and Research, Music Publishing.* 2 vols. 2nd ed. München: K. G. Saur, 2006.

Pavlakis, Christopher. *The American Music Handbook.* New York: The Free Press, 1974.

Performing Arts Yearbook for Europe (PAYE*).* London: Arts Publishing International, 1990– (annual). (Includes free CD-ROM)

Peterson's Professional Degree Programs in the Visual and Performing Arts. Princeton, NJ: Peterson's, 1995– (annual).

SIBMAS International Directory of Performing Arts Collections. Haslemere: Emmett, 1995–96.

Stern's Performing Arts Directory (formerly *Dance Magazine Annual*). [New York?]: DM, 1988– (annual).

Strad International Yearbook. London: Orpheus, 1991– (annual).

String Instruments Buyers Guide: http://www.stringsmagazine.com/ Search/index.asp?WhereFrom=TS.

Uscher, Nancy. *The Schirmer Guide to Schools of Music and Conservatories Throughout the World.* New York: Schirmer Books; London: Collier Macmillan, 1988.

Zietz, Karyl Lynn. *Opera Companies and Houses of the United States: A Comprehensive, Illustrated Reference.* Jefferson, NC: McFarland, 1995.

FUNDING RESOURCES AND GRANTS

Foundation Directory. New York: Foundation Center. (Annual) *Foundation Directory Online* (available on a paid subscription basis: www.foundationcenter.org)

Foundation Grants to Individuals. 16th ed. New York: Foundation Center, 2007. (Biennial) (available online on a paid subscription basis: www.foundationcenter.org)

Geever, Jane C., and Patricia McNeill. *The Foundation Center's Guide to Proposal Writing.* 3rd ed. New York: Foundation Center, 2001.

Green, Laura. *Money for Artists: A Guide to Grants and Awards for Individual Artists.* New York: ACA Books, 1987.

The Grants Register. Chicago: St. James Press, 1969– (annual).

Institute of International Education: http://iiebooks.org/. Various publications, all updated annually, including

IIEPassport: Academic Year Abroad; Short-Term Study Abroad.
IIEPassport Study Abroad Funding: A Guide for U.S. Students and Professionals.
(CD-Rom).
Funding for United States Study: A Guide for International Students and Professionals.
Music, Dance, and Theatre Scholarships: A Complete Guide. 2nd ed. Cleveland: Conway
Greene, 1998.
Niemeyer, Suzanne, ed. *Money for Performing Artists.* New York: ACA Books: Allworth
Press; St. Paul, MN: Consortium Book Sales & Distributor, 1991.
Reiss, Alvin H. *Don't Just Applaud—Send Money!: The Most Successful Strategies for
Funding and Marketing the Arts.* New York: Theater Communications Group, 1995.
Schlachter, Ann, and R. David Weber. *Financial Aid for Research and Creative Activities
Abroad.* San Carlos, CA: Reference Service Press, 1992– (biennial).
_____. *Financial Aid for Study and Training Abroad.* San Carlos, CA: Reference Ser-
vice Press, 1992– (biennial).

Resources for careers in music can generally be divided into two types: those that
offer specific legal and business information, including sample contracts, and those
that offer some of the former along with advice on self-promotion, such as writing a winning resume, or managing an operatic career in Germany. The listing of
the latter sources is quite selective, as visitors to bookstores will find dozens of
other titles in this category, such as *The Complete Idiot's Guide to Starting a Band*
(by Mark Bliesener and Steve Knopper; Alpha Books, 2004) or *Million Dollar
Mistakes: Steering Your Music Career Clear of Lies, Cons, Catastrophes, and Land-
mines (*by Moses Avalon; Backstreet Books, 2005).

BUSINESS AND LEGAL RESOURCES: A SELECTED LIST

Francogna, Xavier M., Jr., and H. Lee Hetherington. *This Business of Artist Management.*
4th ed. New York: Billboard Books, 2004.
Halloran, Mark E., ed. *The Musician's Business and Legal Guide: A Presentation of the
Beverly Hills Bar Association Committee for the Arts.* 4th ed. Upper Saddle River, NJ:
Prentice Hall, 2008.
Krasilovsky, M. William, and Sidney Shemel, with contributions by John M. Gross and
Jonathan Feinstein. *This Business of Music: The Definitive Guide to the Music Industry.*
10th ed. New York: Billboard Books, 2007.
_____. *More About This Business of Music.* 5th ed. Rev. and enl. New York: Billboard
Books, 1994.
Schulenberg, Richard. *Legal Aspects of the Music Industry: An Insider's View.* New York:
Watson-Guptill Publications, 2005.
Sparrow, Andrew. *Music Distribution and the Internet: A Legal Guide for the Music Busi-
ness.* Aldershot, England: Gower Publishing, 2006.

CAREER GUIDES: A SELECTED LIST

Akos, Katherine, Marshall Burlingame, and Jack Wellbaum. *Facing the Maestro: A Musician's Guide to Orchestral Audition Repertoire.* Washington, DC: American Symphony
Orchestra League, 1983.

Baskerville, David. *Music Business Handbook and Career Guide.* 8th ed. Thousand Oaks, CA: Sage Publications, 2006.

Beeching, Angela Myles. *Beyond Talent: Creating a Successful Career in Music.* New York: Oxford University Press, 2005.

Brabec, Jeffrey, and Todd Brabec. *Music, Money and Success.* 5th ed. New York: Schirmer Trade Books, 2006 (biennial).

Burgess, Richard James. *The Art of Music Production.* 3rd ed. New York: Omnibus Press, 2005.

Dunkel, Stuart Edward. *The Audition Process: Anxiety Management and Coping Strategies.* Juilliard Performance Guides 3. Stuyvesant, NY: Pendragon Press, 1989.

Eaker, Sherry. *The Back Stage Handbook for Performing Artists: The How-To and Who-To Contact Reference for Actors, Singers, and Dancers.* 4th ed. New York: Back Stage, 2004.

Gordon, Steve. *The Future of the Music Business: How to Succeed with the New Digital Technologies.* San Francisco, CA: Backbeat Books, 2005.

Heimberg, Tom. *Making a Musical Life.* With a foreword by Lincoln Mayorga and an introduction by Arnold Steinhardt. Backstage Books. San Anselmo, CA: String Letter Press Publishing, 2007.

Highstein, Ellen. *Making Music in Looking Glass Land: A Guide to Survival and Business Skills for the Classical Musician.* 4th ed. New York: Concert Artists Guild, 2003.

Hoover, Deborah A. *Supporting Yourself as an Artist: A Practical Guide.* 2nd ed. New York: Oxford University Press, 1989.

Jakoby, Richard, and Egon Kraus. *Studying Music in Germany: Music, Music Education, Musicology: Study Guide.* 8th ed. Mainz: Schott, 2000.

Knobel, Marita, and Brigitte Steinert. *Singing Opera in Germany: A Practical Guide.* Kassel: Bärenreiter, 2005.

Kolb, Bonita M. *Marketing for Cultural Organizations: New Strategies for Attracting Audiences to Classical Music, Dance, Museums, Theatre and Opera.* 2nd ed. London: Thomson Learning, 2005.

Legge, Anthony. *The Art of Auditioning: A Handbook for Singers, Accompanists, and Coaches.* London: Peters, 2001.

Montgomery, Alan. *Opera Coaching: Professional Techniques and Considerations.* New York: Routledge, 2006. (Includes *annotated* bibliography of sources relevant to opera coaches)

Moore, Steve. *The Truth About the Music Business: A Grassroots Business and Legal Guide.* Boston, MA: Thomson Course Technology, 2005.

Music Schools in Europe: Handbook of European Union of Music Schools. Mainz: Schott Music International, 1995.

Owens, Richard. *Towards a Career in Europe: A Resource Book for American Singers Auditioning in Austria, Germany, and Switzerland.* Dallas: American Institute of Musical Studies, 1983.

Papolos, Janice. *The Performing Artist's Handbook.* Cincinnati: Writer's Digest Books, 1984.

Passman, Donald. *All You Need to Know About the Music Business.* 6th ed. New York: Free Press, 2006.

Seltzer, George. *Music Matters: The Performer and the American Federation of Musicians.* Metuchen, NJ: Scarecrow Press, 1989.

Shagan, Rena. *Booking and Tour Management for the Performing Arts.* 3rd ed. New York: Allworth Press, 2001.

Sullivan, Gail, and Dorothy Maddison. *Kein Angst Baby!: A Guide to German Auditions in the 1990s.* Maplewood, NJ: New York Opera Newsletter Books, 1994.

Summers-Dossena, Ann. *Getting It All Together: A Handbook for Performing Artists in Classical Music and Ballet.* Metuchen, NJ: Scarecrow Press, 1985.

Uscher, Nancy. *Your Own Way in Music: A Career and Resource Guide.* New York: St. Martin's Press, 1990.

Wadhams, Wayne. *Sound Advice: The Musician's Guide to the Record Industry.* New York: Schirmer Books; London: Collier Macmillan, 1990.

Weissman, Dick. *Making Money in Your Local Music Market.* Milwaukee, WI: Hal Leonard, 1990.

_____. *Music Business: Career Opportunities and Self-Defense.* New York: Crown Publishers, 1990.

What the Fach!?!: The Definitive Guide for Opera Singers Auditioning and Working in Germany, Austria, and Switzerland. [n.p.]: Philip Shepard Press, 2007? e-book: www.what-the-fach.com.

Wolf, Thomas. *Presenting Performances: A Basic Handbook for the Twenty-First Century.* Washington, DC: Association of Performing Arts Presenters, 2000.

TRAVEL GUIDES AND GAZETTEERS

See also RISM Series C. *Directory of Music Research Libraries* (pp. 180–181).

Brody, Elaine, and Claire Brook. *The Music Guide to Austria and Germany.* New York: Dodd, Mead, 1975.

_____. *The Music Guide to Belgium, Luxembourg, Holland, and Switzerland.* New York: Dodd, Mead, 1977.

_____. *The Music Guide to Great Britain: England, Scotland, Wales, Ireland.* New York: Dodd, Mead, 1975.

_____. *The Music Guide to Italy.* New York: Dodd, Mead, 1978.

Foreman, Lewis, and Susan Foreman. *London: A Musical Gazetteer.* New Haven, CT: Yale University Press, 2005.

Sadie, Julie Anne, and Stanley Sadie. *Calling on the Composer: A Guide to European Composer Houses and Museums.* New Haven and London: Yale University Press, 2005.

Simeone, Nigel. *Paris—A Musical Gazetteer.* New Haven, CT: Yale University Press, 2000.

Selected Glossary of German Terms

German	English	Abbreviation
Abbildung	illustration	Abb.
Abdruck	offprint, imprint	
Abhandlung	treatise, essay	
Abkürzung	abbreviation	Abk.
Abschrift	copy	
Anhang	appendix	Anh.
Anmerkung	note, comment, remark	Anm.
Anthologie	anthology	Anth.
Anzeige des Erscheinens	notice of publication	
Aufdruck	imprint	
Aufführung	performance	
Aufführungspraxis	performance practice	
Auflage	edition	Aufl.
Aufschrift	copy (in manuscript)	
Ausgabe	edition	
Ausgewählte Werke	selected works	AW
Autograph	autograph	
Band	volume	Bd.
Bearbeiter	arranger, editor	Bearb.
Beiheft	supplement	Beih.
Beilage	supplement, appendix	Beil.
Beispiel	example	Beisp.
Beitrag	contribution, article	Beitr.
Bemerkungen	remarks, annotations, commentary	Bem.
Bericht	report	
Kritischer Bericht	critical commentary	KB
Revisionsbericht	critical commentary	
beschriebenen	with writing	
Besetzung	setting	

German	English	Abbreviation
Besprechung	discussion, review, criticism, conference	
beziehungsweise	respectively; or, or else; more specifically	bzw.
Bibliothek	library	Bibl.
Bildnis	portrait, likeness	Bildn.
Bildtafel	plate in a book	
Blatt	leaf, folio; newspaper	Bl.
Brief	letter	
Briefwechsel	correspondence	
Buchhändler, Buchhandlung	bookseller, bookshop	
Denkmäler	monuments	
Druck	print	
Einband	binding	
Eindruck	imprint	
Einleitung	introduction	Einl.
Einteilung	classification	
einzeln	separate, single	einz.
Entstehungszeit	date of composition, origin	EZ
Entwurf	sketch	
Erstaufführung	premiere, first performance	
Erstausgabe	first edition	
Erst Auflage	first printing	
Exemplar	copy	Expl.
Fälschung	forgery, spurious work	
Fassung	version	
fertiggestellt	completed	
Folge; Neue Folge	series, continuation, issue; new issue	F.; N.F.
früher	earlier	
Fussnote	footnote	
geboren	born	geb.
gedruckt	printed	gedr.
Gegenwart	present time	Gegenw.
Gesammelte Werke	complete works	GW

German	English	Abbreviation
Gesamtausgabe	collected ("complete") edition	GA
Geschichte	history	Gesch.
Gesellschaft	association, society	Ges.
gestorben	died	gest.
gewidmet	dedicated (to)	
Handbuch	handbook, manual	Hdb.
Handexemplar	composer's or author's copy	
Handschrift	manuscript, handwriting	Hs.
Heft	part, number, volume	
Herausgeber	editor	Hrsg.
herausgegeben	edited, published by	hrsg.
Inhalt	table of contents	Inh.
Jahr	year	J.
Jahrbuch	yearbook, annual	Jb.
Jahreszahl	date, year	JZl.
Jahrgang	annual set, volume	
Jahrhundert	century	Jh.
Kapitel	chapter	Kap.
Katalog	catalog	
komponiert	composed (in)	
Komponist	composer	Komp.
Kopist	copyist	
Korigiertes Druckexemplar	corrected printer's copy	
Korrekturbogen	proof sheet	
Lexikon	dictionary	L.
Lieferung	part of a work, fascicle	Lfg.
Literatur	literature, letters, bibliography	Lit.
Manuskript	manuscript (ms)	Ms.
Mitarbeiter	collaborator	Mitarb.
Mitteilung	announcement, communication	Mitt.
Mitwirkung	cooperation	Mitw.
monatlich	monthly	mtl.
Nachdrucke	later printings	
Nachlass	legacy	
Nachschrift	postscript (P.S.)	N.S.

German	English	Abbreviation
Nachweise	cross-references	
Nachwort	concluding remarks, epilogue	Nachw.
Neudruck	reprint	Neudr.
Neue Ausgabe, Neuausgabe	new edition	NA
ohne Jahr	without date	o.J.
Opuszahl	opus number	
Orchesterbesetzung	orchestration, instrumentation	
Partitur	score	
Plattennummer	plate number	
Quelle	source	
quer	horizontal	
Redakteur; Redaktion	editor; editorial matter, editorial staff	Red.
Register	index	
Reihe	series	
revidiert	revised	rev.
Sachtitel	subject heading	
Sachverzeichnis	subject index	
Sammelband	volume containing a collection of essays	Sbd., Smlbd.
Sammelwerk	collected works	Sw., Swk.
Sammlung	collection	Slg.
Sämtliche Werke	complete works	
Satz	movement, theme, process (of composition)	
Schrift	writing, book, periodical, etc.	
Schriftleiter; Schriftleitung	editor; editorship, editorial staff	Schriftl.
Seite	page (p.)	S.
siehe oben	see above, supra	
siehe unten	see below	
Skizzen	sketches, outlines	SK
Stiftung	foundation, organization	
Stimme	part (vocal or instrumental), voice	
Stimmebuch	part book	Stb.
Stück	piece, part	St.
Tabelle	table, chart, graph	Tab.

German	English	Abbreviation
Takte	measures (in length)	T.
Tafel	table	Taf.
Teil	part, division	Tl.
Titelblatt	title page	
Tonsatz	musical composition	
Überlieferung	tradition, inheritance, surviving original sources	
Übertragung	translation, transcription	Übtr.
Übersetzer	translator	
übersetzt	translated	übs.
übersetzt von ...	translated by ...	
Übersetzung	translation	Übs.
Verfasser	composer, writer	Verf.
Verlag, Verleger	publisher	Verl.
verschollen	missing; lost	
Verzeichnis	index	
Vierteljahrsschrift	quarterly periodical	Vjs.
in Vorbereitung	in preparation	i.V.
Vorrede	preface	Vorr.
Vortrag	lecture	
Vorwort	foreword	Vorw.
Wasserzeichen	watermark, papermark	
Weitere Ausgaben	other editions	
Werkzahl	opus number	
Widmung	dedication	
Wochenblatt	weekly periodical	
Wörterbuch	dictionary	Wb.
Zahl	number, numeral, figure	Zl.
Zeitschrift	periodical, magazine	
Zeitschriftenindex	periodical index	
Zeitung	newspaper	Ztg.
zusammen	together	zus.
Zusammenfassung	summary	

Selected Glossary of Bibliographic Terms and Abbreviations

See also index under names of specific terms for page number references.

Abstract   brief summary of a source.

Archive   Repository containing collections of unpublished materials that document the history of an organization or individual; such collections are referred to as *archival* collections.

Bibliographic record   cataloging record or description of a resource in a library catalog.

Boolean search   searches that utilize **and, or,** or **not** to combine words; named for nineteenth-century mathematician George Boole.

Congress report   published proceedings of scholarly conferences, with contributions by different scholars.

Cross-references   *see* and *see also* references within library online catalogs. *See* references refer users to the correct forms of names or titles under which information is found; *see also* references (or "Related Subjects") refer users to additional headings relevant to the topic.

Fair use   exemption within copyright law that allows use of protected works under specific circumstances.

Festschrift   collection of essays by different authors in honor of an individual.

IAML   International Association of Music Libraries.

Incipit   opening notes of a work.

ISBN   International Standard Book Number.

ISMN   International Standard Music Number.

ISRC   International Standard Recording Code.

ISSN   International Standard Serial Number.

LCSH   Library of Congress Subject Headings.

MIC   Music Information Center.

Microform   photographic reproduction with significant reduction of image size; common formats include microfilm and microfiche.

MLA   Music Library Association.

OCLC   Online Computer Library Center; database of library collection holdings worldwide.

Organology   study of musical instruments.

Orphan work   work for which it is difficult to identify copyright holder.

Phrase searching   use of parameters to search words as a phrase, for example "Aaron Copland" or ("global hip hop.").

Proximity searching   Use of terms **near, before, after** to locate keywords within a text.

Rental score   score available from a publisher only for a specific performance.

RIdIM   Répertoire International d'Iconographie Musicale.

RILM   Répertoire Internationale de Littérature Musicale.

RIPM   Retrospective Index to Music Periodicals.

RISM   Répertoire International des Sources Musicales.

RLIN   Research Libraries Information Network; database of holdings of research libraries; merged with OCLC in 2006.

Subject headings   Subject terms available in library catalogs to facilitate broad searches for information on a specific topic.

Uniform title   special title used in library catalogs to bring together different versions of the same work

Union catalog   Combined catalogs or databases that provide access to the holdings of more than one library.

WorldCat   OCLC's union catalog of library holdings.

Other useful sources of information on bibliographic terminology include

Thorin, Suzanne, and Carole Franklin Vidali. *The Acquisition of Music and Sound Recordings: A Glossary.* Music Library Association Technical Reports 11. Canton, MA: Music Library Association, 1984.

See also bibliography of sources on printing and publishing in Chapter 8.

Index

A